THE BOMBING OF LONDON 1940-41

THE BLITZ AND ITS IMPACT ON THE CAPITAL

Matador
Unit E2 Airfield Business Park,
Harrison Road, Market Harborough,
Leicestershire. LE16 7UL
Tel: 0116 2792299
Email: books@troubador.co.uk
Web: www.troubador.co.uk/matador
Twitter: @matadorbooks

ISBN 978 1 80313 487 1

British Library Cataloguing in Publication Data.
A catalogue record for this book is available from the British Library.

The excerpt from *A Chelsea Concerto* by Frances Faviell appears
with permission from Dean Street Press.

Printed and bound in Great Britain by CMP UK
Typeset in 11pt Minion Pro by Troubador Publishing Ltd, Leicester, UK

Matador is an imprint of Troubador Publishing Ltd

THE BOMBING OF LONDON 1940-41

THE BLITZ
AND ITS IMPACT
ON THE CAPITAL

JOHN CONEN

CONTENTS

ACKNOWLEDGEMENTS

Researching this book has taken many years. Volume two of *The Blitz Then and Now* edited by Winston Ramsey, and Alfred Price's *Blitz on Britain 1939-1945* provided an invaluable framework. The Middlesex and LCC archives (particularly MCC/CD/WAR and LCC/FB/WAR) in the London Metropolitan Archives are a valuable source of information on the impact of the Blitz on London as are those of the Ministry of Home Security (particularly HO186) in the National Archives. As with all aspects of German attacks on the UK, wartime restrictions on reporting by the censor mean that contemporary newspaper accounts are of limited use. However, in London, numerous local and personal accounts have been published since the war in many different books and websites. I owe a great debt to the authors and editors of these accounts.

I have had to collate material from a large number of sources, some of which have been little explored in the past. Casualty figures are often difficult to establish, but fortunately the Civilian War Dead Roll of Honour from the Commonwealth War Graves Commission provides a comprehensive record which I have drawn on extensively to explore some of the little-known incidents of the Blitz. Unfortunately, military casualties are not recorded by location and given the number of service people that must have been in London at this time, must be higher than the dozen or so I have come across in various sources.

I am grateful to the staff of the London Metropolitan Archives, the National Archives, the Guildhall Library, the Camden Local Studies and Archive Centre, the Westminster Archives Centre, the Kensington and Chelsea Local Studies and Archives, the Vestry House Museum, Walthamstow, and the staff of public libraries in London for their invaluable assistance in researching this book.

I am also grateful to:

Winston Ramsey, for his past help and inspiration.

Chris Pond for generously giving his advice and copy-editing skills, and for access to the Chigwell Urban District Council war damage cards.

Nicola Beauman of Persephone Books for permission to quote extracts from *Few Eggs and No Oranges* by Vere Hodgson.

Jack McInroy http://walworthsaintpeter.blogspot.com for permission to quote from the memoirs of Rev. John Markham, Rector of St. Peter's Church, Walworth 1937-1944.

Philip Mernick of the East London History Society for permission to quote from Stephen Sadler's article *Terror at Wenlock Brewery* published in East London Record issue 19, 1998.

Nick Baldwin of the Archive Service, Great Ormond Street Hospital for Children NHS Foundation Trust, for permission to quote from the story of William Pendle the boilerman.

Gary Stone of Chingford Historical Society for permission to use extracts from *Chingford at War* and from Chingford Historical Society newsletters.

Alex Mitchell for permission to use extracts from the diaries of his great aunt, Gwladys Cox, which are held at the Imperial War Museum.

Jan Yoxall for permission to use extracts from the webpages *Jimmy's Lambeth*.

The extract from the Westminster Abbey website explaining the Civilian War Dead Roll of Honour is reproduced by courtesy of the Dean and Chapter of Westminster.

Andrew Rootes for permission to include an extract from his book *Front Line County*.

Tim Bryan for permission to include an extract from his book *Great Western at War*.

Eve Hostettler for permission to use the article regarding the bombing of Cubitt Town School which originally appeared in a 2008 edition of *Island History News*.

Rob Pateman for permission to quote from *Kennington's Forgotten Tragedy* published by the Friends of Kennington Park.

Joanna Mack for permission to quote from the memoirs of Len Jones which originally appeared in *The Making of Modern London 1939-1945 London at War* which she co-authored with Steve Humphries.

Capital City College Group for permission to quote from the account of the bombing of Dame Alice Owen's School in the memorial programme produced by City and Islington College in 2005.

Dave Haunton of Merton & Morden Historical Society for permission to quote from his articles in the society's bulletins.

The National Gallery for permission to cite extracts from their website about the Myra Hess concerts.

'The Land Mine in Portland Place' by L D Macgregor is BBC copyright content reproduced courtesy of the British Broadcasting Corporation. All rights reserved.

PREFACE

This is not primarily a social history. I have looked at the Blitz as a battle rather than an experience. There has been, for many years, fascination with the social history aspects of the Blitz and the experience of civilians but usually this is at the expense of the actual events that prompted them. Many distinguished social historians have approached the Blitz from the experience perspective and the works of authors such as Longmate, Calder, Gardiner, Ziegler and White are essential reading and highly recommended. As an experience the Blitz has also been well documented by those on the receiving end with many memories recorded. But how does the battle relate to the experience? I have revisited the London Blitz of 1940-41 looking at exactly what happened in the metropolis in those years, and set out a chronology of events as the Blitz progressed. I have examined what gave rise to those experiences which constitute such a rich London heritage.

Who won the battle? The success or failure of the Luftwaffe's Blitz is often measured solely by the experience of the civilians on the receiving end. Simon Jenkins identifies 'A grim acceptance that this was something that had to be seen through to the end' and 'fortitude' rather than a 'Blitz spirit.'[1] The latter certainly didn't win the battle. 'Blitz' has found its way into many contexts in recent years – even to describe the actions of a food processor. The 'Blitz spirit' now means carrying on through a range of adversarial conditions – in modern times relatively minor interruptions to daily routine. This is perhaps yet another reason to refocus on the original.

The Luftwaffe's Blitz failed partly because the morale aspect was over-estimated. The bombing raids on London and other cities not only failed to break civilian morale but never approached being conclusive in military terms. The raids were not concentrated or heavy enough to deliver 'knockout' blows to the cities targeted. Delivering accurate bombing at night and in poor weather were obstacles never fully overcome by either the Luftwaffe or the RAF in World War 2.

During my childhood in the north-east London suburb of Chingford in the 1950s, World War 2 had only been over for a decade or so, but it seemed very remote to me. The war in Europe had lasted over six years, and for most of those years, aerial bombardment was an ongoing threat, if not always a reality, for Londoners. 'Bomb sites' provided some extra focus for post-war curiosity. Obvious bomb sites were generally to be found in more central locations in London, the amount of damage to shops and houses in Chingford having been relatively small and repaired soon after the war. One has to ask what contribution the destruction of some 295 houses in suburban Chingford made to Germany's air war effort against Britain. It is difficult to assess and I make no apology in returning to Chingford's ordeal during this book as it seems to epitomize the wastefulness and pointlessness of the Luftwaffe's campaign against London.

It also has to be considered that after the war many British

---

1   Jenkins, *A Short History of London* (2019)

people may have just wanted to forget the horrors and hardship they had suffered in the Blitz and in the war generally and concentrate on rebuilding their lives in the difficult post-war environment. Others were scarred by those horrors and trauma to the extent their whole post-war existence was that of unrelieved psychological misery. The military campaigns, however, far from being forgotten, continued to be the subjects of many books and films through the 1950s and 1960s. They naturally involved celebration of the triumphs and victories for the allied military forces against the Axis powers. Perhaps the lack of similar enthusiasm for celebrating London's victory in the Blitz was because the attack on civilians in the Blitz wasn't seen as a 'proper' war, and because there were no tangible or critical battles fought or victories won in this war.

I have included some personal accounts to illustrate the suffering and terror experienced by the civilian population, their personal and material losses, and the grievous damage to London's landmarks. Many heroic actions are recorded during the Blitz. I hope I have done them justice. It is clear that the heart of London did not stop beating, and the population carried on because there was no alternative. We have to appreciate what happened in the capital in the grim years 1940-41 and celebrate and recognise those Londoners who endured it.

John Conen

LIST OF ABBREVIATIONS

Railway companies

LMS	London, Midland and Scottish Railway
LNER	London and North Eastern Railway
GWR	Great Western Railway
SR	Southern Railway

LCC	The London County Council, the local government body for the County of London; that is, modern inner London. There were 28 Metropolitan Boroughs within the LCC's area.
GPO	the General Post Office, the UK's posts and telecommunications authority
ARP	Air Raid Precautions hence ARP wardens etc
HE	High Explosive (bomb)
UXB	Unexploded bomb
X-Gerät, Y-Gerät	German navigation systems used by the Luftwaffe's pathfinder aircraft.
LFS	London Fire Service. London's professional fire service, covering the LCC area (the metropolitan boroughs). Incorporated into the National Fire Service in August 1941

following a review of the performance of local fire services in the Blitz of 1940-41.

AFS   Auxiliary Fire Service

WRNS   Women's Royal Naval Service

VAD   All voluntary aid detachment members (who came to be known simply as 'VADs') were trained in first aid and nursing. At the outbreak of war, the British Red Cross and the Order of St. John joined together again to form the Joint War Organisation (JWO) which had worked so successfully in World War 1. Much of the VAD service was performed in auxiliary hospitals and convalescent homes in Britain.[2]

MoHS   Ministry of Home Security. A government department formed in 1939 to direct civil defence activity in the UK and reabsorbed into the Home Office at the end of the war.

CWGC   Commonwealth War Graves Commission. Custodians of the Civilian War Dead Roll of Honour listing all civilian fatalities in World War 2.

---

2   British Red Cross website http.//www.redcross.org

SOURCES AND RECORDS

When I wrote my account of the Little Blitz of 1944, I frequently consulted sources that covered the whole wartime history of aerial attack on the UK. It was a concern to find so many inaccuracies and contradictions in accounts of the earlier Blitz on London. It soon became clear that there were many differences over the facts of the Blitz of 1940-41, and more understandably, many differing viewpoints on the effects and impact of the Blitz. The advent of the Internet has only compounded the problem. Even when researching his 1959 account of the 10/11 May 1941 raid, Richard Collier found a lack of agreement on the facts regarding casualties, fires and damage. He remarks that 'some historians … have agreed, some have disagreed violently, on almost every one of the points discussed above.'[3]

As with all aspects of German attacks on the UK, wartime restrictions on reporting by the censor mean that contemporary newspaper accounts are of limited use to the researcher. This reflected a need to avoid giving any information away that might be useful to the enemy – the locations of incidents, casualties caused, damage to military targets and essential war industries, transport and utilities. However, for the present-day researcher, local

---

3   Collier, *The City That Wouldn't Die* (1959)

knowledge can be useful in linking these anonymised accounts to actual events. Incidents not involving civilian fatalities can be difficult to track down even if considerable material destruction occurred. Once the location of an 'incident' is identified, a vast amount of information can be found on the Internet – church histories are often helpful. Many local accounts of how the Blitz impacted on London's boroughs have been published since the war and survive in many different books and websites. I owe a great debt to the dedicated local historians who are the authors of these accounts. Much valuable information on the impact of the Blitz on London's railway network is contained in BWL Brooksbank's *London Main Line War Damage*.

Of published sources, Richard Trench's *London Before the Blitz* describes London's streetscape as it was in pre-war days; Sir Nikolaus Pevsner assesses the toll of destruction suffered by London's architectural heritage in the Buildings of England series; Jerry White's *London in the Twentieth Century* gives a colourful account of life in London before the war and insight into how and why the capital's population and industry grew so significantly in the years leading up to that conflict.

The past few decades have seen a huge increase in the recording and dissemination of oral history and the Blitz with its implications for civilian experience is a topic that has benefitted greatly. However, this often exposes the lack of definitive, written information from official sources on the events that led to the experiences recorded. Of the many compilations, the BBC's *WW2 People's War* is an archive which contains many evocative personal accounts from the Blitz era.

The Public Records Act 1958 required central government departments, and certain other public bodies, to identify records of historical value and transfer them for permanent preservation to the National Archives, or to another appointed place of deposit, by the time they are 50 years old. The closure period was reduced from fifty to thirty years by an amending act of 1967 (the Government is currently reducing this timeframe from 30 to 20 years). Covered by this legislation were all the files of the Ministry of Home Security, covering many aspects of the Blitz and the response of the Civil Defence organisation.

Effectively, the 'thirty-year rule' meant that much basic information about the Blitz was not released to the public domain until the 1970s, and in the interim period, hearsay probably became confused with fact in the absence of a definitive history. No doubt secrecy requirements led to many aspects of the Blitz being shrouded in mystery and a proliferation of incorrect information was a feature of the many accounts that were published from the 1970s onwards.

The Ministry of Home Security Daily Intelligence Reports, submitted at 12-hourly intervals in the Blitz period, give a graphic picture of the impact of the raids, as details of damage to London's buildings are recorded. As far as casualties were concerned it was often at least a few days before an accurate assessment was possible. After the first few days of the Blitz, one almost perceives a sense of relief that the situations reported were not anything as bad as had been expected. The minutes of the War Cabinet also seldom record any deep concerns. London's vast acreage was swallowing up the enemy attack.

In his study of Air Raid Precautions services in the London Region, Dr Robin Woolven regrets the lack of a detailed study of the organisation, administration and performance of ARP in London. He thinks 'a sometimes-misleading picture is given in books on 'The Home Front' which tend to over-simplify a complex situation when civil defence is summarised in a few lines or paragraphs'. He highlights that many post-war authors seem to rely on the secondary, rather than the original sources.[4]

---

4   Woolven, R., *Civil Defence in London 1935-1945* (2001)

However, it is understandable that many writers have relied on secondary rather than primary sources. Defining 'primary sources' for the Blitz is in any case difficult. The local Civil Defence organisations generated a vast amount of paperwork much of it in response to demands from their regional HQs, who in turn had to report to the Ministry of Home Security.[5] Naturally these operational monitoring documents and records were not designed to provide or record a history. These primary sources ended up in different places – anything sent to the Ministry of Home Security would have ended up secure and subject to the '30-year rule'[6] which is commonly used to describe the point at which records created by government departments are transferred to The National Archives, and at which most of these records are released into the public domain.

Also, it is often unclear what sources some authors have consulted and where some information has originated. Some are indeed from secondary sources and some are often carelessly transcribed and contain errors. However, the original sources do not purport to tell the history of the Blitz, or of ARP. Also, looking at events solely from the 'experience' point of view clearly has its limitations.

Records kept by the civil defence organisation within local authorities including information on bombing incidents and the response to them were not subject to the thirty-year rule even though summary information sent in to, for example, the Ministry of Home Security was. However, the original records have not always survived, in fact across the ninety-five or so local authorities in the London Civil Defence Region there were wide variations in the extent to which wartime records were preserved. There are occasional discoveries of records even now

---

5   *Chingford at War* includes a comprehensive selection of these forms.
6   From 2013 government papers have been progressively released to the public after 20 years.

after seventy or more years; for instance, a card index of every property damaged in the area of Chigwell Urban District has only recently (2018) come to light. This index was kept for decades by a firm of surveyors, largely to refer to when remediation needed further work. When the firm ceased to trade, it passed into the care of the Loughton and District Historical Society.

Any local history published just after the war can be a useful source, particularly where the authors had served either in civil defence or local government and had access to civil defence records. Later, many of these locally-held records were to disappear. Fire brigade records are very extensive and every fire call has an entry, although the fire brigades did not necessarily attend even a major bombing incident if no fire was involved. The Metropolitan Police also kept their own records and diaries. Official histories commissioned by railway companies, the GPO, and other bodies after the war would also have had access.

Many statistics first appeared at a time when it was desirable to understate the size and effect of a Luftwaffe air raid. As a result, it can be difficult to find consensus about an air raid when it comes to the basics about the number of aircraft that took part, how many bombs they dropped, and how many lives were lost and buildings destroyed. The size of an air raid is usually expressed in terms of the number of aircraft taking part, but British sources may only count the aircraft that were actually observed to attack the target locality. In addition, it was quite normal for Luftwaffe crews to make a second sortie in the course of a night. The number of bombs dropped in any raid must have been very difficult for those on the receiving end to quantify. German sources giving the number and weight of bombs despatched would seem to be the best, even if not all bombs loaded would have been dropped on Britain, if for example an aircraft was shot down or crashed before it had released its bombs. The best measure of incendiaries is to total the number of canisters the Luftwaffe claimed to have dropped, multiplied by the numbers of bombs in a canister.

British civil defence personnel did make great efforts to record the tonnage of bombs dropped but there were inevitably incidents where it was not possible. This was certainly the case in the heaviest air raids, and in locations that suffered particularly intense attacks. Assessing the weight of individual bombs was never going to be 100% accurate. Not all unexploded bombs were traced and some are known not to have been recovered, and unexploded German bombs still turn up from time to time in the course of building and construction work in London. Fortunately, there have been no casualties in Britain from World War 2 unexploded ordnance since 1956. However, there was a tragic incident in June 1942 when a bomb that had lain undiscovered since the raid of 10/11 May 1941 exploded without warning in Southwark, killing nineteen people. It had possibly been disturbed in the course of demolition work nearby. The entry hole of an unexploded heavy bomb could sometimes be confused with the crater of an exploded small bomb. Given its weight and speed of descent, any heavy bomb would cause some destruction even if it did not explode.

So, I am reluctant to baffle readers with a multitude of alternative facts and figures and I hope they will forgive the occasional lack of precision on my part.

PART ONE

THE BLITZ IN CONTEXT

ONE

DEFINITIONS

Those with a little knowledge of German may think 'Blitz' is a strange name for the bombing of London in 1940-41. Blitzkrieg or lightning war was a name given (not by the German leadership) to the Axis attacks on France and the Low Countries, and on Denmark and Norway in 1940, rapid and conclusive attacks which conquered each of these countries in a matter of weeks. Blitz as applied to the German Luftwaffe's attack on London was therefore a curious name for a series of long bombing raids, which became a war of attrition on the civilian population and certainly not a 'lightning' strike. Blitz was soon adopted as a name for a series of bombing raids on a particular town, although the term 'blitz' is often used to refer to London's ordeal alone. Others seem to regard 'the Blitz' and 'wartime Britain' as interchangeable terms.

In 1940-41 most German night attacks on the UK were of this nature and a 'dusk to dawn' ordeal was the lot of most

British cities at various times during this period. This in itself made the raids much more of an ordeal than a sharp attack of around one hour even if the intensity of the bombing was less. Contributing to the 'experience' was the inevitable lack of sleep for the civilian.

'Blitz' as a separate term for a series of air raids has evolved slightly differently. In World War 1, the appearance of German Zeppelin airships and later Gotha and Giant aircraft over British cities caused terror and panic. After all, a decade earlier aircraft had not existed let alone been seen by civilians in Britain, and airships were scarcely more familiar. Terror and panic soon turned to anger as children were killed and little was seen to be done to halt the raiders. Although the scope and effects of air raids in World War 1 were very limited, technology continued to develop. Strategists soon dreamt of huge outcomes from the future use of aircraft to bomb cities, and fiction authors let their imaginations run riot. An air raid was envisaged as a mass attack on a city, brief and in daylight, which would cause huge casualties and force civilians to flee the built-up areas. The experience of Guernica in 1937 was not encouraging for those planning future protection against air raids. This was reinforced by reports of the attacks on Warsaw and Rotterdam in the first year of World War 2.

The 'incident' as opposed to an 'accident' was the term used by the ARP or Civil Defence organisations in wartime Britain for the result of the fall of a bomb. 'Incident' by its very name seems to trivialise and some writers do not like the term. During the Blitz, there was a range of events, from major disaster to minor incident and as Sansom has said, 'no disaster can be greater than the death or maiming of a single person'. The phrase 'only one person was killed' again can trivialise a personal tragedy.

THE GERMAN STRATEGY FOR BLITZKRIEG

Unlike the Little Blitz of 1944, the Blitz of 1940-41was not planned as a single campaign by the Luftwaffe and not only comprised several distinct phases but involved a number of target locations. These the British official historian in *Front Line* classified as 'the Onslaught on London', and under 'the Ordeal of the Provinces', 'the attack on the Arms Towns', 'the attack on the Ports', 'the Countryman's Blitz', and 'Seaside Tip-and-Run'. But the German leadership let alone the Luftwaffe would not have recognised this breakdown.

The significance of the Blitz, which affects all the perceptions of it, is that it was a military attack against a civilian population. Therefore, the Blitz became an experience rather than a battle for the British civilian. The civilian had a passive role, with some limited military input into defence in the form of anti-aircraft fire and night fighters. Neither AA fire nor night fighters, nor the barrage balloons, had much effect on the attacking bombers during the London Blitz, although the official line was that they did (this was the case but not in night-time raids), and civilians also set great store by them.

In the space of less than forty years the aeroplane had been invented, developed as a transport option, adopted by the military and then established as a centrepiece of military strategy. A substantial part of its military usage in World War 2 was dedicated to the destruction of the domestic infrastructure of participating countries. However, by the end of World War 2 the concept of destroying enemy cities with vast fleets of planes delivering equally vast tonnages of conventional bombs was redundant. Technology had continued to develop, and in the end strategic bombing was overtaken and superseded.

A key supporter of the concept was Sir Arthur Harris, appointed Commander-in-Chief of the RAF's Bomber

Command in February 1942. He soon analysed the Luftwaffe's failings in the war to date. Referring to the German attacks on provincial cities, Harris wrote after the war that the Luftwaffe had repeatedly missed its chance, as it had done in the London Blitz to set cities ablaze by a concentrated attack.[7] The notorious attack on Coventry on 14 November 1940 was in Harris's opinion adequately concentrated in point of space but he found little concentration in point of time. This was the result of what Frederick Taylor calls 'shuttle bombing' which resulted in the Luftwaffe's night raids of the 1940-41 period lasting anything up to ten hours. Unimpeded by night fighters and AA fire, the attacking bombers would arrive a few at a time over the target, before returning to base and preparing for a second sortie. An extended bombing raid certainly had some advantages for the attacker, given the debilitating effect on civil defence workers and firefighting personnel. On 14 November 1940 in Coventry the sirens sounded at 19.10 and the 'raiders passed' signal reached Coventry at 06.16 the next morning, although most of the sirens in the city could not be sounded for the 'all clear' due to power failures created by the raid. An estimated 330 Luftwaffe aircraft attacked Coventry.[8] It is interesting to speculate what the outcome might have been if the raid had delivered its tonnage of bombs in half an hour rather than eleven hours.

Despite his criticisms of German efforts in 1940-41, Harris was committed to aerial bombardment of enemy cities to cause the collapse of the enemy war effort and to hasten the end of hostilities. Harris seems to have acknowledged that the Germans had the right idea but they hadn't had the aircraft to follow it through adequately. For Harris, achieving success involved the building of a huge fleet of heavy bombers and a

---

7   Harris, *Bomber Offensive* (2005)
8   Longmate, *Air Raid* (1976)

vast effort to train crews, which took several years to bring to a state of full readiness. When this was achieved, compared to the Luftwaffe, Harris was to have the disadvantage of a long haul for his bombers to reach many German cities with particular problems at night locating the more remote targets such as Berlin, Munich and Nuremberg. As a result, Harris' bombing efforts sometimes suffered from the same lack of concentration that he had criticised in German attacks in 1940-41. But in the end the sheer weight of the RAF's attack achieved results far beyond anything the Luftwaffe could have aspired to in 1940-41.

The 'failure' of the Luftwaffe's various blitzes on Britain is often looked at in the context of the subsequent 'success' of the RAF blitzes on German cities. The Luftwaffe at the time was a support not a strategic function; it took the RAF three years to develop a function the Luftwaffe never aspired to. The weather also was a significant influence on operations throughout the winter of 1940-41.

The German approach initially in 1940 was that bombing would be a 'softening up' prior to an invasion. But the cumulative effect of the 'softening' was wasted as invasion plans did not materialize and had in fact been put on hold by Hitler as early as October 1940. Hitler didn't appear to want to destroy Britain, and his air force in its role as support to the army certainly preferred strategic strikes and specific targets. On the face of it, these would not seem to be incompatible. But the revenge aspect was always there. A popular response by British civilians early in the Blitz was 'we can take it' but with the rider 'give it to 'em back!' The popular press also supported revenge. After the raid of 16/17 April 1941, the *Daily Mail* headlines proclaimed that 'London will not forget – nor forgive'. Hitler's response to the RAF's rather feeble raid on Berlin in August 1940 was to promise retribution in kind, and for the Luftwaffe in doing so to greatly exceed the tonnage the RAF had dropped on Berlin. Similarly, when Munich, the capital of the Nazi movement, received a token effort from the RAF, vengeance was soon forthcoming. Nevertheless, the bombing of cities often seemed to be regarded by both sides as having a 'frightener' role rather than being a centrepiece of military strategy.

Foreign visitors often had a more realistic and perceptive view of the raids. US Military Attaché General Raymond E Lee remarked that he failed to see the point of the Luftwaffe's continuous onslaught against London: 'so erratic and so varied in its objectives I cannot believe it is being directed by a trained soldier or airman'. Later however, he acknowledged that at least Hitler made his attacks at weekends 'when the British automatically forsake their posts'![9] This certainly seemed to be a strategy deliberately employed during the winter months, when the opportunity to attack a city centre on a Sunday night was usually taken. It was unlikely to have been Hitler's personal decision.

At dinner with Churchill and the new Chief of Air Staff, Air Marshal Sir Charles Portal on 13 October 1940, Dowding remarked that the Luftwaffe had been 'almost exclusively lacking in purpose' and had failed to concentrate on detailed objectives. The assembled company wondered why there had not been, for example, a 'mass raid' on one small part of London.[10] Apart from the opening attack of the Blitz on 7 September 1940, the raid on Teddington in November 1940 was the only attempt in this direction. Did the Luftwaffe not seek any feedback on these raids? The big raids on London in the spring of 1941 were potentially a winning formula but there seemed to be no intention to follow them through and by the time of the successful 10/11 May raid the Luftwaffe was already committed to redeploy and support the planned invasion of the Soviet Union.

---

9   Leutze, ed., *The London Observer* (1972)
10 Colville, *The Fringes of Power* (1985)

Not only military experts had doubts. Looking back after the war, Tom Harrisson noted that 'the erratic pattern' of the Luftwaffe blitzes seemed in retrospect to be nearly senseless. He thought that the sequence of raids showed 'no logic, no discernible theory of what such attacks – more or less indiscriminate bombing of all structures within a few limited areas nightly – were supposed to achieve'. He couldn't see why one place was left alone for weeks or months, while another was given 'serial assault, though still never with any consistency.'[11] Harrisson was concerned mainly with the blitzes on provincial cities but the attack on London showed similar characteristics, particularly the randomness of the attacks in the spring of 1941, and the general failure to focus on any particular targets in the London region after 7 September 1940.

The raid on the City of London on 29 December 1940 was a success for the Luftwaffe, but there was a strong element of luck involved. Only 136 German aircraft took part but the raid was given a substantial advantage by the poor state of readiness of the defenders – it was the Sunday night after Christmas in an area with a very low resident population, consisting largely of unoccupied business premises – and the tides had resulted in the Thames being at an exceptionally low level. Firefighters found business premises deserted, padlocked and inaccessible – and in at least one case with guard dogs as a deterrent to entry! Although the pathfinders were not 100% accurate, they did concentrate bombing on the City and Southwark. Again, the Luftwaffe did not seek or receive any feedback which might have shown the seriousness of the damage they had caused. They assumed that because the raid had ended earlier than planned because of deteriorating weather, it could not have been successful.

---

11 Harrisson, *Living through the Blitz* (1978)

Trying to get participation in fire-watching duties was only belated recognised as a major challenge and even the first legislation on this subject in January 1941 did not produce the commitment desired. The end of continuous nightly bombing added to the problem, as each raid-free night added to the defenders' complacency. Night bombing inevitably led to a requirement for fire-watchers, drawn from a diminishing supply of labour. The need for sleep and rest for those working in the day conflicted with the need to have adequate fire-watching cover for homes as well as workplaces at night. The eventual overwhelming of civil defence resistance by fire bombing was an outcome that was spared in Britain by the Luftwaffe focussing on a large number of targets.

The cost of the huge number of high explosive bombs that fell harmlessly in open ground, fell on buildings of no significance to the war effort or simply failed to explode must have been enormous. The incendiary bomb was considering its size far better value and more effective. Blast from high explosive alone did not usually cause irreparable damage to plant and machinery in factories. Fire caused by incendiary bombs was soon to be recognised as the greatest danger facing Britain's industries. The German standard incendiary bomb weighed just 1kg, it consisted of a cylindrical body, 34.5cm long, and 5cm in diameter, made of magnesium alloy and filled with thermite, an incendiary compound, to which was riveted a steel tail with three fins. These bombs did not explode, but on impact, the needle in the igniter was driven into a small percussion cap, which in turn ignited the thermite filling, and ultimately, the alloy casing itself, producing heat that was sufficient to melt steel. It then burned fiercely for fifty seconds, then less fiercely for five minutes. The intense blaze caused by an incendiary could cause the destruction of machinery and equipment that might have survived the blast of a high explosive.

Considerable commitment of manpower was essential to ensure all incendiary bombs were tackled as soon as they fell. But the concept of round-the-clock security of premises against incendiary bombs seemed alien to Britain's businesses. The Civil Defence authorities and ordinary civilians, like Vere Hodgson, seemed to be all too aware of the shameful neglect of ARP by small businesses in London and of the wider vulnerability of London's historic buildings. 'We had further news of the damage to the City – and all through neglect! Always the same … no one wants to take responsibility … let others do it. Common sense should tell us that it is madness to leave buildings to one caretaker, or to no one at all, in times like these.'[12] Even after the raid of 10/11 May, Miss Hodgson, seeing the destruction caused to Westminster Abbey, Westminster Hall and the Houses of Parliament, is moved to write: 'I feel we must have sinned grievously as a nation to have such sacrifices demanded of us. Indeed, future generations will say we have not taken care of what was handed down to us.'[13]

If tackled immediately on falling, an incendiary bomb could be put out by a civilian using a quantity of sand or even garden soil. Once an incendiary had taken hold, unless tackled quickly with a stirrup pump, it could develop into a fire which could only be put out by the fire services, using water pumped from the mains supply. In contrast, the much larger 'oil bomb' (the 250 kg *Flammenbombe* and a bigger 500 kg version) and the later phosphorus bombs were ineffective, often failing to explode or even if they did, to ignite, merely causing an unpleasant mess. Reports of barrels of oil strapped to high explosive bombs are unlikely to have any basis in fact, nor was the idea likely to be more effective than a real oil bomb.

---

12 Hodgson, *Few Eggs and No Oranges* (2010)
13 Hodgson, *Few Eggs and No Oranges* (2010)

One disadvantage of the lack of concentration in time that Harris had observed in the Luftwaffe night raids of 1940-41 was that it reduced the effectiveness of the incendiary attack, whatever the exhaustion it caused for those enduring lengthy periods on duty in fire brigades and civil defence. There appears to have been a lack of appreciation of the potential of incendiary attack as according to Luftwaffe records, the bomb loads in some London raids in the autumn of 1940 had a negligible incendiary content.

Throughout the war, with only limited technology to optimise operational performance, every air raid, whether by the RAF on Germany or by the Luftwaffe on Britain was unpredictable – the variables being the weather, the alertness and readiness of the defences, the preparedness of the civilian population, or just a particular combination of circumstances.

'Is there a foe that bombing cannot break?' was said to be the motto of Feldmarschall Hugo Sperrle, commander of Air Fleet Three during the London Blitz.[14] He had led the Condor legion in 1936-37 in Spain where his forces were responsible for the bombing of Guernica and other Spanish towns. He was responsible for some devastating and successful air raids. But did he actually break any of his foes? Sperrle, despite his unflattering depiction in contemporary photographs, was no sadistic destroyer of cities; he was an experienced bomber commander who even before the war was aware of the immense destructive power of the incendiary bomb. Although he did not apparently favour a strategy of dropping high explosive bombs late in a raid to keep firefighters under cover (he thought that the destruction caused by such bombs would merely act as firebreaks) there is little evidence his air fleet put this into practice.

---

14 Collier, *The City That Wouldn't Die* (1959). I have not seen Sperrle's 'motto' quoted elsewhere.

The Blitz ended without any decisive results for the Luftwaffe. There is little evidence that there was any real desire to break British civilian resistance or that the actual raids were expected to do this.

BRITISH PREPAREDNESS

'In the next war you will find that any town within reach of an aerodrome can be bombed within the first five minutes of war ...I think it is well also for the man in the street to realize that there is no power on earth that can protect him from being bombed, whatever people may tell him. The bomber will always get through'.

This gloomy forecast by Britain's Conservative party leader, Stanley Baldwin, addressing Parliament in 1932, did not take account of the development of defences against bombers, particularly fighter aircraft, which led to daylight bombing soon becoming too costly in terms of aircraft losses. Night bombing too had its own problems both for the attackers and the defences, but most night bombers in 1940-41 got through even if they didn't always locate the target adequately. This pattern would continue throughout the bombing war in Britain and Germany; what happened once the bombers got through remained a significant variable. Even as late as March 1945 in Operation *Gisela*, seventy Luftwaffe night fighters were able to 'get through' and infiltrate British defences under cover of RAF aircraft returning from Germany, and bomb and strafe at will for three and a half hours. If the 'bomber will always get through' theory had been disproved in the daytime Luftwaffe attacks, at night it seemed it would hold true. Leaving aside the weather, which at least led to some nights of respite in the winter of 1940/41, the main deterrents to the attackers were balloons, AA fire and night fighters. These were negligible in their effect on the Luftwaffe, and although the press was keen to emphasise how these defensive measures were operating, most of the successes occurred in daytime. The cumulative totals of Luftwaffe aircraft shot down in 1940 looked impressive but were almost entirely the result of daytime fighter action.

Aerial attack on Britain was long anticipated and official 'precautions' were devised and put in place. The attack was anticipated to start on day one of a conflict and would be in the form of relatively brief daylight bombing attacks. These would be followed by a series of similar daily attacks continuing to cause a huge number of casualties – casualty estimates were initially based on figures from the experience of London in World War 1. They were not to be scaled down. In May 1924 when an ARP sub-committee in the Home Office headed by Sir John Anderson had begun to meet, it was advised that London would be the prime target in the first hours of hostilities. 450 tons of bombs would fall in the first 72 hours, killing 3,800 and seriously wounding twice as many. Therefore over 25,000 deaths could be expected in the first month. The figures were to be enhanced by those who sought to avoid war in the 1930s. Both the weight of attack and in particular its effect in terms of casualties and damage turned out to be grossly over-estimated, but these figures were used by other Government departments for planning purposes. By 1937 the figures had increased based on a figure of fifty to seventy-two casualties per ton of bombs and although this had no statistical validity, it came to form the basis for much pre-war planning.[15] Bomb tonnage to be dropped was estimated as initially 3,500 tons in the

---

15 Harrisson, *Living Through the Blitz* (1973)

first twenty-four hours followed by 600 per day rising to 900 within six months.[16] 700 tons a day on London was forecast by the British Air Staff in the spring of 1939. 3,000 tons had been mentioned but by anti-war supporters at the time of the Munich crisis.[17] But it is what it was thought this would cause – 250,000 casualties and £100 million of damage estimated – that was the most frightening, but in the end very far from realistic.

Harrisson's view was that Sir John Anderson and his advisers were led by these 'dire projections' into overestimating the material impact but at the same time underestimating the human capacity to face up to it. He felt that the individuals in charge – like Anderson – were of the highest intellectual quality but very remote from 'the people' amongst whom it was assumed neurosis and panic would be widespread.[18]

The reality was different. After war was declared, the expected air attack did not materialise and this gave an opportunity to improve defences and 'precautions' further. Quite how comprehensive the attack was anticipated to be was unclear. How much of London could have been affected? How many other cities could be targeted as well? The strength of the Luftwaffe in terms of number of planes was exaggerated. What weight of bombs they could deliver was also exaggerated – no German bombers could attack Britain with a full bomb load from bases in Germany. The aircraft could not carry a full bomb load in view of the fuel needed for distance involved and the need to make an 'operational allowance' for forming up etc. They would be unescorted in view of the distance from their German bases. It seems there was no intention to launch an attack on day one, even if the Luftwaffe had sufficient aircraft

16 Fitzgibbon, *The Blitz* (1970)
17 Price, *Blitz on Britain* 1939-1945 (1977)
18 Harrisson, *Living Through the Blitz* (1973)

available; initially of course, the Luftwaffe was tied up in Poland. Also, Britain had made the first move by declaring war.

Basic questions remained unanswered. How many aircraft were realistically available to deliver this weight of attack? Could it have been done? What number of aircraft and bomb capacity would be needed? Even at the outbreak of war, Price estimates that Fighter Command had sufficient resources to inflict a 13% loss on attacking aircraft, a rate of attrition that would be unsustainable.[19] This would affect not only the weight of bombs that could be dropped but what casualties these would cause. In World War 1 few precautions were in place in the form of warning systems or shelters, and lucky hits contributed to the high casualty rate.

In the event, in the London Blitz, the first major raid on 7 September 1940 – which did have some resemblance to the anticipated format – delivered 320 tons; this figure was only occasionally exceeded in a single raid during the fifty-seven nights of the first stage of the London Blitz. Only once, on 19/20 April 1941, in London was more than 1,000 tons to be dropped in a Luftwaffe raid on Britain in one night.

Post-war, it was estimated[20] that a ton of high-explosive dropped in a night raid actually killed four to five people and injured between ten and fifteen, most of them only slightly. So, the casualty rate was between fifteen and twenty per ton as opposed to the pre-war estimates of fifty to seventy-two casualties per ton. Titmuss attributes this to the 'uncritical acceptance of historical evidence, in the lack of research concerning the effects of high-explosive bombs, exaggerated ideas about the consequences of air bombardment, and, finally, in a general over-estimation of Germany's striking power in the

19 Price, *Blitz on Britain 1939-1945* (1977)
20 Titmuss, *Problems of Social Policy* (1950)

air'.[21] There were some interesting revelations. The Ministry of Home Security found that casualties per ton were 50% higher in day raids than in night raids, one factor being that during day raids many people would be at work or outdoors. The ministry also found that density of population was important – there was a steep decline in the casualty rate even a few miles from the inner-city areas.

Given the scale of the onslaught anticipated, it is not surprising that Air Raid Precautions rather than Civil Defence were the order of the day in pre-war Britain. In particular, taking precautions against the use of poison gas by an enemy was a very important part of pre-war ARP planning and involved the issue of gas masks to the entire population. A civilian anti-gas school was set up at Falfield, Gloucestershire, to train instructors. Also instigated was the provision of decontamination facilities for people, their clothes and food stocks. It is argued that this thorough preparation meant that a poison gas attack on Britain was never seriously contemplated by the German leadership. Another reason may have been that the German developments in precautions against poison gas were far less advanced or comprehensive than those in place in Britain at the outbreak of war.

The Government introduced the Air Raid Precautions Act in 1937 and it received the Royal Assent on 22 December that year. It was designed to ensure precautions were taken to protect people and property from injury and damage in the event of hostile attack from the air. Local councils had to prepare and submit an ARP scheme for the approval of the Home Secretary. The schemes were to include provision of premises and recruitment of personnel and provide for shelter protection for the population.

---

21 Titmuss, *Problems of Social Policy* (1950)

Services to deal with the after-effects of aerial attack had to be detailed in the schemes: air raid wardens' service, first aid post service (including a gas cleansing section), emergency ambulance service, rescue service and stretcher parties, gas identification services, decontamination services, repair of highways and sewers and the provision of a report and control centre.

A major part of the pre-war preparations was the establishment of the role of the ARP warden. The Government anticipated that he was to 'regard himself, first and foremost, as a member of the public chosen and trained to be a leader of his fellow-citizens and, with them and for them, to do the right things in an emergency.'[22] The legacy of World War 1 meant there was a generous potential supply of such people available in 1939. The National Register of September 1939 had a special column for those engaged in these organisations, and it's surprising how many were. Primarily this role was seen as that of enforcing the precautionary initiatives, and inevitably to many it was perceived as 'nannying', as we now call it, especially when no immediate threat was apparent. One can see a parallel with the popular decrying of 'health & safety' in Britain today. Only when air raids began did the role of ARP personnel develop into something more defined and the leadership qualities of the wardens were allowed to develop and be appreciated. Unfortunately, in the phoney war period hostility to 'underemployed' civil defence workers led to loss of trained staff.

There were significant variations in preparedness between districts and boroughs in the London region, and, once the Blitz had started, equally significant variations in the efficiency of their response. This is alluded to by O'Brien,[23] but surprisingly not explored in any detail in his official history. 'Genial, woolly-

---

22 *Duties of Air Raid Wardens* (1938)
23 O'Brien, *Civil Defence* (1958)

headed old duffers' was a less than flattering description of those in charge in local authorities. Civil defence had to be wrested from local control in two boroughs, the Metropolitan Borough of Stepney and the County Borough of West Ham. The ARP services of these boroughs functioned well, but the administration was severely tested by the sheer weight of the attacks. Poplar, by comparison, coped well although it was equally hard pressed.

Barbara Nixon, an active Labour supporter, was a warden in Finsbury and became very disillusioned with that borough's attitude to its people and to its civil defenders. However, it seemed that civil defence matters proceeded smoothly there and shelter provision was good. Nevertheless, things were far from perfect. Nixon, in examining what was wrong with Finsbury's warden service, identifies lack of proper treatment of personnel, appointment of unsuitable people to senior roles, discouragement of any democratic organisation amongst the personnel of the service or among the general public.[24]

The unexpected features of air raids included:

1. Far fewer casualties than expected in relation to the physical damage.
2. The large amount of rescue, repair and clearance work needed.
3. The large number of unexploded bombs necessitating temporary evacuation.
4. The sheer number of incidents in heavy raids (leading to problems in reporting and in directing the rescue services).
5. Problems locating casualties in intense darkness.
6. Extensive welfare services were needed post-raid.
7. Fire was potentially far more damaging than high explosive.

---

24 Nixon, *Raiders Overhead* (1980)

Of these 1 and 3 have relevance to the perceived lack of provision for those made homeless.

Numerous technical limitations became apparent in the Blitz of 1940-41 and were challenging if very much of their time, for example, in telecommunications, in the lighting of incidents at night to aid rescue work, and in the availability of heavy lifting gear to help rescue work, and bulldozers to clear wreckage.

The fire danger from an air raid was expected to provide a challenge completely dwarfing the normal fire occurrences encountered by a peacetime city fire brigade. Hence the establishment of the Auxiliary Fire Service which in terms of manpower was to greatly outnumber (tenfold) their regular colleagues. The initial attitude of 'regular' fire service personnel to their auxiliary colleagues is one of the rare negatives of the Blitz era but may indicate that the likely challenge had not been adequately communicated.

The Government's evacuation policy covered the evacuation of school children, mothers and young children, and invalids, from cities expected to be subject to enemy attack. The country was divided into 'evacuation', 'neutral' and 'reception' areas, and it was anticipated that in the event of war, eligible classes would be evacuated from the evacuation areas to reception areas in safer parts of the country. Some parts of London were initially classified as 'neutral' and were expected to be unlikely to attract the attention of the enemy's bombers; representations by some of these boroughs including Chingford led their status to be changed to 'evacuation'. The logistical aspects of evacuation in Britain were remarkably successful; the human aspects were not afforded the same level of attention. The welfare state was still years away and 'poor law' attitudes prevailed. The evacuation policy was upset by the failure of air attacks to materialise after the outbreak of war which led to probably two-thirds of all evacuees returning home by the time of the 1940 Blitz.

Contemporary letters quoted by Waller and Vaughan-Rees[25] reflect perceptions that dead or injured, the Londoner would be 'wonderfully catered for' but for the homeless there would be 'ludicrously underestimated', mean and inadequate provision. Tea and corned beef sandwiches! A major failing of pre-war planning was not anticipating the homelessness issue that arose in the wake of the night raids of 1940-41. Air raids were expected to result in a huge death toll, but they were expected to be brief and in daylight. Therefore, shelters weren't designed for prolonged habitation, let alone overnight stays, and deaths and provision of coffins, and hospital bed allocation were thought to be more important issues than providing for long-term homelessness. Perhaps it was thought that the sheer numbers of those becoming casualties would leave very few to become homeless? Gas, a major pre-war concern, would not have caused homelessness. Rest centres lacking facilities and equally poorly-equipped shelters were found to be housing hundreds of people with nowhere else to go, an undesirable and dangerous situation. On the first night of the Blitz, the first of many tragedies unfolded as these unprotected rest centres and poorly built or otherwise inadequate shelters were hit by bombs.

After the raids of early September 1940, refugees headed out of the East End into the outer suburbs and were accommodated at designated 'second line' rest centres. The borough of Chingford was required to accommodate 3,000 refugees, mainly from East Ham and West Ham. The Ministry of Home Security Daily Intelligence Reports say 8,000 reached Chingford, with 5,000 more expected! Miss Doris Sortwell, the head teacher of South Chingford Infants School, was perhaps a typical recipient. Most of the school's pupils had been evacuated but teaching had been organised in the homes of pupils who either declined evacuation

---

25 Waller and Rees, *Blitz. The Civilian War 1940-45* (1990)

or had returned – the school could not be used for classes as it had no shelters. She recorded that on 11 September, 170 refugees arrived and the school was closed until further notice. Within a few days, the school was in 'a most disgusting condition and the smell appalling...the outside and staff lavatories are unusable.' On 30 September, the refugees left, leaving the school still in 'a disgusting condition...nothing whatever done to clean school or playgrounds and the place is littered with rubbish.'[26]

On 1 October Miss Sortwell records that 'the schools are still in a filthy state ... the teachers are doing their best but nothing short of complete fumigation will make it habitable'.[27] Whether the school was fumigated is not recorded by Miss Sortwell, but the pupils eventually returned. The refugees and their plight were already a serious concern for the authorities everywhere and lodging them in schools with no facilities or shelters was courting disaster. No mention is made of how these particular refugees were fed (the school had no canteen facilities), but it seems that the WVS somehow undertook this responsibility.

In Richmond hundreds of refugees arrived at short notice on 12 September. The *Richmond and Twickenham Times* reported that 'a thousand men, women and children arrived, after a four-hour journey down river by barge or in pleasure launches. The first relay arrived at about 12 o'clock; a later party were landing just as an air raid warning sounded and so had to take shelter under the arches by the riverside immediately, and the last 600 arrived so late that they could not be billeted ... but had to spend the night at the cinema sleeping on the chairs or the floor'.

Simon Fowler adds that they did not receive a warm welcome.[28] As far as post-raid support was concerned, Barbara Nixon, a warden in Finsbury has commented that Public

---

26 Chingford Historical Society records
27 Chingford Historical Society records
28 Fowler, *Richmond at War* (2015)

Assistance officials could not rid themselves of the idea that they were dispensing charity and it was this attitude that caused even more resentment and anger than the delays.[29]

SHELTERS

When in July 1935, the first government Air Raid Precautions policy was published, it was a 'Protection and Dispersal' policy featuring evacuation, individual shelters and household refuges. Large communal shelters were discouraged. Post-raid services, gas protection – including masks – and public shelters for those caught out in a raid were also planned. The Air Raid Precautions Act 1938 introduced compulsion, and the Munich crisis had an accelerating effect. Sir John Anderson was appointed Lord Privy Seal in October 1938 with responsibility for the Co-ordination of Civil Defence and National Service and with a seat in the Cabinet.

The Government provided Anderson shelters, for use in houses with gardens, and later (in 1941, after the London Blitz had ended) the Morrison shelter for use indoors. Trench shelters, reinforced basement shelters in buildings and purpose-built communal shelters were also provided by local authorities, partly to meet the needs of those without shelters at home and partly for those caught out in an air raid.

Air raids like those experienced during the night Blitz of 1940-41 had not been anticipated. Neither was there any reason to expect raids lasting up to fourteen hours. Warsaw and Rotterdam had been severely bombed but the raids were brief. Barcelona's ordeal in the Spanish Civil War is worth mentioning as it was slightly different. Barcelona had seventeen raids at

---

29   Nixon, *Raiders Overhead* (1980)

THE BOMBING OF LONDON 1940-41

three-hourly intervals in the period 16 to 18 March 1938. Forty-four tons of bombs were dropped and an estimated 1,000 people killed. After this a huge effort was made to construct air raid shelters – over 1,200 of them; this work was done by the citizens, women and children having a prominent role. Altogether Barcelona had a total of 194 raids. On 29 January 1939, the city fell to Franco's forces.

It is alleged that Ramon Perera, who designed Barcelona's air raid shelters, was brought to Britain at the end of the civil war. However, he failed to convince the British authorities to provide shelters 'leaving 40,000 to die because they were only given Andersons'.[30] This is contradicted by others who also say that Perera didn't actually design all the shelters in Barcelona, and in any case, there is little doubt that Britain's Anderson shelters were effective except if they received a direct hit. The fact that people chose not to use their Andersons is also relevant! Barcelona is built on sandstone which is easily tunnelled. London is built on clay which means that tunnels must be lined, and that the Andersons were very wet. Barcelona's population mainly lived in apartments, London's in houses.

Londoners' Anderson shelters were relatively safe, but those who trusted in the larger public shelters were betrayed. Throughout the Civilian War Dead Roll of Honour for the years of the Blitz, the tragic perhaps even reproachful annotation 'died at the X shelter' recurs. Unfortunately, during the Blitz, public shelters, which were never designed to stand a direct hit, were hit, in most cases as a result of a random bomb. It was usually sheer bad luck. The gathering of a number of people in such places only increased the risk of disaster whereas a similar bomb falling on or near to the Anderson shelter of a small terraced

---

30 Ramon Perera, the man who saved Barcelona https.//collections.ushmm. org/search/catalog/bib144964

house might have only caused half a dozen casualties. In some cases, faulty shelter construction was to blame as initially, some street shelters had been constructed with the wrong mortar, although steps were taken to replace them when the situation became known. But in most cases, it was simply the inability to withstand a direct hit. Trench shelters were especially vulnerable.

An examination of the casualties for one month of the London Blitz gives some indication of how public shelters became death-traps. The Civilian War Dead Roll of Honour lists 4,777 civilian fatalities in the London region in October 1940; whilst this total also includes people who died following incidents in September or earlier, it gives a fairly accurate assessment of the total fatalities in the capital caused by bombing that month. Only 287 of these deaths are annotated in the Roll as occurring at a named shelter. However, there are at least 571 further listed deaths that did occur at a shelter although the shelter is not named, or at least the word 'shelter' is not used. The addresses Druid Street Billiard Hall, Dame Alice Owen's School, 157/161 Stoke Newington Road and Balham tube station all had large public sheltering facilities and were the location of some of the worst incidents to occur in the London Blitz. Morley College, another location, was a rest centre which was totally unsuitable to house the numbers that gathered there. Therefore at least 858 people – around a fifth of the total for the month – died at officially designated shelters and rest centres in London in October 1940. There were probably more. In the thousand-bomber RAF raid on Cologne in May 1942, according to the records of the Police President, nearly 40% of the 469 fatalities were in shelters.

Frances Faviell, who was a first aid worker at the time, remarks rather helplessly that it was policy for civilians to be directed to these official shelters.[31] At least they could not be

---

31 Faviell, *A Chelsea Concerto* (1959)

compelled to go, but there were few other options. As can be seen, many of the disastrous bombing incidents in the early part of the Blitz were at public shelters, officially designated for this purpose. In fact, the number of such incidents and the huge casualty lists they caused are appalling, and one would think there was no need to exaggerate these figures. But of course, the actual figures were not publicised at the time. This has no doubt given rise to the many rumours and untruths regarding these incidents which are still perpetuated today. Not only can casualty figures be grossly exaggerated, but it is often stated that the bodies of victims were left unrecovered under the ruins once all attempts at rescue had failed. This is just not true, although unidentified victims were often recovered and taken to mortuaries. If it was the case, one would expect to see many protests from people unable to bury their relatives or trace their bodies. I have never seen any evidence of this, but unfortunately there were incidents where victims of air raids were literally blown to pieces, and there was little left for identification or to put in the coffins.

Despite these incidents, people continued to shelter where they perceived themselves to be safe. Some popular shelters were not, initially at least, officially approved, and by inference unsafe. The stations on the underground railway network, although used during World War 1, came into this category. A major concern here was potential flooding of the deeper tubes, and flood gates were installed at great expense where these lines passed under the Thames. Without these there was a risk that the whole tube network in central London could have been flooded as a consequence of a bomb breaching just one tunnel under the Thames. But this work was not done to make the tubes safer as shelters.

The 'demand' for tube stations to be opened as shelters is something of a red herring. 100 tube stations were identified pre-war for use as shelters, of which only forty-five were considered 'non-vulnerable'.[32] Seventy-nine tube stations were eventually used for sheltering plus several miles of temporarily disused tube tunnel, for example the Holborn to Aldwych branch of the Piccadilly line (from 21 September 1940), and uncompleted lines such as the eastern extension of the Central line from Liverpool Street to Stratford and Leytonstone to Ilford. Some disused stations were brought into use as shelters and the LPTB handed them over to local authorities to run.[33] The stations on the sub-surface (rather than deep level tube) lines which included the Circle, District and Metropolitan lines in central London could not be used as shelters, neither could the stations on the outer reaches of the Bakerloo, Piccadilly and Northern lines, where the tracks ran on the surface. Once the Blitz began, a number of incidents seem to suggest that quite deep tube tunnels could be penetrated by the heavier types of high explosive bombs that the Luftwaffe introduced that autumn. Bombs penetrated 47ft at Eversholt Street on 21 October 1940, and 45ft at Holloway and 32ft at Bounds Green on 13 October 1940.[34] Fortunately the tunnels under the Thames were never breached, although the result of a hit on a disused tunnel only a few days after the Blitz had started was a confirmation that it had been prudent to take precautions. This proved to be the only such incident of the war.

Pre-war civil servants dithered over the tube sheltering issue. It has to be remembered that at this stage, air raids were expected to happen during the day. The reality was that when air raids began, they largely took place at night and for most of the night, the tube service ceased which put a slightly different slant on matters. Initially, sheltering in the tubes was discouraged, but people got around this by buying 1d platform tickets. On

---

32 TNA HO 186/149
33 Graves, *London Transport at War* (1989)
34 Graves, *London Transport at War* (1989)

8 September, a large number gained access to Liverpool Street (underground) Station despite the efforts of staff and police, and on 11 September over 2,000 were able to enter Holborn.[35] Mack and Humphries say that on 12 September, thousands of East Enders stormed tube stations in the east and centre of London. There were no tube stations in East London, only subsurface ones and this seems an exaggeration (Woolven finds no evidence of this and attributes it to a 'folk myth'[36]), although confrontational situations did no doubt arise. In any case the number of deep tube stations in east London was nil – east of Liverpool Street there was only the tunnel dug for the planned extension to the Central Line. However, the Metropolitan Police Diary states that 'on the evening of 9th (before the raid) some 5,000 persons attempted to rush the entrance of the new tube station at Bethnal Green – order restored by Police & Home Guard.'[37] What exactly happened is unclear but the subsequent action was reported by the *Sunday Mirror* on 6 October:

'Herbert Morrison, new Minister of Home Security, beloved by Londoners, is the man who gets things done. Standing on the platform of the uncompleted Bethnal Green Underground station, 65ft below ground yesterday, he asked L.P.T.B and local council officials why it was not being used as a shelter. He was told there were certain technical difficulties. "Is there anything to stop the people using it right away?" he queried brusquely. He was told there were not. "Then open it tonight" said Herbert Morrison. A.A. Shells were bursting in the sky during an alert when Mr Morrison and Admiral Sir Edward Evans arrived to inspect the station. Mr Morrison, after chatting with the experts, reached his decision about the opening of the station as a shelter in five minutes ... Mr Morrison said in an interview. "You can

---

35 Cooper, *London Underground at War* (2014)
36 Woolven, *Civil Defence in London 1935-1945* (2001)
37 MEPO 4/126 Metropolitan Police Diary 12 September 1940

tell the people we are going to utilise every inch of shelter we can find and we're going to do it quickly".'

This is an interesting scenario because it was at the uncompleted Bethnal Green underground station that Britain's biggest wartime disaster occurred in March 1943 when a stampede for the shelter entrance resulted in 173 people dying of suffocation. It had been used without incident by up to 7,000 people nightly since October 1940.

Although Morrison was told there were 'technical difficulties', it was not explained what these were. Of relevance was the fact there was only one entrance from the street and thousands would have to pass through this to the booking hall and this may have been considered a risk. However, the even narrower access from the booking hall to the platforms via two escalators was of greater concern and wardens were posted there every evening to manage the flow. Similar circumstances were present at other very large shelters but Bethnal Green seems to have been the riskiest.

Underground stations had open access with control at the ticket barriers at the top of the escalators. Risks at Bethnal Green were seen as the temporary wooden gates at street level giving way and people falling down the stairs, poor lighting and rainwater ingress. Proposals were made – albeit after the 1940-41 Blitz had ended – to remedy this but were turned down by Regional ARP.

By 1943, sheltering patterns were different to the main Blitz. Then people queued for their place often lining up early in the day and spending all night in the shelter irrespective of whether a raid took place. In 1943 a different attitude had evolved. People would wait around on the streets to see if a raid occurred and on hearing the alert would head to the shelter. Occupants of small shelters might move to larger ones. This would obviously lead to last minute rushes to get under cover which rarely occurred in 1940-41. People perhaps didn't feel confident that the Luftwaffe would not be able to match the RAF's efforts which were widely boasted about in the British media.[38]

On 14 September 1940, there was a political protest when about 100 people led by communist activists invaded the Savoy Hotel. The protest was led by Phil Piratin, a Communist Stepney borough councillor, who claimed that the occupation was designed as a 'pressure stunt' as part of a campaign to open the tube stations. Fitzgibbon says the unexpected sounding of the 'all clear' brought the demonstration to an earlier than expected end, but Bernard Kops saw it as a triumph for the people of the East End[39]. The following Tuesday a crowd encouraged by Piratin broke into Goodge Street station. Churchill had favoured opening the tubes but was opposed by cabinet colleagues; he was surprised at their subsequent change of heart and wondered why their previous strong arguments had been put aside. The Home Secretary never announced that the tubes would be officially opened for shelterers.[40] However, effectively they were and by 27 September, 177,000 people were using the London tubes for shelter, although this total thereafter gradually declined.

Pre-war, there were two arguments against using the tubes for sheltering; the need to keep the service running and linked to that, to avoid people taking up permanent residence in the stations. This would, it was feared, bring many safety and health-related issues into play. An important problem was that there were no toilets on the station platforms, which lie beneath the level of the sewers. The authorities also had a long-standing fear of a deep shelter mentality developing. Amongst the inter-war speculation and fear about the effects of aerial attack was an unchallenged assumption that people, having taken shelter, would refuse to come out. This did happen, although it was

---

38 Anon, *Tragedy at Bethnal Green 1943* (1999)
39 Kops, *The World is a Wedding* (1963)
40 Piratin, quoted in Levine, *Forgotten Voices* (2007)

often people whose homes had been destroyed and had nothing to come out to. But as most people didn't take shelter, the size of the problem was relatively small. As soon as air raids became less frequent, so sheltering declined, which probably contributed to the high casualty toll in the spring raids of 1941. The experience of other countries in air raids, for example Italy and Bulgaria, was that the population fled major cities and refused to return,[41] but this has to be looked at in the context of a lack of commitment to the war by civilians in those countries. Barcelona during the Spanish Civil War turned out to be more resilient when attacked by the Italian air force based in Majorca. In London, the new deep level shelters completed in 1941 were not opened to the public until after the V1 attack started in June 1944.

However, it is unlikely that any fear of shelters was engendered by the incidents referred to, as even in the height of the Blitz in November 1940, only a small proportion of London's population was using approved shelters, either public or at home. A survey made in November 1940 revealed that out of the 40% of Londoners who used shelters, 4% used the tube, 9% public shelters and 25% their own shelters.[42] Unfortunately, the situation often arose whereby people were killed in their local public shelter who would have escaped injury if they had remained at home. Using public shelters did provide company for the lonely, an important factor for some people who may have had their spouses or children evacuated or away on active service. The diarist, Anthony Heap, even expressed his appreciation of the saving in home heating and lighting costs that using public shelters afforded.[43]

Nevertheless, many people were to die in air raids because they did not take shelter at all. Some were caught out of doors or

---

41 Overy, *The Bombing War. Europe 1939-1945* (2014)
42 Ray (quoting Marwick) *The Night Blitz* (2004)
43 *The Diaries of Anthony Heap*

in transit, but mostly they remained in their homes and hoped to remain unscathed. The author's grandfather would always sleep in his bed in Hornsey – because of his arduous lorry driving job he needed a good night's rest and the air raids didn't worry him. A typical London raid of the 1940-41 period might last up to ten hours, but a particular locality might experience activity overhead for only a small proportion of this time even if the alert had been sounded. As a rule, most of London's citizens were not huddled in their shelters experiencing a continuous fall of bombs around them, although this scenario certainly did arise in the most concentrated raids on parts of inner-city London and in some provincial cities.

Incidents at blocks of tenements and flats, and at houses in multiple occupation, could result in large casualty lists. Out in the suburbs, casualties from incidents on modern housing estates might be less numerous. There was a strong contrast with Germany where civilian discipline was tighter and very few people would have failed to obey orders to take shelter. However, far more German city-dwellers lived in apartment blocks than Londoners. Ironically street shelters, originally designed for use in daytime raids, had later to be locked during daylight hours because of pilfering and vandalism. In the outer suburbs, they were seldom fully used.

After the Blitz, there was an increase in 'friendly fire' incidents. This was partially due to people staying outside to watch air raid activity, but British AA shell fuses were displaying a much higher incidence of faults by 1943, causing many shells to return to the ground and explode. By this stage of the war, about a third of all air raid casualties were attributable to 'friendly fire'.

The Commercial Road Goods Depot, known as the Tilbury shelter, was a notorious public shelter. Its name indicated it had once belonged to the London, Tilbury and Southend Railway Company but it wasn't in Tilbury or anywhere near it. It was a massive building in Whitechapel, an eight-storey railway warehouse off the Commercial Road which had been used as a shelter in World War 1.[44] Part of it had in fact been designated an official shelter in the next conflict, but the rest was taken over as an unofficial shelter following which the authorities had to make it at least meet basic standards of hygiene. But initially it didn't meet them, shelterers being camped out amongst cartons of margarine, with no toilet facilities, and visitors were met by a sickening stench. It was probably far from ideal as a shelter, but thousands of local people (Calder records estimates of 14,000 to 16,000[45]) felt safe there.

Private shelters in some business premises were also opened to the general public, but not all. In the centre of London, some were opened to the public in the evening as they were no longer needed to provide daytime shelter for employees during working hours. Street shelters, trench shelters, tunnels and natural caves were all brought into use. The Chislehurst Caves in the Chislehurst and Sidcup Urban District were the most famous of the latter – Lewis Blake's *Bromley in the Front Line* describes how they were taken over as shelters. Railway arches were used as shelters, in south east London in particular. The borough of Bermondsey favoured them, and as a result were able to boast of their extensive provision of public shelter. 55,000 people were provided for by 'the London Borough of Shelter' as Bermondsey was dubbed in the press.[46] However, the railway arches were not safe, as the crown of an arch is relatively thin even if the brickwork of the sides and arches appears sturdy, and inevitably, more tragic incidents occurred, beginning as early as 6 September 1940.

---

44 http.//www.glias.org.uk/journals/2-a.html gives the history of the Com-
     mercial Road Goods Depot. It was demolished in 1975.
45 Calder, quoted in Gardiner, *The Blitz* (2010)
46 Bright, *Southwark in the Blitz* (2016)

TWO

THE BOMBS AND
THE FIRES

One weakness faced by the Luftwaffe in the 1940/41 Blitz was its shortage of heavy calibre high explosive bombs. Initially the Luftwaffe dropped mainly 50 kg and 250 kg bombs. Sticks of ten 50kg bombs dropped across residential areas had very limited effect and raises the question again: what was the Luftwaffe hoping to achieve? Larger bombs – the 1,000kg type was often used – were more effective but if they fell in gardens or parkland their effect would be dissipated when the bomb penetrated deep into the soil. It has been suggested that the 500kg bomb was the optimum size but few were available to the Luftwaffe at the start of the Blitz.

The limited destructive power of the 50kg and 250kg bombs led to the use of naval mines against land targets, a practice opposed by the German navy who naturally wanted them for use against shipping. The 1,000kg mines, dropped by parachute, were effective as their blast effect exceeded that of equivalent high explosive bombs, as the parachute slowed down the descent of the mine which then exploded above ground rather than below – conventional high explosive bombs usually penetrated the ground or buildings before exploding. The parachute mine's blast effect invariably caused casualties over a wide area irrespective of where it fell. The huge explosion of the mine and the extensive blast effect significantly impacted on civilian morale and the 'land mine' as it was known was greatly feared, to the extent that any large and destructive bombing incident would be attributed to a 'land mine'. The 1,000 kg mines were normally dropped in pairs by a Heinkel He111 aircraft, and although their descent was sometimes affected by winds, usually landed within a few hundred yards of each other. They were not the only type dropped – a 500 kg mine was also used but references to it are far less common. There was also the 'G' mine, similar to the 1,000kg mine, but sometimes dropped without a parachute.

As the British government kept quiet about the use of sea mines by the Luftwaffe, the 'land mine' was initially seen as an unknown quantity if it was seen descending. Naturally this weapon became surrounded by rumour, and later fear. The silent descent of the mine was quite slow and likely to be affected by air currents, and this was seen as confirmation that as an aerial weapon it could not be accurate and thus was no more than a terror weapon. Its descent was sometimes confused with that of a German airman descending by parachute, and on one occasion a squad of Home Guard personnel was wiped out when they ran towards what turned out to be a mine rather than a parachutist. I have read that in one case an unexploded mine was thought to be a container of supplies for invading parachutists, and in another incident the mine was thought to be a domestic hot water cylinder blown out of a bombed building, and consequently ignored! Norman Longmate tells the story of the group of men who attempted to move an unexploded mine which was blocking a road in Coventry. It exploded and blew them all to pieces.[47] On landing a mine was fused to explode in fifteen seconds; any bomb fuse could jam but any movement might restart it, another factor which made all bomb disposal work very dangerous and unpredictable. The mine's fifteen second delay was dangerous in itself – in more than one incident those who had laid flat on seeing a mine fall were getting to their feet again when it exploded. But in a number of personal stories, this delay enabled the persons concerned to take cover or maximise the distance between them and the mine.

Dealing with unexploded sea mines was the responsibility of the Royal Navy; mines also had magnetic properties which necessitated using tools for defusing that were not made of steel. This added to the rumours and fear surrounding the weapon. One source describes a parachute mine as a 50-gallon oil drum packed with explosives. In fact, they were a sophisticated device designed to send large merchant vessels to the bottom of the ocean. Another describes how on the opening day of the London Blitz, 'more than a thousand bombs – some strapped to oil drums' fell. There may have been some confusion with the 'oil bomb' which did contain a quantity of crude oil and often failed to ignite.

Confusing references are often made to 'time bombs' and 'aerial torpedoes.' The former are more accurately described as delayed action bombs and were fused to explode at a specified interval after being dropped, disrupting life in the danger zone and if undetected perhaps killing or injuring those engaged in rescue work. Only the lower weights of bombs were fused as 'delayed action' as it would have been an expensive waste of higher calibre bombs. They are not to be confused with bombs

---

47 Longmate, *Air Raid* (1976)

that failed to detonate due to a defect or damage. However, all unexploded bombs had to be treated as 'delayed action' until their true status was established. 'Aerial torpedoes' were only used to a limited extent by the Luftwaffe and not against land targets. They were self-propelled torpedoes dropped from aircraft to continue on course in the sea towards a ship or other naval target as did their equivalents launched from submarines. Price says 'German aerial torpedoes at that time were unreliable and generally ineffective.'[48] The term often seems to have been used both in Britain and Germany to describe a very heavy bomb. It no doubt sounded more impressive but does not tie in with fact!

The weight of bombs dropped also affected casualties and damage. Smaller bombs might demolish a house or two with a direct hit, but when falling in gardens or street the blast effect might be dissipated if the bomb penetrated soft ground. In larger buildings and blocks of flats, a bomb might explode in the upper stories and collapse the building into the basement where people were sheltering. The heavy 1,800kg 'Satan' and 1,400kg 'Fritz' bombs had 'semi-armour piercing' properties and a delay fuse and would pass through a building to explode in the basement or even deeper.

After the commencement of the Blitz, unexploded bombs rapidly became a major problem, although inaccurate reporting was partially responsible for the plethora of incidents awaiting attention. Essential production was held up, road and rail transport disorganised and many residents evacuated until the bombs were made safe. The huge homelessness problem was significantly added to by this. Classification according to importance and degree of urgency was therefore implemented to assist prioritisation in bomb disposal activity.

---

48 Price, *Blitz on Britain 1939-1945* (1977)

The weight of German bombs, which were manufactured and classified in metric sizes, is expressed in kilos. It is often converted to pounds for British and American readers, which serves little purpose. Pounds can even be confused with kilos or are assumed to be the same. In March 2015 discovery of an unexploded bomb (said to date back to the 10/11 May 1941 raid) on a building site in Southwark necessitated the evacuation of hundreds of residents and made national headlines. However, widespread confusion was reflected in the various media reports of the bomb's size – I noted 250kg, 450kg, 500kg, 500lb, 1,000lb and half a tonne in different sources! Another bomb was discovered later that year and caused similar disruption in Bethnal Green, although there was more general agreement on its size.

With regards to fires, this book follows the classifications used by the fire services at the time, categorizing fires as small (one pump required), medium (two to ten pumps), serious (eleven to thirty pumps) and major (over thirty pumps). A conflagration is defined as a major fire requiring over 100 pumps which is spreading out of control. A 'pump' refers to a fire appliance – which might be a standard fire engine, but at that time included trailer pumps which could be towed into action by a variety of vehicles.

DAMAGE

Damage was not of such concern to the British authorities pre-war as the human casualties. Reporting included provision to identify damage to 'key points of national importance' but it seems that such damage soon turned out to be minimal, especially once raids on London became spread over the metropolis and not concentrated in the Docks and other industrial areas. However, damage to buildings and roads soon became extensive. After the first few weeks of the Blitz many roads in London were blocked as a result of unexploded bombs, bomb craters and buildings in a dangerous condition. In 1937, as part of the general planning for war, provision was made for a special labour force to consist of infantry and cavalry reservists to be formed in groups and companies under the general administration of the Royal Engineers.[49] The Pioneer Corps, initially called the Auxiliary Military Pioneer Corps, performed valuable work during the Blitz, clearing roads of debris, filling craters and pulling down unsafe buildings. Special Commissioner Sir Warren Fisher was responsible for calling them into action in October 1940.

By 1942 over one million people in England and Wales were estimated as 'inhabiting houses which had been, or but for the war would have been, condemned as slums'.[50] It is frequently said that a positive side of the Blitz was that bombing cleared much slum housing, and thereby did work that local councils should have done years before. It did, but it also destroyed the cosy unpretentious little homes of thousands of Londoners that were not in any way slums. It also destroyed recently-built replacements for slum dwellings erected by London boroughs and the LCC itself between the wars. Modern inner-city blocks of flats, and semi-detached houses on new housing estates fared no better than their Victorian and Edwardian predecessors when subjected to German high explosive. Curiously, as Scholey has observed,[51] earlier Georgian and Regency houses seemed to have rather better resistance. Only the steel-framed and ferro-concrete construction of some modern factories, blocks of flats and offices offered really adequate resistance. Churchill later recorded his fears that only such buildings would remain

---

49 *The Pioneer* website http.//www.royalpioneercorps.co.uk
50 Titmuss, *Problems of Social Policy* (1950)
51 Scholey, *Bombs on Holborn* (1998)

standing in London if the Blitz continued: 'Our outlook at this time was that London, except for its strong modern buildings, would gradually and soon be reduced to a rubble heap.'[52] Things never got that bad, and the proportion of London's built-up area destroyed by the Luftwaffe remained small. London was just too big a target, and the Luftwaffe could only deliver a fraction of the bomb load needed to destroy it. In fact, Churchill told the House of Commons on 8 October 1940 that 'statisticians may amuse themselves by calculating that after making allowances for the laws of diminishing returns, through the same houses being struck twice or three times over, it would take ten years at the present rate for half the houses of London to be demolished.'[53]

The worst destruction occurred in the East End, where some 30% of the built-up area was destroyed. in Stepney 40% of the housing was destroyed. Similar levels of damage were inflicted in Holborn and the City of London. By comparison most German cities were to suffer the destruction of up to 90% of their central districts by the end of the war. Slums or not, it took years for London's housing shortages to be overcome. After the war, an East Ender quoted by Harriet Salisbury maintained that bombing may have left fewer slums, yet 'a slum was somewhere to live, but we had nowhere to live.'[54] This was only the beginning of the sad break-up of the old East End communities.

Andrew Crisp has pointed out that on a positive note, within the ruins there were some amazing archaeological discoveries. These included a Roman wall at Cripplegate, Roman relics at Austin Friars, an underground chamber below St Mary le Bow, a Gothic doorway at St Vedast's and a seventh century arch at All Hallows Church. Nevertheless, the devastation caused by the Blitz was phenomenal and long-lasting. Many historic buildings

52 Churchill, *Their Finest Hour* (1950)
53 http.//www.history.co.uk/history-of-london/ww2-the-blitz-hits
54 Salisbury, *The War on our Doorstep* (2012)

in London were destroyed or seriously damaged. Some looked at things in a different light for example McDonald Hastings in the BBC's *London Calling* magazine who did not seem to mind that Wren's most beautiful churches and some of the City's most noble and historic buildings were damaged irreparably. He felt that because they had taken with them some of the dreariest and meanest stretches of Victorian office buildings, the Luftwaffe had given an opportunity to 'reconceive' the City on a 'more rational and liveable' plan. This was written at a time when there was little love for the Victorian era and its architecture.

AN EXPERIENCE OR A MYTH?

The bare statistics tell us that during World War 2 London experienced 1,224 red alerts when the sirens were sounded. The blackout lasted for 1,840 days, followed (after 17 September 1944) by 258 days of 'dim-out'. In the period up to the end of the 1940-41 Blitz, London was subject to eighty-five major (over 100 tons of bombs dropped) raids and about twenty lesser attacks. 20,083 Londoners died and 26,019 were injured so seriously they had to be admitted to hospital. 300,000 homes in London were destroyed or badly damaged. 24,000 tons of high explosive bombs were dropped on London in the major raids of 1940-41. But statistics can vary enormously. For example, depending on source, statistics for casualties can refer to different time frames and they can exclude certain categories, for example civil defence workers, police and fire service personnel. German sources may be more reliable when determining tonnage of bombs dropped.

The Blitz did not affect all the boroughs and districts of the London Civil Defence region with the same degree of intensity of attack. In particular, many places on the western edge of the region were affected only occasionally by the fall of bombs, although they were 'under siren' along with the rest of London. In 1941, the raids became more concentrated on the central, south-east and eastern suburbs, and areas to the west of London had even fewer incidents. The urban district of Yiewsley and West Drayton experienced no civilian fatalities in World War 2; in that respect it was unique in the London Civil Defence region. The outer suburbs of south-east London were on the flight path of most Luftwaffe aircraft en route to London. As a result, they suffered a lot of casualties and damage, nearly all of which was to residential property and shops. There was little of military value in the area except the RAF stations at Biggin Hill and Kenley which were pounded with a huge amount of high explosive.

Many modern writers have claimed that the 'Blitz experience' was embellished by propaganda to give the impression of 100% solidarity behind the wartime government. Where this particular myth of solidarity is derived is not clear. Certainly, none of the standard histories of the Blitz – Fitzgibbon, Moseley, Longmate, even Calder – describe it in those terms. If anything, it appears to be more commonly found in newspaper articles and features from the 1980s onwards.

Following the outcry in 1973 when Mass-Observation reports and then the Hodsoll reports were released into the public domain, Tom Harrisson was prompted to comment that the only valid information for this sort of social history of war is that recorded at the time on the spot.[55] However Mass-Observation was not the only 'valid information'. Many people kept diaries during the Blitz, and were no different to Mass-Observation diarists, who in any case received no special training from Mass-Observation. Mass-Observation participants (there were around 1,500 observers and 50 diarists)

---

55 Harrisson, *Living through the Blitz* (1976)

were not representative of the population as a whole, however valuable their observations.

As Harrisson maintains, memories written down thirty years after the event have less claim to validity. Harrisson's concern was the superimposition of the values of the 1970s on the 'what really happened' accounts of the 1940s. What really happened is of course the 'experience' as documented by Mass-Observation and other diarists at the time and not what was officially recorded as history by Luftwaffe units on one side and Civil Defence, Police and Fire authorities in Britain on the other.

To what extent did the myths emerge apart from the reactions in Southampton? Robert Mackay's major study of UK civilian morale[56] devotes some time to the 'Blitz Spirit' and how this has been questioned in post war writing. Mackay makes a convincing case against the exaggerations of the revisionist interpretations. While looting, panic, pacifism, criminality, class antagonisms, bigotry and other divisive elements were certainly present in English society at that time, they never prevailed and were only present in a small minority of the population.

Revisionists say that the population of bombed cities was falsely portrayed as upbeat, cheerful etc. Ziegler identifies two main elements in the myth – 'the comradeship and sense of unity it inspired and the cheerful good humour with which it was endured.'[57] He thinks both were justified by the facts. The focus seems to be on a generally held perception of civilian reaction to bombing; 'plucky and stoical suffering and resistance' was deemed to be ever-present, in fact for 100% of the time. Where this perception manifests itself is not clear but it does not seem to feature in most of the standard histories of the Blitz, both wartime and post-war which are usually well-balanced and do not shirk

56 Mackay, *Half the Battle* (2002)
57 Ziegler, *London at War* (1995)

from the negatives, although a few individual publications do match the stereotype. It certainly gets casual references in the media since the war and writers have enjoyed the concept of debunking this 'myth' by raking over the negatives of the Blitz and other aspects of life in wartime Britain. But negatives were seldom absent – the failings of national and local governments, and of evacuation, the selfishness, snobbery, crime and looting recur in most accounts. Civilian reaction to bombing was a topic which brought much uninformed speculation usually by military commanders or by those in authority in government at various levels. The civilian population had little choice but to 'carry on'.

Writers including Angus Calder in his *The Myth of the Blitz* have been anxious to downplay the 'Blitz experience'. But many of the 'myths' that so infuriate him seem to be a modern phenomenon, dating from when records were opened up and people with no personal memories of the Blitz began to write about it. Then it seemed to be *de rigeur* to write about the Blitz with sentimental and humorous references to gas masks, Anderson shelters and knees up Mother Brown, with the population depicted as uniformly brave and resolute in the face of rather incompetent enemy attacks which were, without doubt, ultimately unsuccessful. The emphasis was on the civilian experience of air raids isolated from the realities of the military attack and the outcomes of that aerial attack. From the 1980s, the Blitz was also seen as an interesting subject for schoolchildren to study, and aspects such as people being blown to pieces and the total destruction of acres of housing were not on the agenda.

It is true that some aspects did not apply to all the population. People were not always brave or resolute, and perhaps more worryingly, not honest, and some in the post-war years were not happy to acknowledge this. To them it seems only 100% was acceptable, which is a myth. In addition, whilst there is no doubt the population was generally brave and resolute, depicting the enemy – professional and highly trained airmen – as incompetent or ineffective in many ways detracts from this bravery and resolution.

Perhaps it's not so much myths but the spin put on the events of the Blitz and reactions to them. Calder gets terribly fired up about the myths and devotes his whole book to them; perhaps the title of his book (myth in the singular rather than the plural) is somewhat unfortunate. The events of the Blitz era happened and of course people have been upset by what they see as implications that they didn't. Surely, if the Blitz was 'a myth', then it didn't happen! Calder does acknowledge 'myth' should not be taken as equating to 'untruth' still less to 'lies'.[58]

There is certainly a suspicion by many modern writers that there was a great government conspiracy to keep information from the general public during the war, in particular to understate casualties and conceal news of disastrous bombing incidents. This has been regularly revived as anniversaries are celebrated. However, there seems little evidence that this is the case. The true situation was not the opposite to the generally promoted 'official' view.

The writer James Hayward has compiled a rather less intense debunking of some of the myths.[59] Hayward tells how Tom Driberg questions a bystander at a bombed house who is claiming dozens of people are buried there, as Driberg knows that only one person has died. The person is evasive and slips away to harangue others. This is a quite common phenomenon. Richard Collier's otherwise excellent account of the raid of 10/11 May 1941 mentions the belief apparently held by 'many people' that 'the dead did walk that night' although nowhere in his book is any evidence of this presented!

---

58 Calder, *The Myth of the Blitz* (1991)
59 Hayward, *Myths and Legends of the Second World War* (2004)

Myths can be divided into those that originated during the war and those that have developed since. Obviously, some myths were the product of the secrecy necessary in wartime. At the time of the Blitz, the authorities could not do otherwise than promote an upbeat view of civilian reaction to bombing and conceal or downplay any incidents with the potential either to lower morale or to reveal Luftwaffe accuracy or damage to vital services. They ensured that incidents when non-military targets were hit were publicised whilst censoring accounts of enemy successes and pictures of alarming damage. Heroism by civilians and civil defence workers was publicised but not cowardice or desertion, panic or demoralisation. What else could a nation fighting for its survival do? When asking how people being bombed are supposed to feel, there was limited evidence based on the experience of London in World War 1 and of the experience of other nations in various campaigns since. A possible explanation is that although the need to be 100% upbeat and positive all the time had disappeared, many writers in the post-war years seemed to think the war was still in progress, Britain was still under threat, and morale must be maintained. The upbeat hearty tone of wartime newsreels accompanied by martial music has jarred for the past few decades, but through to the 1960s all newsreels were presented like that.

Conscientious objectors were undoubtedly seen by some as a sign of a lack of national unity, but attitudes towards them were more tolerant than in World War 1, and the role of those people in non-combatant roles in Civil Defence and Bomb Disposal was especially appreciated by Londoners in the Blitz.

It has to be said that a lot of more recent general accounts (particularly on the Internet) serve only to perpetuate the old myths and some writers seen to have little real appreciation of either the severity of the Luftwaffe raids or what the 'Blitz experience' really meant for the civilian population.

In a situation where the civilian could not retaliate or resist, the attack on him, except in a most modest way, it seemed natural to describe the Luftwaffe's efforts as unsuccessful, although the average citizen could do nothing to influence the success of a particular raid. The AA and night fighter defences were often said to have driven off the attackers, but this is unlikely. Contemporary accounts usually stated that a particular raid had failed, newspaper accounts of each raid at least asserting that although an ordeal had been suffered, London was still there and functioning. What criteria were applied to assess the failure is usually not clear. Usually, failure seems to be whether morale collapsed or not. In Britain's bombed cities it didn't usually collapse and it is not even clear if the German leadership expected it to. Any evidence of collapsed morale would certainly not have been publicised in wartime. The incident at a Bromley rest centre on 16/17 April 1941 recounted by Blake is the only example I have seen. It was reported to Whitehall (presumably the MoHS) that 'a minor panic on Downham housing estate (a large LCC estate) in which about 100 distraught women and children invaded a rest centre reserved for the bombed out' had occurred. Undoubtedly there had been a very unpleasant ordeal in the area that night and Blake suggests that 'exaggerated rumours had been circulating locally'.[60]

Even recent accounts assess the Baedeker blitz on Norwich in the spring of 1942 as a failure because the symbols of that city – the cathedral, the castle and the city hall – were left unscathed. The reality was that a huge amount of damage was done to commercial and residential property in this small compact city. Despite the underlying 'Baedeker' theme (Baedeker was a popular German tourist guidebook, translated into other languages, too), the Luftwaffe targeted communications and

---

60 Blake, *Bromley in the Front Line* (2005)

industry when they attacked Norwich. They may have failed (if indeed they attempted) to hit the well-known buildings that symbolised Norwich, but they destroyed many other historic buildings. Public utilities, shops and services (department stores and laundries were particularly badly affected) were destroyed. Some areas of the city remained relatively unscathed but overall, the destruction was extensive. This was achieved with a relatively small bomber force. As in the 1940/41 Blitz, individual air attacks could be successful but whether they contributed to a long-term strategic outcome is a different matter. The Luftwaffe never attempted to drive home attacks through to a conclusion anywhere although in some British cities it might have been possible. The Luftwaffe attacked too many targets and of these, London was probably too big for their resources (without heavy bombers) anyway. The most successful raids were concentrated on a sector of the capital; for example, the raids of 19/20 March and 19/20 April 1941 which were focussed on east London, and those of 16/17 April and 10/11 May 1941, which were focussed on central London.

Common myths are those that surround the explanations given for bombing incidents. Many personal accounts express conviction that an incident occurred because a German bomber was aiming at a local target of significance. Bombers were alleged to have circled for a lengthy period of time over a particular area before choosing a target. People liked to think that the Luftwaffe had been aiming at a particular local target; then they could triumphantly say that they had missed, even if their own home was destroyed instead. A frequently-quoted example is that someone's home was destroyed because the bomb-aimer was actually aiming at the gas works or factory or power station in the next street. Or that someone had opened a door during a raid and the light thus shown had caused a bomb to be dropped. There was widespread belief that showing any light – even lighting a cigarette – during an air raid would bring down bombs on the miscreant. Some compensation was derived from the fact that in these scenarios, the Germans had at least been made to miss their intended targets!

Civilians on the receiving end would sometimes console themselves by saying that enemy aircraft had been turned back from their target by AA fire and British fighters, and had jettisoned their bombs on them instead. However, pilots of enemy aircraft could not bomb with such degrees of accuracy at night. They would be unlikely to hang around over the target. Small amounts of light for example a cigarette, were invisible to a pilot of an aircraft even as low as 3,000 feet above, and the purpose of Britain's rigidly enforced total blackout was primarily to disguise the location of whole towns and cities.

Ridiculous situations occurred when people were told to put a cigarette out during an air raid, although it was as bright as day as a result of huge fires burning nearby. A fireman having a cigarette whilst fighting fires in the docks was reminded by a policeman that smoking was prohibited in the docks. British searchlights were alleged to have caused bombs to be dropped on houses near the searchlight site, although there might be some truth in this, and there was some pressure from local councils for searchlight sites to be moved. They were certainly visible to enemy bombers, although bombers above a certain height would be out of their range and would not be illuminated by them.

All these are true experiences, recorded by those who were there, not made up by officialdom. The population seemed to want to believe that the Luftwaffe was aiming for valid targets and was only hitting residential property by accident. Incredible stories have also appeared. George Macbeth's 1987 *A Child of the War* relates that in 1944, over a hundred people in a London shelter died from 'silent panic' when a bomb fell outside and blocked their exit to the air. Macbeth explains that 'silent panic' was simply a way of describing the fact that none of them had any physical symptoms of injury. 'They had died of terror'.[61] I cannot trace any incident of this nature. Macbeth was aged 12 at the time and resident in Sheffield. In a contemporary diary by Mary Morrison dated 11 November 1943, Mary, a nurse from a fever hospital in Woolwich, describes a similar incident. The previous night, her ambulance is stopped by an ARP warden in the West End and she is shown to a tube shelter which is found to have many fatal casualties without any obvious injuries.[62] Again, no incident of this nature can be traced.

Looting in the wake of air raids was another negative of life in wartime Britain. It was common and abhorrent, but was certainly not covered up, and seems to have received plenty of press coverage at the time. Looting from bombed houses still seems a shocking crime even today. John Simkin recounts how in the first eight weeks of the London Blitz a total of 390 cases of looting was reported to the police, and on 9 November 1940, the first people tried for looting appeared at the Old Bailey. Of these twenty cases, ten involved members of the Auxiliary Fire Service.[63] By the end of the war, 4,854 cases of looting had come before the courts, but this did not reflect the magnitude of the problem. Looting is a quite interesting topic for people today because the family home of the 1940s contained few of the objects that would make it attractive to looters now. Besides jewellery and money (which people probably kept with them anyway when they went to shelter), looters seized items such as clothing and bedding which were relatively valuable and not easily replaced in wartime. Also targeted were gas and electricity meters which in those days householders fed with coins to pay for their supply.

61 Macbeth *A Child of the War* (1987)
62 Morrison, A *Very Private Diary. A Nurse in Wartime*
63 Simkin, J *Crime in Wartime (1997)* Spartacus Educational Publishers Ltd

Did looting reflect an underlying lack of commitment to the war? Probably not. It was annoying and distressing, particularly for the victims, but unlikely to undermine morale significantly.

LONDON – THE TARGET

At the outbreak of war, London was the second largest city in the world, with a population of 8.6 million, a total that was not to be exceeded until 2015. The importance of London was as the capital city of the British Empire, the seat of government and the centre of government administration. Since 1918 it had expanded enormously both in population and infrastructure.

In 1939 Britain had 163,000 non-industrial (white-collar) and 184,000 industrial civil servants. Many industrials were engaged in supporting the armed services (for instance in the Royal Naval dockyards) or in organisations such as the Royal Mail. By 1944, the totals had reached 505,000 and 658,000 respectively, a grand total of 1,163,000 civil servants.[64] Non-industrial (white-collar) civil servants were in pre-war days largely based in central London, and dispersal to the regions was not to happen until the 1950s and 1960s, when it was necessitated by escalating living costs in London and difficulties in recruitment. In wartime, evacuation to the provinces took place, although this created problems in billeting and finding office space.

The City of London was by no means solely an area of office buildings. There were still many warehouses both alongside the Thames and elsewhere with active wharves. The City also had an important concentration of press activity. At this time, most national newspapers were based in Fleet Street and its immediate neighbourhood, and the papers were printed on

---

64 http.//www.civilservant.org.uk

the premises. An exception was Odhams Press who published the *Daily Herald* in Long Acre near Covent Garden. The daily newspapers continued to appear despite the nightly air raids even if paper shortages reduced their size. In addition, many provincial and foreign newspapers had London offices in Fleet Street as well as press agencies and bureaus such as Reuters. Britain's legal profession has an impressive presence in central London. London's four Inns of Court – Gray's Inn, Lincoln's Inn, Inner Temple and Middle Temple are there as well as the Royal Courts of Justice, and the Old Bailey, the Central Criminal Court for England and Wales lies within the City of London.

Docks

Pre-war London was one of the biggest ports of Europe; one-third of Britain's overseas trade passed through the London docks. In 1938, the Port of London Authority handled a record 44.6 million tons of overseas and coastwise import and export cargoes. This just exceeded the previous record year of 1937, with 42.9 million tons of cargo. The value of the foreign trade of the port reached £605 million.[65] Docks had gradually spread down the Thames estuary since the early nineteenth century, but the City of London still had working docks in the Pool of London. The docks, unmodernised and labour intensive, needed a huge workforce, which was accommodated in the crowded streets of east and south-east London.

Utilities

Before nationalisation in 1948, there were a number of companies in London generating electricity and manufacturing gas, both processes utilizing coal from British coalfields transported

---

65 Port of London Authority website http.//www.pla.co.uk/

to London by rail and by sea. Some local authorities had their own electricity generation plants. Besides Beckton, gasworks making gas from coal were located at East Greenwich, Southall, Fulham, Nine Elms, and many other locations. Gasholders (incorrectly known as gasometers), the distinctive storage tanks each containing about 50,000 cubic metres of gas when full, were located in most London boroughs, and were all too visible to enemy pilots. The Luftwaffe successfully bombed several of them.

Power stations included the massive and iconic Battersea plant with a 245,000kW generating capacity. By contrast Lots Road power station in Chelsea had a generating capacity of 50,000kW but along with Neasden and Greenwich power stations powered most of the LPTB underground railway system and tramways. The Southern Railway, with its extensive electrified network, had a power station at Wimbledon. The North Metropolitan (Northmet) Electric Power Supply Company supplied electricity to a wide area of north London and Middlesex. Its power stations were at Willesden and Brimsdown.

The electricity supply was vulnerable to interruption by bombing severing cables but these were relatively easy to repair, unlike the gas supply where miles of dangerous, pressurized pipes could when hit necessitate hazardous repair effort.

Oil refineries and storage facilities were located at Coryton, Shell Haven and Thames Haven, on the estuary of the River Thames some 28 miles from the centre of London. Coryton Refinery was between Shell Haven Creek and Hole Haven Creek, which separates Canvey Island from the mainland. It was a part of the Port of London and was the last of the three major refineries on the Thames Estuary to remain in operation.

Communications
London's communications were provided by the General Post Office, who at that time operated both the telecommunications

and the postal services. It was then the largest employer in the country. The undeveloped state of telecommunications in the pre-war years is difficult for the present-day user of the internet and other digital services to appreciate. At the time of the Blitz only about 10% of London residents possessed telephones, and 'subscribers' could only dial telephone numbers within London themselves. Anywhere outside London required an operator to connect the call manually, 'subscriber trunk dialling' or STD being at this time a distant dream. London was home to dozens of vulnerable local telephone exchanges, linked by miles of intricate and equally vulnerable cabling. For the many homes that did not have telephones, the only other telecommunication option was the public phone box, or the telegram, which usually printed off at local post offices, and was delivered by hand or on cycles by messengers.

There was an unhealthy concentration of telecommunications in the narrow streets of the City of London, including not only the General Post Office's operational centres but the centres for the overseas operations of Cable and Wireless. The latter company maintained a global network of cable and radio links which were vital in wartime and also extensively used by servicemen and women serving overseas to keep in touch with their families. The GPO had its Central Telegraph Office in Newgate Street and its international telephone exchange in Faraday Building, a modern block only a few yards south of St. Paul's Cathedral.

The GPO's postal headquarters were in St. Martin's Le Grand in the City and its Mount Pleasant complex in Finsbury was one of the largest postal sorting offices in the world. The latter had several narrow escapes from major damage in the Blitz only to fall victim to a lone raider in 1943, a single bomb leading to the destruction by fire of the parcels sorting facility and 100,000 parcels.

Industry

After World War 1, industry boomed in London. Between the wars, old-established industries moved out to expand in the suburbs, but London also acquired a high number of new 'sunrise' industries, making electrical equipment, food and consumer goods. The capital's main industrial sectors were engineering, clothing and shoes, food and drink, furniture and printing and paper. Light industry continued to move west and Hoover, EMI and Coty were amongst companies that built modern factories along the roads leading west out of London – the Great West Road and Western Avenue. On the east side of London, the American car manufacturer Ford opened their huge plant at Dagenham in 1931. Briggs Manufacturing, an American, Detroit-based manufacturer of automobile bodies followed Ford to the United Kingdom setting up a plant for their Briggs Motor Bodies Limited in Dagenham (the companies were associated). In wartime, a workforce of over 36,000 built aircraft gun-turrets, doors, wing components, bomb doors, heavy and medium tank hulls, trucks and ambulance bodies. Also, sites for new industry were established at Park Royal in Willesden, the Lea Valley at Edmonton, and the Wandle Valley and Kingston Bypass in south-west London. The newly constructed Purley Way became the principal industrial district of Croydon in the 1930s. Although Woolwich, Crayford and Erith were other areas for new industry they were unfortunately on the likely route to London of an enemy bombing force. Numerous important factories were therefore conveniently situated for enemy bombers approaching the capital!

Siemens (involved in research, development, engineering and manufacture of electrical cables, telegraph, telephone, signalling and measuring apparatus, wireless equipment, lamps, lights and batteries) had a 17½ acre site at Woolwich with 9,000 employees in 1940. At the time of World War 1, the Royal Arsenal at Woolwich covered 1,285 acres and employed close to 80,000 people, but this had declined to around 32,500 at the beginning of World War 2. After severe damage early in the Blitz, although the production of guns, shells, cartridge cases and bombs continued, the numbers working dropped to 19,000. The numbers employed on site increased later in the war. There were also munitions and explosives factories at Enfield (the Royal Small Arms Factory) and Waltham Abbey (the former Royal Gunpowder Mills). However, pre-war expansion of the munitions industry had wisely spread it out over new sites across the country.

Fortunately, by 1939 no single British city was a dedicated centre for the aircraft industry, which had been initially based in London but was now dispersed to several different locations, but mainly away from Britain's traditional industrial heartlands. Thus, the aircraft industry was well-dispersed by the time the Blitz started, in that the different companies producing the RAF's aircraft were at geographically well-separated sites. Supermarine's factories producing the Spitfire fighter had their activity dispersed across the south of England after both their Castle Bromwich and Southampton works were clearly identified and targeted by the Luftwaffe early in the Battle of Britain. Hawker produced the Hurricane fighter at Weybridge and Kingston upon Thames, and also at Langley near Slough. The de Havilland company made aero engines at its plant in Edgware, north-west London. D. Napier & Son also made aero engines and later developed diesel engines at its plant in Acton. It was taken over by English Electric in 1942. The AEC company, originally formed as a subsidiary of the London General Omnibus Company, manufactured considerable numbers of bus chassis for use in London, with many of the bodies being built at Park Royal. At Southall, AEC switched from making buses to armoured cars and extended its product range to include trucks, tanks, power units and diesel engines, recruiting over 5,000 new employees.[66]

---

66 Upton, *Ealing, Acton & Southall at War* (2009)

London's huge wholesale markets included Smithfield, the meat market employing 7,000 workers, Billingsgate the fish market and in Westminster the Covent Garden fruit, vegetable and flower market, all on their original cramped sites. Covered markets included Borough, Spitalfields and Leadenhall all at central locations.

In 1939 the inner-city areas of London still contained many industrial concerns including the premises of firms that are still household names to this day. Tate & Lyle's Thames Refinery at Plaistow Wharf, Silvertown was the largest cane sugar refinery in the world, producing 14,000 tons a week in 1939. It was hit on numerous occasions during the Blitz. Amongst other food and drink companies, Clarnico was a large sweet and confectionery company based in Hackney Wick. Biscuit manufacturers such as Peek Frean's, Meredith & Drew at Shadwell, and McVitie also catered for the Londoner's sweet tooth. They took on an important wartime role in providing ration packs for the armed forces. The factory of HJ Heinz in Harlesden was only one of the large food manufacturing companies in Greater London established in the inter-war years.

London was home to many large brewing companies, none of which have survived rationalisations of recent years. They employed thousands of workers to produce the Londoner's favourite tipple, and ten times as much beer was brewed as today. In the East End, there was Taylor Walker in Limehouse, Truman, Hanbury & Buxton in Brick Lane, Mann, Crossman and Paulin in Whitechapel Road, and Charrington & Co Ltd, in Mile End Road, Bethnal Green. Watney Combe Reid & Co, brewed at the Stag Brewery in Victoria, Whitbread in Chiswell Street in the City of London, the Cannon Brewery in St John Street Clerkenwell, the Wenlock brewery in Shoreditch, and Guinness, with the only modern plant, in Park Royal. Across the Thames, there was Barclay Perkins in Southwark, once the largest brewery in the world, and Courage in Horsleydown, Bermondsey. Hops, a vital ingredient of beer, were stored and traded in Southwark, a risky concentration of national supplies. During the war, no fewer than twenty-five out of the thirty-seven Southwark hop warehouses were destroyed. In the post-war years, the Hops Marketing Board and the Brewers' Society made a decision to concentrate the trade's activities at Paddock Wood in Kent.[67]

Distilling was another important industry with London gin being produced by amongst others Beefeater in Lambeth, Booth's in Clerkenwell and Gordon's in Southwark. 'British wine' was a popular product (imported wine was a luxury) made from imported grape juice at Kingston upon Thames.

Transport

Four privately-owned railway companies served London, each with their own terminal stations. Each had their associated goods facilities and marshalling yards of which the largest were Temple Mills in east London and Feltham in Middlesex. Feltham Marshalling Yards were built at the end of World War 1 using German prisoner of war labour, the thirty-two miles of track being completed in 1922. They were an important sorting centre for freight in transit between southern and south western England and the rest of the country. All the main lines from London to the north, east, and west were accessible from Feltham, via the West and North London Lines from Kew Bridge junction, through Acton and on to other railway goods yards in north London. In peacetime, as well as during war, a high proportion of rail freight is moved at night, when the railway lines are free of their daily passenger traffic. The marshalling yards at Feltham worked 24/7 in blackout conditions and all weathers throughout the war years

---

67 *The Hop Trade in Southwark* by Stephen Humphrey in The Journal of the Brewery History Society. Brewery History No.123 Summer 2006.

and have been compared to the Hamm yards in Germany. They could turn around 6,000 wagons in 24 hours.[68]

Detailed contingency plans were made to continue the provision of public transport services in the aftermath of air raids. Besides the main line trains operated by the four railway companies, buses, trams, trolleybuses, and the underground railway were operated by the London Passenger Transport Board (LPTB). The vulnerability of the LPTB's underground railway network was a rather more difficult matter and was by far the greatest potential threat to the operation of London's transport systems. Damage to above ground railway lines was relatively easily repaired and continued to be so in both Britain and Germany throughout the war. However, north-west London with its many tunnels under the Northern Heights was vulnerable especially as all the railway companies were sending traffic to other companies through this area. Fortunately, from 1941 this area of London was not affected so frequently by air raids. Much transfer traffic in East London went through heavily bombed areas; and some passenger services were removed to accommodate it.

Extensive works were carried out to install protective barriers so that the tube network in central London was not flooded by a breach of the tunnels under the Thames.

The LPTB had extensive works for their buses and coaches at Acton and Chiswick. At Chiswick, in addition to overhaul, the works also built the complete bodies for a number of vehicles. The works extended to some 31 acres, employing 1,200 staff and maintaining fleets of about 6,000 vehicles. During the war London Transport co-ordinated the London Aircraft Production Group, and their Chiswick Works manufactured parts for

---

68 Clegg and Marshall, *The World War II bombing of Feltham, Hanworth & Bedfont* (2013)

Halifax bombers, with the final assembly being undertaken at the LPTB Aldenham works. The first aircraft flew in December 1941, and production continued until 1945 by which time 710 aircraft had been built.

Park Royal Vehicles Ltd was engaged in the building of bus and trolleybus bodies, which became the major part of the company's work. The company had a competitor in the form of Strachan and Brown, coachbuilders, also in Park Royal. Manufacturing some 1,000 bus bodies per year, the company became one of the largest suppliers in the country, selling to many provincial bus companies in the UK and worldwide. During World War 2 the production changed to military vehicles and bus bodies manufactured under the government-imposed Utility scheme, with vehicles being allocated to authorities with the greatest needs. The company were also part of the London Aircraft Production group and built wings and body components for the Halifax bomber.[69]

The London Transport site at Aldenham had originally been built as a railway depot for the Northern line extension to Bushey Heath, as part of the 1930s New Works programme.[70] Construction of the railway extension was under way and the depot was partially complete at the outbreak of World War 2. The railway works were stopped and the site was modified for use as an aircraft factory, producing Handley Page Halifax bombers as part of the London Aircraft Production consortium, together with Handley Page, Duple, Park Royal and London Transport.

---

69 Acton History Group website http.//www.actonhistory.co.uk
70 The New Works Programme was a major investment program delivered by the London Passenger Transport Board (LPTB), which had been created in 1933 to coordinate underground train, tram, trolleybus and bus services in the capital and the surrounding areas. The programme was to develop many aspects of the public transport services run by the LPTB and the suburban rail services of the Great Western Railway (GWR) and London and North Eastern Railway (LNER).

Charlton tram and trolleybus works took on additional work manufacturing ammunition and gun parts.

LONDON – THE GEOGRAPHY

The country was divided into twelve regions for Civil Defence purposes. Region 5, the London region, was headed by a Senior Regional Commissioner with two additional regional commissioners because of the size and importance of the region. Sir Ernest Gowers succeeded Captain Euan Wallace as Senior Regional Commissioner in January 1941 when the latter resigned on account of ill-health. He died in February 1941. Admiral Sir Edward Evans was a joint commissioner with Sir Ernest Gowers until January 1941 and thereafter with Charles W Key.

The urgent issues highlighted in the early months of the London Blitz led to deployment of 'heavyweights' – three special commissioners being appointed with specific responsibilities. Henry Willink, the MP for Croydon North (homeless people), Charles Key, the MP for Bow & Bromley (shelters) and Sir Warren Fisher, the former head of the Civil Service (damage to roads and utilities, and debris clearance).

The London Civil Defence region, which more or less corresponded to the area of the Metropolitan Police,[71] was divided into nine groups, groups 1-5, the 'inner' groups, comprised the City of London and the twenty-eight boroughs of the County of London (known as the metropolitan boroughs), groups 6-9 the outer groups comprising the boroughs/local authorities of the County of Middlesex and parts of Essex, Hertfordshire, Kent and Surrey.

---

71 Watford was one authority which although within the Metropolitan Police area was not included in the London Civil Defence region.

In this book, I refer to the location of air raid incidents by the names of the districts and boroughs that were in existence at the time. The total of boroughs/districts in the London Civil Defence region varies in different sources but the figure of 95[72] quoted by Longmate appears to be correct although it specifically refers to 1944, a few changes in boundaries having been implemented after 1939.

The war was many years before the re-organisation of London boroughs in 1965 which created thirty-two new Greater London boroughs. These were to incorporate the existing twenty-eight LCC boroughs (which were reduced in number) and expand their area of authority, although there were a few exceptions and a few of the old boroughs were split when creating the new boroughs. Appendix A lists those boroughs, cross-referenced to today's boroughs, most of which fall within the Greater London area. It is interesting to note that today's Greater London corresponds quite closely to the London Civil Defence region of 1939. I have not referred to postal districts in this book as they were not always used in reporting bombing incidents and in any case, as now, they usually did not coincide with political/local authority boundaries. I have not slavishly restricted my coverage of the London Blitz to the London Civil Defence region and I have included events that occurred in neighbouring areas when appropriate.

72 Longmate, *The Doodlebugs* (1981)

PART 2
CHRONOLOGY OF THE BLITZ

THREE

THE BUILD-UP

Establishing a date when the London Blitz started has been difficult and it is still open to dispute. Most sources agree it began on 7 September 1940 with the great raid on the East End and the docks. However, it is worth reviewing the events of the first year of war in that they influenced the experience as eventually endured by Londoners.

On 3 September 1939 at 11.00 the Prime Minister, Neville Chamberlain, broadcast to the nation. The impact of his announcement that the country was at war provoked many varied reactions from the British people, but undoubtedly left civilians stunned and confused. Chingford's official war history conveys it simply: 'Few will recall without a tremor September 3rd, 1939.'

This history also sets out the basics of the switch to war readiness, in dry phrases of understated text:

'During the previous few days, instructions had been received from the government with regard to precautions that should be taken by the local authorities in view of the deterioration in the international situation. On Friday, September 1st, instructions had been received that the sounding of all sirens and hooters should be prohibited, except for air raid warning purposes, and that lighting restrictions were to come into force from the Friday evening. Instructions were received to complete the equipment of all ARP buildings, buying equipment locally if necessary, and on the following day, Saturday, instructions were given that all work involving the opening of roads and footpaths should be suspended at once and the surface made good, the only exception being work of national importance connected with war.

In these last few days before the outbreak of war the local authorities were authorised to put the Civil Defence Services on a war footing, which in many cases meant that with regard to personnel 20 per cent of war establishment should be employed on a whole-time basis, and that Civil Defence Posts and Depots should be manned on rota, both day and night.

During Saturday arrangements were made for the evacuation of school children from the district, to begin on the Sunday morning, and many hundreds of school children, together with mothers and young children, left the borough for safer areas on Sunday, September 3rd.[73]

In some other London boroughs evacuation took place a day earlier or later. As South Chingford School's pupils made their way in LPTB buses towards their destinations in the east of Essex, the announcement of war from the Prime Minister was broadcast, though it is unlikely that the school parties had any portable radios.

---

73 Warburton, *Chingford at War* (1946). Chingford had initially been
    designated a 'neutral' evacuation area but following local representations
    this was amended to 'evacuation'. Although neighbouring Loughton was
    never made evacuable, that's where the first bombing incident occurred!

As previously discussed, after war was declared the expected air attack did not materialise and the period which was to be known as the phoney war followed. This gave an opportunity to improve defences and 'precautions' further. But it did lead to criticism of 'under-employed' workers in ARP, and to the loss of trained staff from this area. People also got used to the sound of the sirens, and the sporadic attacks by day and night during the early summer of 1940 eased people into a state of alertness and apprehension but not of terror.

Enemy air activity after the fall of France was not always clear in its purpose, and even the official history *Front Line*, published in 1942, acknowledged this. It declared that 'until after the war no one will be able to say for certain what the enemy's mind was at this time' although it seemed that he was 'working up to an air assault as a preliminary to invasion'. Ever since the war the Luftwaffe's strategy has continued to baffle historians.

The Battle of Britain was recognised as beginning over the sea on 8 August and over land on 10 August. It soon involved attacks on the RAF's airfields in the south of England and on ports, aircraft factories and oil installations. The battle drew nearer to London but the Luftwaffe had strict instructions that the capital itself was not to be bombed. In 1942, the official historian was not prepared to discuss the issue of the tit for tat this precipitated at this stage of the war!

18 June 1940
Front Line says the first bombs on the London area were dropped on plough-land at Addington, Surrey, although the sirens did not sound in the London Civil Defence Region.

24 June
The sirens sounded in the London area, as they were to do from time to time over the following weeks. Blake says this was only

the fourth time the sirens had been sounded since the outbreak of war, at least in south-east London[74]. But little activity occurred and sightings of enemy aircraft were rare.

26 July

The first fatalities occurred in the London Civil Defence Region when two people were killed in The Drive, Loughton. 'About 8pm in the evening, Chigwell Urban District Council's fire brigade were alerted and officers Chumley, Roberts, Sweeting and Varley were sent to the small shelter post which had been dug on part of the Loughton Cinema car park, opposite no 6 The Drive. They heard aircraft and gunfire and took shelter. It is thought that one of the raiders could have become disorientated and jettisoned a bomb or bombs, one of which exploded here, and one in nearby allotments. A piece of the bomb's casing went straight through James Robert's helmet killing him instantly. The explosion damaged nos 4-14 The Drive opposite, killing an elderly lady, Mrs Jane Page, in no.14'[75].

15 August

The Battle of Britain, as Churchill had memorably defined it, was drawing closer to London, and Croydon airport was bombed in a dramatic daytime raid in the early evening of 15 August, at 19.05. On this warm summer evening, the attack on Croydon was clearly visible to spectators across south London. Croydon was closed as a civil airport on 29 August 1939 and was taken over by the Royal Air Force as a fighter station; it became part of 11 Group RAF and was placed in the Kenley Sector. On 15 August, it seems that the intended target was the RAF fighter station at

---

74   Blake, *Red Alert* (1982)
75   Loughton Town Council press release 29.7.2015. The discovery by the Loughton and District Historical Society of the Chigwell Urban District Council war damage cards has amended some details.

Kenley, about ten miles to the south. The sirens did not sound until seventeen minutes after the first bomb dropped, which led to protests being raised with Sir John Anderson, the Home Secretary. Thirty-six civilians died at the airport, neighbouring factories and housing estates. Berwick Sayers relates how 'the control buildings and hangars of the aerodrome appeared to be intact but the factories, which had been camouflaged as an old English country scene, were now gaping black skeletons of twisted, unroofed girders and fallen rubbish from which surged an evil-smelling smoke. Purley Way was strewn with lumps of chalk and plaster and fragments of glass, and some of the houses looked as if a giant in berserk glee had shuffled tiles and slates, smashed windows and occasionally trampled on a house.'[76] About two hundred houses were damaged and over 180 people had to be re-housed. The all clear sounded at 19.35. The attackers lost seven of their twenty-three aircraft. The H.E. Rollason Aircraft Works was destroyed and severe damage was done to the British N.S.F. electrical components factory, where there were about nineteen fatalities. 'The terminal airport buildings were partially destroyed but no damage was caused to the aerodrome surface or to aircraft on the aerodrome. Casualties to RAF personnel were five killed and a number of injured not yet assessed.'[77] The Bourjois scent factory at Waddon was destroyed. This large modern building was totally burnt out and a smell of scent hung over the neighbourhood for days.

16 August

'The very cloudy conditions meant that 16 August 1940 was a day of confusion for both attackers and defenders. Bombs fell in Esher, New Malden, Wimbledon, Merton and Mitcham, but

---

76 Berwick-Sayers, *Croydon in the Second World War* (1949)
77 TNA HO 202 Ministry of Home Security: Home Security War Room Reports

overall, the German bombing was adjudged "ill-directed and scattered".[78]

Despite this, there were many fatalities in Kingston upon Thames, Malden, Merton and Wimbledon that afternoon when bombs were dropped on residential areas. 'In fact, no fewer than eighty-one civilians lost their lives as a consequence of this raid. thirty-three in Merton and Morden, nine in Wimbledon and thirty-nine in Malden and Coombe. The total for Merton and Morden Urban District included twenty residents, five people who lived in Wimbledon and eight from further afield. One Merton resident was killed in Wimbledon, while two others, the Marriott brothers, died at New Malden Station, which had been heavily bombed and machine-gunned'[79]. From 16.30 a large Luftwaffe incursion took place, some aircraft penetrating to the London area. It is unclear what the intended target of the Luftwaffe was. New Malden station was hit at 17.30 and ten people killed including three railway staff. Merton Park station was also bombed. A Teddington to Waterloo train was strafed by an enemy plane and a passenger killed. Far from terrorising the population, these raids had a novelty value; they drew huge crowds to watch the excitement and no panic was in evidence. Nevertheless, the *Surrey Comet* newspaper reported the raid as 'Nazi frightfulness in Surrey'.

17 August
No daytime bombing occurred, and the night incursions only resulted in a few casualties.

18 August
An attack was made on RAF Kenley aerodrome with disastrous

---

78 Haunton, in Merton Historical Society Bulletins 165-167
79 Haunton, in Merton Historical Society Bulletins 165-167

consequences. At 13.00 around sixty enemy aircraft crossed the coast and fifteen minutes later the airfield came under attack whilst some pilots were still strapping themselves into their machines. Damage to the airfield and its facilities was considerable – three of the hangers were well alight and the equipment stores were destroyed. Four Hurricanes and a Blenheim were destroyed on the ground, and other aircraft damaged. All communications were put out of action. Nine people were killed including the station's much-loved Medical Officer and local GP, Flt Lt Robert Cromie, and a further ten people were injured. Several enemy fighters and bombers were shot down.[80]

Price says the attack on Kenley was made by only nine low-flying Dorniers, although they dropped over 100 bombs.[81] Serious damage was done to the pumping station and waterworks at Kenley, and twelve civilian fatalities occurred, including two at the waterworks.

The air battle over Kent and Surrey that Sunday lunchtime was watched by patrons of the *King's Arms*, Leaves Green, which was very close to RAF Biggin Hill. A Dornier, pursued by a Hurricane crashed a mile north of the pub, with the Addington Home Guard earning publicity in the national press for their alleged role in downing the aircraft by rifle fire. Vehicles in the pub car park were set on fire and in Leaves Green village six died including a family of four in their Anderson shelter.[82]

In the evening, the first bombs fell in the London Metropolitan (London County Council) area, at Woolwich and Eltham, and nine minor fires were caused.

19/22 August
Heavy cloud cover prevented any large-scale Luftwaffe attacks

---

80 Kenley Airfield Friends Group website
81 Price, *Blitz on Britain 1939-1945* (1977)
82 Blake, *Bromley in the Front Line* (2005)

and only a handful of casualties were reported in the London region.

22/23 August

The first bomb of the London night blitz – if you agree 'London' equals the London Civil Defence Region – fell at Harrow at 03.30 on the night of 22/23 August. It badly damaged Barclay's Bank in High Street, Wealdstone. Bombs also fell at Edmonton and Willesden – at the latter location a delayed action bomb exploded about eight hours later. In Edmonton, houses in Sebastopol Road were demolished and the Alcazar cinema and boxing ring in Fore Street were badly damaged.

This wasn't recognised as a bombing of London by either protagonist, so one wonders how Churchill and Hitler defined London.

23/24 August

The London area remained free of bombing raids.

24/25 August

From 24 August, the south-east of England enjoyed seventeen days of continuous fine weather apart from one partly cloudy day.[83]

A critical event occurred this night when the Luftwaffe accidentally bombed the City of London, thus going against explicit orders from Goering. This provoked an RAF retaliatory strike on Berlin the next night – the start of over four years of revenge and retaliation. John Ray points out that this was not by any means the sole reason for the apparent change in the Luftwaffe's strategy at this time. He maintains that the Goering had a variety of reasons for switching to attacks on London

---

83 Article by James Rothwell in *Weather* vol. 67 issue 4

and starting a night time Blitz against Britain. By changing the main assault from the RAF to economic and civilian targets, Goering was thereby able to take pressure off the Luftwaffe and especially his bomber crews. Also, he could also claim that the Luftwaffe was doing no more than retaliating for RAF raids on German civilians.[84] As far as the 'forbidden' target is concerned, it is difficult to envisage where the borders had been drawn and how apparent the boundary between the City of London and the rest of London would be to a Luftwaffe pilot attacking at night!

However, it seems that although the intended target that night was the oil installations at Thames Haven, bombs were dropped across north London and the East End, the sirens sounding at 23.08. Among the districts bombed were Canonbury Park, Tottenham (three killed in Ida Road), Highbury Park, Leyton, Wood Green, Stepney, Islington, Enfield, Hampton Court and Millwall. There were two major fires in east London. a warehouse in the West India Docks was badly damaged by fire, and further warehouses were later reported to be ablaze. One fire required 100 pumps and two fireboats, the other seventy pumps and six fireboats.[85] At 02.40, it was reported that the Imperial Tobacco factory and Carter Patterson's works in Goswell Road, Finsbury were on fire but only slight damage was reported. Malden, Coulsdon, Feltham, Kingston, Banstead and Epsom were also bombed.[86]

Only two Luftwaffe aircraft went astray, releasing bombs that damaged the sixteenth century church of St. Giles Cripplegate in the City of London, which had survived the Great Fire of London. The bombs also started a large fire at

---

84 Ray, *The Night Blitz* (2004)
85 Wallington, *Firemen at War* (1981)
86 TNA HO 202 Ministry of Home Security: Home Security War Room Reports

Fore Street which spread to London Wall. The raid gave a clear indication to the fire services of the ramifications of an air raid, in particular the number of pumps and the manpower required. The Fore Street blaze involved around 200 pumps and was much larger than anything most regular firemen had ever experienced, let alone the men of the AFS.[87]It was truly a baptism of fire for them. Although there were many alerts over the next two weeks, there were few incidents in London and fire crews from London continued to assist at fires outside the London region.

It is said that the errant Luftwaffe crews were summoned to Berlin for punishment, on the orders of Goering himself. This episode features in the 1969 film *Battle of Britain,* but whether the crews were really punished by demotion to infantry is not known.

25/26 August
There were about twenty alerts in the London area over the weekend with machine-gunning of streets reported in Croydon on 25 August. Between 23.15 and 01.58 various boroughs in the London region suffered incidents with five killed in the area covered by Middlesex County Council, and four in Shoreditch.

26 August
A further attack on Croydon by a solitary aircraft did only slight damage but killed two policemen at the Beddington factory estate and one civilian in Croydon.

27 August
Although the alert sounded a couple of times in the London area, no casualties and little damage were caused.

---

87 Wallington, *Firemen at War* (1981)

28 August
During a daylight attack, six people were killed in Addis Close, Enfield. At night, bombs fell on the Cricklewood factory of S Smith & Son which was the only incident where damage to industrial premises was reported – incendiaries caused serious fire damage here. Two high explosive bombs and one incendiary were dropped at two addresses in Woodford Green, but damage was light and only one minor injury was reported.[88]

29 August
The London area saw no activity during the day but at night, a large number of enemy aircraft were over the country. The only significant incident was when seven people died in Barrington Road, Lambeth.

30/31 August
The Luftwaffe made four major attacks targeting airfields in the south-east of England. In addition, at 16.43 the Vauxhall works at Luton was bombed with heavy casualties including fifty killed. 'Considerable' damage was done and fires were started, although production was back to normal in six days. Equally destructive were two strikes on RAF Biggin Hill at noon and at 18.00. Thirty-nine people were killed and another twenty-six injured. Bombs caused a huge amount of damage and all power was lost. Twelve civilians died in Orpington district, mostly in the vicinity of Biggin Hill.

Central London was under alert between 21.50 and 22.13, 22.25 and 23.59 and 00.57 and 03.54. Attacks on this area appeared to be much less severe than those of recent nights, but Pimlico, Belgravia, Finchley, Hornsey, Paddington, Highgate

---

88 https://wansteadmeteo.com/2015/07/31/75th-anniversary-of-the-blitz-in-wanstead/

and Hendon were bombed although there were no fatalities. In Willesden, it was reported that forty-three houses were demolished or rendered uninhabitable, gas and water mains were damaged and there were many casualties – five people were killed in Clarence Road. An unexploded bomb was reported to have dropped at 02.05 close to Brondesbury Park Station, and Kilburn High Road was reported blocked.

31 August
This Saturday saw four daytime raids disrupt everyday activities in London. A Messerschmitt 110 crashed in back gardens in Plumstead, blazing fuel trapping residents in shelters. One subsequently died. Fatalities occurred in East Ham, where seven people died in Milton Avenue, and Plaistow Park Road. Leytonstone, Hornchurch, Stepney and West Ham also recorded casualties.

SEPTEMBER 1940

"In England they're filled with curiosity and keep asking. 'Why doesn't he come?' Be calm. He's coming! He's coming!" (Adolf Hitler 4 September 1940 – speech at Berlin's Sportpalast for the opening of the Winterhilfswerk).

Uncertainty and apprehension hung over London. The pattern of frequent air raid alerts with isolated bombing incidents continued across the London Civil Defence region. Civilians still found these incidents as objects of curiosity worthy of a sightseeing expedition. Gradually they were eased into acceptance of much more heavy and dangerous attacks.

1 September
At 11.05 Tilbury was attacked and considerable damage was

done. A railway station was hit and both up and down lines blocked; gas and water mains were broken; the premises of Harland & Wolff received a direct hit; dockside buildings and workshops were also affected; a number of private houses were demolished and ten shops damaged. Casualties included five dead.

At 14.05 some high explosive and incendiary bombs fell at Orpington, damaging the boiler house and nurses' quarters at a hospital.[89] A family of four died in Farnborough when their Anderson shelter received a direct hit. At 18.00 RAF Biggin Hill was attacked again, for the third day in succession, and its sector operations room was put out of action. As the air battles continued civilians in the target area were increasingly at risk.

3 September

North Weald airfield was bombed at 10.45 by twenty-five to thirty Dornier bombers accompanied by an escort of fifty Me110 fighters. Two hangars, several MT lorries, two Hurricane and one Blenheim aircraft were damaged by fire and the main stores and living quarters received a certain amount of damage. Four RAF personnel were killed. A part of the old Operations Room was demolished, but there was no damage when a direct hit was registered on the new Operations Room. A certain amount of damage was done to communications. The landing ground was left serviceable except for the south and south-west areas where craters and unexploded bombs remained.[90]

4 September

A surprise lunchtime raid left eighty-three dead at the Vickers

---

89 TNA HO 202 Ministry of Home Security: Home Security War Room Reports
90 TNA HO 202 Ministry of Home Security: Home Security War Room Reports

Armstrong factory, an important aircraft manufacturing plant at Brooklands, Weybridge. Over 400 were injured in a raid which is extensively documented. The attack was carried out by fourteen Messerschmitt Me110 aircraft and was over in three minutes, before an alert could be sounded. Six 500kg bombs hit Vickers. It has been suggested that the neighbouring Hawker factory, making the Hurricane fighter aircraft, may have been the real target. However, the attackers' logbooks seem to confirm that Vickers was the target. The damage at Vickers was serious enough – two months production was lost and it was said to be equivalent to the loss of 125 Wellington bombers.[91]

Large fires at Tilbury Docks and in two ships moored on the Thames were attended by London fireboats.[92] St Paul's Church in Charlton became the first church in London to be destroyed, when a lone bomber targeted it at 21.45.

One of the worst incidents in Dartford occurred during the early hours of 5 September 1940 when a high explosive bomb demolished two women's wards at the County Hospital, West Hill, killing a nurse and twenty-four patients. Disregarding her own safety, Sister Gantry, one of the hospital staff crawled in and out of the wreckage to give injections of morphine to the trapped women.[93]

5 September

Blake claims this was the first occasion on which a deliberate raid was made on London[94]. In the late evening, incendiaries fell in the centre of Eltham, in Bromley (forty-eight fires) and at Greenwich. Bombs caused damage and casualties at Hayes and Petts Wood. Total fatalities in London came to eleven. At

91 Ray, *The Night Blitz* (2004)
92 Wallington, *Firemen at War* (1981)
93 Dartford Town Archive © 2000-09 Dartford Grammar School.
94 Blake, *Red Alert* (1982)

Goodmayes, the station and marshalling yard were hit and a passing train derailed.

6 September
'Very vulnerable and visible were the 216 aluminium oil tanks at Thames Haven and Coryton.' A further attack was delivered at 02.20 and fresh oil tank fires were started which were still burning in the early hours of 7 September. Another attack was delivered at 18.00 on 6 September and yet another at 00.24 on 7 September.[95] These were tackled by London fire crews. Twenty-seven tanks were destroyed but the works never closed or refused cargo.

A raid was made on London in the late evening, with many incidents in south-east London. There were civilian casualties across the London region, and these were most numerous in Bermondsey and Southwark. Six died at the Linsey Street arch, a shelter in Bermondsey. Thirty incidents occurred in Canning Town and North Woolwich. Bernard Bennie of Lewisham's heavy rescue squad was awarded the George Medal for his efforts in attempting to rescue families trapped in Engleheart Road, Catford.

95 TNA HO 202 Ministry of Home Security: Home Security War Room Reports

FOUR

THE BLITZ BEGINS

7/8 SEPTEMBER 'BLACK SATURDAY'

As *Front Line* was to say, 'Guernica, Warsaw, Rotterdam, London.'
But although the four locations suffered terrible ordeals, the ordeals
were very different except in the human suffering that resulted.

In London, it was a warm September Saturday afternoon,
and the temperature reached 79F. Football grounds were
turning out their crowds onto the busy streets of east London.
Within a couple of hours, it was a war zone. The spectacle of
348 bombers (quoted by Stansky and Ray – other sources give
differing totals: 318 in Price, 375 in *Front Line*), escorted by over
500 fighters (again many different totals are quoted in various
sources), approaching London in formation, in daylight – the
nightmare come true – was never to be repeated. 'Few civilians
in a peace-time life will have witnessed anything as unnerving
as the approach of this thundering aerial armada.'[96]

---

96 Blake, *Red Alert* (1982)

This short intense raid – the sirens sounded at 16.43 and the all clear at 18.10 – targeted the East End and docks. The raiders reached their target unhindered by RAF fighters. The raid demonstrated concentration of bombing on a strategic target in a short space of time and terrified those on the receiving end. It also alarmed the authorities who had little idea of what reaction it would provoke among the population. It was what many would have considered the ideal format for a bombing raid on London, and left chaos in its wake. As the German aircraft approached London, the Ford Motor Company's factory at Dagenham was one of the first targets. Amongst the destruction done was severe damage at the Beckton gas works in East Ham, described as the largest gas works in Europe or even in the world, which was forced to stop making gas, leaving much of east London without a supply. Although Beckton gas works was to be hit many times during the Blitz, this was the only time it had to halt production.

Fires broke out at the Royal Arsenal and the Siemens works at Woolwich, and at Harland & Wolff's premises at North Woolwich. The Civilian War Dead Roll of Honour records sixty fatalities in Woolwich on 7 September, most of them at the Royal Arsenal. Details of the circumstances behind this death toll are not available. At Purfleet, serious fires occurred at the Anglo-American Oil Works, and other industrial buildings were hit and fires broke out. Seven died including three firemen. In Dockland, principally in the East India, West India, Surrey Commercial and Millwall Docks very serious fires broke out. The boroughs of Stepney, Poplar and West Ham, and on the south bank, Southwark and Bermondsey, were the worst affected by the bombing. In West Ham, Queen Mary's hospital was hit and two nurses and six patients killed. Over twenty-five people died in East Ham High Street. This appears to have been a result of an incident when a bomb fell on the railway bridge and demolished a number of shops, trapping people in the basement of Woolworth's store. The fire brigade struggled to prevent fire spreading to the Palace Theatre. Just before 17.00, a German Messerschmitt fighter crashed in Ranelagh Road, West Ham. It hit an Anderson shelter in the garden of no.75 killing five people in all. The pilot bailed out and landed in Rainham.[97]

Two hours later at 20.10, the sirens sounded again in London, whilst civil defence and fire services were still working on the incidents caused by the earlier raid. The all clear did not sound until 05.50, and the length of the raid was an experience which took most Londoners by surprise, even invoking some Cockney humour, as it was thought by some that the raid should have finished in time for a pint before closing time! There were already far more pressing concerns for Londoners than the availability of their next beer, and there was little scope for such levity.

The raids had left the East End in ruins and its people traumatized. The recollections of Len Jones, who had survived the raid in a public shelter in Limehouse, are oft-quoted. He had witnessed 'the total destruction of where I'd lived ... the church that I'd been to and the school, my old place of work, all smashed to pieces, all in one night ... that night haunted me for more than forty years, it was so awful I couldn't tell anybody about it, it almost destroyed me.'[98] Fitzgibbon has the account of Nancy Spender, the ambulance driver who finds people cowering in shelters in Silvertown, traumatized and unable to speak.[99]

A total of 649 tons of high explosive and 100,000 incendiaries had fallen on London in the two raids. By dawn on 8 September, nine conflagrations, nineteen major and forty serious fires had

---

97 *The Newham Story* website
98 Mack & Humphries, *London at War* (1985)
99 Fitzgibbon *The Blitz* (1970)

broken out. Of the conflagrations two were in the Surrey Docks, one at Woolwich Arsenal, one at Bishopsgate Goods Station and five at various points on the docks. The largest fire was at Quebec Yard in the Surrey Commercial Docks, where an area of one square mile was declared a fire zone, with 250 acres of timber burning. Twenty-foot stacks of timber in addition to the deck cargoes of vessels awaiting unloading were alight within half an hour of the first bombs falling. This fire was thirty or forty times greater than any recent peacetime fire. The fires soon threatened the safety of residents on the riverside areas of Bermondsey, there only being two roads in and out of the Surrey Docks area. Soon after 22.00 the Keeton's Road School in Bermondsey was hit. This building had been brought into use as a rest centre, receiving people who had been evacuated from Rotherhithe because of the fires raging in the docks. Seventy-three people died in Bermondsey that night, many of them at Keeton's Road School. At 19.15 at the Abbey Road Depot in Stratford, used as an ARP cleansing and ambulance station, thirteen ARP and Fire Service personnel were killed when the building received a direct hit.

Railway damage in east London was considerable, with numerous interruptions to services. North Woolwich station was hit at 22.56 and much damage was caused, and the section of line between Stratford and North Woolwich was closed to passenger traffic until January. All LMS lines were closed at Plaistow, and West Ham station was closed for the best part of a year. Elsewhere there was also much disruption on the Southern Railway. A stationary train was hit in Victoria Station and the driver killed. Damage to a viaduct arch outside Waterloo Station closed the station and required urgent repairs.

At the Woolwich Arsenal site, 'London's No.1 military target' there were several huge fires amongst the additional hazards of live ammunition and explosives.

'There were pepper fires, loading the surrounding air heavily with stinging particles, so that when the firemen took a deep breath it felt like burning fire itself. There were rum fires, with torrents of blazing liquid pouring from the warehouse doors and barrels exploding like bombs themselves. There was a paint fire, another cascade of white-hot flame, coating the pumps with varnish that could not be cleaned for weeks. A rubber fire gave forth black clouds of smoke so asphyxiating that it could only be fought from a distance and was always threatening to choke the attackers. Sugar, it seems, burns well in liquid form as it floats on the water in dockyard basins. Tea makes a blaze that is 'sweet, sickly and very intense'. One man found it odd to be pouring cold water on hot tea leaves. A grain warehouse when burning produced great clouds of black flies that settled in banks upon the walls, whence the firemen washed them off with their jets. There were rats in their hundreds. And the residue of burned wheat was "a sticky mess that pulls your boots off".'[100]

In Silvertown, Tate & Lyle's sugar refinery, John Knight's Primrose Soap works, and the Silvertown Rubber Works were all badly damaged. Keiller's factory at Tay Wharf, Silvertown, producing preserves, chocolates and confectionery was almost completely destroyed by the bombing. Silvertown was another community isolated between the docks and the river, and soon it became obvious that it would have to be evacuated. A bomb demolished storage tanks at Burt, Boulton and Hay, who made coal tar products at Prince Regent's Wharf, Silvertown. This sent molten tar flowing into roadways and sewers, presenting a challenging clear-up operation.

In the initial raid, most casualties occurred in the East End and the Thameside boroughs. The second raid had spread

---

100 Anon., *Front Line* (1942)

the destruction westward but there were few incidents there, certainly not enough to give the impression the East End's ordeal was going to be shared by its more affluent neighbours. Fire brigade reinforcements were called up from no.6 region, the Thames Valley and south Midlands.

One of the worst individual incidents of the first night of the Blitz was at the shelter of Columbia Market in Bethnal Green. This was an incident of a type which was to become all too common. Columbia Road Market was a huge Gothic building built in 1869 by the philanthropist Angela Burdett-Coutts to supply affordable food to impoverished East Enders. It never thrived, and when the war began it had been closed for more than half a century, the market having moved to the streets on and around Columbia Road. A 50kg bomb dropped straight down an air shaft and into the shelter below. The memorial lists forty-three fatalities. Also in Bethnal Green, St Matthew's church was left as a roofless shell. A bomb fell outside St George in the East hospital in Stepney, badly damaging the front of the building but not causing any serious injuries to patients or staff.

The borough of Wanstead and Woodford, so far unscathed, sent rescue parties to East Ham to assist but within a few hours, the borough itself became the target of bombing. At 01.25 three high explosive bombs fell in the Grove Park area behind the High Street, Wanstead. Two houses in Grove Park and the central block of the Shrubbery flats collapsed. A row of shops in the High Street was badly damaged by the third bomb which was accompanied by about 500 incendiaries. The bombing left eight dead and another bomb in Highfield Road, Woodford Green, killed three more. Some fifty people were injured across the borough during the raid. Wanstead and Woodford suffered far less damage than other parts of London and a decision had already been taken to accept 2,000 evacuees from the East End.

By Sunday lunchtime the first of these began to arrive in buses and lorries.[101]

The East Ham fire brigade noted that by 02.00 on the Sunday morning, there was no doubt that their personnel were flagging for want of food and drink. There was no water, gas, or electricity south of the Barking Road. However, by 06.30, most of the fires in East Ham were out. By Sunday evening, the only thing that was left burning was the coke dump at Beckton gas works, which was finally extinguished on the Monday.[102]

Albert George Dolphin, aged 44, was posthumously awarded the George Cross for the heroism he displayed in Deptford during the night raid:

'A high explosive bomb fell on the kitchens of Ward Block 1 at the South Eastern Hospital, killing four nurses who were in the ground floor kitchen and injuring the night Sister and patients in the adjoining ward. A nurse, who was in the ward kitchen on the first floor, was thrown through the collapsing floor into the passage below. Together with other helpers, Albert George Dolphin, one of the porters of the hospital, rushed to the site and found her pinioned by a block of masonry across her legs. While they were working the wall was heard to crack and subsequently collapsed. The workers had ample time to jump clear before the masonry fell, but Dolphin remained where he was and his body was subsequently found lying face downwards across the nurse with his head towards the wall which collapsed on top of him. When found he was dead, but the nurse, who was subsequently extricated, was still alive, though severely injured. There is no doubt that Dolphin, although aware that the wall was about to collapse, deliberately remained where he was and threw himself across the nurse's

---

101 https://wansteadmeteo.com/2015/07/31/75th-anniversary-of-the-blitz-in-wanstead/
102 East Ham Fire Service (*The Newham Story*)

body in an endeavour to protect her. This he succeeded in doing at the cost of his own life.'[103]

Old Kent Road bus garage was badly damaged. Suburban Bromley and adjacent areas inevitably suffered incidents as the huge air armada passed over – eleven deaths were reported near Beckenham including four residents at a nursing home.

8/9 September

There was no daytime raid on Sunday, but it was a day of rumour and suspense, following the issuing of the codeword 'Cromwell' indicating an invasion was imminent. During the day the Prime Minister Winston Churchill visited the East End, touring scenes of destruction including the Columbia Market shelter.

The *Daily Express* was to report that 'Goering restarted his great blitzkrieg on London ... promptly at black out time'. The evening raid began at 19.59, half an hour after Goering had made a triumphal broadcast to the German nation.

In the East End, the docks were again targeted and in St Katherine's Dock warehouses were shattered and vegetable oils and paraffin wax were soon blazing on the surface of the water. In the Millwall Dock, 1¼ million gallons of rum were ablaze. K block of the Peabody estate in John Fisher Street, Stepney received a direct hit and seventy-eight residents and visitors were killed in the shelter. In 1995, a marble memorial plaque was placed on the estate to commemorate the victims. I was unable to trace any further details of this incident and perhaps find out why the casualties were so numerous, but it seems that a bomb hit the building and collapsed it into the basement shelter. The adjacent Block D of the Peabody estate was also badly damaged and later demolished. Whitechapel fire station in Commercial Road was hit, causing several casualties among fire service personnel.

---

103 London Gazette 17 January 1941

St. Thomas' Hospital, prominently located opposite the Houses of Parliament, next to Westminster Bridge, sustained its first damage when a large bomb fell on Block 1, which included Gassiot House, which served as the hospital's nurses' home. Six members of hospital staff were killed including two nurses.

The war made its first impact on the borough of Holborn when two 250kg bombs fell in High Holborn, causing much damage along the thoroughfare. One fell on the corner of Red Lion Street and Featherstone Buildings, the other on the corner of Great Turnstile, and twenty-nine people were killed. Twenty-seven fatalities are detailed in the Civilian War Dead Roll of Honour. Twelve victims of this raid died at Lincoln House in High Holborn (which is on the south side, numbered as 300 High Holborn) although one is recorded as dying outside Lincoln House, eight died 'at High Holborn', three at 280/1 High Holborn, three at Featherstone Buildings and two at 303 High Holborn. Possibly there was a public shelter and or ARP depot there, as is indicated by the quotation below. Five of the victims are ambulance staff, two AFS & one a heavy rescue man. There is also one ARP warden and one Home Guard sergeant among the victims. Scholey says further bombs fell whilst rescue squads were still at work, which may explain the above.[104] Edward Redknapp, a member of an ARP Rescue Party, received the George Medal:

'Some buildings were severely damaged by high explosive bombs and three large fires started. Redknapp was a member of one of four rescue parties sent to this incident. Several persons were known to be trapped in a basement shelter. Shortly after the commencement of rescue operations a second bombing attack was made, causing heavy casualties to A.R.P. personnel and disorganizing the rescue work. Redknapp and the remainder of

---

104 Scholey, *Bombs on Holborn* (1998)

his party, who by then had penetrated to the basement shelter, were ordered to get away. Soon afterwards, however, Redknapp led ten of the men back to the basement shelter and, under his leadership, rescue operations were resumed. Technically, the work was extremely difficult and dangerous. The general insecurity of the masses of debris was rendered more acute by the volume of water being poured over the burning building and flooding through to the basement. The careless movement of any part of it was liable to cause a subsidence which would have buried the rescue party along with the casualties already trapped. In spite of this ever-present danger, Redknapp worked coolly and continuously for nearly four hours, inspiring, by his own example, the efforts of the rest of the squad, until the last live casualty had been extricated.'[105]

One of the first bombs on the borough of St Pancras wrecked a number of houses in Harrington Square, Camden Town. Falling at 03.35, it blew a bus up against the row of houses providing a famous Blitz image, but fortunately the bus crew and passengers had already taken shelter. However, there were many trapped casualties, including eleven deaths, and R D Stewart and A G Palmer of the rescue and stretcher parties received the George Medal for their work. Later in the night another bomb fell on an Anderson shelter in Allcroft Road, Kentish Town, near the ARP depot in the old William Ellis School, and a total of sixteen people were killed in this incident.[106]

Once again, public shelters were hit and serious incidents resulted. Sixteen people were killed at the Annette Crescent trench shelter in Islington. The Cadogan House shelter in Chelsea received a direct hit. This was a public shelter under a block of flats in Beaufort Street. Sixty-one died including the

---

105 London Gazette 7 March 1941
106 Newbery, *Wartime St Pancras. a London borough defends itself* (2006)

shelter warden Jean Darling, and this was the worst incident in Chelsea in the 1940-41 Blitz. Frances Faviell recalled this incident 'Our first casualties at FAP5 were quiet and shocked. None of them wanted to say much – I think the dirt and mess with which they were all covered and their anxiety for missing relatives and friends was uppermost. The casualties' indifference to injuries, cuts, and abrasions astonished us just as the dirt upset all our arrangements. The effects of shock when they first arrived, although we had been trained to recognise them, varied very much in individual cases. What did emerge from this first unfortunate tragedy was a feeling that shelters were not safe – that had the victims stayed at home they would still be alive. To this there was no answer – it was the duty of all Civil Defence personnel to encourage the public to use the shelters.'[107]

The situation report summarises the position in London. 'Reports show that very considerable damage was done to rail and road communications and many serious fires occurred. Three hospitals were hit and Fulham Power Station was set on fire.' Hasker[108] says the turbine house of the power station received a direct hit causing extensive damage and killing several workers. 'The heaviest bombing was in the riverside districts but minor indiscriminate bombing was widespread.' Clearly there was an official perception that most enemy bombing was not indiscriminate, but this was soon to be disproved.

Sixty local authority areas, including every metropolitan borough, were bombed during that night. Major damage was done in Acton, Leyton and Poplar and all lines were blocked at Broad Street station. The Thames Embankment was flooded by a burst main at Chelsea. A serious fire occurred at Chiltern Court (this is the massive block of flats that incorporates Baker Street

107 Faviell, *A Chelsea Concerto* (1959)
108 Hasker, *Fulham in the Second World War* (2005)

station) and at Madame Tussauds waxworks, the cinema and over 350 head moulds were destroyed by a bomb falling near the junction of Marylebone Road and Allsop Place. Shoreditch had serious incidents at Worgate Street and Whitmore Road. In Homerton, the vast Berger Paints factory was set ablaze by a direct hit on the varnish storage tank rooms where thousands of gallons of varnish and other highly inflammable liquids were stored. Only strenuous efforts by firefighters prevented destruction of the whole site.[109]

At Southgate, the Metal Box Company's factory and the Lindley Aircraft Company's works were damaged, affecting work on government contracts. Hornsey had its heaviest night of the Blitz, with thirty-eight incidents recorded. Casualties however were relatively low in Hornsey – twenty-one in all, with four killed.[110] St Michael and All Angels Church in Sydenham was totally destroyed along with the vicarage at 02.30.

9/10 September 1940

The next day there was a daylight raid on Chelsea in the late afternoon. A German bomber was chased along the King's Road by a British fighter, releasing four bombs. One fell in Bramerton Street where there were eight fatalities, including the wife and son of local GP Dr Richard Castillo, who was at the time working with the Chelsea mobile squad at various incidents. His daughter was rescued after ARP workers dug for four days in the ruins of their house.[111]

The Metropolitan Police Diary gives the start of the evening raid as 20.36 with the all clear not sounded until 05.41. 'Widespread bombing affecting all divisions except C and

---

109 Golden, *Hackney at War* (1995)
110 Hornsey Historical Society Bulletin no.33. *Home Fires. A North London Suburb at War* (1992)
111 Faviell, *A Chelsea Concerto* (1959)

Y. Extensive damage to property & to public utility services. Damage at Buckingham Palace. Victoria Embankment wall damaged for 50 yards between Waterloo & Blackfriars. H.E. bomb on Hungerford Bridge & train services suspended. Bombs on Waterloo (new) Bridge, Somerset House & Royal Courts of Justice.'[112]

The capital's most vulnerable people soon became victims. Fifteen elderly people were killed at the Central Home in Leytonstone. This was the former Union workhouse, later Langthorne Hospital, run by West Ham Borough Council, who had renamed it the Central Home Public Assistance Institution, a home for the chronically ill, aged and infirm.

A school in Agate Street, Canning Town received a direct hit. The South Hallsville School tragedy is an early Blitz incident about which rumours still abound, one being that there were 400 fatalities – the *Daily Mirror* in an article on 19 September 2010 even gave a total of 600. The circumstances where the authorities failed to evacuate bombed-out families promptly from an unsafe building with no sheltering provision or facilities are particularly emotive, and clearly still arouse strong feelings today. However, although initial civil defence estimates were 225-250, the death toll is officially seventy-eight. Apparently, coaches to transport the evacuees away were organised and instructed to rendezvous at the *George* pub. Various explanations are given as to their failure to appear, including that the coaches went to the wrong *George* pub, either one in another borough or one 'on the wrong side of the river'. Another source says the coaches made their rendezvous, but it was then too late in the day to start the evacuation, another that sounding of the siren halted the evacuation. Yet another says the coaches went to Camden Town instead of Canning Town. The *Daily Mirror* reports that the Queen Mother unveiled a

112 Metropolitan Police Diary 12 September 1940

plaque at the school in 1990 (this does not mention any fatality numbers) and opened a memorial garden.

In Camberwell, at least twenty-eight died when two bombs struck the shelter under Wheatland House on the Dog Kennel Hill estate. The King and Queen visited the scene two days later when bodies were still being recovered. Eighteen people were killed at the Ewer Street shelter in Southwark – most of them were from the nearby flats in Union Street. The shelter received a direct hit and a broken gas main fuelled a blaze. Four policemen were killed when a bomb hit Greenwich Police station, and fifteen AFS men were killed at Poplar Fire Station in East India Dock Road. Bethnal Green had heavy casualties in Hersee Place and Teesdale Street, where twenty people died.

Bombs fell across the southern part of St. Pancras in Argyle Street, Guilford Street, Frederick Street and Birkenhead Street where there were seventeen fatalities. Two high explosive bombs and incendiaries fell in Mecklenburgh Square and one bomb demolished part of Byron Court, which was in use as a hostel, and five women were killed. Another bomb fell in the gardens next to trench shelters, but failed to explode. It exploded the next day damaging several buildings including no.37 the London home of Leonard and Virginia Woolf of the Bloomsbury Group. Further damage later in the month forced the Woolfs to abandon their home.[113]

At 22.20 a bomb destroyed most of the parish church of St. Mary Islington, leaving only the tower and spire intact. A 1,000kg bomb demolished eleven houses in St. James' Lane, Muswell Hill and two people died. Ten ARP workers were killed in Fulham when a delayed action bomb exploded whilst they were engaged in rescue work at the Munster Road end of St. Dionis Road.

---

113 Newbery, *Wartime St Pancras. a London borough defends itself* (2006)

Buckingham Palace was bombed for the first time, the North Lodge being damaged, but the King and Queen were at Windsor. Somerset House and the Royal Courts of Justice were also both damaged for the first time.

It was already being concluded that apart from attacks on railways, bombing appeared wholly indiscriminate and extensive damage was being done to private property. One factor behind the reluctance of the RAF to attack Germany in 1939-40 was that private property might be damaged!

Just after midnight the Great Ormond Street children's hospital in Holborn was hit by a 250kg bomb 'which tore a clean hole through the roof of the west wing, shattering four wards. The sixth floor was wrecked.' The various personal accounts of the bombing of this world-famous hospital diverge on several factual aspects but it seems that the bomb heavily damaged the top floor of the modern western wing dating from 1938. But damage to the boiler rooms caused the greatest threat to the hospital and William Pendle, the boilerman, received the George Medal.

'When this hospital was bombed, the explosion shattered the furnaces and burst gas and water mains. Pendle was in the stokehole when the explosion blew the burning coal from his furnace into the rooms. Three water mains and a gas main were burst, the gas catching fire. Through the openings into the stokehole flames could be seen rising to a height of 70 feet and water in enormous volume burst into this part of the building, filling up the coal bunkers below and then rising rapidly in the stoke-hole itself. Through all this inferno Pendle calmly proceeded to draw his fires, shut off steam and made all as safe as possible, not leaving until this was done. By this time the water was swirling up to his waist and he then had to struggle to the narrow staircase through floating debris to reach ground level.'[114]

114 *London Gazette* 17 January 1941

Pendle described what happened and how he dealt with the fire:

As soon as I went up the stairs to the back of the boiler room, I could see what had happened. The bomb had busted the lot, broken the water mains and fired the gas. Seeing what was going on, and the water coming along like a river, I went back to my boiler to draw the fire and get the pressure down. It was lucky I only had one of the three boilers working. It was summer time, and also not working to full strength on account of the war. The pressure being steady at 36lb, I began to rake out the fire and I went on raking until the pressure dropped to nothing.

He also described the aftermath of the incident:

I walked through the wards and corridors. The lower ground floor was like a deep river. From the first to the fifth floors all was dark and forlorn. On the sixth there was utter devastation. Battered and twisted cots mingled with shattered telephones, children's toys, story books, fallen masonry and rubble … There had been no children recently in this shattered ward, but a toy cupboard had burst open giving an added and authentic horror to the scene.[115]

Most of the hospital's patients had already been moved off-site due to the war situation, and none were injured during the raid.

On this night, large fires were caused in the City and many other fires elsewhere. St. Augustine's church, Watling Street, in the City of London received a direct hit and firewatchers

---

115 GOSH during WW11 https.//www.gosh.nhs.uk/file/47806

nearby observed the spire collapse into the nave.[116] Charing Cross Station and Fenchurch Street Station were both put out of action and lines were blocked in other places. The huge LNER warehouses at Goodman's Yard by the tracks just outside Fenchurch Street station were completely gutted and partly demolished together with the freight wagons alongside. There was a serious fire at Woolwich, where Greenwood & Batley's Ltd cordite shed was blown up; at Woolwich Arsenal a large building was set on fire. At Westminster part of the Embankment had to be closed and major damage was reported from Lambeth, Southwark, East Ham and West Ham. There were also large fires at warehouses at the Docks. Chingford received a 1,400kg bomb which penetrated some 30 feet underground but failed to explode. It was eventually exploded in situ by a bomb disposal team. Gas supplies were still affected by the opening raid on 7 September and reduced pressure was being experienced even at factories in west London.

As far the railways were concerned Brooksbank succinctly sums up: 'On the morning of Monday 9 September, the situation was dire.'

10/11 September

The lovely weather that had been a backdrop to the opening of the Blitz had gone and diarist Anthony Heap noted that it was now cool and dull with some rain.[117] The weather was much less settled until the 22nd. It was often cloudy with mostly poor flying conditions – except on the 14th and 15th.[118] There was no daytime raid on London on 10 September.

The War Cabinet met at 10 Downing Street at 12.30. The Home Secretary, Sir John Anderson, informed the War Cabinet

---

116 Kynaston, *City of London* (2011)
117 The Diaries of Anthony Heap
118 Article by James Rothwell in Weather vol. 67 issue 4

that a difficult situation was arising in regard to people in the East End of London who had been made homeless. 'This matter had not, perhaps, been very well handled by all the local authorities, but arrangements had now been made for the matter to be taken over by the London County Council'. A special organisation was also being set up in Whitehall. It was proposed to transfer the homeless people from the East of London to districts further West. An appeal would be made to householders to find accommodation. Continuing, the Home Secretary said that the Lord Mayor wanted to start a fund for the relief of distress caused by the bombing of London. It would be difficult to refuse to allow this fund to be started, more especially as the American Ambassador and the Lord Mayor of Melbourne had opened similar funds. It should, however, be made clear that the scheme was intended to supplement the compensation provided by the Government, and would deal with the sort of items of expenditure which could not be covered by the Government's scheme. The War Cabinet gave the go-ahead for the Home Secretary to inform the Lord Mayor of London that there was no objection to the opening of a fund on these lines.

In the night raid, bombing took place between 20.40 and 04.27 'there was considerable use of incendiary bombs which caused a number of fires, particularly in St. Katherine's Dock. In all there were four major, eight serious, twenty-six medium and 204 small fires in the County of London and twenty-one medium fires and ninety-six small fires in Outer London. All these are under control except one at a timber yard in Mile End Road'. This was Durrell's Timber Yard.

The major damage was at St. Katherine's Dock, where a raging fire was reported to be out of control and at London Docks where two large warehouses were on fire, probably set alight from the St. Katherine's Dock fire. These seven-storey buildings were packed with inflammable wool, copra, hides, hops and wax. According to Lewey, flames reached 100ft into the sky, cranes collapsed and cables fell. Blazing barges had to be sunk.[119] 130 pumps attended at this fire. High explosive bombs fell on the Millwall entrance lock.

Serious fires also broke out in the West India Dock – North Quay, at Islington, in the City – Golden Lane (75 pumps), Barbican (40 pumps) and Aldgate Avenue; at Shadwell, where the East End Maternity Hospital was set on fire, at Stepney (a major fire in Cable Street – 50 pumps), at Millwall (hydraulic mains burst), at Paddington, St. Marylebone and Bayswater Road. Marylebone station was closed after a bomb fell at 23.35 in the station yard and four UXBs were found in the station and goods yard, and services terminated at Wembley Hill until mid-morning on 11 September. The Metropolitan Water Board's pumping station at St Michael's Road, Willesden, was seriously damaged but was still operating. In the West End, Burlington Arcade was wrecked.

At the Wenlock brewery in Windsor Terrace, Shoreditch, where the basement of the brewery was used as a public shelter by several hundred people, at least eleven people died:

'Just after 4am, 11th September, a series of explosions shook the brewery. The adjacent Wenlock Road School and surrounding houses had been bombed. Debris from those buildings fell into the road and smothered brewery basement doors trapping the occupants inside. Meanwhile, bomb damage in the brewery sent masonry falling on to the refrigeration plant and caused it to leak ammonia gas throughout the basement via the ventilation system. Some of the debris blocked an internal door, the only way in and out of the room where the card school sat. This disaster resulted in Warden's Post L phoning dramatic messages to local ARP Emergency Services. One hand written report

---

119 Lewey, *Cockney Campaign* (1944)

reads, "Proceed to Wenlock Brewery, Wenlock Road. Ammonia plant Exploded". Another reads "Send police to control crowds to Wenlock Brewery".[120] The men in the card school managed to force their way out onto the street via gratings in the pavement. They were badly affected by ammonia fumes. 'Terror began for the many people already cringing in fear in the main shelter. Falling masonry brought thick dust. That dusty air rapidly became more polluted with a white vapour. With their lights still miraculously working the victim could see their plight. Eyes streaming choking and gasping for breath they rushed for the external doors and found them jammed tight. Some people, badly affected by the ammonia gas collapsed, in the rush they were trampled underfoot. In the midst of it all a frightened shout "it's a German gas attack" caused even more panic among the trapped people'.

Eventually a door leading to the street was opened and they were able to escape. Soon the local St. Leonard's Hospital and others were full of victims severely affected by ammonia gas, and several of the victims were to die in hospital over the next few days.

Since the Blitz proper began on 7 September, *Front Line* observed that 'by the end of five or six days, Londoners appreciated the fact that they were in for a long siege.'

11/12 September

The War Cabinet met at 10 Downing Street at 12.30. The First Sea Lord, Sir Dudley Pound, reported that the damage to shipping during the raids of the last few nights on the London Docks had not been so considerable as had at first been thought. The tonnage of ships totally lost was about 29,000. In addition,

---

120 Stephen Sadler *Terror at Wenlock Brewery* in East London Record issue 19, 1998

15,000 tons of shipping could probably be salvaged on a long-term basis. Ships totalling 72,000 tons had suffered minor damage. Such an attack had been anticipated with the result that there was not so much shipping in the Thames as usual. The Admiralty were taking further steps to arrange for extra shipping facilities in the North-West ports.[121]

During daytime combats over Croydon, a Spitfire crashed on houses in Hartland Way, Shirley, and petrol from the blazing wreck poured into an Anderson shelter, killing the four occupants.[122] Warehouses and sheds were set on fire and heavy damage done at the Surrey Commercial Docks as a result of an attack at 16.23. Around the same time, a street shelter in Albion Way, Lewisham was hit and thirty-six people died. Then a bomb hit the Central Hall in Greenwich and at least twenty-three more people died. Joseph Hoyle of the Greenwich rescue squad received the George Medal for his work in extricating victims from the debris. The AFS station in the King's Warren High School in Plumstead had a direct hit and two firemen were killed. There were many fires in south-east London.

The night raid, which commenced at 20.20 was very heavy and lasted for some nine hours, resulting in 356 fatal casualties. The Central Telegraph Office, St. Martins Le Grand in the City was hit by bombs at 20.42, the upper storeys being heavily damaged. The emergency telegraph and telephone schemes were put into operation by the GPO. At 22.34 three bombs caused serious damage to the London Docks. Sheds were set on fire and a fire float was sunk at the quay. The Star Works of Thomas de la Rue Ltd in Bunhill Row, Finsbury was gutted by fire at about 23.20 but no casualties were reported. At Poplar, major damage was caused to the Manganese Bronze and Brass

---

121 TNA CAB 65/9
122 Ogley, *Surrey at War* (1995)

Company's Wharf by bombs at 23.33. At 01.00 a major fire was caused by incendiary bombs at the Finsbury works of the Ormond Engineering Company.

The main London-Brighton railway line was temporarily closed during a search for suspected unexploded bombs near the Merstham tunnel. The Southern Railway's line at Bickley was blocked as a result of five bombs at 01.30; their line was also obstructed between Holborn low level and Farringdon Street station, stopping all traffic from north of the Thames to the south on this system. The Crystal Palace low level station sustained major damage by bombs at 02.10. At Camberwell a serious fire broke out at the works of the Anti-Attrition Metal Company and surrounding factories were reported to be involved.'[123] Camberwell Tram Depot was also seriously damaged, with many trams destroyed, and thirteen died at the Guinness Trust flats in Page's Walk, Bermondsey.

The Park Hospital in Hither Green was hit by high explosive bombs and fire broke out. John Foley of the hospital's maintenance staff received a George Medal for his work in rescuing a badly burned nurse.

London's AA barrage finally opened up, although even General Sir Frederick Pile himself would argue that it wasn't a true barrage. Pile had been appointed Commander-in-Chief A.A. Command in July 1939. The night Blitz brought huge problems for his inadequate resources. After a few days of the Blitz, he and his staff determined that 'whatever had gone before, we would meet the enemy that night with a barrage the like of which had never been seen or heard before.'[124] As ordered by General Pile, every available gun fired and 13,500 rounds were fired in all. The barrage (particularly its noise) was enthusiastically welcomed

123 TNA HO 202 Ministry of Home Security: Home Security War Room Reports
124 Pile, *Ack-Ack* (1949)

by Londoners and was perceived as a visible form of 'hitting back' at the enemy. As far as hitting enemy aircraft it was known to be very inaccurate and the results in terms of enemy aircraft shot down were poor and of no real significance throughout the London Blitz. It is said that the barrage forced the attackers to fly at higher altitude with consequent effect on accuracy, and that it forced them to drop their bombs early or even turn back. But the Luftwaffe's night raids continued to gain in strength and effectiveness, and its aircraft losses remained very low throughout the Blitz. The sheer length of the attacks put AA defences under pressure. Wear and tear on the guns, the number of guns needed and the conflicting needs for their deployment, as well as the personnel available were all problems. This was shown again during the later 'Baedeker Blitz' of 1942 when cities not anticipated to be strategic targets were attacked and rapid re-deployment of gun batteries was necessary.

12/13 September

Diarist Anthony Heap noted that the damage in Holborn was by far the most extensive he had observed. However, bomb damage was becoming more obvious all around central London. A 1,000kg bomb fell in Dean's Yard outside St. Paul's Cathedral but failed to explode, posing a great threat to the cathedral. The recovery of the bomb was fraught with difficulty – it had penetrated thirty feet or more and continued to move in the clay soil – but it was eventually brought to the surface by a bomb disposal team led by Lt. Robert Davies, who alone had then driven it away to Hackney Marshes and detonated it. This was a story of suspense and bravery maximised in the story as given to the press – the reality was perhaps not quite so glamorous, although Lt. Davies' bravery was never in doubt. James Owen[125]

---

125 Owen, *Danger UXB. The Heroic Story* (2010)

maintains that a bomb of this size was unlikely to be a 'delayed action' type and its failure to explode was no doubt due to a defect. It has also been alleged that Lt. Davies did not in fact drive the bomb away himself and unfortunately, he was later dismissed from the army in disgrace for fraud and looting.

The evening raid, which began at 21.15 is recorded as having been on 'a very minor scale'. However, at least eighteen people were killed at the Orb Street shelter in Walworth. London's churches continued to fall victim to the Luftwaffe. The Catholic church of Our Lady of Victories in Kensington High Street was destroyed by incendiary bombs; the modern church of St. Catherine Coleman on Westway, Shepherds Bush, was destroyed by high explosive bombs along with the vicarage and four houses. St. Thomas' Hospital was damaged again by two further bombs.

13/14 September

London had a lengthy daylight alert, being under siren from 09.45 to 13.55, and thirty-one people were killed and 224 injured in various incidents. Home Security reports state that at 10.43 Ravenshill School in West Ham, 'which was occupied by families evacuated from their homes was demolished by high explosive bombs. Fifty casualties have so far been reported.' Fortunately, it appears that none were fatal, as no fatalities appear in the Civilian War Dead Roll of Honour for West Ham on that date.

At 11.10 Buckingham Palace was hit by six bombs in a deliberate attack, a German aircraft approaching up The Mall, and two bombs exploded in the courtyard only a short distance from where the King and Queen were watching. It was widely reported that the Queen felt that henceforth she would be able to 'look the East End in the face'. Just before noon incendiary bombs caused slight damage at Scotland Yard, the Admiralty and the War Office.

In St. Marylebone, a fire was started at Great Titchfield Street, and in St. Pancras the Euston Road was blocked as a result of high explosive bombs which fell at 15.50. Fifty-nine casualties were reported. Fatalities also occurred in Camberwell, Chelsea, Kensington and Hampstead.

Nine people were killed at the Independent Church, Brixton Road, Lambeth. Queen Anne's Mansions, a huge old eleven-storey Victorian block in Westminster received a direct hit, a section of the building being sliced away, but there were no serious casualties, the building having been requisitioned for government use as offices.

At 11.00 the War Cabinet met at 10 Downing Street, despite the enemy air activity over London, and discussed the situation in the London area. The minutes by civil servants describe the events of the past few days in measured, calm and unemotional, but emphatically positive tones. They give little clue as to the actual degree of emotion expressed. The Minister of Health, Malcolm Macdonald, reported 'a remarkable improvement in the morale of the people during the preceding thirty-six hours, largely owing to the heavy anti-aircraft fire' but it was not explained how this improvement had been measured or recorded. However, it had to some extent impeded the evacuation of the homeless. People who earlier had clamoured to be taken away were now reluctant to leave their homes. Nevertheless, the evacuation arrangements were said to be functioning reasonably well and large numbers from the East End had been moved into west London boroughs or into Essex. The Lord Privy Seal, Clement Attlee, told of a complaint that homeless people were to be billeted, although houses were empty and could be taken over for the purpose of accommodating them. The Minister of Health said that the sewage situation was unsatisfactory. A vital part of the sewage pumping machinery had been damaged and the main sewers broken in several places. As a result, sewage was draining into the river Lea instead of into the Thames. The Minister added that he was very dissatisfied with a report that the damage to the sewage system might take several months to repair. He was looking into the matter personally. Fortunately, he was able to report a few days later that the situation was better than reported and repairs would complete in a few weeks. The Silvertown district had been evacuated owing to the water supply being cut off. The supply had been restored, but it was not proposed to allow the people to return to their homes at present. This is not clear because the usual explanation is that Silvertown was evacuated on 7 September because it was surrounded by fires. In parts of London people were reluctant to use Anderson shelters and street shelters, preferring other underground accommodation such as church crypts, schools and public buildings. This was acknowledged by the Home Secretary to be the result of direct hits on a number of street shelters.

The Minister of Health said that this overcrowding might necessitate inoculation against diphtheria and scarlet fever but public opinion would have to be prepared before such measures could be put into effect. He had appointed a committee to report at an early date on these matters. The committee included Lord Horder (Chairman), Sir Wyndham Deedes, and representatives of the Ministry of Home Security and the Ministry of Health. The Lord President of the Council, Neville Chamberlain said that he had had two meetings with the ministers concerned, to review the steps taken to deal with the damage caused by air raids in the London area to public utility services, transport and food supplies, etc. He said that whilst considerable damage had been caused, in no case had more than two days' consumption of any food commodity been destroyed. Steps were being taken to disperse further stocks. However, the loss of flour mills, cold storage plant, margarine factories and oil and cake mills in the

London docks was more significant than loss of actual food stocks.

The possibility of increasing air raid shelter accommodation by use of the tubes was discussed and rejected. The Minister of Transport Sir John Reith still agreed with the conclusions of the committee which had examined the question before the war, namely, that it was more important to keep the tubes available for transport services. Sir John Anderson as Secretary of State for Home Affairs and Minister of Home Security said that the Commissioner of Police strongly deprecated the use of the tubes as shelters. The public had been educated to use shelters and there was broadly sufficient shelter accommodation available for the majority of the population. Advice urging the public to use shelters was continually being given, and new shelters were being built as soon as material was available. Materials for air raid shelters did not, however, enjoy a very high priority, and the supply presented some difficulty. The War Cabinet agreed that the public should be encouraged to take shelter during air raids, and that the shelters provided, while not affording immunity from a direct hit, offered the best protection available.

On the effect of bombing on the railway network, the Minister of Transport said that more than half the trouble was caused by unexploded bombs. He thought that vital points on railways should receive higher priority; that inspection should be made as soon as possible to determine what were unexploded time bombs; that additional units should be made available, and that a number of bomb disposal units should be specially allocated for use on the railways. The Secretary of State for War said that steps had been taken to increase the number of these units in the London area from twelve last Tuesday, to twenty-two. A further increase to twenty-eight was contemplated. The Secretary of State for War was instructed to determine, in consultation with the Minister of Home Security and the Minister of Transport, the best means of ensuring that a due proportion of the available bomb disposal units was made available for dealing with unexploded bombs on the railways.

During the meeting, the War Cabinet were informed that a dive-bombing attack had been carried out on Buckingham Palace. The War Cabinet invited the Prime Minister to send the following message on their behalf to His Majesty the King:

'The War Cabinet offer their hearty congratulations to their Majesties on their providential escape from the barbarous attack made on their home and Royal Persons.' They also agreed that, subject to His Majesty's consent, the fullest publicity should be given to this message. It was.[126]

The night raid on 13 September was relatively light, only 125 tons of bombs being dropped. A bomb in Adelaide Road, Hampstead killed twelve people. Several high explosive bombs fell at Clapham Junction station, causing extensive disruption to services whilst damaged arches were reconstructed. At West Dulwich station on the Chatham line, the Alleyn Park Road bridge was destroyed – its replacement needed 100 tons of steel. In Fulham, one of eleven bombs killed eleven people at a large surface shelter in Bucklers Alley, North End Road. At 21.40 the Fulham telephone exchange in Lillie Road received a direct hit by bombs which caused the death of three operators and put the exchange completely out of action.

14/15 September

The principal attack on London was made at 16.00 when bombs were dropped in Camberwell, Lambeth and in Battersea, where a gasholder was hit and slight damage was done to Battersea power station and Battersea Council's electrical generator. The Russell Street Bridge which carries the lines out of Victoria

---

126 TNA CAB 65/9

Station over those from Waterloo was hit by two bombs and extensive damage caused. Fortunately, repairs were completed within a few days. At 18.35 the Church of the Holy Redeemer in Upper Cheyne Row, Chelsea sustained a direct hit. Between eighty and 100 people were sheltering in the crypt when a high explosive bomb crashed through both the west window and the floor, before exploding in the crypt, killing nineteen people, including the air raid warden, Bert Thorpe. There were twenty-one deaths in Chelsea that day.

There were only a few incidents in London during the night – these occurred between 21.31 and 21.50 and between 01.16 and 03.29.

15/16 September

Celebrated as Battle of Britain day, 15 September saw much aerial activity over London. At 13.07 the UXB that threatened St Paul's Cathedral was removed. Buckingham Palace was bombed but both bombs failed to explode. A Luftwaffe Dornier aircraft crashed on a jeweller's shop at Victoria station, the pilot of the Hurricane fighter that shot it down bailing out in Hugh Street after his aircraft suffered damage. Another German plane crashed in Lambeth, the pilot being confronted by hostile local residents. More casualties resulted from the daylight raids on London: 'in Battersea at 12.10 railway bridges between Victoria and Clapham Junction were hit and bombs also fell on the West London extension line, and at 23.25 bombs fell on the Projectile Engineering Company's works in Battersea causing major damage. Damage was done to utility mains and roadways in this district. In Lambeth at 12.15, water and gas mains were damaged by bombs, and Norwood Road and Brixton Hill were blocked. An unexploded bomb at the Telephone Manufacturing Company caused production to be suspended.' At 15.00 the Penge railway tunnel was penetrated by a bomb and collapsed; repairs were to take over three weeks.

'At 20.29 a major fire was caused at the Brixton School of Building and other extensive fires as well as damage to gas and water mains resulted from bombing with high explosive and incendiaries. At East Croydon, the railway track was closed and damage has been done to the property in the vicinity by bombs which fell at 00.30. Shepherd's Bush. high explosive bombs have fallen on private property near the electric substation, which has been put out of action by the resulting blast. There is no current on the Hammersmith & City Line.'[127] Bombs fell at Kilburn High Road which was blocked as a result, and severe damage was done to the railway bridge, used by LPTB and LNER services, that crosses it. Repairs took a week to complete.

At 22.53 high explosive bombs fell outside Cadby Hall in Hammersmith (the headquarters of the caterers J Lyons & Co), damaging gas and water mains and completely blocking Hammersmith Road. At 02.20 further bombs fell at the junction of Uxbridge Road which was also blocked. Utility mains were damaged and a LCC sewer was fractured. Shell Mex House on the Strand suffered heavy damage at 00.47 by high explosive bombs. The central tower was demolished and the top storey was in danger of collapse. No photographs seem to have survived of this damage to an iconic building. The Strand was blocked from Adam Street to Aldwych. Bombs also fell near the Gaiety Theatre and serious flooding occurred as a result of burst water mains. Bombs fell at Vauxhall Bridge Road which was blocked by craters and debris. St. Thomas', Guy's and Lambeth Hospitals were all hit by bombs but initially no serious damage or casualties were reported.[128] However, Bright says it was Guy's Hospital's first incident of major damage and

---

127 TNA HO 202 Ministry of Home Security: Home Security War Room Reports
128 TNA HO 202 Ministry of Home Security: Home Security War Room Reports

a trapped doctor had to be rescued. Two fatalities are listed.[129] At St Thomas' a very heavy bomb made a direct hit on the main hospital corridor, causing the collapse of the medical outpatients' department, wrecking the kitchen, canteen, dispensary and administrative blocks, and putting all essential services at St. Thomas' out of action. There was a 20-pump fire and two doctors and a nurse were killed; three members of staff were critically injured, and thirty-eight other patients and staff also suffered injuries. Two rescue workers received George Medals for their work. Queen's Buildings in Scovell Road, Southwark, the shelter at Bermondsey Town Hall and the Neptune Street shelter in Rotherhithe were all the scene of serious incidents.

Two serious fires, two major fires and thirty-four medium fires were recorded. There were incidents in East Ham, West Ham, Dagenham and in Ilford where there were fourteen fatalities, mainly in Winding Way and Roman Road.

16/17 September

The War Cabinet met at 12.00 in the Cabinet War Room. On 14 September, the Lord President of the Council, Neville Chamberlain, had reported on air raid damage in the London area. He was able to bring the information in his report up to date following a further meeting that morning. The news seemed quite positive – no further substantial damage had been sustained to electricity, water and gas utilities. The statement in his report that it would take several months to repair the sewage pumping machinery was inaccurate. The pumps had been repaired, and it was hoped that the breached sewers could be repaired in two or three weeks.

No further major damage had been sustained in the docks and on the railways and there had been a very definite

---

129 Bright, *Southwark in the Blitz* (2016)

improvement in the marshalling yards and depots. In the three days ended 16 September nearly 60 per cent, of the normal war traffic had been carried. The Southern Railway was still the line most affected. Regarding food stocks, the amount of sugar lost now amounted to a week's supply. Some copra (used for margarine) had also been lost. The damage done to cold storage plants might make it necessary to build further plants. Effect was being given to the steps outlined in the report for the further dispersal of stocks of raw materials. The numbers in rest centres had dropped from about 17,000 to 10,000 or 11,000, and the centres were functioning much more satisfactorily. The delegation of powers to Regional Commissioners to authorise evacuation in cases of special emergency was being communicated to them that day.

The Prime Minister referred to a report in the Press about the 'invasion' at the Savoy Hotel. 'Episodes of this kind could easily lead to serious trouble' he said. 'The Home Secretary said that there were some signs of organised demonstrations, especially by persons who came from the East End into the West End, where they thought that better shelter could be found. He agreed with the Prime Minister that it would be necessary to take strong action to prevent demonstrations of this kind, which if allowed to grow, might easily lead to serious difficulties.'

The Lord Privy Seal, Clement Attlee, stressed the need for publicity for the measures which the Government was taking to deal with air raid damage and to assist homeless people. Unless these measures received proper publicity, it was apt to be assumed that nothing was being done. The Minister of Health, Malcolm MacDonald, said that he was arranging a press conference that afternoon for this purpose. The Prime Minister suggested to the Lord President of the Council that he might make a statement on this subject in Parliament on the Wednesday. The meeting 'recorded the view that strong action should, if necessary, be taken to prevent organised demonstrations by bodies of people purporting to seek better shelter accommodation.[130]

At this time, the *Daily Mirror* was still insisting 'there is still time ... to get on with further evacuation schemes and the provision of deep shelters, hitherto rejected with unparalleled obstinacy by Sir John Anderson.' It is unclear if the newspaper appreciated the time required to construct deep shelters, or even if it did, how long it envisaged the air raids on London would last.

The Ministry of Home Security reports tell how 'bombs were dropped in some districts of the capital, and attacks were made on several RAF stations, but on the whole very little damage and few casualties were caused during this period. As soon as darkness fell, the attack on London was renewed, and many heavy high explosive bombs were dropped in the West End and the City, starting serious fires, most of which however, came under control after a time. Minor bombing is reported from most districts in Greater London, and communications have been interrupted, but it would appear that no vital targets have been hit, and damage is comparatively light.'

At Thames Haven a serious fire was started at the oil wharf by high explosive and incendiary bombs at 21.04 and involved two oil tanks. In Hackney at 23.00 bombs fell at the Victoria Park LMS signal box, damaging the track and stopping all traffic. Bombs also fell on the railway bridge at Homerton causing heavy damage. High explosive bombs in Poplar caused damage to the East Ferry Crane and Engineering Company at 23.40. At 00.20, a direct hit was made on the Southern Railway arch at Guildford Street, Union Street Junction, Southwark. Another serious incident occurred at a shelter in Bermondsey; twenty-six people died at the Linsey Street arch.

130 TNA CAB 65/9

A major incident occurred at St. Pancras Hospital when the reception ward was demolished by high explosive. Although nobody was hurt, many patients had to be evacuated. At 20.45 a parachute mine fell in the Euston Road outside the St. Pancras Goods Yard causing damage to St. Pancras Town Hall, the *Euston Tavern*, the Euston Cinema and other buildings along the Euston Road, but few casualties. Ilford Limited making photographic products in the eponymous town, and now operating under the auspices of the Ministry of Aircraft Production, was hit at 21.50.

Many serious fires were reported during the night including at Ordell Street, Bow (30 pumps), Farringdon Street station and market (30 pumps), West Smithfield (80 pumps), Old Bond Street (30 pumps), Bermondsey (50 pumps), Great Portland Street (30 pumps), Clerkenwell (40 pumps), Eastcheap (30 pumps), Tower Hill (20 pumps) and Old Broad Street (20 pumps). Three firemen from Euston fire station were killed whilst firefighting in Great Portland Street.

A spectacular incident occurred in Twickenham when a 250kg bomb completely destroyed Radnor House, a large Italianate mansion overlooking the Thames.

17/18 September

This evening saw the first of three heavy night attacks. It lasted around nine hours and killed 256 people in London. 'Bombs fell in many districts in central and greater London causing damage to buildings and communications and some fires broke out; many of these have since come under control, an exception being the fire at Thames Haven, control of which is difficult owing to strong wind.'[131]

Fires were reported at Bermondsey (20 pumps), Old Kent Road (20 pumps), Stockwell Road (10 pumps), Poplar (40

131 TNA HO 202 Ministry of Home Security: Home Security War Room Reports

pumps), Millwall Dock (20 pumps), East India Dock Gate (30 pumps), Deptford (20 pumps), Lewisham (15 pumps) and Islington (20 pumps).[132]There was always a significant impact on Londoners when well-loved buildings were hit. The Blitz came to Oxford Street and the landmark John Lewis store was totally destroyed by fire, despite 30 pumps attending. Bourne & Hollingsworth, Peter Robinson, Selfridges and D. H. Evans were also damaged with 40 pumps attending at the latter store. The Greenwich telephone exchange received a direct hit which put it out of action until 3 October.

An incident that Sansom, Westminster's official historian, calls 'a grave disaster' occurred at Marble Arch. The bomb penetrated the subway – a pedestrian tunnel under Park Lane, the blast ripping tiles from the walls and turning them into lethal weapons. Mosley says it was 'one of the unluckiest tragedies of the Blitz. It was only a small bomb … but the nose cap … found a tiny hole between two girders and exploded. The force ripped along the corridor of the station with a fantastic impact'.[133] Sansom states there were forty casualties with over twenty dead. They are listed in the Civilian War Dead Roll of Honour under Westminster and St. Marylebone, with another dying a few days later in hospital. However, the fatalities come from locations all over London not just from these boroughs, and were undoubtedly sheltering. The reference to the station appears to be incorrect as the LPTB underground station was not affected.

Nick Cooper however seems to suggest there were also casualties at the station but the use of 'subway' may have been confusing, as this is a term used for underground stations in other countries.'[134]

---

132 TNA HO 202 Ministry of Home Security: Home Security War Room Reports
133 Mosley, *London Under Fire 1939-1945* (1972)
134 Cooper, *London Underground at War* (2014)

Several people were killed at the Halton Mansions shelter in Islington, and at the Camberwell Green shelter over twelve died. In the latter incident, a couple who had been married that day were killed, along with all the groom's family and other people. They had left the *Father Red Cap* pub, where the celebrations were held, to take shelter.

The first reports of parachute mines falling in the London area were received. Forty fell in London, half of them in south-east London. In one of the incidents, twenty-three died in Ladywell Park, Lewisham. An immediate problem was the failure of a number of these mines to explode; only the Navy had the required expertise to deal with them. Large-scale evacuation of residents had to take place in Lewisham and Deptford.

18/19 September

The Minister of Aircraft Production reported to the War Cabinet that during the previous night the Murex Magnesium factory at Rainham, Essex, had been set on fire and seriously damaged.

The Prime Minister announced that the enemy had dropped magnetic mines on this country on the previous night. The blast of the explosion from magnetic mines was very great and would destroy glass over a wide area. He had already given directions that the supply of glass should be investigated and the utmost economy practised in its use. He thought it should be the rule that, where glass was broken in large windows, only part of the windows should be replaced by glass, the rest being filled with some other material. It might also be necessary to direct that the glass should be taken out of some of the panes of large windows in particularly exposed localities and stored as a reserve. Churchill could never be criticised for lack of attention to detail!

The night's raid was the heaviest of the Blitz to date, lasting from 19.53 to 05.26. Fires were reported at Taylor's Depository, Pimlico (30 pumps), County Hall (30 pumps),

Hackney (20 pumps), Millwall (20 pumps) and Waltham Holy Cross (8 pumps). Major damage was reported at Edmonton, an unexploded bomb being suspected at De La Rue, Thomas & Co.'s factories, necessitating all production being stopped. Casualties were severe; in West Hampstead seven bombs fell destroying nineteen houses and killing nineteen people. In Willesden, there were twenty-three fatalities at Compton Road and Willesden Lane, and there were eighteen fatalities in Walthamstow. Six people were killed at the Vicarage shelter in Eltham and thirteen were killed in Mitcham. West Hackney Parish Church was demolished by a bomb; this church, St. James in Stoke Newington Road, was the work of Smirke, the architect of the British Museum Reading Room.

A bomb fell through the tunnel roof at Euston Square tube station at 01.20 killing two railway workers and although it is said flying glass injured passengers on a train, it would seem unlikely that passenger services were still running at this time. There were twenty-seven deaths in St. Marylebone, at Beaumont Street, Montagu Square and at Jackson's garage, Rathbone Place. The latter three-storey building was used as an AFS station and was completely demolished by a direct hit, killing eleven firemen and other people who were presumably sheltering there. Harry Errington, who rescued two of his colleagues who were trapped in the blazing building, was one of only three members of the fire services to receive the George Cross during the war:

'High explosive and incendiary bombs demolished a building. Errington and two other Auxiliary firemen were the only occupants of the basement of the building at the time of the explosion. The blast blew Errington across the basement, but although dazed and injured he made his way to the other two Auxiliaries, whom found to be pinned down, flat on their backs, by debris. A fierce fire broke out and the trapped men were in imminent danger of being burnt to death. The heat of the fire was so intense that Errington had to protect himself with a blanket. After working with his bare hands for some minutes he managed to release the injured men and dragged them from under the wreckage and away from the fire.

While he was so engaged, burning debris was falling into the basement and there was considerable danger of further collapse of the building. He carried one of the men up a narrow stone staircase partially choked with debris, into the courtyard, made his way through an adjoining building and thence into the street.

Despite the appalling conditions and although burned and injured, Errington returned and brought out the second man.

Both Errington's comrades were severely burned but survived. He showed great bravery and endurance in effecting the rescues, at risk of his own life.'[135]

Wallington alleges that unfair treatment was accorded to Errington after the incident. His injuries were slow to heal and as a result he was compulsorily discharged from the fire service in accordance with the provisions of the Civil Injuries Act.[136]

More parachute mines were dropped, again mainly falling in south-east London, and the tremendous damage caused by these mines was becoming apparent. It was reported that there were two unexploded bombs in the quadrangle of the War Office, a fire on the roof of the Foreign Office and a burst water main at the Scottish Office. At least twenty-four ARP stretcher bearers and ambulance staff were killed at the Cubitt Town School in Saunders Ness Road, Poplar. The school 'had been newly built in the 1930s and the spacious, airy building was, in many ways, ideal for a Civil Defence base. It had kitchens, offices, teaching rooms and open spaces for drilling and for storing vehicles. Civil Defence was largely the responsibility of

135 *London Gazette*, 8 August 1941
136 Wallington, *Firemen at War* (1981)

the local Council and after the children were evacuated in 1939 the School had become home to an Air Raid Warning Post, a Stretcher Party, and a Mobile Unit. The Ambulance and Fire Services also had units based there. The School often housed large numbers of personnel, either actually on duty or taking a break between shifts, recovering from action or waiting to be called out. Fireman A. F. Sharpe recalled in his memoirs that the Hall of the School had been specially strengthened with iron girders and that this was where they waited, fully rigged, for a call … As the raid began, the centre of the building took a direct hit. A fireman stationed in Millwall Fire Station recalled later that the explosion had literally flung a girder out of the building across the road into the warehouses opposite. Fireman Sharpe, who was on duty inside the School, recorded his memory of a dull thud and a bright flash, the crash of falling masonry and a desperate rush for the exits, then a roll-call and the missing girls, of trying to climb the staircase to the women's rest-room, but it was ready to come down at any moment and the centre of the school had been flattened. "Are you there?" he called. There was no response.

Eventually, the rescue workers penetrated the solid mass of rubble that had been the School. The remains of the dead were discovered and identified. On the 10th October 1940, they were buried together in a local authority grave … 14 members of the Stretcher Party died that night. All the members of the Mobile Unit died – a nurse, a doctor, two First Aid workers and a driver. Four of the eight ambulance drivers died. The one Warden on duty was killed.'[137]

A parachute mine landed on the Bermondsey Labour Institute in Fort Road at 22.40 and totally destroyed the Institute and surrounding buildings. Two of the rescue workers, John

---

137 The Island History Trust

Bradley and Ernest Playford, received the George Medal for bravery:

'A building (a wardens' post) was demolished by a bomb. The basement collapsed and a Post Warden was trapped in the debris. A Rescue Party led by Playford began digging and the trapped Warden was found ten feet beneath the debris. The work was rendered highly dangerous by the fact that a wall of an adjoining church hall was liable to collapse. Suddenly the wall started to fall. Bradley and Playford, who were in the excavation, made no move to leave the entombed man and Playford made a bridge with his body to protect the head of the Warden. The wall fell across the casualty and the two rescuers and they were buried under the mass of bricks and rubble. Rescue squads made frantic efforts to release them and Playford and Bradley were brought out severely injured. The Warden also was eventually rescued alive.'[138]

It appears that four other wardens at the post were killed.

19/20 September

The King and Queen visited Chelsea where they were shown where Dr Castillo's daughter was rescued, and the church of the Holy Redeemer, the site of the incident on 14 September.

After some daytime enemy activity, an evening raid took place beginning about 21.00. Trench shelters at Downhills Park Road, Tottenham were hit and out of sixty casualties, at least forty people died in this horrific incident. Forty-five people died in Tottenham that night, including some residents of Walpole Road which is near the trench shelters but was struck by another bomb. The ARP log books state that the public trench shelters, located just inside the entrance to Lordship Park from Downhills Park Road, were completely demolished. A contemporary local

---

138 *London Gazette*, 3 October 1941

newspaper report states 230 people usually sheltered there. Other sources say 300 or 400, and survivors said the shelters were very crowded.[139]

Police Inspector Ernest Newark was awarded the BEM for leadership and gallantry. The official citation in the London Gazette reads as follows:

'A bomb was dropped near some shelters. With a police rescue party under his command, Inspector Newark quickly restored a situation fraught with grave danger. He organized the work of stretcher parties and, with his men, worked for nearly three hours during a heavy raid. It was largely due to the Inspector's leadership and organizing ability that one hundred persons trapped in the shelters were rescued.'

This is another Blitz tragedy which did not receive commemoration until well after the war, when in September 2010 a 70th anniversary ceremony was held in Lordship Park.

Elsewhere there was further disruption to cross-London rail traffic due to bomb damage – in fact most cross-London lines were not working and considerable railway freight congestion was building up in the London area. Twelve people died in Tadworth Road, Cricklewood. Eight members of the Stacey family died in Starfield Road, Hammersmith. In Chingford, considerable damage was done to residential property and incendiaries fell on Chase Lane school which was being used as a rest centre, and on British Latex Products (the London Rubber Company), where the company's new factory extension was burnt out[140]. This was probably the only occasion during the Blitz on which significant damage to a war industry occurred in this borough.

Clapham Tram Depot was seriously damaged, and as a

---

139 This incident has been extensively documented in recent years – see
https.//tottenham-summerhillroad.com/downhillsheltertragedy.htm
140 Warburton, *Chingford at War* (1946)

result of bombing at 02.19 on 20 September, the thoroughfare from Parliament Square to Whitehall Place was blocked.

Shortly after midnight, a Junkers 88 bomber crashed on houses in Richmond Avenue, Merton, killing three of the crew. A fourth member managed to bail out. There were no civilian casualties as the occupants of the houses had taken shelter[141].

20/21 September

At 12.10 a high explosive bomb exploded in Heston, killing six men of the Bomb Disposal Section, Royal Engineers. Whilst working on an unexploded bomb on the Great Western Road, Corporal George Mundy phoned his barracks to get some advice but his superiors were not available – both were out on another job at the time. It seems that Corporal Mundy then went to a garage, borrowed a rope and crow bar and went back to the bomb. The events after this are unknown except for the fact that the bomb detonated, killing Corporal Mundy and five sappers.[142].

In the evening, activity was on a very much smaller scale than on the previous night. However, much railway damage occurred, including an incident where a bomb hit railway arches in Southwark necessitating the assistance of the Royal Engineers in making major structural repairs. Fire damage was extensive in Bermondsey and Southwark. Several industrial premises were affected in Bermondsey, and St. John's Horsleydown church was gutted. W T Henley's Telegraph Works in North Woolwich was seriously damaged at 03.50 by high explosive bombs and Stepney power station was put out of action.

Gillian Tanner was awarded the George Medal while stationed as an auxiliary fire officer at Dockhead Station,

141 Ogley, *Surrey at War* (1995)
142 The Royal Engineers Association Bomb Disposal Branch website
    https.//www.royalengineersbombdisposal-eod.org.uk/

Bermondsey: 'Six serious fires were in progress and for three hours Auxiliary Tanner drove a 30-cwt. lorry loaded with 150 gallons of petrol in cans from fire to fire, replenishing petrol supplies, despite intense bombing at the time. She showed remarkable coolness and courage throughout.'[143]

Newbery states seventeen people were killed and fourteen were injured outside Kings Cross Station by an AA shell which struck the pavement outside a café at 21.42.[144] However Brooksbank states two dead and twenty-seven injured, and the Civilian War Dead Roll of Honour also only lists two fatalities, one at Jack's Café and another at the 'snack bar'. However, there may have been military casualties as a result of this incident.

Twenty-six were killed in Tottenham, in incidents in Clonmell Road and Walpole Road. Twenty died in Richmond when at 02.40 two parachute mines fell at Peldon Avenue and Courtlands. At the latter location, a mine demolished a block of flats – Runnymede House – but although the website of the estate claims there were no casualties, it seems at least nine people died there. Most of Peldon Avenue was demolished by the other mine. The local paper observed that 'the area resembled part of Ypres in the last war.'[145]

21/22 September

Lt Cdr Richard Ryan RN and CPO Reginald Ellingworth from HMS Vernon, the Royal Navy Mine Warfare Establishment, died while attempting to defuse a parachute mine in Dagenham. They were both posthumously awarded the George Cross for gallantry and devotion to duty.

The Grand Union Canal was bombed at 10.30 and the explosion cracked the wall of Limehouse Cut and also damaged

---

143 *London Gazette* 31 January 1941
144 Newbery, *Wartime St Pancras. a London borough defends itself* (2006)
145 Fowler, *Richmond at War* (2015)

part of a warehouse. Navigation was closed from the Thames to Britannia Bridge. Major damage was reported at Allen & Hanbury's, the manufacturers of pharmaceuticals and medical equipment at Bethnal Green, and production was halted. Poplar was bombed at 00.16 and an 80-pump fire was reported in progress at Howard's Timber Yard. A serious fire occurred at 00.40 at the South Metropolitan Gas Co in Lambeth and more than fifty casualties were reported. In West Ham, fires were caused at 01.25 at J Rank's flour mills and also at the Corporation Electricity Supply. Bombs were dropped at 02.07 on Shoreditch and one railway arch was completely demolished and a direct hit on the track attained. Forty yards of bank by the Kingsland Road Bridge was reported to have fallen into the canal.[146] Six people were killed at the wardens' post at St Mary's church, Peckham. Yet another Bermondsey shelter was hit, in Llewellyn Street.

A parachute mine fell in gardens between Carlton Road and Stanley Avenue in Romford and caused what was said to be the biggest crater of the war in Essex, the parachute of the mine probably having failed to deploy. Over 100 houses were damaged but there were no fatalities.

Ten people were killed at Church Path, Acton, where a sea of devastation is shown in contemporary photographs.

22/23 September

At 17.16 Hendon ARP were requested to send six ambulances to Mill Hill barracks, but the military authorities refused to give reasons for this request. However, Lieutenant John Hunter of the Royal Engineers is known to have died at the barracks that day. It seems that Lt Hunter, engaged on bomb disposal duties, had brought a fuse back to the barracks for investigation. The

---

146 TNA HO 202 Ministry of Home Security: Home Security War Room Reports

fuse detonated, killing Hunter and injuring several members of his team, two seriously.

In Woolwich, a fire in the Royal Arsenal timber field was the result of the previous night's bombing, but by 03.28 on the 23rd this had increased to two major conflagrations involving the Arsenal. However, it was later reported that the fires were in hand at 04.32 hours, but damage was not known. In Lambeth at 23.30 bombs damaged the Southern Railway generating station by the Canterbury Theatre, Westminster Bridge Road. A parachute mine exploding at 21.40 in Ilford was reported to have demolished 100 houses and damaged 100 (This may be the previous night's incident; the Civilian War Dead Roll of Honour only indicates eight fatalities in a number of localities). Poplar and Lambeth reported direct hits on two air raid shelters and it was reported that between thirty and fifty people were killed in addition to numerous others injured. The Civilian War Dead Roll of Honour confirms that twenty-five died at the Orsett House shelter in Lambeth and sixteen at what was presumably a shelter at 419 Old Ford Road, Poplar. The situation report refers to the Poplar shelter as 'Kidd's' and this could have been John Kidd & Co Ltd – a memorial plaque exists at 419 Wick Lane, a general war memorial for this firm's employees.

In an incident at Dolphin Square, Pimlico, a bomb exploded in a basement shelter underneath Hawkins House. Seven were killed and fifty-eight rescued, many of them badly injured. The situation report states refugees were killed, but the victims appear to be local residents, who had been evacuated there because of an unexploded bomb nearby.

J Rank at Victoria Dock, West Ham, reported that their flour mills, hit the previous evening, would be out of commission 'for the duration', and 1,800 employees would be affected. A fire at Briggs Body Works in Dagenham was still raging at 06.00 and was not yet reported to be under control. In the early hours of

23 September an incendiary bomb fell on the East Wing of the British Museum. The resulting fire was put out by the museum's firefighters, but not before it damaged an important part of the King's Library Gallery and destroyed 400 of the books collected by King George III.

23/24 September

The War Cabinet recorded their concern that work both in government departments and in factories was ceasing on receipt of a red warning and that there was a need to avoid dislocation of production. The solution seemed to lie with the provision of roof spotters. However, daylight raids soon died out and the problem ceased.

At night, London experienced another heavy attack, with 261 aircraft delivering 300 tons of high explosive and a significant incendiary load. There were four major, eleven serious and 106 medium fires. At 21.07 the Stevenage Wharf in Wandsworth was hit and petrol was leaking into the river from the tanks of the National Benzole Co. During a later attack, bombs were dropped on Wandsworth Common station, resulting in a complete blockage of the London to Brighton line. In Walthamstow, a fire completely gutted the ARP transport store and garage at Low Hall Farm, but all the vehicles were saved. At 23.25 Clarnico's Factory in Poplar was set on fire and approximately 100 people were believed trapped in a shelter under the factory. Eleven people were killed at the Southill Street shelter in Poplar. In West Ham at 00.07, serious fires were caused at the LNER running shed at Stratford, at various factories (including Dextrine Ltd.) and at Upton Lane School. At 03.00 a direct hit was registered on Mile End Road underground station. Nearly thirty people died at Risinghill Street, Finsbury, and thirty died at 742 Romford Road, East Ham; the latter was probably a shelter incident as the home addresses of victims vary. The Mills Equipment Co in

Fountayne Road, Tottenham was partially destroyed by fire, but only one fatality occurred. Before this attack on Mills Equipment Co it was reported that 'Nos 3 and 4 Factories cannot continue production. However, nos 1 and 2 factories hope to recommence production in a few days.'[147]

At 00.30 a high explosive bomb fell at the junction of Regents Park Road and the North Circular Road at Finchley, blocking roads. The North Circular Road then had to be closed because of flooding. Incendiaries destroyed the Muller factory in Acton. A parachute mine fell in the Stanley Road area of South Woodford, killing seventeen people – the highest number of deaths recorded in any single incident in the borough of Wanstead and Woodford.[148] The next two nights' raids were also heavy.

24 September

The Royal Warrant laying down the conditions of the award of the George Cross was published following the announcement in a broadcast to the nation by the King:

'The men and women in the factories or on the railways who work on regardless of danger, though the sirens have sounded, maintaining all the services and necessities of our common life and keeping the fighting line well supplied with weapons, earn their place among the heroes of this war. No less honour is due to all those who night after night uncomplainingly endure discomfort, hardship, and peril in their homes. Many and glorious are the deeds of gallantry done during these perilous but famous days. In order that they should be worthily and promptly recognized I have decided to create at once a new mark of honour for men and women in all walks of civilian

---

147 TNA HO 202 Ministry of Home Security: Home Security War Room Reports
148 Wanstead Meteo.com 31 July 2015

life. I propose to give my name to this new distinction, which will consist of the George Cross, which will rank next to Queen Victoria Cross, and the George Medal for wider distribution'.

Despite the heroic actions of civil defence personnel under enemy air attacks, they were not eligible for the highest British award, the Victoria Cross which had to be awarded for deeds 'in the face of the enemy'. This new award for gallantry was to be received by many civil defence workers and forces personnel working on bomb disposal. The warrant also made provision for living holders of the Empire Gallantry Medal to have their medal replaced by the George Cross. Churchill himself set great store by the medal as a morale raiser for civilians although the majority of awards for the George Cross and the George Medal (for lesser acts of heroism) were to go to members of the armed forces.[149] Churchill did express disappointment with this. The British Empire Medal and OBE were also awarded to civilians in recognition of their work in Civil Defence. Thomas Hopper Alderson (1903-1965) was the first person to be directly awarded the George Cross after its creation. He was an ARP warden in Bridlington, Yorkshire. The Order of the British Empire was used to reward acts of gallantry not at the level required for a George Medal. The award reflected the rank, grade or level of responsibility of the recipient.[150]

Owen describes how on the day the George Cross was announced, 16 and 17 BD Sections had been to a funeral for half a dozen sappers from 60 Section, and the mood in the pub that morning was sombre. They had been killed whilst digging for a UXB near the railway in Dalston.[151] It was deemed to have been 'a premature bomb explosion' but there were no witnesses,

149 Smyth, *The Story of the George Cross* (1968)
150 https.//www.nickmetcalfe.co.uk/
151 Owen, *Danger UXB. The Heroic Story* (2010)

nor survivors. This was one of several such incidents where what actually happened will never be known.

24/25 September

The first raiders headed for London about 19.30 and bombing activity continued with some lulls almost until daybreak. The raid was more extensive than had been the case in recent weeks. Over 200 people died and many fires – over 700 – were started in central London. The West End was badly affected, the East End only lightly. There were four major, ten serious and eighty-one medium fires, as well as a conflagration in Holborn. At 21.00 incendiaries fell on the offices of the Sunbeam-Talbot Motor Works, Kensington, which were damaged by fire. It was recorded that production was not likely to be affected. It was also reported that Warwick Road was blocked and Earls Court station closed. Damage was caused to the new West Central police station in Savile Row (only opened in July 1940) by bombs and a mine falling nearby. At least two policemen were killed and many injuries were caused by glass partitions in the station being shattered.[152] St George's Hall, built in 1865 and located next to the Queen's Hall was home to BBC Variety performances from 1933 and had a famous theatre organ. It was set alight by incendiaries; the whole auditorium was burnt to the ground and the organ was destroyed.[153] Two high explosive bombs fell on St Anne's Soho at around 23.38 and the seventeenth century church suffered severe fire and structural damage.[154] The Queen's Theatre in Shaftesbury Avenue was the first London theatre to be bombed. It was extensively damaged and as a result closed.

Hungerford Bridge and signal box were on fire, together with the church of St. Margaret's, Westminster. Bombs dropped

---

152 Westminster City Archives www.westendatwar.org.uk
153 Westminster City Archives www.westendatwar.org.uk
154 Westminster City Archives www.westendatwar.org.uk

on the Southern Railway track at Broughton Street, Battersea and the line from Battersea to Clapham Junction was blocked. Major damage was reported at platform 10 at Waterloo Station, involving approximately thirty casualties. Incendiaries were reported to have fallen on the west wings of the North Middlesex and St. David's hospitals in Edmonton. At 21.15 bombs slightly damaged Plessey's at Ilford. Major damage occurred at 02.17 in the City of London at Blackfriars station, *The Times* offices, Queen Victoria Street, and Upper Thames Street.[155]

Further bombings were reported at Hammersmith (seventeen fatalities), Islington (twenty-one fatalities), Kensington (twenty-two fatalities), Hendon, Tottenham, Wimbledon, Hornsey, Wandsworth, Richmond, Barnes and Ealing. Very heavy casualties occurred in Hackney on the Pembury Estate at Adisham House, and in Downs Park Road; in both incidents, shelters were hit. Fifty-four died in these and other incidents in Hackney, but few details are recorded as to the circumstances. The other incidents occurred in Bethune Road and Glyn Road. In Wood Green nine people died in Hornsey Park Road and at Barratt's confectionery factory.

Thirty-one people died at the Stanfield House shelter in Frampton Street, St. Marylebone. A parachute mine demolished the *Blue Posts* pub in Tottenham Court Road, also blasting the Central YMCA, and causing many casualties. About twelve people died in Tottenham Court Road in addition to six at the YMCA. The British Empire Medal was awarded to John Wilkins, leader and Jack Weeks, labourer, from the Holborn ARP Rescue Party:

'Owing to enemy action buildings collapsed and caught fire. People were trapped in a ground floor room and Wilkins,

---

155 TNA HO 202 Ministry of Home Security: Home Security War Room Reports

followed by Weeks, reached it through a service hatch. Two brick columns leant over towards a wall and between these was a large heap of debris. Hindered by the fire raging on the other side of the wall and drenched by fireman's hoses, Wilkins and Weeks removed the debris. Because of the removal of this support to the leaning columns, the whole of the wreckage was liable to collapse on to them. They were finally successful in extricating a woman, who was passed to safety through the service hatch.'[156]

A report by the Officer in Charge of the Rescue Services, Holborn, adds further details: 'At about 21.30 hours on the 24th September 1940, a mine fell in Tottenham Court Road outside the Central Y.M.C.A. premises. Wilkins was the leader of the first rescue party to arrive and he proceeded to help in searching for casualties on the upper floors and in their removal to the basement. On the completion of this work he and his men came out of the building. Wilkins was then informed by a Warden that there were trapped casualties in the rear premises at the side of the Blue Posts Public House on the opposite side of Tottenham Court Road at the corner of Hanway Street. On this side of the road many buildings had collapsed and fierce fires were raging. Wilkins was taken into a ground floor room and shown the adjoining room where the casualties were. He gained access to the latter room through a service hatch the small size of which would only permit one of his men, Weeks, to follow.'

Extensive fires in Holborn resulted in the destruction of the Chancery Lane Safe Deposit building and although the vaults were untouched, there was damage to the valuable books and manuscripts held in the building. 100 pumps were needed at Southampton Buildings near Chancery Lane. A bomb caused damage at St Pancras hospital and elsewhere in the borough of

---

156 *London Gazette* 27 June 1941

St. Pancras, fires caused serious damage at London University library, Maple's department store and Oetzmann furnishers in Hampstead Road.

Ten people died at Chaucer Avenue, Cranford in the borough of Heston and Isleworth, Middlesex, and incidents in Kentish Town resulted in eight deaths. The AEC factory at Southall, producing armoured cars rather than buses as in peacetime, was struck by a bomb and as a result of the serious damage caused, a large part of the building was put out of action for six months. Fortunately, all the workers on the night shift were in the factory's shelters.

25/26 September

The evening raid again commenced soon after 19.30 and continued through the night. North and west London experienced the most activity: 'Railway property in and around London seemed to be one of the enemy's main objectives, damage and traffic interference being caused as follows: at 22.40 hours a crater was made on the GWR line near Ruislip Gardens station. High explosive bombs were dropped on the GWR and LMS (West London Joint) Railway at Addison Road, Kensington at 05.00, lines being completely blocked by debris. The railway bridge over Thames Road, Chiswick, was hit by bombs at 00.55'.[157]

Major fires were started at Wandsworth, Edmonton, Tottenham, Old Kent Road and Hammersmith. In the course of these fires damage was caused to the British Oxygen Company's plant at Edmonton, and the GWR sheds at Hammersmith. At 22.45 approximately 300 incendiary bombs were dropped on RAF Hendon which caused only slight damage. An oil bomb was also dropped and rebounded off a hangar and exploded but

---

157 TNA HO 202 Ministry of Home Security: Home Security War Room Reports

did not ignite. At Highgate, a parachute mine hit the ARP depot in North Hill at 21.32, causing two deaths and seven serious casualties.

Suburban Greenford was devastated by two incidents. in one the *Load of Hay* pub received a direct hit and was demolished, the licensee and his family being killed. The other caused extensive casualties (twenty-one killed) and damage on the Medway estate. The King and Queen visited. Another suburb to receive royal visitors was Hampstead Garden Suburb where the tranquillity had been shattered by a number of bombs which wrought substantial destruction in Willifield Green and Coleridge Walk, and killed ten people at the latter location. There were further deaths in Golders Green, Mill Hill, Sudbury and Kingsbury.

Colindale station on the LPTB Northern line was hit by a high explosive bomb at 20.45, and then by a second at 22.45 the same night which killed staff and passengers, and injured others. The station's surface buildings were reduced to rubble. The Civilian War Dead Roll of Honour records eight fatalities at the scene.[158] Fortunately as Colindale was and is an 'overground' station, it would not have been used as a shelter. Three high explosive bombs hit Hendon Isolation Hospital. Five children died and several members of staff were injured in one of two wards badly damaged in the attack. Over twenty incidents and seven fatalities were recorded in Hornsey.

A number of incidents in the borough of Hammersmith caused fifty fatalities, twenty-one people being killed at the *Sun Inn*, Askew Road, which was hit just before closing time. The pub was one of the oldest in the borough and was totally demolished. Fulham was also subject to heavy bombing (fifty-two high explosive bombs fell, killing thirty people, mainly in Reporton

---

158 Cooper, *London Underground at War* (2014)

Road), and fourteen people were killed near Kew Gardens, at Beechwood Avenue and West Park Road. A parachute mine killed a number of people in Brookwood and Willow Avenues in Barnes. Ten people died in incidents at Clarence Road and Lamb Lane, Hackney. In Southwark seven people died at Danson Road and two at the *Bricklayers Arms* pub in the Old Kent Road. Casualties in St. Marylebone included eleven killed at Bryanston Mews and Bryanston Square.

26/27 September

Enemy aircraft did not approach London until 20.30 when the 'Red' warning was received. The all clear sounded at 03.55, but the warning was renewed about an hour later. The damage in the London area was not so severe as on the previous night. In St. Pancras, there were major incidents at Parliament Hill Mansions, Belmont Street, Harrison Street and Ferdinand Street. At 23.15 about five bombs were dropped on RAF Northolt but little damage was done and no aircraft were damaged or destroyed. In the Westminster district, one bomb fell outside the Houses of Parliament, blasting windows and the statue of Richard Coeur de Lion, and another in front of the steps leading from King Charles Street to St. James' Park.

At the *Queen's Arms* in Kilburn, ten people died after the pub received a direct hit. For the second night running the borough of Barnes was heavily hit. Sixteen people were killed at a public shelter in Trinity Church Road – two of those killed were shelter marshals. In Islington, there were thirty-two deaths mainly at Mitford Road and Sussex Way.

A 500kg bomb, having demolished two houses in Carlton Hill, St. John's Wood, penetrated the tunnel carrying the main railway line into Marylebone station. The station had to be closed and although repairs were due to be completed within a week, a further bomb was to fall a few days later. In Wood

Green, part of the railway track between Park Avenue and Palace Gates stations was damaged. Castlehaven Road railway bridge in Camden Town was badly damaged and there was also a large fire on the Southern Railway Crystal Palace line.[159] Five people died at a public shelter in London Road, Norbury.

27/28 September

There were three daytime raids in which enemy aircraft attempted to reach central London. In a lunchtime raid a bomb struck the shelter at the headquarters of Freemans, the largest catalogue business in the UK, at 139 Clapham Road, Lambeth. Nineteen female employees were killed.

After three nights when the attack had targeted western and central areas of London, a much wider area suffered bombing. In the evening, it appears that damage was of a less serious nature than on previous nights although communications were again affected and several fires started. A fire was started at the Thames Ammunition Works in Erith but the damage was negligible. Holland House, an architecturally important and impressive seventeenth century mansion in Kensington, was largely destroyed by fire, after incendiary bombs fell. There were nearly 200 fatalities in London, although these almost entirely occurred in residential areas. Incidents with fatal casualties occurred in South Ealing Road, in Faraday Road, Acton, Coventry Road in Ilford, and in Wandsworth. More serious was the situation in St. Pancras where thirty died, mainly in Kentish Town, where twenty-one high explosive bombs fell. In Lambeth, there were further incidents and fatalities following the lunchtime events.

Four people died at 23.45 after a parachute mine incident at The Fortune, a house in Fortune Lane, Elstree.[160]

---

159 TNA HO 202 Ministry of Home Security: Home Security War Room Reports
160 Bard, *Elstree & Borehamwood Through Time* (2011)

28/29 September

Enemy aircraft activity during the day was on a much-reduced scale, but a small number penetrated to London and bombs were dropped in Poplar, Deptford and Woolwich shortly after 10.00.

The night raid was the first of four quite heavy raids although the incendiary content was much lower after the first night. Major damage was reported at Ottway's Orion Works in Ealing, caused by incendiaries at 00.08. 200 incendiaries and twenty high explosive bombs were dropped opposite the Vickers works at Weybridge, blocking the road, but there was no damage to the factory. At 23.40 bombs at the Acton works of Messrs S & G Brown Ltd, caused severe damage to the offices and the destruction of part of the factory roof.[161] Five people died at the Skylux shelter in Telford Way, Acton. Fifteen were killed in Willesden where there were incidents in Hamilton Road and at St Matthew's Hall. The latter received a direct hit from a bomb and seven people sheltering in the boiler house were trapped and drowned because of a broken water main. At the AFS station in Denmark Hill, Camberwell, thirteen firemen were killed when the shelter was hit. Two parachute mines fell in Croydon; one in the Park Hill recreational ground shattered windows over a wide area of the town. The other landed next to the Town Hall but did not explode until two days later; fortunately, the bomb disposal experts working on it were able to get clear in time. Damage was extensive locally although the Town Hall mainly suffered damage to its windows.

Several hospitals were hit including West Middlesex, Heston, Staines Emergency, St Bernard's (Uxbridge) and Barnes Isolation. The Friern Mental Hospital in Friern Barnet was a very large hospital with over 2,000 patients although part of it had

---

161 TNA HO 202 Ministry of Home Security: Home Security War Room Reports

been designated an emergency hospital, dealing with casualties from air raids from all over London. Confusion surrounds what happened here. Sources state five villas were destroyed and thirty-six patients and four nurses were killed, but these figures may refer to a total of casualties and include those that occurred in a further incident on 16 November. Ramsey states twenty-four were killed on 28 September, but the Civilian War Dead Roll of Honour for Friern Barnet lists fifteen, all women with a number of foreign nationals and one nurse. The local ARP log books only mention four fatalities, and local historians Reboul and Heathfield do not mention any incidents at the hospital at all.

29/30 September

After nightfall, much industrial damage occurred in north-west London. Willesden power station at Stonebridge Park was hit and put out of action for three days. Twelve died in Villiers Road, Willesden, where one victim was impaled on the railings outside the Working Men's Club opposite.[162] At Bowden (Engineers) Limited and G Beaton & Sons Limited of Acton, production was affected by failure of the electricity supply. Also in Acton, a fire occurred at Renault's factory. At LEP Transport, Chiswick, the roof of the bonded warehouse and a lathe were damaged and at the Celotex Factory in Beresford Avenue, Wembley, a fire caused by an incendiary bomb destroyed 500 tons of wood pulp.

Railway damage included a high explosive bomb on the locomotive shed at Nine Elms, Crystal Palace main level line blocked and at Woolwich Dockyard and Station, unexploded bombs on the embankment and at Well Hall Station, as a result of which most services were suspended. The LPTB Central line service was suspended between North Acton and Ealing Broadway, and Ealing Common Station was out

---

162 Whitehead, *Brent's War* (1995)

of use because of an escape of gas due to bomb damage. The LPTB Metropolitan Line was closed between Kings Cross and Moorgate and suspended between Latimer Road and Addison Road. Fenchurch Street and Marylebone were also affected. Incendiary bombs dropped at 20.05 set fire to railway rolling stock at Willesden.

Nine ARP staff were killed at their post in the basement of a chapel in Great Guildford Street, Southwark. The building was demolished by a direct hit and there was only one survivor. Generally, although there was some fire damage and interruption to railway services, casualties were low in London.

30 September/1 October

Thirty-four people died in a daytime attack in the borough of Ealing. At 13.50 six Luftwaffe aircraft attempted to attack RAF Northolt but their bombs – over 100 were dropped – fell short of the target, in residential areas of Greenford, before the alert was sounded and before people could take cover. German planes were also alleged to have machine-gunned the area. Ben Wicks includes the memories of three-year-old Brenda Duer whose mother is fatally injured in Greenford when they are returning from shopping.[163] Upton includes two further personal accounts of this raid including the equally tragic experience of Ray Lawlor, who also lost his mother and was seriously hurt himself. Greenford Baptist church was among the buildings destroyed.[164]

After dusk, raids once again built up over London, the north and north-east suburbs being most affected. At 20.45 a fire was started at CAV Ltd, Acton but was brought under control and did not affect production. An unexploded bomb was reported at the AEC Works, Southall.

---

163 Wicks, *Waiting for the All Clear* (1990)
164 Upton, *Ealing, Acton & Southall at War* (2009)

At midnight, three parachute mines fell in Chingford, the borough experiencing one of its worst nights of the Blitz. Eighteen people died, twenty-two were seriously injured and over fifty were slightly injured. More than sixty houses were destroyed, and thousands of houses were damaged. AFS fireman John Llewellyn Davies was awarded the George Medal for his efforts at the incident in Royston Avenue, and ARP Warden Benjamin Stanley Musgrave was awarded the British Empire Medal:

'During a heavy air raid, several houses were destroyed. The debris caught fire and blazed fiercely. Fireman Davies' house was severely damaged and he was badly shaken. Immediately he had recovered he went to a wrecked house in which two persons and a child were trapped under a bed. Having located the casualties, he burrowed into the debris with his bare hands. He succeeded in reaching the bed and, finding the baby, he passed it out to the Wardens. He then tried to release the other victims. This he could not do unaided and Warden Musgrave volunteered to help him. Davies then levered up the debris with his body whilst Musgrave crawled under the bed and allowed himself to be pulled out with the woman on his back. Still taking the weight of the debris, Davies, after fifteen minutes, succeeded in releasing the remaining trapped person, who was then drawn to safety. Davies was in a state of collapse and had to receive first aid treatment but, when it was reported that another child was trapped, he again crawled under the wreckage and continued working for the rest of the night. His heroic action saved many lives.'[165]

Mrs Churchill visited the borough on 4 October in connection with these incidents, as the Prime Minister was the MP for Epping, the constituency which included Chingford.

---

165 *London Gazette* 28 March 1941

'Jock' Colville, Churchill's private secretary, accompanied Mrs Churchill and in his memoirs, describes meeting homeless refugees in a school.[166] Presumably these were not the refugees from the East End referred to by the headmistress of South Chingford School – they had moved on by then – but homeless local residents who would have been accommodated at Chase Lane School, the dedicated rest centre for South Chingford. However, there may still have been refugees from the East End at other locations in Chingford.

In Ponders End, Enfield, a bomb hit the *Two Brewers* pub in South Street penetrating to the basement shelter where men attending a Buffaloes meeting had taken refuge. Recent reports say twenty men died although the Civilian War Dead Roll of Honour only lists five with a further person dying in hospital the next day.

The Metropolitan Water Board reported that 42-inch and 48-inch diameter mains from Kempton Park to Cricklewood were broken at about 20.30 and that supplies in north and north-west London would be seriously affected and the supplies to west London would be affected to a lesser extent. The damage log books state that at 20.31 serious flooding – no doubt the result of the above – affected Tokyngton Avenue in Wembley and four people were drowned in an Anderson shelter at No.164. However, the Ministry of Home Security Daily Intelligence Reports suggest a reservoir may have burst at Stonebridge Park power station.

---

166 Colville, *The Fringes of Power* (1985)

FIVE

OCTOBER 1940

By the end of September 1940, it became clear that the Luftwaffe had settled down to a war of attrition in which all the boroughs and districts of the London Civil Defence region were suffering bombing incidents. In these incidents, most of the buildings affected had no strategic significance whatsoever. Neither was there any concentration of bombing, and the perceived risk to individual Londoners was small. But over all this the threat of invasion remained; the bombing was intended as part of a softening up process.

Many of the raids in the last few weeks of September were on a relatively small scale, but they maintained their effect on a tired population, particularly, in many of the raids, with an increased use of incendiary bombs. Perhaps only a dozen or so boroughs were seriously affected each night but by the latter part of the month the pressure had been taken off the East End and the riverside boroughs. October brought worsening weather and the Luftwaffe's raids were initially less heavy, although the nightly ordeal continued without respite. From the second week of October however, the raids once again became more intense. German sources say 7,160 tons of HE and 4,735 IB canisters were dropped on London that month.

Front Line regards 7 September and the following four weeks of attack as an attempt to deliver a 'knockout blow' on London, but this does not appear to have been the case. By 5 October, however, the perception was that the Luftwaffe had accepted that the RAF retained mastery of the air and further daylight mass bombing attacks were not going to be feasible. After this daylight raids on London were on a small scale. The US journalist Quentin Reynolds narrated a film tribute 'London can take it'. Americans admired British resilience under aerial attack, memories of the effects of the 'War of the Worlds' radio broadcast[167] no doubt being fresh in their minds.

1/2 October

It was perhaps a little unfortunate that the *Evening Standard* announced that Regional Commissioner Admiral Evans was to a be 'shelter dictator for London' albeit with commendable powers 'to marshal all the available shelter resources, to create new ones, and to see that every Londoner has a safe and reasonably comfortable refuge when the bombers come.' Evans was very popular amongst civil defence workers in London.

This evening's raid was mainly focussed on north and north-west London. Six died at trench shelters in The Fairway, Acton, and sixteen at the Hanger Hill Park trenches in Ealing. At 01.59 in the morning of 2 October, three high explosive bombs fell on Hanger Hill Park, one of which made a direct hit upon the shelter there, killing sixteen people. Strangely, the history of

---

167 A memorable dramatization of HG Wells' science fiction novel in a 1938 radio programme in the USA allegedly caused public panic among listeners who did not know the Martian invasion was fictional.

the Hanger Hill Garden Estate does not mention this incident although it does mention the building of the shelters. At 23.45 a bomb penetrated the roof of the railway tunnel north of Marylebone station, exploding inside and blocking all lines, leaving a massive reconstruction challenge. The station could not be re-opened until 25 November, and trains had to terminate at Neasden, where temporary platforms were constructed by the Royal Engineers so that passengers could transfer to LPTB services.[168] In Hampstead, a parachute mine fell on North End village, and the *Hare and Hounds* pub was destroyed along with other old buildings but no fatalities were caused. But in Fordwych Road, West Hampstead, six houses were demolished with ten fatalities. Ten people were killed in Lena Gardens, Hammersmith and there were also fatalities elsewhere in London; Lambeth, Lewisham and Paddington had the worst casualties. Seventeen incidents in Hornsey caused thirty-three casualties including eight fatalities. A bomb scored a direct hit on Barclay's brewery in Southwark causing serious damage. The Holborn Restaurant, a popular banqueting venue, was badly damaged by high explosive. Over 100 Londoners are listed in the Civilian War Dead Roll of Honour on 2 October; most of them died on the night of 1/2 October with the exception of around eighteen who died in the daylight raids the following day and early evening.

At 20.38 the fire service was called to Lymington Mansions, West Hampstead and in their dry formal way reported 'A building of 4 floors & basement about 100x60ft (used as residential flats). Top floor & contents severely damaged by fire & most part of roof off. Rest of building & contents slightly by fire, heat, smoke & water.'[169] On the top floor was the home

---

168 Brooksbank, *London Main Line War Damage* (2007)
169 LFS records in the London Metropolitan Archive

of Gwladys Cox, who later wrote 'My neat and orderly home was a scene of indescribable desolation. The dining room was completely burnt out, neither of our windows remained ... what remained of the furniture was covered with a shining layer of molten lead from the burning roof. The carpet was inches deep in a wet mixture of ceiling plaster and burnt rafters.'[170] To add to the Coxes' distress, looters had also been at work. Like thousands of Londoners, they had lost most of their possessions and were homeless.

2 October

At a meeting of the War Cabinet, the Prime Minister referred to a statement by the editor of *The New Statesman and Nation*, which had been brought to his notice, giving an account of conditions in 'the large shelter at Stepney', undoubtedly the Tilbury shelter. In parts of this building, which had not been thought suitable for a shelter, and had not therefore been recognised as such, and suitably equipped, indescribable conditions had prevailed. The Prime Minister urged the need for strong action to prevent large numbers of people crowding into this building until the necessary work had been done to make it safe. From all he learnt of the position, drastic action was called for, and the Air Raid Precautions Officer (Controller) in Stepney should be immediately superseded. The Home Secretary said that steps were being taken to deal with the Stepney shelter, and Admiral Evans, Regional Commissioner, had been given the fullest powers to deal with this matter, including supersession of this particular Air Raid Precautions Officer. As a result of this the officer concerned was indeed superseded rather than sacked, presumably reverting to his peacetime role.[171] Woolven relates

---

170 IWM Private papers of Mrs G Cox
171 TNA CAB 65/9

a slightly different sequence of events and does not mention conditions at the Tilbury shelter as a trigger.

2/3 October
Daylight attacks affected south London, and fifteen people were killed and thirty-one sustained serious injuries. This was followed by the quietest night since early September. A 30-pump fire at St. Quintin Park & Wormwood Scrubs station in Hammersmith was the only major incident; this station on the West London line was hit by an oil bomb and burnt out. There was also some other railway damage and disruption in north and north-west London.

3/4 October
Some strategic targets linked to the aircraft industry came under attack. The De Havilland factory at Edgware was bombed at approximately 11.30 and a large assembly shed and the technical school received direct hits and were set on fire, and a sheet metal shop was destroyed.[172] The Desoutter factory in The Hyde was also hit. However, the most serious attack was on the De Havilland factory at Hatfield where twenty-one people were killed by a direct hit when a low flying Junkers 88 aircraft dropped four bombs. A further seventy were injured. An anti-aircraft gun on the administration building roof damaged the Junkers sufficiently to force it to crash land at Hertingfordbury, the crew being taken prisoner. Amongst the wreckage of the factory was eighty percent of work in progress on the Mosquito aircraft, and as a result all Mosquito work was widely dispersed to avoid further disruption due to enemy attack.

---

172 TNA HO 202 Ministry of Home Security: Home Security War Room Reports

Not so strategic was the First Aid Post at Ruckholt Road, Leyton where four members of the staff were killed. The Territorial Army HQ at nearby Whipps Cross was also hit with twelve casualties. But overall, as the situation report says, enemy activity was on a very restricted scale.

4/5 October
London was under alert for about five hours during the day, and widespread bombing by small numbers of aircraft continued through the night. About sixty people were killed and 200 injured but damage was mainly confined to residential areas. A direct hit on the Victorian North Bastion of the Tower of London killed a warder but exposed much older fortifications. A bomb falling in The Vale, Golders Green, severed a 42-inch water main and caused extensive flooding. The Park Royal Coach Works were severely damaged, and seven people died in Stanhope Street, Camden Town.

5/6 October
Of four daytime attacks, two reached London and killed twenty people; more were killed during the following night's activity which continued until dawn. Twenty-five were killed in Dagenham – in an incident at Halbutt Street, ten members of the Mann family died. Six died at a shelter on Wanstead Flats in East Ham.

Willesden Power Station received a direct hit which caused its closure for the second time in a week. The initial reports indicated that the damage was extensive, but eventually it turned out to be not as great as feared.

6 October
At 13.15 an attack was made on RAF Northolt, killing three airmen. Bombs also fell in Hayes and Hillingdon, and in

Montague Road, Uxbridge where eleven people died. A bomb hit the nurses' quarters at Friern hospital, but there were no casualties.

Although there had been activity with damage and casualties during the day, on the night of 6 October very few bombs (*Front Line* claims only one) fell on London, but for Londoners this was enough to support their later claim to have experienced fifty-seven nights of continuous bombing. However, Cheshunt residents were complaining that the barrage was starting up before the sirens were sounded!

7/8 October

An unexploded bomb in Dagenham was being moved when it exploded, killing five men of a bomb disposal squad.

During the night raid, sixty-five were killed in a heavy raid on London, and there were also three serious fires. 145 Piccadilly, the former home of the King and Queen when they were Duke and Duchess of York, was hit and demolished, although fortunately it was unoccupied at the time. At 19.45 Shaftesbury Avenue (Soho) fire station was hit and five people killed, of whom two were fire service personnel. The building was badly damaged, in fact virtually demolished. A number of incidents occurred across south London and fourteen people died at Prospect Vale, Woolwich. Sutton emergency hospital was extensively damaged and one wing demolished. A nurse and at least sixteen others died but it is not possible to say if all the deaths were a result of the bombing of the hospital. Severe damage occurred to the Catholic church of St Benedict Ealing Abbey at 21.25 when a bomb fell between the Priory Church and the gym, wrecking the organ chamber and damaging the War Memorial Chapel. Another bomb which fell through the roof of the church exploded at 06.00 the following morning. It demolished the east end of the Priory Church, turning the sanctuary and the choir into a single crater filled with debris[173]. A bomb caused heavy damage to the offices at the LPTB's Neasden depot.

8/9 October

A daylight raid at 08.48 hit rush-hour London. One source believes the raid was probably carried out at least in part by Messerschmitt 109E fighters carrying 250kg bombs. Charing Cross station was hit by oil bombs and high explosive which damaged the track, signalling, roof and girders. A train was blasted and at least four people killed and the Hungerford footbridge over the Thames was damaged. The station had to be closed whilst steel girders were replaced and was not fully operational again until January. At 08.50 a high explosive bomb penetrated the roof of Charing Cross (now Embankment) underground station, and exploded on the District line track, although fortunately there was no damage to the river wall or an adjacent water main. The ticket hall was wrecked, killing one person and injuring nineteen more, and the station had to be closed.[174] This was called 'the Whitehall Raid' because bombs were also dropped in the area of government offices, which suffered in consequence. The Paymaster General's office received a direct hit, and the Ministry of Agriculture and Great Scotland Yard were also damaged. Somerset House's south wing was extensively damaged and the Nelson rotunda staircase was largely destroyed. A stick of four bombs hit the War Office, causing only superficial damage but killing one person. Otherwise, despite a further seven hits during the Blitz, this building remained relatively unscathed, the damage mainly confined to its upper levels.[175]

---

173 http.//www.ealingabbey.org.uk/04history4.htm
174 Cooper, *London Underground at War* (2014)
175 The former War Office building is located on Horse Guards Avenue at its junction with Whitehall. In 1964 the War Office was absorbed into the MOD. The building was sold off for development in 2016.

Later the attackers targeted Holborn and a stick of three bombs fell; one killed five people at Endell Street and Shelton Street and another killed at least thirty-two people in High Holborn – Trench states the fatalities were on a bus that was blasted, and the Civilian War Dead Roll of Honour entries indicate that the victims came from a variety of locations[176]. This was one of those disastrous Blitz incidents that have seldom been written about. It seems that the bomb hit Manzoni's Restaurant at 12 High Holborn and demolished the building. A passing bus was blasted and came to a halt just a few yards eastwards. All but four of the victims (the restaurant owner and family, plus another man who lived or was present at 12 High Holborn) came from addresses around London and were certainly killed on the bus or on the street. Ten of the deaths are recorded in St Pancras or the City of London and are those who were taken to the Royal Free Hospital and died later. The location of the incident is variously given for fatalities as Holborn, High Holborn, 329 High Holborn (the premises opposite), High Holborn by Chancery Lane, High Holborn between Gray's Inn Road and Chancery Lane or Gray's Inn Road. The remaining bomb fell in St. Giles' churchyard.

At 09.19 there was damage at the Bricklayers Arms goods station where four staff were killed. The AFS station in Churchdown School, Catford was hit at 12.50 with one killed and twenty-five injured. Altogether sixty-three died in London.

The evening raid was rather more serious than those of previous weeks with 138 killed, and numerous fires started. A conflagration at LEP Transport Ltd in Chiswick and a major fire at Hay's Wharf, Tooley Street, Southwark were the worst fires. Both required fifty pumps. There were five serious fires and forty-eight medium fires, and gasholders were set on

---

176 Trench, *London Before the Blitz* (1989)

fire at Battersea and St. Pancras. St. Clement Danes church was damaged by blast, and a high explosive bomb fell in the courtyard of the Royal Courts of Justice. Finsbury Park station was hit at 20.40 and seven people in a waiting train were killed. Victoria station had to be closed as a gas main was on fire on the Grosvenor Road bridge. Eight people died at the recreation ground in Lillie Road, Fulham; presumably this was a shelter incident. The Church of the Sacred Heart in Camberwell was destroyed.

At 21.23 St. Matthew's Hospital in Shepherdess Walk, Shoreditch was seriously damaged when a quarter of the ward accommodation was destroyed by a high explosive bomb. Initially it was recorded that ninety casualties were trapped. One account claims fifty male patients, thirty-three female patients and three nurses were killed. The Civilian War Dead Roll of Honour is not clear as to whether the fatalities were a result of the bombing of the hospital or whether they were brought to the hospital from other incidents. A number of fatalities are recorded at St. Leonard's Hospital, and possibly the people concerned may have been taken there from St. Matthew's. Nevertheless, it was one of the worst incidents of bomb damage and casualties involving a hospital during the Blitz. The thirty-three fatal casualties are listed as occurring on 9 October in the Civilian War Dead Roll of Honour. However, on 10 October there are a further nine people listed whose deaths might be due to the same incident, and on 11 October a further ten. Unfortunately, few details are given merely 'died at St. Matthew's Hospital' or 'died at St. Leonard's Hospital'. Clearly the hospitals were under great pressure – St. Matthew's was evacuated and closed a couple of days after the incident.

9/10 October

A daylight raid in the afternoon caused seventy-seven fatalities in London. The Royal Courts of Justice were hit and about twenty died at a shelter in Fetter Lane in the City of London. Vere Hodgson mentions a bomb falling in Fetter Lane after the all-clear was sounded.[177] People were also killed at a shelter in Anerley Road, Penge, the worst incident to happen in Penge during the Blitz. Serious damage to a main sewer at St. Johns Wood meant that untreated raw sewage had to be discharged into the Grand Union Canal for several months. 190 people were killed during the evening raid, and there were two serious fires. There were heavy casualties at Lymington Avenue in Wood Green, Shakspeare Walk in Stoke Newington, and other locations. Ten died in Finsbury at the Leysian Mission and at the *Weavers Arms*, Lever Street. At 22.25 a bomb hit Victoria station damaging platforms 15-17 and rolling stock, and another bomb on the station damaged the forecourt and the Grosvenor Hotel. At 20.05 a bomb fell on Spriggs Oak House, a home for expectant mothers in Palmers Hill, Epping, killing eight women and injuring fourteen. The women had been evacuated to the house from the East End of London. Towards the end of the raid at 06.00, St. Paul's Cathedral received a direct hit by a bomb which exploded in the roof above the high altar which was as a result severely damaged by falling masonry.

10/11 October

Bomb disposal continued to be a hazardous occupation, and even experienced men could be caught out. A 250kg bomb had been recovered with a badly damaged fuse. and it was decided by the bomb disposal team that it was no longer capable of functioning. It was loaded onto a truck and taken to the Duke of York's barracks in Chelsea, where the men stopped to eat their evening meal. Lieutenant Lionel Carter saw the bomb with the fuse in position and decided it should have been taken directly

---

177 Hodgson, *Few Eggs and No Oranges* (2010)

to the bomb cemetery, which had been established in Regents Park. The driver of the vehicle asked permission to have the rest of the evening off and Lieutenant Carter agreed to this as he was prepared to drive the vehicle himself. A number of other men volunteered to come along, not only to help move the bomb, but also so they could be dropped off at a pub on the way back. As they were driving up the Marylebone Road, near Madame Tussauds, the bomb exploded without warning and all six men died in the blast.[178]

At 20.40, services between Wembley Park and Stanmore were suspended again (they had been suspended that morning because of the discovery of an UXB), this time because of a derailed and damaged Metropolitan line train near Forty Lane bridge.[179]

Many casualties occurred across the London area at widely scattered locations. Over 150 people were killed and one major and four serious fires were recorded.

11/12 October

Night raids commenced at 18.35, but by 22.45 they were slackening off and gradually diminished in number and by 02.20, the country was clear of enemy aircraft. Operations were probably curtailed on account of fog.[180] First reports of the new explosive incendiary bombs were received. These were a great hazard for firefighters as the explosive charge would detonate after five minutes, when they were likely to be tackling the bomb with sand.

Overall although this was a relatively light raid and bombs were widely scattered, there were 108 fatalities in London. Most

178 The Royal Engineers Association Bomb Disposal Branch website
179 Cooper, *London Underground at War* (2014)
180 TNA HO 202 Ministry of Home Security: Home Security War Room Reports

activity was over east London where many of the casualties occurred in Leyton. At 19.53 at least fourteen people were killed there, the entries in the Civilian War Dead Roll of Honour giving the place of death as the junction of Markhouse Road and Lea Bridge Road, and several of the casualties were from outside Leyton. A trolleybus driver and conductor were among the fatal casualties. According to an account on the Walthamstow Memories website, a bus received a direct hit outside the *Royal Standard* pub. In addition, a 24-inch water main was severed. The Home Security Report states thirty deaths. This incident was one of several in Leyton, another bomb hitting the trolleybus depot.[181]

At 22.00 a bomb caused all railway lines to be blocked outside Waterloo Station. At Hammersmith, severe damage was caused to water and gas mains by bombs at 21.25 and Shepherds Bush Road and Uxbridge Road were blocked. A 30-pump fire was caused by incendiary bombs at the Convent of the Sacred Heart, Roehampton Lane. The school had been evacuated and was relocated to a new site in 1945. A lesser fire occurred at Queen Mary's Hospital, Roehampton. Westminster had a long casualty list but many other locations were affected, including Wandsworth where the tram depot was damaged by bombs. Even Merton and Morden, and Mitcham, had casualties.

12/13 October

The Luftwaffe made attacks on London intermittently between 19.20 and 23.00. In Trafalgar Square, a bomb fell at 20.45 near King Charles' statue and penetrated to the hall at the bottom of the escalator at Trafalgar Square underground station, where it exploded, killing seven people and injuring another thirty. The War Office received a direct hit. Several incidents affected rail services in west London, but it seems that whilst an incident

---

181 Image on LT Museum site

at Wembley Central station (an express train collided with a luggage trolley which had been allowed to roll onto the tracks) was not the result of enemy action, the LMS had to suspend all its freight traffic to London.

In Islington, seventeen people were killed in Isledon Road, a bomb falling on rescue personnel working on an earlier incident. Brooke House in Clapton was severely damaged by a high explosive bomb. This building, originally an Elizabethan manor house, dated back in parts to the sixteenth century and was of great architectural interest.

13/14 October 1940

A long raid which lasted nearly eleven hours. The biggest shelter incident of the London Blitz occurred at the Coronation Avenue flats in Stoke Newington Road, when at 21.00 a heavy bomb caused part of the building to collapse into the basement shelters. More people (154) died here than in any other single incident in the London Blitz of 1940-41. The flats were part of a complex of five-storey apartment blocks built by the Four Per Cent Industrial Dwellings Society in 1907. It seems most of the deaths were due to drowning, the victims being trapped under layers of compacted debris as mains water flooded the basement. Cranes and other lifting gear had to be brought in and it took over a week to recover all the bodies. John Cochrane Easthope of Stoke Newington Council's Engineers department was awarded the George Medal:

'Mr. Easthope was on duty in the Control Room and, hearing that a large number of persons were trapped in a Public Shelter, he volunteered to go to the scene of the incident. He arrived and entered the middle compartment of the shelter through a window at the rear. In spite of the danger of a further collapse of the debris and of the fact that the water was then about 4 ft. deep in the shelter, Mr. Easthope worked his way over and under the debris into this compartment in an endeavour to rescue anybody who might be there, but primarily to carry out a reconnaissance to direct the squads who were working above. He found debris blocking the centre compartment up to a distance of 15 ft. from the point of entry. Several persons were pinned under the wreckage. Mr. Easthope then came out and entered again – through the emergency exit into the north compartment and crawled along the top tiers of the bunks in an effort to discover whether any persons were still in that compartment. The water was several feet high and appeared to be rising. Mr. Easthope emerged from the shelter again and reported on the conditions inside. He then, re-entered the shelter and confirmed the position of the debris. Regardless of the danger of being crushed to death at any instant, or of being trapped and drowned. Easthope made four separate visits to the shelter through the hole he had made, fully aware of the risk he was running while searching for trapped people.'[182]

A mass burial of eighty-six victims took place at the Abney Park cemetery and twenty-four Jewish victims were interred at a ceremony by the Jewish Burial Society. The remaining victims received private burials. The King and Queen visited the site, accompanied by the Senior Regional Commissioner for the London Civil Defence Region, Ernest Gowers and Admiral Sir Edward Evans, the Regional Commissioner.[183]

There were a number of other bombing incidents in Stoke Newington that night – seventeen are recorded – but fatalities only occurred at Nevill Road. Hackney received over thirty high explosive bombs and suffered several serious incidents, with twenty-six fatalities. Among these were six people killed in an Anderson shelter in Richmond Road.

---

182 *London Gazette* 7 February 1941
183 Hyde in Ramsey, ed., *The Blitz Then and Now Vol.2* (1988)

Several incidents at tube stations occurred on this night. The first was at Bounds Green station on the Piccadilly line. At 20.55 a bomb fell on two houses in Bounds Green Road directly above the southbound platform, demolishing them and damaging the tunnel some thirty feet below. The northern end of the southbound tunnel collapsed with 200 tons of debris filling the tunnel, trapping dozens of people sheltering on the platform. Fortunately, the escalators continued to run and the station lighting was not affected, which assisted the rescue parties. Doctor Malcolm Manson, the medical officer of health for Wood Green was a leading figure in the rescue efforts and persisted with his rescue efforts although seriously injured by a fall of debris. He was awarded the George Medal.

'A heavy H.E. bomb fell, causing a tunnel to collapse. A number of people were trapped under the debris and the clay which had fallen through the cavity. Dr Manson arrived on the scene within a few minutes of the occurrence, and immediately assumed the direction and leadership of the rescue work. For nearly three hours he worked without intermission actively participating in the release of persons trapped in the debris heap, giving medical aid where it was needed and all the time keeping effective control. Throughout this period he was in grave personal danger from frequent falls of clay. It seemed likely that a further portion of the tunnel would collapse. At one period he was lying full length on the heap endeavouring to release a man partially buried when there was a shout from the lookout man of "Run for it!" The Doctor ignored the warning and continued his efforts for the trapped man. There was a large fall of clay and the Doctor was struck by a large piece full in the back. He was partially buried and had to be dragged out feet foremost. He rested for a few minutes, and then, in spite of severe pain, carried on with the work. Dr Manson's pertinacity, courage and disregard of personal safety set a wonderful example to the men and was no doubt responsible for the saving of a number of lives which otherwise would have been lost. He sustained serious injuries during the rescue operations.'[184]

Some controversy exists about the nationality of the nineteen fatal casualties, several sources – beginning with Charles Graves in 1947[185] – saying they were mainly Belgian refugees. However, it seems according to the Civilian War Dead Roll of Honour that only three were Belgian and the rest British nationals. A simple explanation could be that one account may have mistakenly transposed the nationalities. The memorial plaque in the station dating from 1994 is also incorrect – it states '16 Belgian refugees and three British citizens.' Repairs to the station were not completed until 12 December and traffic resumed four days later.

Another station incident was at the LPTB Metropolitan line station at Praed Street, Paddington,[186] which was hit by several bombs at 23.33. Many people were trapped and eight died.

At Holloway Road Piccadilly line station, the tunnels were severely damaged by a bomb which fell just south of the station at 21.30. This prevented a through service running until 5 December, but no fatalities are recorded.[187] Pictures in the LT Museum collection clearly show the tunnel blocked by debris and the subsequent repair work.

The convent in Lawn Road, Hampstead, was destroyed and five nuns were killed. At least twenty-eight people died at 294 Clapham Road in Lambeth; it seems this was the address of the *Prince of Wales* pub, which was partially destroyed. The borough

---

184 *London Gazette* 7 February 1941
185 Graves, *London Transport at War* (1947)
186 Now Paddington Metropolitan line station
187 R07 *The Piccadilly Line – An Illustrated History* (Desmond F. Croome, 1998, Capital Transport Publishing, ISBN 1-85414-192-9) quoted in Cooper, *London Underground at War* (2014)

of Lambeth was becoming one of London's worse-bombed. It already had experienced shelter incidents at the Brockwell Park shelter on 15 September, the Bowater's shelter on 20 September and at the Orsett House shelter on 22 September.

14/15 October

'The moon is full ... so God help us.'[188]

The newspapers announced that 5,000 members of the Pioneer Corps had been deployed in London to begin work in clearing debris, pulling down dangerous buildings and salvaging materials. The Royal Engineers were also on hand to restore communications and repair roads. By the next morning, they had even more work to do.

'A full-scale attack on the capital was launched after dark, and bombs were falling in most districts including the West End until an early hour on October 15th ... most of the damage, however, was of a minor character'. This seems to support the assertion by Hill & Alexander that the Ministry of Home Security played down the severity of this raid, a strategy that did not go down too well with Londoners.[189]

It was in fact a heavy raid with 240 killed and one major and twenty-four serious fires. Incidents occurred in many of the inner London boroughs. Shortly after the sirens sounded, fires broke out all over the inner London area. In St. Marylebone, the London Fire Brigade reported numerous fires due to incendiaries; but in this neighbourhood between Oxford Street and the Marylebone Road most did not develop into serious fires. Later Chelsea, Fulham and West Brompton were similarly affected. However, larger outbreaks occurred at the Western Hospital, Mawer's furniture depositary and

---

188 Hodgson, *Few Eggs and No Oranges* (2010)
189 Hill & Alexander, *The Blitz on Britain* (2010)

West Brompton station which suffered severe fire damage. Kensington Court and the Milestone Hotel also sustained severe damage. In Goswell Road, Finsbury, there was a 30-pump fire at Cater Patterson carriers and a 20-pump fire at JC King stationers. In Great Marlborough Street, there was a 10-pump fire at a carpet manufacturer's and in Berners Street two 10-pump fires. Numerous fires across the West End and Soho engulfed many garment manufacturers and there was also a 20-pump fire at Rathbone Place. The ordinary citizens as well as the aristocracy suffered as homes, mansions, businesses and clubs alike were hit. The *Harp* pub in Carnaby Street, the home of the Duke of Devonshire in Carlton Gardens and J Lyons in Shaftesbury Avenue were targets. The Reform Club and the RAC in Pall Mall were alight. A direct hit on the Carlton Club in Pall Mall (which was affiliated to the Conservative party) wrecked the building. At 19.48 a bomb penetrated the roof and exploded in the library. 220 people were in the club at the time and probably half the British War Cabinet, including the future Conservative Prime Minister Harold Macmillan were dining in the Club on the floor below. Although badly shaken, they all escaped injury. But two fatalities were recorded outside, including a soldier killed by a lamp post blown along Pall Mall.[190] Catesby's garage in Maple Place, Bonham Auction Galleries and Tooth & Sons Art Dealers in New Bond Street were all severely damaged by fire. Ridgmount Street had a 20-pump fire. George Medals were awarded to two wardens who carried out a precarious rescue in a bombed building in Lowndes Street. After midnight, the City and Camden Town were affected. Stationers' Hall in the City was destroyed and Tower Pier was hit killing two people.

---

190 Westminster City Archives www.westendatwar.org.uk . This has several personal accounts of the Carlton Club bombing.

Some rather more valuable targets were hit including the LMS Depot in Kentish Town Road and Primrose Street near Broad Street Station where two people were killed and railway infrastructure destroyed blocking all the lines into Broad Street station, which was as a result out of action for four weeks. More deaths occurred locally and extensive damage was done in Bunhill Street and Worship Street, and three AFS men were killed. A police section house in Shepherdess Walk was destroyed in addition to other damage in Hoxton. The gas works at Nine Elms was hit and a gas holder destroyed. The factory of Negretti and Zambra in Barnsbury, making scientific and optical instruments, was gutted by fire caused by an oil bomb. Rollasons Aircraft Instruments Ltd in Mitcham was severely damaged by bombs at 21.55 causing production to be suspended. Radio Transmission Equipment Ltd, Wandsworth was set on fire by incendiary bombs. One section of the Siebe Gorman factory in Old Kent Road was destroyed by fire, and a fire also occurred at Austin's (Metal Refiners) factory at Hackney.

Bombs fell at the Croydon gasworks at 21.15 causing one large and two small fires and demolishing one gas holder. The hit on a gasholder caused 'an enormous uprush of white light, like a gigantic mushroom with a huge black cap, which threw the whole district to the farthest horizons into dazzling illumination.'[191] The adjacent electricity works was undamaged. An electricity distributing station, in Popes Lane, Ealing, was hit by high explosive bombs at 21.00, and part of the switchgear and some transformers were damaged, causing a temporary failure in the electric supply to the Ealing area. The LMS sustained much damage: at 20.15 the very large and ornate Highbury and Islington station was set on fire and badly damaged; at 01.39, a bomb fell at Lismore Circus, penetrating through the crown of

---

191 Berwick Sayers, *Croydon in the Second World War* (1949)

a tunnel and exploding on the LMS line from St. Pancras, which was blocked until 19 October.

One of the worst disasters of the London Blitz occurred at Balham tube station, when at 20.02, a 1,400kg semi armour-piercing bomb penetrated 32ft underground and exploded just above the cross passage between the two platforms. Balham High Road outside the station was cratered. Debris, sand and gravel cascaded onto the platforms, washed down by a torrent of water from broken water mains and sewage pipes. The station lights failed, plunging the platforms into darkness, there was a strong smell of gas, and panic ensued. LPTB staff were to able open the emergency exits and led most of the 600 people sheltering to safety. Nevertheless, sixty-seven died. The Northern line remained out of action until 19 January 1941, unsurprisingly as seven million gallons of water, sewage and silt had to be removed from the line between Clapham Common and Tooting Broadway. Above ground, a bus crashed into the crater providing one of the classic pictures of the Blitz.

Camden Town tube station was hit at 20.57, much damage being done to the surface buildings on the west side, but fortunately not to the platforms which were used for sheltering. Nevertheless, five people were killed, but trains continued to run. Other fatalities occurred locally in Oakley Square. The Holborn Empire, one of London's grand old music halls, was destroyed. Fortunately, the theatre was empty having been evacuated the previous evening because of an unexploded bomb. *The Times* building in Printing House Square off Fleet Street was damaged. Much damage was done around the Monument although the obelisk itself escaped serious harm.

Fires and high explosive caused much damage in the Piccadilly area. A 20-pump fire severely damaged St. James's church in Piccadilly. The church was hit by high explosive and incendiary bombs at 19.54; the blast severely weakened the brick and Portland stone fabric. the north wall was fractured and pieces of shrapnel lacerated the building's east end. The next morning it was a burnt-out ruin, open to the elements. The Middle Temple Hall, 'probably the finest example of an Elizabethan Hall in London' was seriously damaged by a parachute mine which destroyed Elm Court, blowing the masonry through the east gable end of the Hall, smashing the minstrels' gallery and reducing the Elizabethan screen to rubble.

At 19.50, a high explosive bomb fell on the Dean's Yard facade of Church House, Westminster, the new headquarters of the Church of England. The building had been officially opened only in June. The bomb smashed through the fifth and fourth floors and exploded on the third floor. Church House contains at its centre a circular Assembly Hall and the explosion blasted a gap thirty yards wide in its walls. Thanks to its sturdy construction – Church House had been built on a steel frame – there was little other damage, and the three hundred people who were sheltering in the basement were unhurt. However, six people were killed by falling masonry inside Church House.[192] Church House was the emergency chamber or 'annexe' as it was known, designated for the House of Commons.

55 Broadway, headquarters of the London Passenger Transport Board, was another modern, steel-framed building. It received a direct hit from a high explosive bomb which penetrated the roof of the west wing on the 9th floor, passing through successive floors down to the 5th floor, where it struck a steel girder and exploded. A fire broke out and a sizeable section of the upper west wing was gutted. No casualties were reported among London Transport staff but the building's Portland stone facade and sections of its interior were badly damaged. One floor level collapsed downwards and debris fell into Broadway.

---

192 http.//www.winchestercollegeatwar.com/archive/hichens-william-lionel/

Bombs in Whitehall hit the Treasury, causing massive damage. Damage was also done to no.10 Downing Street, where the kitchen, pantry and offices were shattered by blast. Fortunately, the Prime Minister was dining in the basement and was unhurt, and he had ordered his staff to the shelter. This prompted a review of the Prime Minister's security in terms of sheltering arrangements. John Colville, Churchill's Private Secretary, was staying overnight at no.10 and had not long fallen asleep before the crash of a falling bomb woke him. He found the air thick with smoke and the choking smell of sulphur and gunpowder. The Treasury was hidden in a dense cloud of smoke and there was a huge crater outside the Home Office. When the smoke cleared, Colville saw that a large part of the Treasury had been destroyed.[193] Three Treasury staff who were on Home Guard duty were killed.

A 250kg bomb hit the BBC's Broadcasting House – many accounts say whilst Bruce Belfrage was reading the 9 o'clock news bulletin, but it seems the bomb fell soon after 20.00 but did not explode until the news was being read. The bomb destroyed the BBC switchboard before penetrating to the Music Library on the fifth floor. Some sources say that BBC staff tried to move the bomb by hand, but it exploded during the attempt. The bomb was a delayed action type and it is quite probable that it exploded without intervention. There were eleven casualties including seven killed.

Part of the fifth and sixth floor façade of Broadcasting House were blown out into Portland Place and debris littered the roadway. A small fire also broke out but was quickly brought under control by the BBC's own fire teams. Covered by dust in his basement studio, Belfrage, displaying admirable sang-froid, paused briefly then finished reading the news bulletin. The

---

193 Colville, *The Fringes of Power* (1985)

building continued to be in operation, although the telephone service was interrupted. Authorisation had just been received to paint Broadcasting House's original white Portland Stone facade with camouflage paint![194] Too late, unfortunately.

Five died in Green Lanes, Stoke Newington, and there were further fatalities in Hackney. Further out in the suburbs the housing estate belonging to the John Groom's Crippleage charity in Upcroft Avenue, Edgware was hit by high explosive and four women were killed. Damage in the East End and south of the Thames was not so extensive.

15/16 October 1940

'From nightfall onwards, London was subjected to a very heavy attack, which appeared to be directed mainly on railway communications and on the City and dockyard area, where several factories suffered damage by fire. Major damage reports have been received from many districts of the Capital, and many other fires were started; it is notable that the enemy has resumed the use of the parachute mine, which has caused considerable devastation and casualties'[195].

Unlike the previous night official comment seemed to be realistic. The night's raid turned out to be much heavier than those in previous weeks, with a full moon again assisting the attackers. The raid lasted from 20.40 to 04.40, and central and north London were the areas most affected. 430 people were killed in this raid and there was a huge amount of damage to water, gas and electricity supplies and to five major railway stations.

In West Ham, there were fires at Silvertown Lubricants (40-pump), Pinchin Johnson Ltd (25-pump) and Venesta Ltd. W T

194 Westminster City Archives www.westendatwar.org.uk
195 TNA HO 202 Ministry of Home Security: Home Security War Room Reports

Henley's was hit again. At 20.00 bombs fell adjacent to the South Metropolitan Gas Works at Greenwich, damaging a gas holder. The gas ignited but the fire was out by 21.00. Waterloo Station was attacked twice during the day at 09.16 and at 20.10. Serious track damage resulted from the first attack, and in the second, platforms 3 and 4 were hit, and a train was wrecked. At Hendon, the LMS lines were damaged at 23.30 by high explosive bombs and at 01.30 bombs fell in the GWR Goods Depot at South Lambeth, causing a large fire.

The Metropolitan line at Whitechapel High Street was penetrated by high explosive bombs at 20.05. At Victoria Dock, L warehouse was gutted by fire, and bombs fell inside no.2 Shed and on a garage; no.10 Shed, Surrey Commercial Docks was damaged by bombs at 20.35. A 40-pump fire was in progress at Ranelagh Road, Westminster. The Theatre Royal in Drury Lane received a direct hit and was badly damaged. At 23.45 bombs wrecked the Salvation Army Congress Hall in Linscott Road, Clapton, along with many houses in the road and Lower Clapton Road.

In the City of London, a parachute mine almost totally destroyed the Dutch church in Austin Friars, a mediaeval monastery church which had been handed over to the Dutch community centuries before. James Pope-Hennessy found 'nothing upon its site but pieces of stone, lengths of sodden planking, smashed tiles, red telephone books hurled from a nearby office by the bomb blast, a mound of curled lead ... and a stack of iron railings.'[196] Two ARP wardens died. Stationers' Hall in Ave Maria Lane was badly damaged. Twenty-two were killed in Baldwins Gardens, off Gray's Inn Road, Holborn when a bomb hit a block of flats and a delayed action bomb later exploded

---

196 James Pope-Hennessy *History under Fire* (Batsford,1941) quoted in Trench, *London before the Blitz* (1989)

amongst rescue workers. Another bomb in Holborn killed fourteen people in a shelter behind Queen Square belonging to the National Deposit Friendly Society, and a parachute mine blasted the buildings around Lincoln's Inn Fields.

A serious incident occurred at Morley College, Lambeth, an adult education college then used as a rest centre, which was hit by a 1,000kg bomb:

'On the night of 15th October at precisely 19.55 hours a heavy H.E. bomb fell, entering the roof on the King Edward Walk side of the college and exploding on the floor above the room used as the restaurant. The bomb shattered the building from one end to the other, only the new extension escaping destruction. The force of the explosion broke up and threw huge sections of masonry, brickwork and reinforced concrete into the air which in turn fell on the adjoining houses on both sides of King Edward Walk, totally demolishing them.

The wardens on duty at Post no.3, about 200 yards away, felt a heavy thud at the time the bomb fell, preceded by a terrific swishing noise. They went out to investigate and ran into a huge cloud of dust in Westminster Bridge Road that completely blotted out the general view, and it was some moments before they were able to discern the actual spot, although it was a bright moonlight night. Making their way towards the cloud of dust, huge sections of debris impeding their progress, the wardens came across a scene of desolation and immediately noting the position of the occurrence sent a report to the Post which was 'phoned to the Report and Control Centre at precisely 20.00 hours. Whilst the express message was being 'phoned the M.1 (the standard report form) was being made out. The M.1 report was received at the Control Centre at 20.10 hours and before this time the express services of ambulance, stretcher party and sitting case cars were on the spot.

Meanwhile the wardens were conducting several people

from the college to the Post and minor injuries were attended to. At 20.20 hours rescue squads and more stretcher parties arrived on the scene and very soon the whole area was alive with rescue parties and first aiders attending to the casualties. At 20.30 hours the A.D.W. (Assistant District Warden) took over as Incident Officer and organisation was set up to deal with the situation. In order to relieve the work at the post where sixty people were being attended to, the Hall at St. Thomas's Church, opposite the college, was opened up as a temporary first aid post. A mobile hospital unit arrived and doctors administered morphia to trapped casualties who were seriously injured and were being released from the debris. Many people were trapped between the floors and walls of the upstairs rooms which had collapsed into the basement. Many were dead in this wreckage and the bodies were taken out in the morning, the time being utilised to seek those who were still alive.

The wardens and rescue parties (some twelve in all, including two parties from Southwark who did excellent work at the beginning) carried on with their work throughout the night. During the whole time, heavy A.A. fire was going on directly overhead and bombs were falling in considerable numbers in the locality. Whilst there were many runnings and duckings for cover the work went on until dawn, when a better opportunity availed to survey the damage caused and plan out the continuation of the work. Relief systems had to be evolved in order to give wardens and rescue workers some rest.

This incident, the first major incident the Post had experienced, gave the wardens many practical lessons, and they were able to learn much from their successes and mistakes. The Report and Control Centre was continually in touch with events by the various supplementary reports and messages that were sent from time to time and we are pleased to say that all our requests were promptly dealt with. In conclusion, out of 195 actually in the building at the time of the occurrence, 84 came out alive and unhurt, 54 were sent to hospital and 57 were killed, 10 of whom died in hospital and one of whom is still unidentified.'[197]

Dame Alice Owen's School, Finsbury, where there were 110 casualties, was also open as a public shelter. The following is taken from the memorial programme produced by City and Islington College:

'On this night about 150 people, who mainly lived in the surrounding area, had come to sleep in the public air raid shelter in the basement of Dame Alice Owen's Girls' School. The school building stood fifty metres south of the commemorative panels. There were many families with children and elderly people. At 20.07 hours, as people were settling in for the night, a large parachute high explosive bomb – a land mine – hit the school directly and most of the building collapsed. The explosion also shattered the major water main (the New River) in front of the building, which ran to the reservoir near Sadler's Wells. People were crushed or trapped in the basement, which began to fill with water.

Local people started rescue work immediately. They were later joined by uniform services, who were dealing with incidents all over London. Some people were rescued, including the school caretaker's wife, Mrs Burley, who was photographed being carried from the ruins 17 hours after the bomb fell. The picture was sent all over the world and became an icon of the London Blitz. This picture is shown on the panels. But the majority died in the shelter or afterwards in hospital. The last bodies arrived at the mortuary on 8 November after more than three weeks of recovery work. Seventeen of the bodies were unidentified. The names, which are known of those who died, are recorded on the panels.'

---

197 Anon., *Front Line* (1942)

The school, whose pupils had been evacuated to Bedford, was almost totally destroyed. Over 100 people are said to have died, although the Civilian War Dead Roll of Honour shows that in all there were ninety-five deaths in Finsbury that night. On Tuesday 18 October, 2005, a memorial to the people who died was officially unveiled at Owen's Field, City and Islington College, Goswell Road.

Three parachute mines exploded in the borough of St. Pancras. Prospect Terrace, a block of seventy flats off Gray's Inn Road, built in 1906, was demolished and there were 100 casualties with over thirty killed. Another mine fell at Cromer Street causing a large amount of blast damage in neighbouring streets and eight fatalities. The third mine fell at St. Pancras station, fortunately not exploding until after evacuation had taken place. But the station was severely damaged and as a result, had to be closed until 21 October. A fourth mine in Gray's Inn Road failed to explode but necessitated the evacuation of the Royal Free Hospital. There were also casualties in Ampton Street which may have been as a result of the Prospect Terrace incident. Major incidents also happened in St. Marylebone at Cumberland Place but no fatalities appear in the Civilian War Dead Roll of Honour. Forty-eight were killed in Islington, at incidents in Barnsbury Road, Britannia Row and Eden Grove. Over 100 people were trapped in trench shelters in Market Road Gardens, Islington, many being overcome by fumes and several killed. Twenty-three died in Hackney, in a number of incidents including those at the *Adam and Eve* and *Middleton Arms* pubs. Six died at the Salvation Army barracks in Homerton High Street and the church of St. Mary Haggerston was demolished by a direct hit.

Trench shelters at Cadogan Terrace in Poplar were hit as well as other shelters in Southwark (Flint Street) and Westminster. In the latter location, a bomb fell on the huge upmarket block of flats known as Dolphin Square and penetrated to the underground car park. Most of the 160 cars garaged there were damaged or destroyed. This was only a few yards from a depot and shelter used by ARP workers. Nearby there was a large fire in a furniture warehouse and later another bomb caused further damage at Dolphin Square and blocked access to the basement. A parachute mine landed in nearby Alderney Street destroying or damaging over 150 houses, killing twenty-three and injuring about sixty people. The *Six Bells* pub in the King's Road, Chelsea, a favourite of the literary set, was badly damaged and two members of staff killed.

In Victoria Park, an air raid shelter had been built underground just inside St. Marks Gate. A bomb made a direct hit, trapping around a hundred inside and killing fifteen. The fatalities were all Poplar residents.

Twelve people were killed at Barrie Street, Paddington, when a bomb landed in the roadway wrecking the entire street and surrounding property, including an ARP depot. In the borough of Willesden two parachute mines fell in Mortimer Road, Kensal Green and in Christchurch Avenue, Brondesbury Park, in addition to other bombs, and at least eleven people died.

Very serious damage was done to the New River Bridge in Edmonton which drastically affected the water supply to central London. The river Lea supplied 48 million gallons of water a day to London via the New River. At 21.30 the New River was reported to be overflowing, flooding local roads in Edmonton. The New River, which was designed as an aqueduct to bring drinking water from the river Lea in Hertfordshire to central London, was in fact breached at Bush Hill Park. Early the next morning Regional Commissioner Euan Wallace met with the Metropolitan Water Board's Chief Engineer and by 09.30 had agreed a solution – to commandeer 2,000 soldiers to dig out half a mile of the former course of the New River west of Edmonton.

This would be used to divert the river away from the breach. Later that day they were already at work digging out this culvert which was blocked with rubbish and silt whilst the Pioneer Corps had to be called in to repair the banks. The fire service was required to provide a relay to by-pass the breach. Twelve pumps and seventy-two men were continuously engaged for over three days on this task until the breach was repaired on 19 October.[198]

Railway damage was particularly severe with several lines being closed until the next day for examination. The damage at St. Pancras has already been mentioned. Waterloo station was hit by bombs at 09.16 and again at 20.55. As a result of the damage, all platforms were not back in use until 26 October. At 03.44 a bomb penetrated the LPTB Metropolitan railway tunnel between Kings Cross and Farringdon at Clerkenwell. As a result, the Metropolitan line and the Metropolitan Widened Lines were flooded when the Fleet sewer burst, in addition to being filled with gas leaking from fractured mains. A bomb near Queen's Park station threw debris onto the track, derailing the engine of an express to Inverness. Fortunately, it was only travelling at 20 mph and there were no casualties except the fireman who was seriously injured. A further bomb also blasted debris onto the track at the station and the electric lines (used by LMS and LPTB services) were blocked by flooding and power failure. Mainline trains were able to continue to run but it was not until 26 October that all lines at the station were back in action.

The Southern Railway's power station at Durnsford Road, Wimbledon, was hit by bombs which put half its boilers out of action and demolished a chimney stack. The capacity of the station was reduced by 50%, and repairs took nearly four months to complete. Much disruption was caused to train

---

198 Wallington, *Firemen at War* (1981)

services around Waterloo, London Bridge and Clapham Junction stations.

At 20.05 part of a trench shelter in Kennington Park, Lambeth, took a direct hit from a bomb. Fred Armer, then a small boy in a different part of the shelter, recalls 'the whole ceiling lifting up and banging back down again. Then there was an eerie silence for a few seconds. Then a call for help.' Rescue workers spent hours digging out the dead and wounded, despite the pitch darkness and the bombs that continued to fall around them. A man who helped rescue efforts reported that 'the whole thing was blown to bits. There were heads and arms and legs and feet lying about. The only way you could tell the girls from the men was because of their hair.'

> 'At 7am the next morning, a request was made for 100 shrouds and a large lorry for the removal of bodies. No official death toll was announced at the time but the figure is now believed to be 104 fatalities. Forty-eight bodies were recovered and buried in Streatham Cemetery; the remainder still lie beneath the park.
>
> A memorial at Lambeth Cemetery commemorates Lambeth's civilian World War 2 casualties. But those killed in the shelter were largely forgotten until a memorial service, initiated by Councillor Marietta Crichton Stuart, took place at St. Mark's Church in 2003. The Friends of Kennington Park raised funds for a permanent memorial in the park and commissioned local sculptor Richard Kindersley. The memorial was unveiled in 2006 in front of more than 100 local people.'[199]

It will be noted that the author quite confidently asserts that bodies of victims were left unrecovered. The Civilian War Dead

---

199 Pateman, *Kennington's forgotten tragedy* (c2007)

Roll of Honour lists fifty fatalities. In addition, in Lambeth six died at the sawmills in Hercules Road, and three in Aveline Street. Queen's Buildings in Scovell Street, Southwark was a large complex of old tenement blocks. It was hit by a parachute mine and a number of blocks demolished, and this accounted for most of the forty-six people who died in Southwark that night.

Forty-one night fighters took off but only two succeeded in intercepting a German aircraft. A Defiant of 264 Squadron shot down a Heinkel, which crashed at Ingrave in Essex.[200]

16/17 October

At a meeting of the War Cabinet held at no.10 Downing Street, the Minister of Home Security said that relatively serious damage had been suffered during the last two nights. Public morale was good, but he thought 'we should look ahead, as morale might begin to suffer if the public felt that our reply to night bombing was ineffective. It was of the utmost importance that every effort should be made to press ahead as quickly as possible with the means of countering night bombing. During the last two or three nights two tube stations had been pierced. The effect had been to make the public realise that practically no kind of shelter was invulnerable'. Reference was made to the very serious structural damage to the Carlton Club, where the building had been wrecked but virtually no personal injury had been sustained by the large number of people in the club. Here of course, many cabinet members had been dining so there was some personal stake! In some other cases, large numbers of casualties had been sustained at individual shelters, e.g., the refuge under the Stoke Newington block of flats. While the effects of high explosive bombs were freakish, everything pointed to the advantages of

---

200 Price, *Blitz on Britain 1939-1945* (1977)

dispersal. The War Cabinet were also informed that the Germans had recently announced publicly that their air attack was to be directed against the big hotels and clubs.[201]

Only slight enemy activity was observed during the day and no bombs were dropped in the London area. The evening raid was much less severe than the previous night, possibly because of very wet weather – 'less intense' was the phrase used in the situation report. In Dagenham, fires were reported at May & Baker, the Ford Motor Works, Briggs Motor Bodies and the Pritchett & Gold & EPS Company. Several civilian fatalities occurred. Richings Park Mansion in Buckinghamshire was reported severely damaged by a parachute mine with another unexploded mine in the vicinity. The house was occupied by the Air Ministry and had formerly served as Bomber Command HQ.[202] An unexploded bomb in the slaughter houses of the Caledonian Market threatened distribution of meat in north London. Other rail disruption was reported at Crayford, between Orpington and Chelsfield, Sutton and Wimbledon (residents alongside evacuated) and Chadwell Heath (LNER station). Leicester Square was badly blasted with the AA building and the taxi rank outside being particularly affected. More shelter casualties occurred in Lambeth, this time at the Model Dwellings shelter on the Albert Embankment where eight people died. In Chelsea, St Stephen's Hospital was hit with over eighteen fatalities.

Once again Hackney was badly hit with thirty-three fatalities. Of these, at least ten people died at a shelter in Victoria Park. Eighteen died in Hornsey, many of them at the trench shelters in Broad Lane, which were hit at 00.52; forty-four people were rescued.

---

201 TNA CAB 65/9
202 Richings Park mansion was demolished after the war

17/18 October

A huge explosion from the direction of Shoreditch was heard by bomb disposal men on their parade ground in City Road. A parachute mine had exploded, killing two of their colleagues who were attempting to defuse it.

At 15.25 a bomb fell in Wilkin Street, Kentish Town. Three people were killed, ten injured and one hundred were believed trapped.[203] The Civilian War Dead Roll of Honour indicates that Dell's factory in the adjacent Ryland Road was hit. At night, incidents occurred in more than a dozen boroughs. The Holloway trolleybus/tram garage in Pemberton Gardens was hit and a number of vehicles destroyed. At approximately 21.35 there was a direct hit on the fire station in Mitcham Lane, Streatham. Two heavy appliances were wrecked and there were twelve fatal casualties among AFS personnel together with eight injured. Later in the night bombs hit the Home Office and the Scottish Office in Whitehall, but only one casualty was recorded.

Padstow House is a modern council block of flats in Three Colt Street, Stepney, which had been completed only in March 1939. At about 19.45 a bomb hit the flats, demolishing one wing and trapping 170 people in the shelter. Eight people died.[204]

18/19 October

A serious water deficiency was affecting factories in north London. The evening raid resulted in forty-five fatalities in London, in incidents scattered across the capital.

The *Rose and Crown* pub in Lambeth was completely demolished at 20.25 by a direct hit. Early estimates were that there were two dead, six injured with a further forty trapped, 'for

---

203 TNA HO 202 Ministry of Home Security: Home Security War Room Reports
204 Taylor & Lloyd, *The East End at War* (2000)

whom little hope of survival can be entertained'[205]. The Civilian War Dead Roll of Honour shows twenty-one people were killed at 1 Crown Lane but doesn't mention the pub by name. Clyde Street school in Deptford, a busy ARP station was hit and six personnel killed.

At 21.25 a bomb fell at Harrow & Wealdstone LMS station killing four people and blocking the road. An oil bomb fell in the goods yard causing a fire and minor damage[206]. At 22.00 a bomb dropped near the corner of the Air Ministry Unit annexe on the main road at Harrow and four airmen were killed. 'Telephones are out of action but Operations are safe and an emergency line from main shelter is in order. The gas main is broken but no serious damage is reported to main buildings'[207]. A few bombs fell in the vicinity of Coastal Command Headquarters at Northwood at about 21.25. Nine people died at Twyford Avenue, Acton. Walthamstow trolleybus depot was damaged although this incident is not mentioned in the account by local author, Ross Wyld. At the tail end of the raid, Beckton gas works was set on fire.

19/20 October

After a few daytime incidents, bombing became widespread after dusk over the London area and continued all night. The situation report noted that 'a particularly vicious attack was launched against London and surrounding suburbs.' This was the first of two quite heavy raids, although the incendiary content was not high. In Acton, the Dubilier Condenser Company was badly damaged. The electrolytic condenser shop was completely

---

205 TNA HO 202 Ministry of Home Security: Home Security War Room Reports

206 Brooksbank, *London Main Line War Damage* (2007).

207 TNA HO 202 Ministry of Home Security: Home Security War Room Reports

wrecked by a direct hit. The spray shop, impregnation shop and other departments were less severely damaged. No casualties were reported.

Incendiaries set fire to the roof of the Great Hall at Euston Station and high explosive bombs cratered platforms 2 and 3, damaged the station roof and damaged the LMS offices in Drummond Street and the west wing of the Euston Hotel. However, this was the only occasion during the Blitz on which this important London rail terminus was substantially damaged. Hampstead Heath station received a direct hit which scattered debris over the tracks, blocking all lines. In Wimbledon bombs fell near the Southern Railway's Durnsford Road power station and thirty casualties were reported, some of whom were trapped in a passenger train. Bombs fell through the railway arch at Filwood Street, Deptford causing major damage. At Brentford, a bomb fell on the Southern Railway track south of Chiswick Station. Well Hall Station in Woolwich was damaged by fire, and much other railway damage was caused.

In Stepney at 21.25 a bomb partially demolished 'D' Block of the Mile End Hospital. Damage was caused at a number of locations in London's docks, including at Redline-Glico, manufacturers of motor oils in West Ham. The Rev Sidney Marsh was killed at his church, St. Phillip's in Parkholme Road, Dalston, along with two others, and in the same area several people died at the Connor Street shelter. Fires included a 50-pump fire at Goswell Road, Clerkenwell, a 30-pump fire at the gas works in Poplar, and 20-pump fires at Smeed Road in Bow, Hopton Street in Southwark, the Medical College in Charterhouse Square and College Hall at St. Bartholomew's Hospital.

174 people were killed, with Camberwell and Croydon having the worst casualties. At least six people died at the Fulham Palace Road school, which was used as a rest centre. A number of people died in Waterloo Road, in an incident outside

Waterloo station. Firefighters managed to put out fires at St. John's East Dulwich, but the church was to be hit again on 8 December and gutted.

20/21 October
Thirteen were killed during daytime incursions by German aircraft, and seventy-six during the night raid. Lambeth Palace was bombed for the first time and the drawing room was demolished. The Central Middlesex Hospital's nurses' home in Park Royal and the British Museum's depository at Hendon were damaged. A bomb hit the edge of an underground shelter in the New Kent Road, Southwark, where twenty-six people were sheltering. Most of them died.

In Battersea, at least fifteen people died at the Tennyson Street shelter. The Eagle Court shelter in Finsbury was the scene of another tragedy, seven people being killed, as was the Gordon Grove railway arch shelter in Loughborough Park, Lambeth. A number of people died at Frederick Street, Stratford but the circumstances are not known.

Addison Road LPTB station in Kensington was hit and badly damaged and this forced the closure of this short branch line until after the war[208]. Addison Road (now Kensington Olympia) had served as a railhead when hospitals were evacuated at the outbreak of war and later for the reception of refugees from Belgium and Holland.

21/22 October
At a meeting of the War Cabinet held at no.10 Downing Street, reference was made to the effect of air raids on public morale. There was comment that the AA barrage had decreased, and some disappointment that more enemy bombers were not brought down

208 Cooper, *London Underground at War* (2014)

at night. Press statements to the effect that an antidote to the night bombers might be expected shortly had not been realised, with the result that Londoners were at the moment a little pessimistic. The Lord Privy Seal stated that the Prime Minister had held a meeting that morning at which the question of the best means of combating night bombers had been fully dealt with.

Referring to the Tilbury shelter, the Home Secretary said that the public had been excluded from this shelter while work was in progress on the structural improvements. When an air raid warning had sounded the shelter had not been opened quickly. Some disorder had followed, and a party had attempted to rush the ARP Control Office in Stepney. The police had drawn their truncheons, and a number of men had been arrested. The *Daily Worker* had made a strong complaint about the police action, but as far as he (the Home Secretary) could see, the police had been fully justified.[209]

The evening's raid saw a number of incidents scattered across London with over 100 fatalities. At 22.16 a 500kg bomb which made a crater of over 40ft in diameter, fell at the junction of Eversholt Street and Phoenix Road, at the side of Euston station, causing serious damage to the LPTB Northern line tunnels between Euston and Mornington Crescent stations. A 36-inch gas main was fractured and set on fire, and a large water main was broken allowing water to enter the tube tunnels fifty feet below, although pumping was soon started and the flood was controlled. Even with the assistance of the Royal Engineers, repairs were not completed and traffic resumed until 22 February.

22/23 October

At 21.45 Whiteley's, the large department store in Bayswater, received a direct hit, a 1,400kg bomb penetrating to the

---

209 TNA CAB 65/9

basement. A gas main was fractured, causing the subsequent 30-pump fire. This was brought under control by midnight. Seven people were killed, but overall that night fatalities in London only came to twenty-five, and enemy air activity over the capital ceased by 23.00.

23/24 October

Enemy activity was again restricted due to poor weather, and civilian casualties were accordingly low. In the afternoon, there was a surprise when a delayed action bomb suddenly exploded at 13.40 in the National Gallery in Trafalgar Square, causing extensive structural damage. The National Gallery had closed just before the outbreak of war, its paintings being sent away for safekeeping. 'With the pictures evacuated, the director waited for notification that the gallery would be requisitioned for administrative purposes, saddened by its inability to offer Londoners comfort just when they needed it most. Then one day, just a few weeks after the outbreak of war, he was visited by the famous pianist, Myra Hess. She shared his dismay. The arts, she believed, played a powerful spiritual role in the health of the nation at the best of times – and would play a greater role now during wartime.' A series of concerts began which turned out to be highly popular. But '... at 11am on 15 October, Myra Hess was told by phone that a time bomb had fallen and required the immediate evacuation of the Gallery. For a brief period, it seemed as if the concerts' continuous run might finally be broken but within half an hour an alternative venue had been found. A boy was positioned in Trafalgar Square to redirect the audience to the library of nearby South Africa House, where several hundred people heard the Griller Quartet and Max Gilbert play Mozart String Quintets. The concerts returned to the National Gallery the next day, only for another unexploded bomb, this time a 1,000lb one, to be discovered buried in the wreckage on the 18 October. Undeterred, the audience was shepherded to a room in the east wing to hear the Menges String Quartet while the bomb disposal team got to work. Then on 23 October at 1.30pm, in the middle of a Beethoven quartet, a third device exploded under the old board room of the Gallery, away from Room 36 where there was a concert taking place. There were no casualties. According to one account, no one in the audience moved and the Stratton Quartet continued their performance without missing a beat.[210]

In the evening, a minor raid began and three bombs fell just north of St. Pancras station at 18.47. These caused considerable damage, including a large crater on the London main line and two holes through a bridge; property and rolling stock also suffered severely. Five railwaymen were killed and five injured. Despite being faced with a scene of widespread devastation repair gangs were able to get most lines reopened within twenty-four hours. The North London line was also affected where it passes over the lines from St. Pancras.

24 October
Bombs were dropped at Hayes at 14.34 and a serious fire was started in Keith Road at the works of the Fairey Aviation Co, where the main store was damaged. There were five casualties, and production was expected to be temporarily affected.

25/26 October
Seventy aircraft attacked London in the morning of 25 October and a further thirty in the afternoon. At Battersea, a bomb which failed to explode was dropped on Dorman

---

210 See https://www.nationalgallery.org.uk/about-us/history/the-myra-hess-concerts/myra-hesss-wartime-concerts (accessed 7 January 2022).

Long's yard at 09.30, causing delay to important government work. In Westminster, the Air Provost Marshal's department was hit by a bomb at 13.30, killing four RAF personnel and injuring eight. Factories at Willesden were also damaged, and four workers were killed at the Guinness brewery in Park Royal when the ice house was struck by a bomb[211]. Damage was also done to the LPTB Piccadilly line tracks at Park Royal station.

During the day raids, there was much damage to railway property. The worst of this was at 09.50 when Blackfriars Road railway bridge was hit, five trams parked under the bridge being blasted – two of them were wrecked and five drivers and two conductors killed in addition to bridge repair and railway staff injured. Considerable repair work was being carried out to the bridge following the raid on 16 October and further major engineering work now became necessary. The nearby Ring, a former chapel which was now a boxing venue, was also badly damaged and had to be demolished. Thirty-five died in all in London.

During the night raid at about 21.00, there were six serious fires and forty-three medium fires. A 50kg bomb which hit a railway arch shelter killed 105 people and injured fifty-eight – virtually everyone who was in the shelter was a casualty[212]. The Druid Street Billiard Hall in Bermondsey was a social club which was used as a shelter at night. According to Harvey[213] the casualties represented the largest number of people killed and injured by a single bomb in London. It was certainly Bermondsey's worst incident of the whole war. There were also fatalities at the Richard House shelter in Cottington Street, Lambeth. Cobb's department store in Sydenham – said to be the most prestigious

211 Glover, *Brewing for Victory* (1995)
212 TNA HO186/1862
213 Harvey, *Collision of Empires* (1992)

in south-east London – was hit by incendiary bombs and largely destroyed in the ensuing 20-pump blaze. Greenwich power station was hit with thirteen fatalities including members of the Home Guard. Eight people died in the Ruislip area including two policemen but the circumstances are not known nor is it known at what time of day this happened.

26/27 October

Daylight raids on central London inevitably resulted in heavy casualties. At around noon on 26 October, a high explosive bomb struck the red brick St James's Residences, built in 1883-86, on Brewer Street, Soho. Whilst it was lucky that the bomb struck when it did, as many residents were away at the time, the bomb was still highly destructive. It resulted in a total of forty-five casualties: five dead, twenty seriously injured, and twenty slightly injured.

Around the same time a high explosive bomb hit Curzon Street House in Mayfair, detonating at the base of the building and resulting in around thirty casualties, and at least twenty-one fatalities appear in the Civilian War Dead Roll of Honour. At this time, Curzon Street House – a 1930s block of flats – was being used by the War Office. The casualties were among workmen engaged on decorating the building but there may have been military casualties as well. The blast had dislodged a large (60-ton) girder leaving the building appearing to hang in the air unsupported.

The rescue workers' job was complicated by a large crowd of civilian onlookers. These bystanders broke through the ARP cordon and hampered those working at the scene. In one case, a rescue worker reputedly knocked out a gawping civilian with his helmet.[214]

---

214 Sansom, *Westminster at War* (1990)

At night, 164 Londoners were killed in a moderately severe raid which lasted over twelve hours. A major fire was started at Saffron Hill, Clerkenwell, necessitating the attendance of fifty pumps. In Chelsea, the Royal Hospital, home to the Chelsea Pensioners, suffered a direct hit but there were no casualties. In Hammersmith, at least ten people were killed at the *Telegraph Hotel*, a pub in Shepherd's Bush Green. The District line of the London Underground kept running although the roof of the tunnel was blown away in Queen Victoria Street. Another crater was opened up in Seymour Street alongside Euston Station. Croydon (Waddon) power station was put out of action.

27/28 October
Over forty people were killed in incidents scattered across the London region.

28/29 October
Overall, casualties were light on 28 October although ten people died at the electricity showrooms in Croydon, when a bomb penetrated the basement shelter of this modern building. There were over 100 casualties in all, but the shelter was quickly and efficiently evacuated. A 50-pump fire broke out at the Royal Arsenal, Woolwich but was under control by about 02.00 on the morning of 29 October. The most serious incidents occurred when a stick of 50kg bombs fell across Walworth. At 01.40 St. Peter's Church in Liverpool Grove, Walworth was hit by two bombs which exploded amongst shelterers in the crypt. Sixty-five were killed and nearly 250 seriously injured. John Markham, Rector of Walworth from 1937 to 1944, gives a detailed description of the night in his memoirs:[215]

---

215 http.//walworthsaintpeter.blogspot.com

The crypt shelter was full, even before the warning. Everybody had their usual settling down period – perhaps a few songs, families talking, eating the food they brought with them, before they lay down to get some sleep in their usual places, on improvised bedding, deck chairs and even on the bare stone floor.

Jenner and I returned to the Post, and then decided that we would make a circuit of the area, to contact the wardens on patrol, whom we had not been able to see for several hours. As usual, we mounted our blitz bikes, brakeless, lampless, and started off down the street alongside the churchyard.

We heard the explosions of one or two bombs in the distance, and carried out our usual drill – falling off the bikes without stopping. As we hit the ground, five bombs exploded around us, so that we could see the orange flashes; two in the churchyard beyond the church, two others, as it turned out in the church and one in the garden of one of the small houses beside us, throwing some of the dirt on us as we sprawled in the gutter. We got up, and rushed round to the other side of the church, which appeared, in the moonlight, to be undamaged, expecting to find that the houses on the other side of the churchyard had been hit. No signs of damage there. Then I heard a dull confused murmur from the crypt, and a dusty figure struggled among the sandbags in the doorway at the foot of the steps, leading to the shelter, crying "Help".

Markham together with his wife and survivors worked tirelessly through the night to rescue the many injured from the devastation. He later recalled the grief and shock felt by the community at the terrible sight of so many dead amongst the rubble.

'I had all the bodies taken straight into the undamaged

West End of the church, where they were laid out in rows in one of the aisles. In the morning there were 35 stretchers of the remains waiting for the vans. Their blood stained the stone flags. I was glad that I was able within a week to establish our altar on that very spot, where we offered the sacrifice of our worship and prayer for them and ourselves, and all the world, during the following years. I shall always remember them.

Dawn and the 'All Clear' wailing of the sirens found us very weary, particularly my wardens, many of whom had plunged into the work of extracting the injured from the tangle of debris and darkness of the crypt ... Inevitably, those who had been down amongst it all were suffering from shock, as were the whole neighbourhood, when they came out of their shelters, checked up on their friends and relatives, many of whom were in the crypt. There was a shocked feeling about, heightened by the belief that many had cherished, that the crypt was a safe shelter – an illusion which I had never shared.

In Walthamstow, after three bombs had fallen, two women and two children were killed when they fell into a *camouflet*[216] in the garden of a house in Marlowe Road.[217]

29/30 October

There were fatalities in Battersea (at the trench shelters on Wandsworth Common), Bermondsey and Camberwell, and

---

216 A *camouflet* is formed when a bomb or shell penetrates the ground and explodes forming a cavern under the surface rather than a crater on the surface. It is not visible on the surface or only an entry hole is visible and is thought to be that of an unexploded bomb or shell. It is very dangerous, as the hole can collapse when trodden on and the toxic gases in the *camouflet* can kill.
217 Wyld, *The War over Walthamstow* (1989)

further out at Dagenham, Croydon and Bromley where a shelter was hit at Queens Mead Road. A severe fire was caused at Wray Optical Works in Lewisham by incendiary bombs dropped at 19.40. It was reported that the centre part of the factory was completely gutted, the factory heating system was damaged and the store containing all raw materials for glass work was burnt out. This was an effective strike on a valuable target and production was seriously curtailed.

Home Security reports state a new five-storey block of flats in Stepney was hit at 19.55 – 'Fortunately most of the tenants were in public shelters and consequently casualties were small.' According to the Civilian War Dead Roll of Honour eight people were killed at Brunswick Buildings in Goulston Street, but this was not a modern block.

30 October

The War Cabinet met in the Cabinet War Room, where it considered a memorandum by Herbert Morrison, the Minister of Home Security on air raid shelter policy. He explained that air raid shelter policy had been governed by the assumption that raids would be comparatively short, and that shelters must be readily accessible. Prolonged night raiding meant people were seeking shelter, irrespective of warnings, towards nightfall and staying there until morning. The arguments against deep shelters which had hitherto prevailed were, therefore, no longer entirely valid. While it was impossible to apply any widespread policy of deep shelter which could be applied evenly over the vulnerable areas of the country, Morrison felt that it would not be right, on this account, to dismiss the possibility of deep shelters. He accordingly suggested that work should be put in hand for providing additional shelter by tunnelling. In London this construction would be linked with the Tube system. In the provinces tunnelling would be carried out where the physical

The docks ablaze after London's first major air raid, 7 September 1940.
Everett Collection / Mary Evans

The Ring, formerly the Surrey Chapel, in ruins, 25 October 1940.
© Historic England Archive / Mary Evans Picture Library

Firemen at work in the London docks, September 1940.
Everett Collection / Mary Evans

The Surrey Commercial Docks, Rotherhithe, 7 September 1940.
©London Fire Brigade / Mary Evans Picture Library

A bomb has blasted trams under a bridge in Blackfriars Road, 25 October 1940.
©London Fire Brigade / Mary Evans Picture Library

The Houses of Parliament and Big Ben viewed across the Thames in 1940.
Mary Evans Picture Library/James Eadie

Chancery Lane 25 September 1940. The Safe Deposit building reduced to a mass of rubble.
©London Fire Brigade / Mary Evans Picture Library

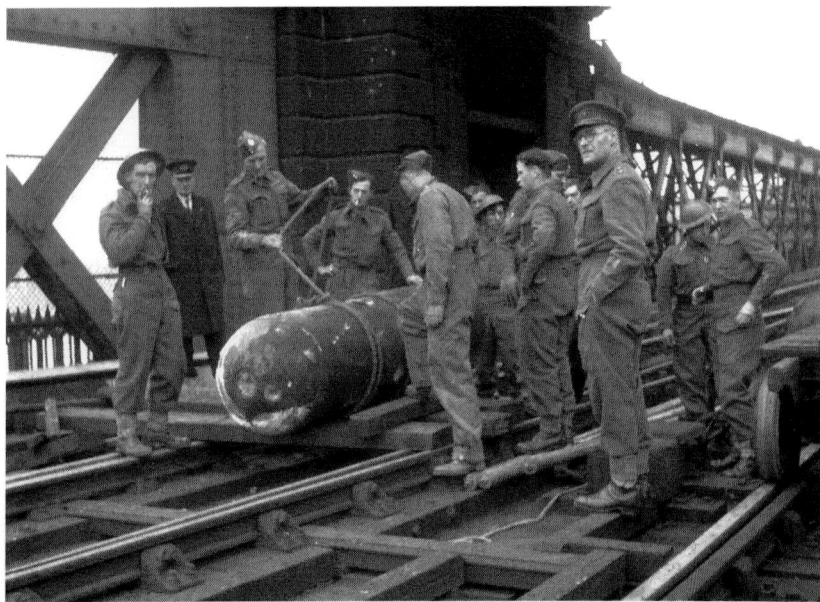

Soldiers use a trolley to remove a defused parachute mine from the Hungerford railway bridge at Charing Cross, 17 April 1941.
©London Fire Brigade / Mary Evans Picture Library

Invicta Road Greenwich, 14 November 1940. Rescue workers, firemen and ambulance personnel search the ruins of a fire station. Fifteen firemen died.
©London Fire Brigade / Mary Evans Picture Library

A burnt-out cargo ship in the Surrey Commercial Docks, Rotherhithe, September 1940.
©London Fire Brigade / Mary Evans Picture Library

Oil tank fire at Thames Haven, 8 September 1940.
©London Fire Brigade / Mary Evans Picture Library

Bomb damage at the Bank Underground Station, January 1941.
Museum of London/by kind permission of The Commissioner of the City of London Police

The notorious Tilbury Shelter: the massive Commercial Road Goods Depot as it was in 1905.

A vital industrial target, Rank's flour mills at the Royal Albert Dock, was put out of action in September 1940.
PLA Collection/Museum of London

The Mazawattee Tea Warehouse, Tower Hill by Cross, Arthur; Tibbs, Fred. This monstrosity, photographed after the raid on 8/9 December 1940, faced the Tower of London.
Image © London Metropolitan Archives (City of London).

features made this practicable. He added that he was anxious, in a broadcast which he would have to make shortly, to deal with 'mischievous Communist agitation' on the deep shelter question. He felt, however, that it would be impossible for him to deal with the situation adequately if he adopted a wholly negative attitude towards the provision of deep shelters where this was practicable. In a preliminary discussion the view was expressed that, if Morrison's proposals were adopted, the advocates of deep shelters would claim that the case for deep shelters had been conceded in principle, but that the measures proposed to provide them were entirely inadequate. It was also argued that to provide deep shelters for a very small proportion of the population would do little good and would have unfortunate psychological results. To this it was replied that the people of this country were too sensible to wish to see a remedy negatived (*sic*) merely because it could not be universally provided.

Neville Chamberlain, the Lord President of the Council said that Morrison's proposal did not really represent any fundamental departure from existing policy. Deep shelters had been approved in a number of cases where suitable deep tunnels could be made available; e.g., Ramsgate, Rochester and Luton. While, however, there was everything to be said for an extension of this policy where feasible, the proposal to drive tunnels linked with the Tube system would require very careful handling. There was the risk that if this proposal was taken up by public opinion in the wrong way, it might be used to discredit the whole shelter policy. Morrison thought it was important to mention publicly the proposal to make new tunnels connected with the Tubes. This point was reserved for further discussion.

The general conclusion expressed in this preliminary discussion was that the question at issue was mainly one of emphasis in presentation. The general line to be followed might be as follows. Morrison would start his statement by stressing the importance of spreading the risk and of popularising the smaller shelters. He would explain that there was neither time nor material available for the construction of deep shelters for large numbers of people. But this was no reason why such measures should not be taken to provide additional deep shelter accommodation where this was feasible. The statement should not be represented as a reversal of existing policy. The War Cabinet took note of this preliminary discussion and invited Morrison to submit to the War Cabinet a draft of the statement which he proposed to make on this matter.[218]

30/31 October

Very little air raid activity took place, although the sirens sounded twice in London during the night. The Odeon cinema in Haverstock Hill Hampstead, which was opened on 29 September 1934, was badly damaged by a bomb, and it was closed down for many years.

At the end of October, a bomb had landed on the apron of Teddington Weir. The breach caused by the bomb's detonation created a reduction in the depth of water at Teddington Reach by six feet, making navigation impossible except at high tides. Full navigation was not restored for seven weeks[219].

---

218 TNA CAB 65/9
219 Twickenham Museum website. http.//www.twickenham-museum.org.
    uk/ This incident also had implications for London's water supplies.

SIX

NOVEMBER 1940

During November, the weather increasingly interfered with and thwarted Luftwaffe plans. On 1 November the *Evening Standard* claimed that the previous night's gales in the English Channel had stopped night raids on London. November 1940 proved to be one of the wettest months in British meteorological records. As a result, raids were on a small scale until the middle of the month. From mid-November the Luftwaffe began heavy attacks on centres of industry across the UK. On 14 November, their attacks switched to Coventry, with devastating effect. From this point onwards, the Luftwaffe began to drop heavier bombs on the UK, and technology in the form of the X-Gerät and Y-Gerät was employed to direct these onto specific targets. In this new phase thirteen major raids took place before the end of the month including three on London (15, 16 and 29 November).

1/2 November
The issue of evacuation of children was still topical. Efforts were

being made to persuade the remaining children (over 279,000) to leave London. A few weeks later concern was expressed that 50,000 of them were not even attending school.

A few aircraft reached London during the day, but casualties and damage were slight. However, many serious incidents were to occur after dark, including one at an AFS station in Poplar. Ricardo Street School, a three-storey London County Council Elementary School, received a direct hit and the firemen and women on duty were buried under the rubble. Five died including 20-year-old Joan Ridd.[220]

The Reeves paint factory in Ashwin Street, Dalston, was hit and rapidly became an inferno. John Cain, a 15-year-old costermonger joined four policemen in rescuing people from the basement shelter under the factory. Six men were brought out despite the very hazardous circumstances, and shortly after, the building collapsed. The rescuers all received the George Medal.[221] The factory was largely destroyed and five people killed. Nine were injured, including five AFS men.

In Chelsea, twelve people died when a heavy bomb hit Shawfield Street, causing a large crater, demolishing nine houses, and damaging about twenty others so badly they had to be pulled down. Faviell relates the horrific scenes facing the ARP teams in the pitch dark, a cloud of dust hanging over the scene of the incident like a thick fog. The rescue efforts went on all the next day.[222]

Camberwell bus garage was extensively damaged with eleven buses destroyed and another eighteen damaged,

A Heinkel bomber, hit by AA fire, crashed in gardens in Hornchurch, its blazing fuel engulfing an Anderson shelter where three members of the Bird family were killed. Two of the

---

220 http.//www.firemenremembered.co.uk
221 Golden, *Hackney at War* (1995)
222 Faviell, *A Chelsea Concerto* (1957)

aircraft's crew also died in the crash but the other two survived, bailing out a few miles to the east.

2/3 November

In Kent at Bromley, at 10.00 a bomber dived and made a direct hit on the Springfield AFS station, killing two men of a team who had spent the previous night fighting a big fire at Walthamstow.

There were a number of scattered incidents in London, and a number of serious casualties occurred when a single raider released parachute mines on Tilbury Dock; eleven men died aboard the Port of London Authority tugs *Deanbrooke* and *Lea*.

London had its first raid-free night since the Blitz began, marking the end of fifty-seven nights of Blitz, although some sources imply there was further activity and incidents. A slackening off of the Luftwaffe attacks was even noticed by the Prime Minister and could not be entirely attributed to the weather although this was very rainy for the first week of the month.[223]

3/4 November

On a day of poor weather, a lone low-flying Heinkel 111 approached London from the south west, returning the AA fire from batteries at Richmond Park and West Wimbledon with machine-gun fire. Around 13.45 it arrived over Hornsey in north London and dropped three bombs and two oil bombs in the vicinity of Hornsey station. A man was killed and much damage was done to the sidings and track, as well as the footbridge. In this extraordinary attack, the aircraft spent at least fifteen minutes in the area, dropping further bombs in Mountview Road, and machine-gunning the streets and a train travelling between Crouch End and Highgate. Although engaged again by the

223 Colville, *The Fringes. of Power* (1985)

Finsbury Park AA batteries, the Heinkel escaped and returned to base.[224]

4/5 November
Another night when although Luftwaffe activity was slight and scattered, it extended through to daybreak. A large fire broke out at the gasworks in St. Mary Cray, Orpington, two of the gasholders being burnt out, three people killed and another nine injured.[225]

5/6 November
London was under alert from 18.16 to 08.20 although again incidents were scattered and damage not significant. South Lambeth Road school in Lambeth was hit and at least twelve people killed; some of these were stretcher bearers so possibly the building was in use as a first aid post.

In the early hours of 6 November, a 1,000kg bomb fell in The Avenue, Chingford, killing ten people including a family of four Belgian refugees.[226]

6 November
Another long night when casualties were higher than in recent raids, partly due to some unlucky bomb strikes. Twelve policemen and one civilian were killed at a section house (a residential facility for policemen) in Salusbury Road, Kilburn. It received a direct hit and those killed were apparently trapped in the basement shelter. This was the largest number of Metropolitan Police personnel ever to die in any incident, in war or peace. In

224 Travers in *Hornsey Historical Society Bulletin no.33. Home Fires. A North London Suburb at War* (1992)

225 Blake, *Bromley in the Front Line* (2005)

226 Warburton, *Chingford at War* (1946). The Avenue was renamed Chingford Avenue after the war.

all, thirty died in the borough of Willesden – other incidents happened in Granville Road and the North Circular Road. Finchley had thirteen fatal casualties, mainly in Lodge Lane. In the borough of Wandsworth, thirteen firemen and women died when the AFS station in Cavendish Road School in Balham was hit. This is not mentioned by Shaw and Mills, the local historians. There were seven other fatalities in Wandsworth, and many casualties in Barnet, Golders Green, Islington and Wembley.

7 November

The House of Commons met for the first time at Church House in Westminster. This modern building, the headquarters of the Church of England, was only completed and opened in 1940, and had stood up well to a direct hit by a bomb on 14 October, although six people had died. Therefore, it was adjudged to be a much safer venue than the Palace of Westminster, and cabinet meetings were also held there. The House of Commons sat in the Hoare Memorial Hall and the Lords in the Convocation Hall, and there on 21 November King George VI, accompanied by the Queen and the Dukes of Gloucester and Kent, opened the 1940-41 session of Parliament. Throughout the course of the Blitz, Parliament assembled at Church House at various times in November and December 1940, and between April and June 1941, during which time the House of Commons Chamber was destroyed.

In the evening raid which occurred between 19.00 and 01.00, seventy-six people died in London. The railway network suffered much damage. St. Pancras station was badly damaged, the LMS tracks were blocked at Kensal Green, and there were eight incidents on the Southern Region. Twenty people were killed in Wandsworth and twelve in Lambeth, and of other incidents the worst casualty list was probably nine killed at Sheen Court, a block of flats in Mortlake.

8/9 November

About 100 people died in London, in incidents across the capital. Croydon (Sonning Road in Woodside, South Norwood), Ealing and Lambeth had the worst incidents in terms of deaths. In the borough of Ealing twelve people died at incidents at Templeman Road, Hanwell, and in St. Leonard's Road, Ealing. Much damage and many casualties occurred in Hackney, and Kingsland Congregational Church was badly damaged.

9/10 November

Over 150 died according to the Civilian War Dead Roll of Honour. At 10.40, twenty people – railway workers – were killed at Kings Cross goods station in York Way, when bombs caused extensive damage. Further incidents occurred in London in the afternoon and scattered bombing occurred throughout the night. Thirty-seven bombs fell in Beckenham, Bromley and Orpington but the worst incident occurred when a Heinkel bomber, damaged by AA fire, crashed at Bromley Common. Three crew members and one civilian died, and great efforts had to be made to extract others from the debris, despite the presence of thirty unexploded bombs. Sergeant David Grigg of the Metropolitan Police, and Dr Kenneth Tapper, head of Bromley's casualty services were both awarded the George Medal.[227]

'A German aeroplane crashed on two dwelling houses demolishing both and burying the residents. Four persons were rescued, slightly injured. Shortly afterwards, four more bombs were dropped nearby, only a few yards from the Police and Rescue Parties, causing them to suspend operations for a few minutes. When the rescue work was resumed, it was discovered that a number of bombs, several of which were still

---

227 Blake, *Bromley in the Front Line* (2005)

attached to parts of the machine, were amongst the debris. Two more persons were trapped underneath and it was necessary to remove the bombs before they could be extricated'.[228]

Police Sergeant Grigg volunteered to carry the bombs from the wrecked houses and removed three of them from the wreckage. He was about to return for a fourth when it was suspected that one or more were about to explode. Nevertheless, Grigg again entered the wreckage and removed the bomb. The Sergeant then crawled beneath the debris and located one of the trapped victims, who was eventually rescued. Grigg, who had no special knowledge of bombs, showed great courage and devotion to duty'.

'Dr Tapper has on many occasions during enemy air attacks crawled under wreckage to search for and give treatment to injured casualties pinned down by debris. When people were buried beneath the wreckage of a German aeroplane and two houses Dr Tapper gave medical aid to the victims whilst large unexploded bombs were removed. Dr Tapper has shown great gallantry in his efforts to relieve suffering amongst air raid victims'.[229]

10 November

Over 150 people died in London where the main period of bombing activity was between 18.00 and 21.00. Ten people died at the technical college in Denzil Road, Willesden, when at 19.49 the college's shelters were hit. The George Medal was awarded to off-duty ARP Stretcher Bearer Bernard Ireland who rescued four people trapped in a boiler room.[230] The British Empire Medal was awarded to Frederick Palmer, a leader in the Willesden Civil Defence Rescue Service.

---

228 *London Gazette* 7 July 1941
229 *London Gazette* 7 July 1941
230 Whitehead, *Brent's War* (1995)

'Bombs damaged a building, the underground boiler room of which was used as an air raid shelter. A Rescue Party, led by Mr. Palmer, began the work of extricating the occupants. Mr. Ireland, who was off duty, went down into the boiler room and brought out a man who had been rendered unconscious by coal gas. He then returned and rescued a woman. There was a strong concentration of coal gas in the boiler room, and hot water to a depth of a foot. Notwithstanding this Ireland again went back and was instrumental in bringing out another casualty. On reaching the open air he was overcome by the effects of the gas. Recovering, he once again went into the wrecked compartment to make sure that no other person remained. Members of the Rescue Party suffered from gas-poisoning and five of them, including Leader Palmer, collapsed and were taken to hospital. Palmer, however, recovered consciousness on arrival and demanded to be taken back as he remembered that two members of his squad were last seen in the boiler house. When he returned, he found that his men had been taken to hospital. Palmer then organised a search for the recovery of two persons still believed to be entombed'[231].

Fifteen died in Wellington Way, Poplar, at a depot for stretcher bearer parties. Factories at Brentford and Southgate were hit, and railway incidents included serious damage at Bow LPTB station. Scenes of other incidents were the Evelina Children's Hospital in Southwark Bridge Road and the Horne Bros factory in Hackney which was set on fire.

Just after 20.00 in the evening a bomb made a direct hit on the *Morning Star* inn, crowded for a darts match, causing Swanscombe's worst wartime disaster. All that was left after the explosion was a 'heap of bricks and twisted rafters round the gaping hole of the cellar, although the staircase leading

---

231 *London Gazette* 3 October 1941

to the clubroom upstairs extended up out of the wreckage. Distressing scenes occurred as the families of those known to be in the pub at the time gathered at the street corners awaiting news of the casualties as bodies were gradually recovered from the ruins.

The official casualty lists revealed the death toll to be twenty-seven, with six others seriously injured and five people slightly hurt. 'The landlord was amongst the dead, although his wife and son survived. The barmaid who was killed had given notice the week before the raid but had stayed on that evening because of the match. One of the other victims was a merchant seaman on seven days' leave who had spent two days travelling from Scotland to see his wife and children and was having a drink with his father in the pub at the time of the bombing. both were killed.'[232]

11 November

In the late afternoon a solitary intruder aircraft dropped three bombs, one of which hit a printing works in Great Peter Street, Westminster, trapping many people under heavy debris. Twenty-five people were found to have died. Deptford and Lambeth were among a number of places where bombs caused casualties.

12/13 November

An evening raid began at about 18.30. There were heavy casualties across the London region, fatalities occurring in locations as far apart as Acton, Beckenham, Croydon and Kingston upon Thames.

Sloane Square tube station was being rebuilt when war broke out and only the building at the ground floor level had been completed by March 1940 when the station was formally re-

---

232 Rootes, *Front Line County. Kent at War 1939-45* (1980)

THE BOMBING OF LONDON 1940-41

opened. Fortunately, perhaps, as at 21.50 the station was hit by a 1,800kg bomb that demolished the station buildings and caused heavy debris to fall on a departing train, as well as destroying the escalators leading to the platforms. There were thirty-five fatal casualties, and another two died later in hospital. Amongst the casualties were LPTB staff using the station canteen, who suffered appalling injuries. Frances Faviell relates how there were thirty-eight stretchers of human flesh to piece together, and two gallons of disinfectant had to be used.[233]

Faviell, a VAD,[234] received a phone call to report to the Royal Court Hotel where many of the casualties were taken. 'The square presented an amazing sight – two great flaming jets guarded the pit which had once been the station.' Firemen told her that the newly built station had just disappeared into the depths below. This caving in of the station had muffled the sound of the explosion and it was not realised in the hotel that such an incident had happened so close at hand. Fortunately, the bomb did not breach the 8ft diameter pipe that carries the Westbourne River over the station. Rescuers had to access the station via the track from South Kensington, as the flaming gas mains made access from above impossible.

At 20.00 a trolleybus and a bus were hit by a bomb outside 150/152 Lower Clapton Road, Hackney, and a passenger was killed and two others seriously injured. A bomb hit the Granada cinema in Wandsworth Road, Lambeth, and killed eight people, and twenty-one people died at 184 Wandsworth Road; this appears to have been a public shelter but no information about this can be traced although fire brigade records state that houses and a surface shelter were hit in Thorparch Road, which is nearby.

---

233 Faviell, *A Chelsea Concerto* (1957)
234 'a voluntary unit of civilians providing nursing care for military personnel'

13/14 November

13 November saw various daytime Luftwaffe attacks scattered around England. Between 06.00 and 07.00 there was an incendiary attack on Hounslow[235] with Woolworths and other stores being burnt out. There was little other damage in London, and few casualties.

14/15 November

Whilst provincial cities had been the subject of attacks since the summer, they had not been at the centre of Luftwaffe strategy. From November, the Luftwaffe demonstrated its ability to subject smaller cities to raids that turned out to be rather more effective than the nightly blitz on London had become. They were not intended to be 'knockout blows' but their cumulative effect might have been brought more results than chipping away at the vast area of London. The experience for these compact communities was to be different to London's. Coventry with its concentration of key industrial sites in the very city centre was devastated on 14 November; Birmingham, Bristol, Sheffield and Manchester were to receive major attacks in the weeks before Christmas. *Front Line* dubbed this 'the attack on the arms towns.' The Luftwaffe was also increasingly aware of the vulnerability of cities to Sunday night attacks.

On the night of the Coventry Blitz, the Luftwaffe also attacked London. Fifteen AFS firemen were killed when a parachute mine hit Invicta Road School in Greenwich which was used as a fire station. Six died in Deptford and eight at St Mary Abbot's Hospital in Kensington where block 'C' was rendered unusable, and a water main was damaged. Far worse damage and casualties were to be caused at this hospital by a V1 flying bomb in 1944.

---

235 There is film footage of this.

15/16 November

For the first two weeks of November, the Luftwaffe's raids on London had been modest in scale with a low incendiary content in the bomb loads. However, the Luftwaffe followed their raid on Coventry with another heavy raid on London, with only a small number of aircraft being assigned to attack Coventry again. The raid lasted from 17.50 to 04.00 and poor weather affected concentration. 358 Luftwaffe bombers dropped 414 tonnes of bombs and over 41,000 incendiaries, and 142 people were killed and over 430 injured. The material destruction was more notable than the human toll. Some heavy bombs of 1,400 kg and 1,800 kg were used. One such bomb must have been responsible for the devastation in East Finchley when at 22.10 the AFS station on the High Road was demolished and an acre of destruction caused in the streets around. It was several weeks before all casualties were accounted for and all reports of body parts in the debris had been followed up. The final death toll was twelve, which was surprisingly low. Another 1,800kg bomb fell at the GPO's Mount Pleasant sorting office in Finsbury but failed to explode, necessitating evacuation of the building. It was the first occasion on which bomb disposal teams had to tackle this type of bomb and according to James Owen[236] it took over a week to dig it out. It was buried under the nearby underground railway track which made it doubly important to neutralize it. When it was eventually recovered, it was found to have a defective fuse.

In Barnet, a parachute mine fell in Bell's Hill killing seventeen people including residents at the *Oakmere* guest house (some sources say *Oakmere* was an old people's home but this does not appear to be the case). High explosive and incendiary bombs as well as seven parachute mines fell on Enfield at around 22.00. One of the mines fell in London Road near the church of Our

---

236 Owen, *Danger UXB. The Heroic Story* (2010)

Lady and St George, which was damaged beyond repair, and although the convent opposite was wrecked, the nuns escaped with minor injuries. Houses in London Road were badly damaged and some had to be demolished. Shop windows in Enfield Town were shattered and there were injuries from flying glass. At least twelve people were killed.[237] In Loughton, a mine exploded on open land, The Stubbles, the blast causing damage to a very wide area.[238]

Twenty-three people (all but one are women, and include three nurses) are listed in the Civilian War Dead Roll of Honour as dying at Friern Emergency hospital, where a parachute mine fell at 04.04. Together with the incident on 27 September this gives a total of thirty-eight killed in total at the hospital – various sources say forty (thirty-six patients and four nurses) were killed here in 1941, implying a single incident, although presumably the year is wrong. It is unclear whether the victims were existing mental health patients or people admitted with injuries sustained in air raids elsewhere. It is also said that five 'villas' were destroyed, and it is likely that these were accommodating mental health patients. However, during the war the hospital also accommodated people other than air raid casualties as in-patients who were not mental health patients.

Much destruction occurred in Westminster, involving the National Gallery, old houses in the St. James's area, the Wellington Barracks where three people died and the Carlton Hotel. Fires included one at Trafalgar Square and another at a tyre factor's in Rochester Row. A large possibly 1,400kg bomb was defused and recovered from Shaftesbury Avenue.

The highly-decorated Léon Pierre Alphons Dens, a Belgian senator and minister for war, died at the Savoy Hotel this

---

237 Enfield at War https.//enfieldatwar.wordpress.com/
238 Chigwell Urban District Council war damage cards

evening, along with another Belgian subject. Yet another Belgian died at the Carlton Hotel. The Savoy Hotel was hit at 02.15, a bomb detonating on its north eastern corner. Besides the two people killed, the area around room 421 of the hotel suffered major damage.[239] Another bomb fell at the same time outside the Strand Palace Hotel.

Thirty pumps attended a fire at Southampton Buildings in Chancery Lane, the offices of the Westminster Bank. Twenty-two people were killed in Huntingdon Street, Islington, another scene of devastation after a large bomb fell. After this incident, Dr John McCarthy was awarded the OBE for gallantry for treating the injured at the site. Six others were also recognised with awards for their bravery in the incident. Thirteen were killed in Kimberley Avenue, East Ham, and a number of people at the Royal Albert Dock, West Ham. Amongst the buildings hit during the night were the Postal Sorting Office at Croydon, the RAF depot at Wembley exhibition grounds, the Ministry of Labour in Richmond and the National Portrait Gallery. Although this was expected to be a 'full moon night', cloud and rain spread in from the Atlantic and as a result bombing was spread across the London region and beyond. Dagenham, Hornchurch, Ilford and Loughton had incidents with fatalities. Twenty-five people including ten members of the Abbott family were killed at 82 Greyhound Road, Fulham, when a bomb hit a shelter. Two Auxiliary Fire Service personnel were killed at Mansfield Road AFS station in Kentish Town. Beckenham had several incidents, including two parachute mines, as did the small community of Knockholt. Parachute mines in Bournemouth killed thirty people and Chalfont St Peter in Buckinghamshire sustained its only fatalities of the war.

---

239 Westminster City Archives www.westendatwar.org.uk

16/17 November

Eighty-seven aircraft attacked London, the raid falling into two phases – 17.45 to 01.00 and 04.00 to 06.15. Damage was spread over a wide area. One of the boroughs worst affected was Wembley, where fifteen people died in residential roads, although factories and the exhibition grounds were also targeted. Willesden also had fatalities with factories and the Central Middlesex hospital hit and the Ace Café (to become an iconic biker rendezvous after the war) on the North Circular Road totally demolished. The Café's website history[240] insists the raid was targeted on the nearby railway marshalling yards. In Ealing, St. Saviour's Church in The Grove was gutted by incendiary bombs, and although a parachute mine exploded in mid-air over Boileau Road, it caused no casualties[241]. However, there were nineteen fatalities in Ealing at the Golf Clubhouse, in Townholm Crescent and in Felix Road.

In Wandsworth, an oil bomb hit the fire station in West Hill, killing six fire service personnel and causing a large fire. This was the third fire station in Wandsworth to be hit in a month. Bombs also hit Courland Road and Alford Road, causing a further seventeen fatalities. Twenty-two people died in Hackney, mainly at Alkham Road and Northwold Road.

Wimbledon was hit by a number of bombs which fell at the end of the raid at 06.00 causing eight fatalities in Woodside, at Queen Alexandra's Court in St. Mary's Road and in Hartfield Road.

17/18 November

The Luftwaffe's main target was Southampton but forty-nine aircraft were directed to attack the government quarter of London. The attack lasted from 17.55 to 04.56. It appears that

---

240 https.//london.acecafe.com/history/
241 Upton, *Ealing, Acton & Southall at War* (2009)

in addition, three Heinkel 111 aircraft attacked Battersea power station using Y-Gerät. But the actual damage recorded in London indicates that these targets were not accurately bombed.

18/19 November
No major attack took place but London was under siren from 18.05 to 06.10. Southampton, Liverpool and Coventry were also attacked. Thirty men of the King's Own Scottish Borderers were killed when a parachute mine struck their billet at Yates' Retreat in Theydon Bois.

19/20 November
At Dellwood Gardens, Ilford, bomb disposal teams had partially uncovered an unexploded bomb fused with a clockwork time delay. After checking the fuse was not ticking, digging continued to check if another fuse was fitted. As this was being undertaken the bomb detonated and two of the team were killed. Three other men were injured and taken to hospital. It is believed that the vibration caused by the digging may have started the clockwork fuse, or another fuse was fitted which could have been of the anti-disturbance type.[242]

In the evening, there was a major attack on Birmingham with a small force of some fifty aircraft attacking London. Casualties were scattered around different localities in London and included twelve people killed at Levita House, Chalton Street, St. Pancras, seven in Wallington and three in Long Acre, Covent Garden. Four people died at the gas works in Rickmansworth, but damage does not seem to have been significant anywhere. Just before 05.00 a stick of ten bombs fell across Walthamstow killing seven people.

The following week was mainly quiet in the London region.

---

242 Royal Engineers Association

20/21 November

The Luftwaffe's main attack was again on Birmingham, but a secondary attack was made on London by forty-five aircraft. Damage and casualties were insignificant.

21/22 November

No major attacks occurred because of poor weather. About fifteen fatalities were recorded, mainly in north London.

22/23 November

Birmingham was targeted for a third time, with London a subsidiary target, and forty-three aircraft attacked central areas over the period 19.30 to 07.06. Fatalities occurred in Coulsdon and Southall.

23/24 November

As a critical water situation now existed in Birmingham, it was fortunate that the Luftwaffe shifted its attack to Southampton.

24/25 November

The Luftwaffe's main attack was on Bristol. In an early evening raid on London, two bombs fell on Croydon before the alert was sounded. One fell on the Town Hall, destroying the ARP Control Centre but not causing any casualties, as the centre was empty, which would not have been the case had the siren sounded. However, this did not help the response to the other bomb, which fell on the Liberal Club in Scarbrook Road. The building was demolished and twenty-five people – all but seven of those present – were killed, including the stewardess and her daughter.[243] Later there were fatalities in Wimbledon.

For the next two nights Bristol was the subject of small

---

243 Berwick Sayers, *Croydon and the Second World War* (1949)

attacks but overall little or no other activity took place over the UK.

27/28 November
The main attack was on Plymouth with a subsidiary attack on London by sixty-five aircraft. Little damage was done and there were relatively few casualties, but eight people died in Derby Road, Edmonton. Other fatalities occurred in Lambeth. As the attack was in three waves, this must have caused disruption to Londoners' sleep for the whole night.

28/29 November
This was intended to be a major attack on Liverpool but incidents also occurred all over England although London was largely unaffected.

29/30 November
At 19.00 Teddington in the borough of Twickenham was subjected to an intense bombardment unparalleled in the London Blitz. The raid opened with a fall of incendiaries, followed by high explosives, and within the space of half an hour, enormous damage and casualties were caused. At least sixty-one people died, and 150 houses were destroyed and hundreds more damaged. Amongst the serious incidents, the *Willoughby Arms* pub was hit with eight people killed including the licensee and his children, and thirteen people were killed in Shacklegate Lane. Another ten people were killed in Church Road, and the Baptist church in Walpole Road was burnt out. Nine bombs were dropped around the National Physical Laboratory, but although little damage was caused to this institution, the bombs killed eight people at the public trench shelter in the grounds. A huge blaze at the Baltic timber yard could be seen for miles. Bombs also fell in Twickenham itself

blocking the railway to Whitton and blocking Waldegrave Road with a large crater.[244]

This raid was too concentrated to be regarded as indiscriminate and it was certain to have been a deliberate attack on the National Physical Laboratory, and possibly also Tough Bros boatyard, and as Richmond was also heavily bombed, with twenty-five killed, Richmond Park. As such it was an effective raid: all three locations were undertaking vital government research and contracts. In Richmond, the Town Hall was hit by a bomb and the building was gutted by fire. The Public Library was also damaged and eight people died at the shelter at the British Legion Poppy Factory, and others at Eton Street, Townshend Road and Sheen Park.[245] In St. Margaret's, 'Mr and Mrs Sydney Clark and their dog were killed by the sheer concussion of a large bomb 5 feet high and 18 inches wide that crashed into their dining room. The bomb failed to explode'. The Beaumont Furniture Works in Beaumont Road, St. Margaret's was set on fire.[246] Fifteen were killed in the neighbouring borough of Sunbury on Thames, eleven in Feltham and eight at East Sheen in the borough of Barnes. In fact, the raid was concentrated on this part of south-west London and most of the 190 fatalities that night occurred in this area. The all clear sounded at 23.15.

THE FIRST THREE MONTHS OF THE LONDON BLITZ

After the first six weeks of the Blitz, public pressure and feedback from many sources led to the setting up of the Horder committee

244 Barnfield, *When the Bombs Fell* (2001)
245 Fowler, *Richmond at War 1939-1945* (2015)
246 St Margaret's community website https.//stmargarets.london/

of enquiry (Lord Horder was chairman of the British Medical Association (BMA)) to investigate conditions in the tubes and shelters. Titmuss[247] was aware of a race between the rate of damage and the rate at which people were rehoused. Initially people had to be transferred out of the East End to relieve pressure on the rest centres, but not all were willing to move out of a familiar neighbourhood. Large numbers of people had been forced to leave their homes because of UXBs rather than bomb damage. By the end of September, over 25,000 people were in rest centres in London, over 14,000 of them in the LCC area. Probably about a third of these had been displaced by UXBs, and these were not therefore casualties or suffering any material loss. The disruption caused by UXBs was enormous and not brought under control until after three months. As a result of the action taken by the end of September, even the severest critics saw a substantial improvement in the London rest centres.

An appreciation report was drawn up by the Research and Experiments department of the Ministry of Home Security and was based on an analysis of three months (September/October/November 1940) of the London Blitz, and also details the lessons learned. It is a quite scientific and detached analysis which does not touch on the human suffering.[248]

In September 1940 two groups of LCC boroughs had a bombing density rate of more than one high explosive bomb per ten acres. One group comprised the City, Holborn, Stepney, Shoreditch, Bethnal Green, Southwark, Bermondsey and Deptford. Of these, Stepney had the highest density at two bombs per ten acres. The other group was Chelsea and Fulham. In October, the densities were lower with only Holborn, Shoreditch and Bethnal Green recorded as having one bomb

---

247 Titmuss, *Problems of Social Policy* (1950)
248 TNA HO186/1862

per ten acres. In November the City, Holborn, Westminster, Chelsea, Stepney, Shoreditch, Bethnal Green, Bermondsey and Finsbury were the heaviest bombed but they only recorded a density of eight bombs per 100 acres.

No systematic bombing of objectives was noted except in daylight raids. The 'factory zones' of London were said to be little affected although these zones are not defined. The intensity of attack was adjudged insufficient once a switch took place away from the docks to more general targets. Although bombing was effective it was far less in terms of tonnage dropped than claimed and it was stressed that the figures as claimed by German sources should not be used as a basis for defence planning.

It was estimated that 3,440 tons of high explosive or 10,120 bombs were dropped on London in the three months. The effects were analysed as transient or durable. The transient effects were morale, which was seen mainly as down to a 'surprise' factor, plus general disruption to utilities, railways and UXBs. The durable effects were the 13,000 killed, 50,000 injured, and the 20,000 houses destroyed.

The Ministry of Home Security did not gain the same perception of parachute mines as did the public. When a mine fell within 15ft of a concrete shelter or within 30ft of an Anderson shelter, the investigators were impressed that the inhabitants survived. The exceptions were the badly constructed surface shelters. But the extensive damage to windows and the discomfort factor the mines created was acknowledged.

It was also acknowledged that the number of UXBs was much exaggerated in the first few weeks of the Blitz but the development of effective bomb disposal squads had helped reduce reports to realistic levels. Around 7% of bombs dropped failed to explode and most UXBs were found to be duds.

Much research went into assessing the effects of high explosive bombs on buildings and people. Most bombs that did not strike buildings penetrated 10ft before exploding, as did many that did in fact strike buildings. In the bomb crater everything would be destroyed and the movement caused would demolish buildings. Damage fell into two categories.

1. Primary. the immediate destruction caused by the bomb
2. Secondary. the collapse of the building. The effect of this was worst in tall buildings without a frame structure of reinforced concrete or steel. Halls, churches and theatres were particularly poor. Buildings heavily constructed in brick e.g. public buildings, hospitals and offices led to serious difficulties in rescue and recovery. Framed buildings were immune from all but a direct hit although Whiteley's department store in Bayswater was hit by a 1,400kg bomb and survived without any structural damage, as did Broadway House in Tothill Street, Westminster.

A 50kg bomb which hit a railway arch shelter (presumably this is the Druid Street shelter incident) killed 105 people and injured 58 – virtually everyone who was in the shelter.

In November, 27% of shelterers occupied brick-built public surface shelters. But it is interesting that twenty-two out of thirty such shelters destroyed were unoccupied at the time.

Trench shelters, said the report, 'behaved badly' when bombed and very few were still in occupation by the time the report was drawn up. Wooden and precast liners were particularly vulnerable and likely to lead to the roofs of such shelters collapsing. Basement shelters were likely to be dangerous if bombs burst at the side or in the road outside or in neighbouring buildings. Large unframed buildings had been the scene of 'disasters' (defined as incidents where 20 or more were killed).

Casualties were divided into:

1. Primary – as a direct result of the explosion.
2. Secondary – knocked over or thrown about by blast.
3. Tertiary – by debris/collapse of the building. This caused most casualties but they were not always fatal.
4. Quaternary – by drowning, escape of gas, burns.

Ministry of Home Security statistics showed that on average one ton of bombs destroyed ten houses, rendered twenty-five uninhabitable and slightly damaged eighty. It made eighty people temporarily homeless and thirty-five permanently so (this would have included the fatalities). On average one ton of bombs would have killed six people and wounded twenty-five.

The Ministry of Home Security also looked at a number of the largest 'disasters' that occurred in the three months:

1. Morley College. A 1,000kg bomb hit an old building used as a rest centre and exploded in the reception rooms that were housing 195 refugees. Fifty-seven were killed and fifty-four seriously injured. This adult education college clearly should not have been used as a rest centre.
2. Columbia Market. This was a 'strutted basement' shelter. Although it was seen as unlucky that the bomb entered via a light well the effect would have been no different if it had been a direct hit as the casualties – thirty-eight killed and thirty-eight seriously injured – were all a result of blast and splinters.
3. Druid Street Arch. Of the 200 in the shelter, 105 were killed and seventy-five seriously injured by blast and splinters.
4. Kennington Park trenches. A 300 ft length of a trench

was destroyed killing forty-seven and seriously injuring twenty-one. This trench comprised precast slabs that collapsed.

5. Stoke Newington Road. A 500 or 1000kg bomb hit the building which collapsed into two of the three basement shelter compartments, each housing 100 shelterers. All those in the first compartment died. Some bodies were found around the exits but no reference is made in the analysis to the alleged drowning of the victims. However, thirty escaped from the second compartment. This was another 'strutted basement' where the strutting was supported on brickwork which collapsed.

6. Whiteley's. The bomb penetrated to the basement of this department store and disintegrated a brick wall between the bomb and the shelter. Seventeen were killed but if the wall had been reinforced concrete rather than brick they might have survived. No collapse of the building occurred.

7. Bounds Green station. A (probably) 500kg bomb penetrated 10ft below ground and exploded causing a collapse of the platform tunnel roof, opening a 20ft by 10ft hole. Twenty-three were killed and twenty-six seriously injured.

The Ministry of Home Security also analysed forty-one 'disasters' during the three months. See appendix B.

In summary, the problems were that most Blitz bombing incidents had to be dealt with in darkness, there were fewer casualties than expected but more rescue, repair and clearance work was required. Obtaining details of building occupants was often a problem.

This report wasn't published until February 1941 by which time the nature of the Blitz had changed and provincial cities were increasingly the focus for Luftwaffe attacks. Many lessons had been learnt and much remedial action was instigated and led by the special commissioners appointed in October 1940.

SEVEN

THE GREAT FIRE, DECEMBER 1940

Poor weather meant that the Luftwaffe could only attack the UK on sixteen nights during December. Three 'major' (100 or more tons of HE) attacks were made on London, but no 'other large' (50-99 tons) attacks. 625 tons of HE and 4,129 IB canisters in all were dropped on London according to German sources. On 2 December, the *Daily Express* announced 'London Blitz switched to Southampton.' Two raids on Southampton were later to generate great controversy about the ability of that city to cope and the effect on the morale of its civilians. However, the attack soon switched back to other targets including London.

3 December
Five died at the LMS Queen's Park Station in Willesden when at 22.07 a bomb fell blocking all lines and damaging the station buildings. All lines were restored the next day. Over thirty

people died at 49 Queen Caroline Street, Hammersmith, and the Home Security Situation Report states that there was a direct hit on a shelter, believed to be that at St. Vincent's convent at the above address. Other fatalities occurred in Leyton, Paddington and Wembley. In Woodford, bombs fell in Nelson Road, Woodford Road and Eagle Lane, but only damaged road surfaces. Later the same night, houses in Wellington Road and Elmcroft Avenue were badly damaged by bombs, but no fatalities occurred.

4 December
About forty-two aircraft attacked London between 18.20 and 23.29. The results of the raid were insignificant but two wardens were killed when a bomb hit their post in Beckenham, and eight people died in Watford.

5 December
London was the target of a subsidiary raid, Portsmouth being the main target. A number of suburbs were affected and five people died in Spearpoint Gardens, Ilford, and a similar number at a shelter in Croydon.

8/9 December
This intense raid was the heaviest on London for two months and was said to be revenge for the bombing of Düsseldorf by the RAF the previous night. In London, 250 people were killed and over 600 were seriously injured. 413 aircraft dropped 387 tons of high explosive and 115,000 incendiaries, a record number. The raid lasted from 18.12 to 06.35 and nine major and twenty-four serious fires were started. Many parachute mines were dropped and caused heavy casualties and damage in a number of locations. The raid was concentrated on the inner-city boroughs, most incidents occurring in Lewisham, Lambeth, Finsbury, Islington,

Hackney, Bermondsey, Stepney, St. Marylebone, Southwark, Shoreditch and Poplar.

One parachute mine landed outside the BBC in Portland Place, St. Marylebone. A Mr L Macgregor, a member of the BBC's staff recorded a vivid account of this incident. The actual recording has not survived but a transcript is in the BBC's archives:

On the night of 8th December, 1940, I left the B.B.C. shortly after 10.45 and accompanied by a colleague, Mr Sibbick, went to the cycle shed in Chapel Mews. The customary nightly air-raid was in progress, and as we left the cycle shed, we could hear the distant sound of aircraft and A.A. gunfire. We were just entering Hallam Street from the mews when I heard a shrieking whistling noise like a large bomb falling. The noise continued for about three seconds, and then abruptly ceased as if in mid-air. There was no thud, explosion or vibration. I particularly remember this, as I'd heard this happen once before, and was curious as to what caused it and why it stopped. Then came the sound of something clattering down the roof of a building in the direction of Broadcasting House. I looked up thinking it might be incendiaries, but this was not so. We slowly walked round to the entrance of Broadcasting House, and I estimate we took about three and a half minutes in doing so. My colleague went inside, returned the cycle shed keys, cycled off towards Oxford Circus. I remained outside the entrance, talking to two policemen, and enquiring about possible diversions on my route home. Their names were Vaughan and Clarke. A saloon car was parked alongside the kerb some distance round from the entrance, and I could see to the left of the car the lamp-post in the middle of the road opposite the Langham Hotel.

The policemen had their backs to this, so did not observe what followed. Whilst we were conversing, I noticed a large, dark, shiny object approach the lamp-post and then recede – I concluded that it was a taxi parking. It made no noise. The night was clear, with a few small clouds. There was moonlight from a westerly direction, but Portland Place was mainly in shadow. All three of us were wearing our steel helmets; my chinstrap was round the back of my head, as I had been advised to wear it shortly after I was issued with the helmet.

A few seconds later I saw what seemed to be a very large tarpaulin of a drab or khaki colour fall on the same spot; the highest part of it was about ten or twelve feet above the road when I first saw it, and it seemed to be about twenty-five feet across. It fell at about the speed of a pocket handkerchief when dropped, and made no noise. Repair work was being carried out on Broadcasting House and I, not unnaturally, concluded that it was a tarpaulin which had become detached and had fallen from the building into the roadway. There were no other warnings of any imminent danger. I drew the attention of the policemen to it. They turned round and could see nothing. It had collapsed, and from where we were it was partly screened by the car, and the roadway at that point was in shadow. They told me they could not see anything. Then followed some banter, but I persisted in saying that I had seen something fall in the road. Then they decided to go to investigate. A third policeman, Mortimer, had meanwhile approached us – he was about to conduct a lady across that part of the road. But after hearing that I'd seen something he told me he was taking her inside the building while they found out what it was. Vaughan drew ahead of Clarke, who stopped at the kerb to ask me just exactly where it had dropped. I went towards him, calling out that I would show him it. It was about a minute since I'd seen the dark object. I went towards the tarpaulin and had reached a spot to the left of Clarke about six feet from the curb, and twenty-five to thirty feet from 'the thing', when Vaughan came running towards me at high speed. He shouted something I did not hear. At that moment, there was a very loud swishing noise, as if a plane was diving with engine cut off – or like a gigantic fuse burning. It lasted about three or four seconds; it did not come from the lamp-post end of 'the thing' but it may have come from the other end.

Vaughan passed me on my left and Clarke, who apparently had understood the shout, also ran towards the building. Realising that I would have to turn right about before I could start running, I crouched down in what is known as 'prone-falling position no.1.' Even at that moment I did not imagine that there was any danger in the road, and thought it was coming from above, up Portland Place. My head was up watching, and before I could reach 'position no.2' and lie down flat 'the thing' in the road exploded. I had a momentary glimpse of a large ball of blinding, white light and two concentric rings of colour, the inner one lavender and the outer one violet, as I ducked my head. The ball seemed to be ten to twenty feet high, and was near the lamp-post. Several things happened simultaneously. My head was jerked back due to a heavy blow on the dome and rim of the back of my steel helmet, but I do not remember this, for, as my head went back, I received a severe blow on my forehead and bridge of my nose. The blast bent up the front rim of my helmet and knocked it off my head. The explosion made an indescribable noise –

something like a colossal growl – and was accompanied by a veritable tornado of air blast. I felt an excruciating pain in my ears, and all sounds were replaced by a very loud singing noise, which I was told later was when I lost my hearing and had my eardrums perforated. I felt that consciousness was slipping from me, and that moment I heard a clear loud voice shouting. 'Don't let yourself go! Face up to it – hold on.' It rallied me, and summoning all my willpower and energy I succeeded in forcing myself down into a crouching position with my knees on the ground and my feet against the curb behind me and my hands covering my face.

I remember having to move them over my ears because of the pain in them, doubtless due to the blast. This seemed to ease the pain. Then I received another hit on the forehead and felt weaker. The blast seemed to come in successive waves, accompanied by vibrations from the ground. I felt as if it were trying to spin me and clear me away from the kerb. Then I received a very heavy blow just in front of the right temple which knocked me down flat on my side, in the gutter. Later, in our first-aid post, they removed what they described as a piece of bomb from that wound. Whilst in the gutter I clung onto the curb with both hands and with my feet against it. I was hit again in the right chest, and later found my double-breasted overcoat, my coat, leather comb-case and papers had been cut through, and the watch in the top right-hand pocket had the back dented in and its works broken.

Just as I felt I could not hold on much longer, I realised that the blast pressure was decreasing and a shower of dust, dirt and rubble swept across me. Pieces penetrated my face, some skin was blown off, and something pierced my left thumbnail and my knuckles were cut, causing me involuntarily to let go my hold on the kerb. Instantly, although the blast was dying down, I felt myself being slowly blown across the pavement towards the wall of the building. I tried to hold on but there was nothing to hold on to. Twice I tried to rise but seemed held down. Eventually I staggered to my feet. I looked around and it seemed like a scene from Dante's Inferno. The front of the building was lit by a reddish-yellow light; the saloon car was on fire to the left of me, and the flames from it were stretching out towards the building, and not upwards; pieces of brick, masonry and glass seemed to appear on the pavement, making, to me, no sound; a few dark huddled bodies were round about, and right in front of me were two soldiers; one, some feet from a breach in the wall of the building where a fire seemed to be raging, was propped up against the wall with his arms dangling by him, like a rag doll. The other was nearer, about twelve feet from the burning car; he was sitting up with his knees drawn up and supporting himself by his arms – his trousers had been blown off him. I could see that his legs were bare and that he was wearing short grey underpants. He was alive and conscious. He appeared to be shouting for assistance. I made for the entrance of the building to get help … it was obscured by dust, smoke and fumes and I nearly fell over a large steel plate which had fallen down and was blocking the entrance. I shouted for help several times, and then realised that no one could get out until the obstruction had been removed. Fearing that the car's tank might explode and envelop the injured soldier in flames, I hurried back to him and, with him clinging to me, we were able to reach the entrance where he sat down as entry was still blocked.

I told him to hang onto an upright at the entrance and to shout like hell for assistance should he see or hear anyone approaching. I went back to look at the other soldier. He was still in the same posture and I fear that he was dead. I looked around. There was a long, dark body lying prone, face downwards close to the kerb in front of the building – it may have been Vaughan. There appeared to be one or two dark, huddled bodies by the wall of the building. I had not the strength to lift any of them. I wondered where the water was coming from which I felt dripping down my face, and soon discovered that it was blood from my head wounds. I could see no movement anywhere, and thought I would look round for my steel helmet and gas mask, which I had slung round me at the time of the explosion. I soon found the gas mask and picked up a steel helmet which was not my own.

I was then joined by my colleague who had returned, and went with him to the entrance where I shouted for assistance for those outside, and for someone to bring fire-fighting appliances to put out the car fire, as I was afraid the glare would bring down more bombs.

I walked down to our First Aid Post, where I was treated and then to Listening Hall 1 where I rested until I was taken away by the stretcher party and sent to the Middlesex Hospital. Here I received every possible attention and kindness. Later on I was told that 'the thing' had been a land mine, and that its explosion or blast had lasted for nine seconds. The effect of the blast on my clothes is possibly of interest, I was wearing bicycle clips round the bottoms of my trousers at the time; after the blast was over my double-breasted overcoat was slit up the back and torn in several places, but was held together by the belt. My trousers and underpants were pitted with small cuts about an inch long, but presumably the bicycle clips had prevented the draught getting up my trousers and tearing them off. A woollen scarf, which was knotted around my neck, undoubtedly saved my neck and chest from small fragments such as were removed from my face, which was not covered.[249]

Mr Macgregor was very fortunate to survive; the police constable, John Vaughan, was killed. The next day's newspapers – although not mentioning the BBC by name – stated that almost every window in the building was broken and many people were injured by flying glass.

All Souls, Langham Place, a distinctive Anglican church commissioned by George IV, designed by Regency architect John Nash and opened in 1824, was damaged by blast from this parachute mine as was the Langham Hotel; the roof of the church was wrecked and its clock tower and Gothic-style spire damaged. No casualties were reported although the Verger and his wife – Mr and Mrs Deham – were badly shaken. Damage was such that the church wasn't re-opened for worship until 1951.[250]

The Langham Hotel in Portland Place is a large Victorian hotel, opened in 1865. In the blast from the mine at the BBC, four floors of the Langham's east wing were destroyed, killing a guest in one of the bathrooms. Fire then broke out on the hotel's roof and its main water tank burst, flooding the building in many places. Fires also burned in surrounding buildings in Langham Place.[251]

Over twenty people died at Maybury Mansions in Marylebone Street, four blocks with a total of seventy flats, built in 1900. At 22.55 two of the blocks with thirty-six flats were demolished by a parachute mine. The blocks were reduced to a mass of rubble which filled the basement and reached up

249 BBC Written Archives Centre Document R49-321
250 Westminster City Archives www.westendatwar.org.uk
251 Westminster City Archives www.westendatwar.org.uk

to the second floor and spilled into the street. The other two blocks were badly damaged. This was an unusual incident in that a number of complaints were subsequently lodged against the civil defence services and the police. Complaints were made concerning the rescue efforts, primarily that there appeared to be a lack of diligence and that the efforts were called off too early when further casualties might have been rescued. Dissatisfaction with the response from the local authority led to the Regional Commissioner ordering an enquiry. This was very thorough and concluded with a number of action points for future incidents. It seems that there was a lack of co-operation between the police and the rescue squads but various other circumstances conspired to give wrong impressions. Also, there was fire in one part of the site, a gas leak in another and unsafe walls, and the emergency services were hard-pressed as a result of earlier incidents.[252]

The major incident in St. Marylebone was at Druce's Depository (Druce & Co Ltd), a large furniture and upholstery showroom and warehouse located at the corner of Baker Street and Blandford Street, a very large site. It was hit by incendiaries and gutted by the ensuing fire. The adjoining streets were sealed off until the fire was controlled and debris and shattered glass cleared. No casualties were reported but the building suffered serious fire and structural damage and its contents – bedding, furniture, carpets, antiques and decorations – were largely destroyed.[253] What was left of the building was destroyed on 10/11 May 1941, although Collier seems to imply that the critical fire occurred on the latter date.[254]

At 19.20 a train was hit by a bomb at Caledonian Road & Barnsbury station, killing four passengers and one railwayman,

---

252 TNA HO 186/641
253 Westminster City Archives www.westendatwar.org.uk
254 Collier, *The City that wouldn't Die. London May 10-11, 1941* (1959)

and injuring eight others. All lines of this important cross-London freight link were closed until the following afternoon. The Waterloo and City line was put out of action by a bomb which fell outside Waterloo mainline station and penetrated the tunnel. Such was the damage (an enormous crater at the foot of the steps) the service could not be restored until 3 March. Marylebone station, (where a bomb fell at the end of platforms 1 & 2), and Fenchurch Street station (where one bomb demolished the signal gantry at Leman Street and another damaged a bridge) were also temporarily put out of action. A parachute mine at London Bridge Station was successfully defused by a naval officer, thus avoiding huge destruction.

Amongst buildings damaged were the Royal Mint, where three people were killed, the Ministry of Pensions in John Islip Street, the Port of London Authority building and Southwark Town Hall. At the Palace of Westminster, extensive damage was caused by two bombs – a high explosive and an oil bomb – which hit the cloisters and the Members' cloakroom. A bomb fell in Cloister Court near Westminster Hall causing considerable damage, and the Lollards' Tower at Lambeth Palace was set on fire by incendiaries. The John Bull arch in Bermondsey was the scene of another shelter incident, fifteen people being killed. Many of the historic buildings of Greenwich were damaged, bombs falling on the National Maritime Museum, the Royal Naval College and the Greenwich Observatory. Albert William Brittan, of the Greenwich Rescue Service, was awarded the George Medal for his bravery in releasing victims trapped in a bombed house in Charlton Lane. In Woolwich, Siemens suffered another large fire and Lewisham was hit by three parachute mines and thirty-seven other high explosive bombs.

Churches hit include All Hallows Barking near the Tower of London, known for its Toc H connections, which was severely damaged along with the neighbouring Mazawattee tea company's unloved building. Incendiaries in a later raid in December reduced the church to a shell. In the Middle Temple, the library was seriously damaged by a parachute mine. Its large oriel window was destroyed, stained glass was blown in, many bookcases smashed or splintered and books scattered amongst earth, broken glass and rubble – it was later estimated that approximately 50,000 books had to be retrieved and cleaned.[255]

In Finsbury, a large amount of destruction occurred in Rydon Place, where eighteen houses were severely damaged, St. John Street and Rosebery Avenue, where Sadler's Wells Theatre was also damaged. Also in Finsbury, ten people were killed at blocks G and H of Peabody Buildings in Farringdon Road. A large number of fires was caused by incendiaries in Finsbury and other central areas although few casualties were recorded. The public baths in Ironmonger Row, Finsbury, the premises of Nurdin & Peacock in Wells Street off Oxford Street, where an NFS man was killed, the United Services Club in Pall Mall and the City church of St. Mary-le-Bow were all damaged by fire. Tottenham Court Road also had several fires.

A large number of fires were caused by incendiaries in Blackheath, Lewisham, New Cross and Peckham, Camberwell, Eltham, East Dulwich and Forest Hill. Having survived an incendiary attack on 19 October, St. John's Church in East Dulwich was severely damaged and burnt out. Ten pumps were called to the Minet Library in Knatchbull Road, Camberwell which was also severely damaged. St. Giles' Hospital in Camberwell was hit with A Block being demolished and four people killed. Thirty pumps were called to office and stores premises in Brixton Road and there were fires at the South-Western Police Court in Balham High Road and Tooting Graveney LCC Schools. The brewing industry in Southwark

---

255 http://www.cilip.org.uk/

suffered badly, with fires occurring at Barclay's and Jenner's breweries, and also at Gaskin's, the hop factors. In Lambeth, forty-seven people died in major incidents in St. Lawrence Road, Mostyn Road, Montford Place and Eastcote Street. At the Lambeth Hospital in Brook Drive, D Block and the chapel were severely damaged. Thirteen people were injured when a bomb struck the railway arches in Hercules Road. St. John's Church, Waterloo was struck by a bomb that tore off the roof and wrecked the interior. The vicar and 150 of his parishioners, who were sheltering in the crypt, escaped injury.

But there was also bombing in the outer suburbs of London. Ealing had serious incidents and in West Ealing fourteen people died and seventy-five were injured when a parachute mine fell between Hartington Road and Broughton Road.[256] A further mine, dropped in Endsleigh Road, failed to explode. Serious incidents also occurred in Woodford. 'The final raid of the year, on the evening of December 8th, saw yet more tragedy befall the boroughs. Just after 7pm a high explosive bomb fell in St. Albans Road, killing three people. And at 10.25pm a paramine was dropped on Wordsworth Avenue, South Woodford, killing 14 people and injuring 41'.[257]

Nine firemen were killed at the Gainsborough Road school in West Ham, which was apparently being used as an AFS station. In Romford, the telephone exchange was partially destroyed by a parachute mine and the gas works was struck by three bombs that ignited two of the gasholders. Two members of the gas works staff, engineer John Grayston and Bert Poole, shift foreman, received the George Medal for their efforts in extinguishing the blaze under very difficult circumstances.

'When bombs were dropped near a group of gasholders,

---

256 Upton, *Ealing, Acton & Southall at War* (2009)
257 https.//wansteadmeteo.com/2015/07/31/75th-anniversary-of-the-blitz-in-wanstead/

fragments penetrated in several places, and the return main was fractured. The escaping gas from some of the fractures was ignited and, as unconsumed gas was escaping from other fractures, there was a grave possibility of a serious explosion. With complete disregard for their personal safety, Grayston, who had been blown to the ground with the force of the explosion, and Poole, entered the blazing premises. This entailed passing over a timber platform, fifteen feet above the ground, which was actually on fire. Grayston and Poole succeeded in closing the main inlet and outlet valves of the damaged purifiers and thus the Fire Brigade were able to deal with the fire on the premises without danger from escaping gas. When Grayston and Poole had finished this operation, their clothes were on fire. Fragments from the second bomb pierced a gasholder in over twenty places and more than half of these ignited. Grayston, accompanied by two labourers, ascended the gasholders and, working from ladders, succeeded after many attempts in extinguishing all ignited gas and stopping the leaks in the two holders. In the course of this work, Grayston fell into the tank of the larger of the holders and was dragged out by one of the workmen. Repair work was continued under the leadership of Grayston and Poole throughout the night and during most of the time aircraft were overhead, bombs were being dropped and gunfire was almost continuous.'[258]

Parachute mines also fell on the Romford brewery and on the ARP depot in Oldchurch Road; there were six fatalities in Romford. Gasholders were also set on fire at Carshalton and Mitcham.

10 December

All the members of a bomb disposal squad – an officer and six

---

258 *London Gazette* 24 January 1941

men – were killed in Chestnut Avenue in Bushy Park, Teddington when attempting to defuse a bomb that had probably fallen in the raid of 29 November.

11 December

For two nights, the weather had prevented the Luftwaffe launching any raids. 11 December however was a moonlit night and the Luftwaffe attacked Birmingham, but London was one of a number of other locations where incidents occurred. Over twenty people died in Westminster, when at 22.30 a bomb hit a sub-surface shelter next to a block of flats in Page Street. Sansom relates how more people than usual had gathered in this shelter because of a noisy dispute about who could use the shelter[259]. A 1,800kg bomb which fell near the Serpentine in Hyde Park failed to explode. Its recovery from the marshy ground was a major challenge for the bomb disposal team, and in fact took three months. At 22.40 a bomb dropped on the Hovis Flour Mill at 147-149 Grosvenor Road, on the north bankside wharves south of Vauxhall Bridge. This bomb completely destroyed the mill (built in 1912), spilling debris and equipment into the Thames and onto an adjacent barge. The building's entire foundations were shifted and the majority of its facilities, including the laboratory, joiners' shop, mills stores, electric stores, small offices, part of the gantry and saw bridge were completely demolished. In addition, about 70ft of the embankment wall was destroyed, which was of some concern to the river authorities. No one was working in the mill at the time and no casualties were reported[260]. At another incident seven people died in Mayfield Road, Acton. The following night the Luftwaffe made a concentrated attack on Sheffield.

---

259 Sansom, *The Blitz. Westminster at War* (1990)
260 Westminster City Archives www.westendatwar.org.uk

13 December
Captain Max Blaney, along with another Royal Engineers officer, a staff-sergeant, a lance-corporal, five sappers and a police inspector were tragically killed in Manor Park when a bomb which they were endeavouring to render safe exploded in their midst. The bomb had fallen five days earlier at 590 Romford Road. Max Blaney was posthumously awarded the George Cross for his bomb disposal work.

14 December
Luftwaffe operations were limited by fog but in the early evening two parachute mines were dropped on Chatham, causing a great deal of damage to houses and killing fifteen people.

16 December
In the morning two bombs fell at the Sidney Burnell School in Highams Park, although no warning had been sounded. There were no casualties and only slight damage.

17/18 December
No Luftwaffe operations took place over the UK.

21/22 December
The Luftwaffe carried out a second major attack on Liverpool and Birkenhead. A few aircraft attacked London, one dropping a very heavy bomb on the railway tracks outside Victoria station at 18.52. This was a 'Max', the Luftwaffe's 2,500 kg bomb, a recent development and evidently very expensive as only certain crews were authorised to drop this bomb, and it was reserved for use on specific targets. Invariably it was dropped during special sorties by the authorised aircraft and crews and not during a general air raid, and the Y-Gerät equipment was used. This was the first 2,500 kg bomb to be dropped on the UK, although to

William Sansom, writing his account of Westminster's war in 1947, it was clearly still a mystery. Like the Hendon bomb of February 1941, it was observed as apparently being on fire as it slowly descended. Its explosion was massive and one eye witness said 'it sounded as though they had dropped a *train*'.[261] Vere Hodgson in Notting Hill heard that it was a bomber which had crashed with all its bombs, a scenario also reported by others. It caused immense damage to the railway outside Victoria station which is assumed to have been the target. The central signal box was demolished and lines blocked, there was huge damage to signalling and telecommunication cabling and many buildings up to half a mile from the explosion suffered bad blast damage. There were fifty-seven serious casualties but fortunately only three deaths. Repairs were not complete until 9 January, personnel from Westinghouse[262] and the Royal Corps of Signals having to be drafted in to assist railway staff.

22/23 December
23/24 December

The Luftwaffe hit Manchester very hard in a double attack on that city. As a result, 200 London firemen were sent to Manchester on 24 December to assist local firefighters. A few aircraft attacked London on 23/24 December, and at about 21.00 a stick of bombs hit the New Cross area. The *Railway Tavern* received a direct hit and fifteen people enjoying a pre-Christmas drink were killed, with many more seriously injured. Damage was also done to the railway at New Cross Gate. In Willesden, Neasden power station was damaged and a worker killed, and damage was also done to LNER and LPTB property.

---

261 Sansom, *The Blitz. Westminster at War* (1990)
262 The signals division of the Westinghouse Brake and Signal Company was responsible for the signalling equipment of most British railway companies.

A Christmas 'truce' (Mortimer says this was brokered by the German Embassy in Washington[263]) is said to have led to no bombs falling on the UK between 24 and 26 December. The diary of Generalfeldmarschall Erhard Milch (As Air Inspector General, Milch was in charge of aircraft production) states this was on the specific orders of Hitler, but there seems little evidence that it was officially sanctioned by either side. The weather in any case was poor and would have restricted operations.

27 December

Although the attacking force was relatively small (156), this was quite a heavy and effective raid, commencing at 18.45 with the all clear sounding at 22.32. Many casualties occurred, and fourteen were killed, in Silver Street, Edmonton. Here, a parachute mine fell, blocking the street and causing extensive damage to neighbouring streets and the North Middlesex Hospital. According to Ramsey, a shelter in Southwark was hit with fifty casualties but no fatalities are recorded by the Civilian War Dead Roll of Honour.[264] Casualties were also recorded in Finsbury, at the Amias House shelter in Central Street where nine were killed and in Hackney where twenty-seven were killed in Middleton Road, Glaskin Road and Oldhill Street. In Deptford twenty were killed, all at the New Cross tram depot, which was seriously damaged. In Tottenham thirteen people were killed by a parachute mine at Asplins Road, and forty were taken to hospital. At 20.17 two parachute mines caused extensive damage in Heron Road, Conley Road and Essex Road, Willesden, over 100 houses being destroyed and many people being made homeless. There were nine fatalities. Two pairs of heavy bombs fell in Walthamstow at 20.20 causing extensive

---

263 Mortimer, *The Longest Night* (2005)
264 Ramsey, *The Blitz Then and Now vol.2* (1988)

damage and four fatalities. Seven died in Easebourne Road, Barking, and Romford received two parachute mines, one of which failed to explode.

Damage was also done to bus garages in Chelsea, Dalston and Nunhead. Damage to railways included a tunnel collapse caused by a bomb at Tulse Hill, which was not cleared until 10 January, and fires were also widespread. Warwick House in Salisbury Square, the headquarters of the publishers Ward Lock & Co was damaged, and two nights later what remained was to be burnt out by incendiaries.

This raid was on a similar scale, both in terms of aircraft participating and bombs dropped, to the raid two nights later, but in terms of destruction was far less significant. The concentration by the pathfinder force was clearly not as good. However, it does not seem there was any intention that the 27 December raid was to be continued with further sorties by the participating aircraft.

29 December 1940 – 'the Second Great Fire of London'

This was the night when the Luftwaffe carried out a devastating fire raid on the City of London. Worsening weather at French airfields fortunately prevented the Luftwaffe returning for a second attack that night. Three conflagrations developed in the City – to the north of St. Paul's, to the south east of the cathedral, and in the Minories area. Some sources give other totals for the number of conflagrations that occurred (O'Brien states six), but there is no doubt that the fire situation was extremely serious. On a Sunday night, the mainly business and commercial area of the City of London was deserted, and the absence of fire guards contributed significantly to the fires developing rapidly and to the destruction that ensued. After the raid, the War Cabinet noted 'the danger of relaxing vigilance in Civil Defence at weekends was disastrously illustrated; and, in this connection, it is of interest to note that of the nine Sundays in November and December, seven were the occasions of major raids directed at the largely depopulated areas of the big cities.'

This raid was said to be retaliation for a raid on Berlin by the RAF on 20 December, but there had been no opportunity for a substantial raid since Christmas because of poor, foggy weather. This restricted the raid on 27 December but there was clearly an intention that the raid scheduled for two nights later would be much heavier. Significantly, Manchester, the subject of two nights of incendiary-biased attacks on 22 and 23 December, had been caught out in the first raid by the usual 'Sunday night' situation – a deserted non-residential area with offices and factories locked up for the weekend. Large expanses of the city centre were burnt out. The Luftwaffe wished to repeat their Manchester strategy and also take advantage of the low tides in the Thames. However, although the London raid did not turn out to be on the scale planned, it stood out as a significantly destructive raid.

There are considerable variations in the various accounts of this raid. Most are agreed that a large area of the 'square mile' of the City of London was burnt out by fire, and that St. Paul's Cathedral was fortunate to escape destruction.

X-Gerät was employed by the Luftwaffe's pathfinders. However, it was not the first raid of this type on London. X-Gerät had been used on 27 December, but on that occasion, the raid wasn't adequately concentrated. The Coventry raid on 14 November was the first to employ X-Gerät, and it was also used at Manchester. However, attempts to 'bend' the beam at Coventry and misdirect the attackers were said to have failed due to a British error.

I have seen a claim that on 29 December around 100,000 bombs fell in just a few hours, causing a firestorm across most of the City's square mile up to Islington. This is inaccurate; nothing like 100,000 bombs fell; a firestorm was not initiated although some of the fires might have developed into one. A change in the weather meant the cold, cloudy, foggy weather in southern England was pushed away by an approaching Atlantic depression which gradually reached northern France and later southern England. This may have accounted for the change in wind direction and speed noted during the raid, and this may not have represented the beginnings of a firestorm. It is not clear if cloud cover was 100% during the raid – Ramsey seems to indicate it was not and as a result, later bombers could bomb visually. The raid was said to have been 'compressed' so attackers could get back to France before the weather worsened.

Only 136 bombers took part, but the raid opened with a concentrated drop of incendiaries on the City and Southwark. Soon after 18.00, within minutes of the sirens sounding, incendiaries began to fall. Despite the cloud cover, the target, the City of London, was accurately marked by the fire-raisers of the Luftwaffe's legendary pathfinder group *Kampf Gruppe* KG100, carrying a bomb-load comprised exclusively of incendiaries. The group comprised ten Heinkel He111 H2s (Johnson says twenty) equipped with the X-Gerät and was led by Hauptmann Friedrich Aschenbrenner. Each aircraft carried thirty-two containers of thirty-six incendiaries. A few minutes after the Luftwaffe's pathfinders had departed, the main attacking force arrived, finding the target already well-illuminated by numerous fires. In all the raid delivered 127 tonnes of high explosive bombs and 22,068 incendiaries. Ramsey says the incendiary content was made up of 613 BSK canisters of 36 incendiaries which gives a total of 22,068 bombs.

The pathfinders, flying at 6,000 ft, just above the cloud cover, went almost undetected until they approached London; only a few minutes elapsed between the alert being sounded and the first bombs landing. It was one of the shortest warnings of the Blitz. The first bombs fell at 18.17, the last at 21.30, and the all clear sounded at 23.50.

David Johnson says the lead pathfinder (Aschenbrenner himself) dropped his bombs short, on Southwark, although presumably he dropped them when X-Gerät told him to. He then waited whilst the remaining pathfinders dropped their bombloads. As the cloud cover was 100% none of them would have been able to see the target. A remarkable success for X-Gerät. The main bombing force arrived soon after and identified the target by the fires lit by KG100.

Basil Collier, the official historian, says the beam was laid across London from south-west to north-east, Wimbledon through Chelsea and Westminster to Tottenham, but the bombs fell east of this with the incendiaries falling within a two-mile radius of St Paul's Cathedral and high explosives over the riverside boroughs from Westminster across to the Isle of Dogs, and down into Camberwell. It is unclear if any British attempt was made to counter the beam on 29 December.

On paper, the high-risk City of London was well-protected by its fire services, there being five fire stations within the Square Mile. St. Paul's Cathedral had its own fire guard:

The St. Paul's Watch was a voluntary organisation first formed in June 1915 to protect the Cathedral from bombing raids. It was disbanded at the end of the war but reformed again in 1939, with a new leader, Godfrey Allen, Surveyor to the Fabric. They kept watch over the Cathedral, reporting to the London Fire Brigade any instances of gunfire, incendiaries or damage to the building. They also received training on dealing with fires, incendiaries and gas attacks, which was to come in useful during the Blitz. The Watch drew its members from various professions, and included architects, academics, businessmen, civil servants, and members of the clergy. As a result of this talent and diversity the Watch was sometimes known as 'the best club in London'.[265]

Other large public buildings in the City such as Guildhall, the Whitbread brewery and Bart's Hospital also had well-organised fire-watching teams. These were soon fully stretched by the number of incendiaries that fell. Blast could break all the windows of a building enabling sparks and embers to blow in from nearby burning premises. Smaller premises with only a token fire-watching presence were soon overwhelmed and buildings without any such provision had no chance whatsoever. Incendiaries would often be concealed by the irregular roof lines of City streets and fire-watchers would be unaware of their fall until fires had taken hold, by which time only the fire services could help.

The Dean of St. Paul's later wrote that in half an hour, fires were raging on every side of the Cathedral and the Watch had to tackle the many bombs which had fallen simultaneously on different parts of the Cathedral roofs. Watchers on the roof of the *Daily Telegraph* building in Fleet Street, who had a full view of St. Paul's thought that the Cathedral was doomed and later told of a veritable cascade of bombs hitting but glancing off the dome. The Dean relates how besides the bombs which fell on the roofs, others landed in the Cathedral gardens 'producing a fairylike effect amongst the trees and shrubs on the north and south sides.' Twenty-eight incendiary bombs fell on St. Paul's and its precincts. The numbers of bombs and their dispersal over a wide area of roofs presented a severe challenge for the Watch.[266]

St. Paul's vulnerability lay in its famous dome. Between the dome and the inner dome above the cathedral nave lay an expanse of dry timbers; at this height, a fire in this would easily be fanned into an uncontrollable blaze. Early in the raid an incendiary

---

265 www.stpauls.co.uk
266 Matthews, *St. Paul's Cathedral in Wartime* (1946)

bomb lodged in the lead covering of the dome. Fortunately, as it burnt it fell outwards into the Stone Gallery and was quickly extinguished. Journalists were on the verge of telling the world that the cathedral was burning to the ground. Guildhall was less fortunate, the situation being made worse by the failure of the water supplies. But the real culprit was the neighbouring church of St. Lawrence Jewry. Locked and unprotected by any fire guards, its steeple caught fire and eventually part of it crashed into the nave, sending huge showers of burning debris over Guildhall. By 23.00, with no water available to the fire crews, the order had to be given to abandon the building.

By 19.30 a strong south-west wind had developed, worsening the fire situation by spreading embers from burning buildings into previously untouched premises. But this heralded worsening weather which curtailed the Luftwaffe attack. Ray quotes a witness who recorded that by 19.30 the south-west wind had increased to gale force and as that person was living in Westminster a few miles from the area most affected by fires, this was unlikely to be a herald of a possible firestorm. It seems a miracle that a firestorm did not start, because soon after the raid began the water supplies ran out because important mains were breached by high explosive bombs. Low tide at the time the raid began meant inaccessibility of water from the Thames, and fire boats could not be used. It seems it was partially because the raid ended prematurely and partially because water supplies were restored. The tide had begun to come in by midnight.[267]

The all clear sounded a couple of hours after the last Luftwaffe plane bombed. Sperrle reluctantly had to accept that further attacks would be impossible in view of the rapidly deteriorating weather at French airfields.

---

267 http.//www.london-fire.gov.uk/news/LatestNewsReleases_the-second-great-fire-of-london

Because only a small proportion of high explosive bombs was dropped, casualties were relatively low and mainly occurred in neighbouring boroughs rather than in the City itself. In the City, no residents died but three AFS men and a member of the Home Guard were killed there, as were four other men whose home addresses were in outer London and were presumably on fire watching duties or working in the City for whatever reason.

Concentrated as it was, the raid did not only affect the City. 'The actual working of the docks was interfered with in three cases—Surrey Commercial, Millwall and London Docks. The most considerable damage was, however, to warehouses and sheds, with their inflammable contents. Four important food factories in the Dock area were hit, but fortunately damage was not significant. Buck and Hickman Ltd in Whitechapel, makers of machine tools, was burnt out; otherwise, Key Point factories escaped serious damage.'[268] Trinity House was gutted by fire. Damage was also done to the Royal Courts of Justice, the Tower of London, the British Museum, the Public Record Office, County Hall and Westminster City Hall.

The boroughs of Camberwell and Southwark were also badly affected, and major incidents involving heavy damage to industrial premises occurred in Lewisham and Greenwich. The area between Waterloo and London Bridge was severely damaged by incendiaries, and both Guy's Hospital and London Bridge Station were surrounded by fires. Guy's Hospital had to be evacuated and other hospitals and nursing homes were damaged in Holborn, Lambeth, Waltham Cross, Bermondsey, Stepney and Camberwell. The worst casualties occurred in Camberwell where fifty-four people died including sixteen at Longcroft Road, an incident at a shelter. In Lambeth eighteen died, in Southwark nineteen, including twelve at the Keyworth Street shelter, and in

268 TNA CAB66-14 War Cabinet weekly resume (no. 70)

Shoreditch fifteen, mainly at Drysdale House in Drysdale Road. In Westminster five people were killed when a tram was hit by a bomb on the Victoria Embankment, at the junction with Horse Guards Avenue. Inevitably, given the weather conditions over London, some Luftwaffe crews missed their target. Kingston upon Thames, where sixteen fatalities occurred in Elm Road, was presumably not intentionally bombed.

The material damage in the City was considerable, with telecommunications being particularly badly hit. O'Brien states the night's attack inflicted the worst blow of the war on GPO telecommunications plant.[269] The GPO's Central Telegraph Office in Newgate Street along with three automatic telephone exchanges in a new building in nearby Wood Street were destroyed. At about 19.00, a high explosive bomb fell near the Wood Street building, blowing in all the windows and allowing burning debris to be blown into the building, which gradually filled with heat and smoke. Staff carried on, but with all the adjacent streets on fire, by 22.00 the building together with all its valuable equipment (15,000 exchange lines terminated in the building) had to be abandoned. The Central Telegraph Office, which housed 3,000 staff engaged on maintaining the country's inland and overseas telegraph service, was also set on fire by burning debris that blew in from other buildings. Fortunately, an emergency facility had been established in the basement of the neighbouring King Edward building, and this was able to take over communications needed for vital defence services[270]. Faraday Building, the vast modern complex just to the south of St. Paul's, housing London's overseas telephone links, also survived although it was filled with smoke and fumes from buildings burning nearby. Cable and Wireless's own Central Telegraph

269 O' Brien, *Civil Defence* (1955)
270 Hay, *The Post Office Went to War* (1946)

Office in Moorgate survived, despite being surrounded by fires and blasted by high explosive. All communications ceased probably as a result of water from fire hoses penetrating the landlines, but fortunately the change of wind direction noted by several observers meant that the worst fire threats here were removed.[271]

Damage to railways around the City was extensive. Services into Broad Street were halted by a UXB at Dalston Junction. Fenchurch Street was similarly affected with the signalling out of action and debris on the line. Liverpool Street was, surprisingly, soon back in action after fires were put out. London Bridge station was consumed by fire, the station buildings and offices being badly damaged (£500,000 estimated costs) along with several trains. Only the 'high level' platforms (which carry the service through into Waterloo station) were unaffected.[272] Waterloo itself was crippled by serious damage to signalling cables which took a week to repair, staff from LPTB, the Royal Corps of Signals and Callender's Cables being drafted in.[273]

Eight Wren churches were destroyed – St. Andrew-by-the-Wardrobe, Christ Church, Newgate Street, St. Bride's in Fleet Street, St. Mary Aldermanbury, St. Vedast Foster Lane, St. Alban's Wood Street, St. Stephen's Coleman Street and St. Lawrence Jewry. Johnson gives the total of Wren churches destroyed as thirteen plus four churches that pre-dated the Great Fire, and states only eight were rebuilt, which does not appear correct for 29 December; it is the total for the whole Blitz. Gardiner quotes ten churches as per Pope-Hennessy's survey taken the next day, and includes Wren's St. Augustine with St Faith; however, this church had already been badly damaged by bombing on 9/10 September.

---

271 Graves, *The Thin Red Lines* (1945)
272 Brooksbank, *London Main Line War Damage* (2007)
273 Brooksbank, *ibid*

Guildhall was at the time a fifteenth century structure that had burnt in the Great Fire, with a later porch added by Dance in 1788. The 19th century roof was totally destroyed along with the statues of the legendary giants, Gog and Magog. The City of London Police A Division Headquarters in Moor Lane were damaged by high explosive and subsequently burnt out. Twelve police officers were injured and the building was so badly damaged it was abandoned and work transferred to temporary premises. The London City Mission in Bridewell Place and Brewers Quay by Tower Stairs, one of the oldest wharves in the Port of London, were destroyed. The losses of the City's livery companies included Saddlers' Hall, the Barber-Surgeons' Hall, Cordwainers' Hall, Brewers' Hall and Haberdashers' Hall. Brewers' Hall, which dated back to 1673, was totally destroyed. Old houses – some of which had survived the Great Fire, including 37 Great Tower Street – were wrecked.

North of St. Paul's Cathedral, Paternoster Row with its publishing firms was wiped out with the loss of five million books. This was a huge blow to the book trade and the publishing industry, already suffering because of wartime restrictions on raw materials. Simpkin Marshall Ltd, described as the greatest distributor of English books in the world and carrying the largest comprehensive stock, lost approximately four million books when their various premises near St. Paul's were entirely destroyed. The textile warehouses in the St. Paul's Churchyard and Ave Maria Lane area were also hard hit. Vere Hodgson later noted that 80,000 businesses were destroyed in the City, and 50,000 typewriters were lost![274] This seems somewhat of an exaggeration, but on the Monday morning following the raid, numerous workers commuted into the City, only to find their place of work had been destroyed. Graves relates how

---

274 Hodgson, *Few Eggs and No Oranges* (2010)

staff heading for Cable & Wireless's office in Moorgate found that it entailed 'a walk through streets lined on both sides with hundreds of trailer pumps, all working and creating a terrible din. Hose was everywhere, running in all directions, and each street-crossing resembled a plate of gigantic spaghetti.' The fires, although now under control, were still burning fiercely. The telecommunications situation was that all telephone and telegraph lines were out of action, and the nearby London Wall telephone exchange completely destroyed. At dusk the whole City area was brilliantly lit by huge fires.[275]

Buildings that survived included the Redcross Street Fire Station, the Cripplegate Institute and the Whitbread Brewery in Chiswell Street. The brewery suffered some damage including the destruction of the hop loft together with 1,800 pockets of hops worth over £40,000. However, brewing was able to re-start in four days, the main problem being the water supply. The national newspapers on 30 December reported the deaths of eighty dray horses at a brewery. In her diary the next day, Ruby Side Thompson also mentions eighty horses killed at a brewery.[276] Gardiner says eighty dray horses were killed at Whitbread's, and Gaskin also mentions eighty horses killed by a high explosive bomb at a Moorgate brewery. Whitbread was the only brewery in the area, but the company's fire brigade log books[277] state not a single horse was injured, and all were led to safety from the stables in Garrett Street. However, it seems that many dray horses were killed and injured by a parachute mine falling at Mann's brewery in Whitechapel. This is mentioned in the brewery history and contemporary newspaper accounts. Dr Johnson's house in Gough Square off Fleet Street was saved, albeit with some fire damage to the roof, only to be more

275 Graves, *The Thin Red Lines* (1945)
276 Washuk, ed., *World War II London Blitz Diary vol. 1 – 4*
277 Quoted in Glover, *Brewing for Victory* (1995)

seriously damaged by a flying bomb in 1944. The Honourable Artillery Company's premises in City Road were saved by the efforts of the London Fire Service despite limited water resources.

Although reports were received from Luftwaffe crews of many fires taking hold in the initial stages of the raid, it seems that German intelligence remained unaware of the true impact of the raid, truncated though it was. Partly this was due to poor visibility, but it seems that it was assumed that as the raid had been brief and had not been continued as planned, substantial damage could not have occurred. Also, the weather prevented any photo-reconnaissance flights. Fitzgibbon emphasises how the raid was not a particularly big one and certainly much smaller than the raids on 15 November and 8 December – on the latter occasion three times as many incendiaries were dropped.

Nick Metcalfe estimates that the raid resulted in forty-four gallantry awards – one MBE, eight George Medals, twenty-two British Empire Medals and thirteen Commendations for Brave Conduct – more than for any other single event during the Blitz.[278] Over 9,000 fire service personnel were deployed to central London and they suffered sixteen fatalities with hundreds being injured.[279]

The *Daily Herald* on 30 December underplayed the raid and maintained that enemy aircraft were driven off by night fighters and thus the raid ended prematurely. In fact, night fighters had little effect and no enemy aircraft were lost. The early ending of the raid was due solely to weather factors. After the 11 January raid this newspaper again attributed the early finish to AA fire driving off the attackers!

---

278 http.//www.nickmetcalfe.co.uk/gallantry-during-the-blitz-29-december-1940

279 Demarne in Ramsey, ed., *The Blitz Then and Now Vol.2* (1988)

The next day, the War Cabinet agreed full publicity should be given to the 29 December raid emphasising the lack of military objectives and the damage to historic buildings such as Guildhall.

A week later, Vere Hodgson 'went up to the City about 1pm … it was gently snowing. Walked up Ludgate Hill. I was by no means the only person in the City. There were hundreds and hundreds there. Firemen were still about. The church on Ludgate Hill is undamaged, but above that it began. Everything is a shell … all burnt out inside. Smoke was still coming from one building. All Ave Maria Lane was closed to the public. I just looked down … burnt out. So I believe is Paternoster Row. On the right Debenham's big building – burnt out. Lots of men working on it.

We had to file through St Paul's Churchyard. Cheapside is closed, so went along Watling Street. On left only remains of buildings. Friday Street … just vistas of destruction wherever one looked. Went along Bread Street into Cheapside, and saw poor Bow Church still looking down sorrowfully on the ruins around. Went along Coleman St – it has pretty well gone. St Stephen's just has the walls. I found Guildhall … roped off. Union Jack was flying bravely above it. Men working hard and no one allowed near, St Lawrence Jewry, the church that caused Guildhall to ignite, was only a shell.

Reached London Wall, but no one is allowed along. Cranes and engines were working on the ruins. Fore St also closed. Got back to Moorgate, and the left side took part in the blaze. The station closed … just one mass all behind of charred walls. Ropemakers and Chiswell St were blown up in part – I just arrived to see some of the walls falling. It is like a battlefield. Walked to the Bank and tried to find Austin Friars. With great difficulty found the little curved lane, and was standing in front of what was once the church, when I heard a familiar drone overhead. Felt I was not in a healthy spot. Sirens went and thought I had better move from that part of London in which so much interest has been taken.'[280]

---

280 Hodgson, *Few Eggs and No Oranges* (2010)

EIGHT

A HARD WINTER

One of the outcomes of the 29 December raid was that Home Secretary Herbert Morrison pushed through legislation for the establishment of a fire guard in all business premises. He announced new fire watching obligations and signed an order compelling all eligible civilians between 16 and 60 to register. The reaction anticipated was that people would resent being compelled to safeguard their bosses' property, particularly as they still had their own homes to safeguard. Not all firms' employees responded with loyalty and enthusiasm as had the staff of the textile wholesaler Hitchcock, Williams & Co in St. Paul's Churchyard at the outbreak of war. However, their efforts were in vain as on 29 December the company's premises had to be abandoned to burn[281].

The new regulations, the Civil Defence Duties (Compulsory

---

281 Hitchcock, Williams & Co employed hundreds of staff at their mainly modern premises next to St. Paul's, including 150 who lived on the site. The story is told in *Operation Textile* by H A Walden (1947)

Enrolment) Order, introduced on 15 January 1941 gave the Ministry of Home Security powers to compel men and women within certain age bands to perform part-time civil defence duties. The regulations were not popular and were difficult to implement. As will be seen they did not prevent an even greater potential disaster occurring on the night of 10/11 May 1941.

The raids of September to December 1940 had affected the whole of Greater London, but from February 1941 raids were to be more concentrated on central and east London and many boroughs, particularly to the west and north-west, were to be hardly affected by the air raids of 1941. There seems to have been a deliberate attempt by the Luftwaffe to focus on the seat of government and the commercial heart of the capital. As such it proved to be a more successful strategy than the blanket approach of the previous autumn when many bombs fell in residential suburbs with little or no strategic importance.

The Luftwaffe continued to target a number of provincial cities, with London serving as a secondary target, this no doubt serving a diversionary role by confusing the night fighter force. Attacks in January and February were limited by weather, which was extremely poor from the third week of January 1941. Frost and snow featured in the London region, but the Luftwaffe took advantage of the weather to make a number of daylight raids. However, Civil Defence was given a challenge to ensure vehicles were serviceable and ready for action at night in the very cold weather. At night, Cardiff, Bristol and Portsmouth each received a heavy raid, and Swansea received two. Over the period March to May the attacks were to be mainly concentrated on the ports.

JANUARY 1941

In January there were two major attacks on London and three

other large attacks. The Luftwaffe could only achieve 45% serviceability in its bomber force at this time.

1/2 January

The amount of Luftwaffe activity was small but widespread, and the London area was under siren for a considerable part of the night although relatively few incidents occurred. A parachute mine in Theobalds Road at 00.15 destroyed a terrace of houses in Gray's Inn, and badly damaged houses in Theobalds Road, including Disraeli's birthplace at no.22. Five people were killed here, but apart from two people killed in Aldgate there were no other civilian fatalities in London. A mine fell in the Middle Temple a few minutes later and caused seven casualties amongst men at a barrage balloon unit.

4 January

At 05.30 two people were seriously injured in Hendon, and shortly after three people were killed in Edgware.

5 January

Weather conditions by day on 5, 6 and 7 January enabled the Luftwaffe to resume harassing tactics with single aircraft.

There was some evening activity over London, and bombs fell in the eastern suburbs. Seven were killed in Meadway, East Barnet – this incident is featured in the BBC People's War archive.[282] In Ilford, fifteen people were killed in Green Lane. There were thirty-four casualties in Walthamstow, where seven bombs fell at 21.30 in the Highams Park area, followed by two parachute mines an hour later. There were also fatal casualties in East Ham. At 19.20 two people were killed by high explosive

---

282 https://www.bbc.co.uk/history/ww2peopleswar/stories/88/a2755488.
shtml

bombs in Southern Row, north Kensington, with eight injured and thirty-three houses damaged. Later incendiaries fell in Finsbury, Holborn and St Pancras and fires were reported in the Highway and Limehouse. In Stoke Newington bombs fell in Howard Road, Wordsworth Road and St. Matthias Square. St. Matthias Church, the work of William Butterfield suffered severe damage and the vicarage was totally destroyed. Nine people died in St. Matthias Square, and a large amount of damage was done. Two hundred people were made homeless, twelve houses were demolished and hundreds damaged. A parachute mine in Cricklewood near the *Windmill* pub failed to explode. At 21.20 a bomb hit Waterloo Station, between the general offices, platforms and York Road. It destroyed offices, blocked the LPTB booking hall with debris and damaged the lifts to the underground. Debris blocked platform 21, and platforms 19 and 20 were closed due to the danger of falling glass.

6 January

There was some daytime activity over London, and machine-gunning of barrage balloons was reported. Fires broke out in West Ham and Tottenham, and at the Thames Ammunition Works in Crayford, firemen had to fight a blaze while shells exploded around them. The Luftwaffe cancelled night operations because of bad weather. London Civil Defence Region sent assistance to Bristol, where the city had suffered a long heavy raid in freezing temperatures on 3/4 January.

7 January

In a daytime raid, four people were killed in Hampstead including two ambulance drivers at the ambulance station at the North Western Hospital in Lawn Road when the canteen was hit at 15.45. The Civilian War Dead Roll of Honour lists three civilians killed in Gilden Road and one in Oakfield Crescent, Kentish Town.

This is presumably the incident referred to by Newbery whose account states three bombs fell near Lismore Circus at 15.45 on an unspecified date and ten members of the Pioneer Corps working on a nearby site were killed.[283] Eight members of the Pioneer Corps died in the UK on 7 January and three on 8 January, but as with all military casualties, no locations are given.

Luftwaffe night operations were again cancelled.

8 January
Very little daytime activity was experienced and there were no night operations by the Luftwaffe.

9 January
The main attack was on Manchester with two secondary attacks on London by sixty-two aircraft. There was little concentration in the bombing. In the late evening incendiaries fell in Shepherds Bush and neighbouring areas. St. Alphege's Hospital in Greenwich was hit and there was some generally minor fire damage across south London. However, Myer's bedding factory in Vauxhall Walk was seriously damaged. Further incidents occurred into the early hours. Four people were killed at Willesden, six at Egham and four at Chertsey. Five died at Hartley's shelter in Tower Bridge Road, Bermondsey and twenty-three were injured. 2,000 tons of jam were destroyed at Hartley's factory. Muswell Hill appears to have suffered a 'major incendiary attack', according to Travers.[284]

10 January
The main evening raid was on Portsmouth, where great damage was caused. In London, a few bombs fell and four people died in

---

283 Newbery, *Wartime St. Pancras* (2006)
284 Travers in *Hornsey Historical Society Bulletin no.33. Home Fires. A North London Suburb at War* (1992)

Wembley when a bomb fell at 00.08 at the junction of Wembley Hill Road and Harrow Road, blocking the road with a crater and interrupting the trolleybus service for two months. Another suburb with casualties was Kingston upon Thames where seven people died in Balmoral Road.

11 January

The Luftwaffe continued to use heavier bombs, in particular the 1,400 kg and 1,800 kg types in their raids of the New Year 1941. This may account for the devastating impact of the bombs dropped in some incidents at this time.

On this night 145 bombers attacked London, dropping 144 tonnes of high explosive and 598 canisters of incendiaries. Despite the extent of the destruction on 29 December 1940 and 10 May 1941, on these occasions, civilian casualties in the City of London were very low. However, on 11 January, more people were to die in the City than in all the other raids put together, although the raid only lasted from 18.25 to 21.30. The disasters on this night were caused by two bombs falling at about 20.20 – one penetrating the subway at Bank Underground station, causing fifty-six deaths, the other falling outside Liverpool Street Station causing another forty-three. The fatality total is often quoted as 111 for the Bank station incident alone, but that would appear to be incorrect. In fact, a number of different versions of the casualty figures appear for the Bank and Liverpool Street incidents. Most of the casualties were resident in other parts of London, presumably being either people sheltering or commuters heading back into Liverpool Street station. In total 226 died in London.

The bomb at Bank station exploded in the booking hall, which is only a few feet below the roadway at the important and busy junction outside the Bank of England. The blast travelled down the escalator shaft, which collapsed, to the Central line platforms, blowing people onto the track just as a train entered the station. The roadway collapsed into the station booking hall and a huge 120-ft wide crater opened in the road, completely blocking the road junction. The Bank of England, Mansion House and the Royal Exchange, overlooking the crater, were undamaged.

With the full participation of the Royal Engineers, a temporary bridge was completed by 3 February thus enabling through traffic to cross the junction. It was even formally opened by the Lord Mayor! The station itself was re-opened by 17 March and by May 1941, the temporary bridge had been removed and the permanent junction restored. A mammoth feat of engineering helped, as in all incidents of this time, by the large military resources available – many skilled personnel were to remain under-occupied in Britain until D Day. As a result of this incident, orders were given to clear all underground station booking halls when the sirens were sounded.

The Liverpool Street incident occurred when a bomb fell on the buildings on the west side of Bishopsgate, blasting buses setting down passengers for the station. Fifteen buses were involved and four of them were severely damaged. Two bus drivers and a conductor were killed. Gristly scenes were recorded with bodies strewn over the roadway and buildings blasted and on fire. The modern Bishopsgate police station on the east side of the road was badly blasted and its Art Deco façade pitted by shrapnel. Fires broke out further north in Leonard Street, Shoreditch, where several fatalities also occurred at Allen's Buildings. City Road, Kiffen Street, Tabernacle Street and Britannia Walk suffered heavy damage by high explosive. The fire brigade log books state St Augustine's church, Watling Street, in the City of London received a direct hit and was seriously damaged by fire at 20.30 – this church had already been badly damaged on 9 September and 29 December.

This raid was also notable for the number of incendiaries used which caused a number of fires (mostly categorised as 'medium' fires requiring 2 to 10 pumps) across the central areas of London, mostly in commercial premises. The Royal Army Medical College on Millbank was hit, and also 20 Kensington Palace Gardens then as now 'Millionaires Row' and home to Sir John Ellermann at the time said to be Britain's richest man. Devonshire House, an office block incorporating Piccadilly LPTB station was built in 1933 to replace the historic London residence of the Dukes of Devonshire. It was seriously damaged by high explosive.

In St. Pancras, the diarist Anthony Heap noted 'a short but fierce blitz' and eight people were killed in Coley Street off Gray's Inn Road. Damage was done to the borough council power station off St Pancras Way and to the canal pumping station. At the Covent Garden fruit warehouse of Elder & Fyffes in Bow Street, a large bomb penetrated to the basement shelter and exploded, collapsing the five-storey building. Twenty people including the company's ARP staff and shelterers from nearby flats died, and there were only a few survivors.

At an incident at Green Park station at 20.18, a bomb fell between the two entrances to the station, damaging the ticket hall. Seven people were killed, including two ambulance drivers on duty outside the station. The *Daily Express* described how six nurses and four other people were killed at one hospital, which was probably Lambeth Hospital, and three nuns at another, the Catholic Nursing Institute in Lambeth Road, Southwark. The latter hospital, half of which was destroyed, had only just been completed and had not even been formally opened. No patients were killed in either incident.

Some damage and fires occurred in Holborn, and a large fire at 140 Kensington Church Street consumed the Rowley Galleries. The *Daily Express* however commented on the failure, once again in this raid to post firewatchers, necessitating ARP workers having to break into locked premises. The newspaper reported how the firewatchers at a drapery store were able to save their premises but could nothing about adjacent properties. In Tottenham sixteen flats were demolished in Ladysmith Road and Burbridge Way, and several people died. 'Yellow bombs' were reported in Edmonton, Enfield and Walthamstow. These seem to have been from a 'free balloon barrage' – a British anti-aircraft device. In the latter borough AA shells also fell, causing one minor casualty.[285]Five people died in Ilford.

12 January

This was another short, concentrated attack of a similar weight to the previous night, beginning at 18.37 with the all clear sounding at 22.05. Although the damage caused was not as serious, over ninety people died. Most damage and casualties occurred in east and south-east London, where nine people were killed in Belvedere, Erith. Fatalities were also recorded in other locations including ten in Greenwich (Ormiston Road) and nearly thirty in Woolwich. No casualties were recorded at Woolwich Arsenal despite extensive damage caused by high explosive and incendiaries. The offices and warehouse of Twining's, the oldest tea dealer in Britain, in Devereux Court, Strand, were destroyed. The *Daily Express* seemed to find the firewatchers' response in this raid better than on the previous night, which may have contributed to its lesser impact.

15/16 January

The German air attack focussed on the Rolls Royce works at Derby, but bombing was scattered all over the United Kingdom. There only seems to have been one major incident in London.

---

285 Wyld, *The War over Walthamstow* (1989)

At 03.56 on 16 January, a German 'Satan' 1,800 kg bomb hit a men's hostel at 92 Westminster Bridge Road in Lambeth, where 107 men were in residence. Thirty-seven were killed here, and the shock-wave severely damaged the southbound tunnel of nearby Lambeth North station, and injured twenty-eight people sheltering there, one of whom died in hospital fifteen days later. Thirty-seven rings of the damaged tunnel had to be completely replaced, fifteen partially replaced, and eighty-six feet of platform rebuilt. Traffic through the station did not resume until three months after the incident. The nearby St. Thomas' Church was badly damaged. There were seventeen casualties, including five fatalities, in Walthamstow after a heavy bomb fell in Ravenswood Road, and other fatalities occurred in Greenwich, Manor Park and Southwark. Ten pumps attended the *Daily Telegraph* building in Fleet Street where stores and offices were on fire. In Holborn, Bartlett's Buildings and Thavies Inn – a former Inn of Chancery – were severely damaged.

Few air raid incidents were to occur in London over the next few weeks. The weather was poor although far less so than in the previous winter which was one of the worst on record. However later in January heavy snow fell in northern England and Scotland. The Luftwaffe by and large restricted its operations to brief daytime raids.

On 16 January two bomb disposal personnel were killed in Southwark Street. The 17th century Ravenscourt House in Hammersmith, in use as a public library, was burnt out by incendiaries, but it is not clear whether this happened on the evening of 16 January or during the previous night's raid.

17/18 January

Two bombs fell in St. Pancras at 01.50, before the siren sounded, causing damage in the vicinity of the Town Hall in Euston Road. The *Kentish Arms* pub in Mabledon Place was partially demolished but the licensee, local councillor Claud Blackmore and his wife escaped from the wreckage unscathed.

21 January
A daytime raid saw nine high explosive bombs fall at Millcrest Road in Goff's Oak, Hertfordshire, but only one fatality was recorded.

26 January
The bomb census investigators of the MoHS recorded their concern at the number of instances of people interfering with unexploded mines and shells. Seven incidents had been recorded in the past week most of which had involved fatalities. In one, an AFS man had been killed by a bomb detonator that exploded at his sleeping quarters.[286]

28 January
In another daytime 'tip and run' raid, three people were killed at Varley's Magnet Co in Woolwich and another person in the same borough. Many other incidents occurred in the London area but only one other fatality occurred, in Southgate.

29 January
In the evening, only thirty-seven aircraft set out to bomb London, and incidents were mainly scattered over the eastern and south-eastern suburbs. The most affected was Walthamstow where at about 22.00, seventeen people were killed in various incidents in Beaconsfield Road and Boundary Road, including a number of boy scouts assembled for a meeting, and twenty-two were injured. It was probably the worst night of the Blitz for Walthamstow. Other fatalities occurred in Bexley, Bromley,

---

286 TNA HO 203/3 Ministry of Home Security Daily Intelligence Reports

Leyton, Barking, West Ham, Greenwich and Thurrock. The LCC food store in Edmonton was completely demolished by a high-explosive bomb. The urban district of Staines also recorded incidents, in Laleham.

30 January

There were two significant daytime raids. At lunchtime eight bombs fell in Woolwich, ten people being killed at the Royal Arsenal and others at a restaurant in the borough. Later in the afternoon four people were killed at the Mills Equipment factory in Angel Road, Edmonton, and production was seriously affected for a week. Other nearby factories were also damaged and the railway blocked. At the same time in the afternoon, incendiary bombs fell across the adjacent areas of south Chingford, with many fires caused in residential and business premises.[287] Factories were also bombed at Park Royal at 16.00 with nine people seriously injured. In the morning bombs also fell at Camden Town where twenty pumps had to attend a blaze at Bowman's furnishers. The casualties were said to be the heaviest in a daylight raid since 25 October.

31 January

In the course of another daylight raid, a bomb fell on a grocery store in Hampstead Road, St. Pancras at 13.45 killing ten people. Stretcher Party Instructor W J Smaje received the George Medal for his efforts in attempting to rescue a trapped man.

'A man was trapped beneath a considerable amount of burning and unstable debris which was itself surmounted by a damaged three storey building. A Stretcher Party Leader went in under the debris and attempted to reach the man but was forced to retire owing to the spread of fire and the dense

---

287 Warburton, *Chingford at War* (1946)

smoke which resulted. He was able to report that the casualty was still alive. Mr Smaje, after repeated attempts, while the fire was still burning and at a time when it was known that a large tank of paraffin was likely to explode at any moment, succeeded in reaching the man and persisted in his efforts to release him until he collapsed as the result of partial asphyxiation. Smaje, although warned against entering the tunnel, continued in his efforts with complete disregard of the great risk to his own life.'[288]

Around the same time, bombs also fell in Highams Park and Walthamstow, causing a number of casualties, but no fatalities. There was a 20-pump fire at Taylor's Furniture Depository in Southwark and in other incidents three hospitals and the Albany Street Barracks were hit.

FEBRUARY 1941

On 6 February, Hitler's War Directive No. 23 – 'Directions for Operations Against the English[289] War Economy' was issued in Berlin. It gives a clue to the revised focus of air attacks on Britain over the following months. In reviewing the effect of operations to date against Britain, the Directive recognised that contrary to the previous view the greatest impact of operations against the British war economy was in the high losses in merchant shipping inflicted by sea and air warfare. This impact was enhanced by the destruction of port installations, the elimination of large quantities of supplies, and by the reduced use of ships when compelled to sail in convoy. This was expected to increase in the course of 1941 by the wider employment of U Boats, and was

---

288 *London Gazette* 13 June 1941
289 The German government invariably used England and English rather than Britain or British.

thought likely to bring about the collapse of British resistance within the foreseeable future.

It was admitted that the effect of direct air attacks against the armaments industry was difficult to estimate. But it was thought that the destruction of many factories and the consequent disorganisation of the armaments industry must lead to a considerable fall in production. This was probably over-optimistic.

Significantly the Directive concluded that 'the least effect of all (as far as we can see) has been made upon the morale and will to resist of the English people.'

This was to lead to consequences for future planned Luftwaffe operations. In the spring of 1941, there would be an increase in attacks on harbours, shipping and the aircraft industry to support and supplement German naval and U boat operations against Britain. This anticipated that air attacks would eventually be greatly reduced as aircraft were diverted to other theatres of operations. So, with better weather attacks were launched on Plymouth, Portsmouth, Southampton, Plymouth, Liverpool, Hull and Clydeside, and all these towns were to receive more concentrated attacks than in the previous Autumn.

No major attacks were made on London in February, as the weather continued to be unfavourable to the Luftwaffe. In the first two weeks of the month, only on 5 and 6 February were fatalities recorded from a night attack on London. A number of deaths from injuries received in earlier raids are also recorded in the Civilian War Dead Roll of Honour. Of provincial targets, most destruction was achieved in Swansea which was attacked on 19, 20 and 21 February.

5 February

At 20.40 Cholmeley Crescent in Hornsey was struck by a bomb which according to one source killed nine people and demolished four houses. However, the Civilian War Dead Roll of Honour only lists three fatalities. Two died in Sidcup.

13 February – the Hendon bomb

On the evening of 13 February, a single Heinkel aircraft of KG26 – the only Luftwaffe unit authorised to drop the 2,500 kg 'Max' bomb – set out for London, the target according to Ramsey being the de Havilland plant in Edgware.[290] The War Cabinet was told that from the direction of the aircraft, it did not seem it would be attacking London. At 20.11, before the siren sounded, the bomb fell between Borthwick Road and Ravenstone Road, West Hendon, about 3,000 yards from the target. It had a catastrophic impact. Houses in the two roads and Argyle Road were flattened and it seems most of the inhabitants were killed – fatalities occurred in all the houses around the crater. Eighty people died in all and 148 were seriously injured. The Civilian War Dead Roll of Honour lists seventy-seven including several who died later from injuries received, and one sailor, presumably on leave, is known to have died. Details of damage vary widely between accounts, but it seems that over 300 houses were destroyed or made uninhabitable. This would seem to tie in with a figure of 1,500 people made homeless by this incident. A large area was affected by blast damage; houses as far away as Kingsbury sustained damage as did factories in The Hyde.

The incident is surrounded by a certain amount of mystery. An eye-witness J Hamilton-Williams (location not given) described how around 21.00, he heard the sound of distant anti-aircraft fire to the north, although no siren had been sounded. A little later, 'what was undoubtedly a crashing aircraft descending with its engines at full throttle' came from the north, heading southward towards West Hendon. It was also clear that it was

---

290 Ramsey, ed., *The Blitz Then and Now Vol.2* (1988)

on fire as the aircraft passed over; his room became as bright as if the light had been turned on. Shortly, there was the loudest explosion that he had ever heard and he speculated that the aircraft was carrying a full load of bombs. A few moments later the air raid siren sounded.

A strange phenomenon was noticed – the windows in Mr Hamilton-Williams' house were sucked out rather than being blown in. Whether this was the result of the explosion or the aircraft fire was not clear. He claimed that the whole area was immediately placed under security restrictions and the explosion was attributed to a large bomb. He was absolutely certain, as were others who lived underneath the flight path, that the incident was caused by an aircraft that had been shot down. He speculated from which air force it came![291]

The 'security restrictions' were probably the usual cordoning off of the affected area to allow unimpeded access for rescue workers and to prevent looting; no explanation has ever been given for the illumination of the falling bomb and the noise accompanying its descent (a similar phenomenon was experienced with the Victoria 2,500kg bomb which fell on 21 December 1940) and nothing has apparently been forthcoming from German sources. Vere Hodgson in Notting Hill hears that it was the 'result of a land mine. The parachute failed to open and it dropped like a stone – and the authorities thought it was a new type of bomb.'[292]

14 February
During the day six members of a bomb disposal team were killed when attempting to defuse a bomb that had fallen outside Purley Oaks School in Croydon during the night of 4/5 February.[293]

Sixteen aircraft attacked London between 19.40 and 22.10

291 *Daily Telegraph* Britain at War, Readers' Memories 31 Oct 2008
292 Hodgson, *Few Eggs and no Oranges* (2010)
293 Ogley, *Surrey at War* (1995)

and there were fatalities in widely separated localities – Hanwell, Hornchurch, Kentish Town and Southwark. An independent attack was made by five He111s of KG26 on the de Havilland aero engine factory at Edgware – the same target as the previous evening. One aircraft carried a 2,500kg bomb, which again missed the target, falling this time on Queensbury Park in Harrow where at 19.50 it killed a woman in Winchester Road. Over sixty houses, mainly in St. Paul's Avenue were damaged and fifty people were made homeless. The Ministry of Home Security investigated this and the previous night's incident and seems to have concluded they were a result of a very heavy bomb falling. The 'Max' may have been used before but obviously it had either not yet been recognised by the defenders as a new weight of bomb; or perhaps its effects were being wrongly identified as those of a parachute mine.

Four other aircraft from KG26 also attacked the de Havilland aero engine factory at Edgware, also using the Y-Gerät on this very cloudy night. They were somewhat more accurate. One high explosive bomb fell at the junction of Stag Lane and Princess Avenue in the industrial area which borders the A5 trunk road. De Havilland was located in Stag Lane. Seven people died and two were seriously injured at the Eucos factory in Carlisle Road, when the works was gutted by fire. Damage was also inflicted on the factories of Zenith Carburettors in Honeypot Lane and the Eric Resistor Co. Two more factories are named in the log books as receiving damage.

The Luftwaffe must have looked very carefully at the future use of the 2,500 kg 'Max'. Accurate though Y-Gerät could be, it was presumably not accurate enough to justify the expense, and few 'Max' bombs were to be dropped over the next few months.

17/18 February

A very harrowing incident occurred at Stainer Street which

runs under the arches carrying the railway track heading east out of London Bridge station. At 22.25 a bomb hit the Central Section concourse of the station near the entrance to platforms 20 and 21. It penetrated to the public shelter below, falling amongst those sheltering under the arches. Some five hours later a further delayed action bomb exploded nearby causing further casualties amongst rescue workers. Ramsey gives a total of ninety fatalities but according to the Civilian War Dead Roll of Honour, sixty-six were killed and are listed under the boroughs of Bermondsey and Southwark. Apart from this there were casualties from incidents at Camberwell, Deptford (Dennett's Road), Willesden and Hampstead (four killed in South End Road), and bombs also fell out of London at Newmarket and Norwich.

19/20 February
The Luftwaffe's main target was Swansea but a subsidiary attack was made on London around 21.00. It was particularly unfortunate that the only significant incident was at St. Stephen's hospital in Fulham Road, Chelsea where twenty-two people were killed.

21/22 February
The Luftwaffe again directed its main attack at Swansea, the third major attack on that city on consecutive nights. A few aircraft attacked the London area. Four large bombs fell in south Chingford before the siren sounded[294] and caused heavy damage to residential property and one fatal casualty.

26/27 February
A mid-evening raid targeted a number of locations in

---

294 Warburton, *Chingford at War* (1946)

southern England, but mist prevented accurate bombing. Four parachute mines hit East Ham although these were the only local incidents that night. The Civilian War Dead Roll of Honour shows that over thirty people were killed at Gladstone Avenue and Hollington Road in East Ham. Two mines fell near East Ham station, and although one failed to explode, the other in Gladstone Avenue killed twenty-two people. A mine in Hollington Road killed twelve and another mine seems to have caused a serious incident when it hit a military hospital canteen. If the fatalities were confined to military personnel, they would not appear in the Civilian War Dead Roll of Honour. However, the MoHS Bomb survey confirms the location as the Isolation Hospital in Roman Road. The Newham Story archive does have a photograph of destruction at the East Ham Isolation Hospital on this date so this must be the hospital referred to.[295] Photographs of both incidents show considerable damage.

27 February
The day was notable for an attack on the Parnall aircraft factory at Yate near Bristol where thirty-three died. In London, a fatality occurred in Finchley.

28 February
Although Ramsey indicates no aerial activity occurred, the Civilian War Dead Roll of Honour records that fatalities occurred in Barking. Also, in Ruislip, three died in King's College Road after a stick of bombs damaged 500 homes in the locality and made twenty-nine people homeless.

---

295 The Newham Story website

MARCH 1941

Despite much improved weather, the first week of March 1941 was quiet for the London area, although serious incidents did occur down river on 5/6 March; the tug *Silverstone* sank after hitting a mine in the River Medway above Rochester, and the tug *Sun VII* was mined and sank in the Thames Estuary with the loss of five crew.

8/9 March 1941

A clear night after a rainy day. This was the first major raid on London since 11 January and London was under siren from 19.48 to 00.03. Bombs mainly fell on the inner London boroughs, but the bombing was not concentrated and no parachute mines were dropped. However, a notable incident occurred at the Café de Paris in Coventry Street off Leicester Square. This was an underground restaurant noted for its entertainment and was popular with the upper classes, including officers on leave. It was also reputed to be very safe from bombs. However, although deep underground, only a ceiling separated it from the ground floor of the building above, the Rialto cinema. There was no special reinforcement. At 21.40 two 50 kg bombs penetrated the Café de Paris. One exploded in front of the band, killing the band leader Ken Johnson and another member of his West Indian Orchestra and killing at least thirty-four others, including diners and members of staff. The fatalities are given as thirty-four in the Civilian War Dead Roll of Honour but of course these do not include any servicemen or women. Undoubtedly there were fatalities amongst servicemen and women at the Café de Paris, but they are not listed anywhere. Many others – probably over eighty – were seriously wounded. This may be the reason some accounts claim eighty people died. The other bomb failed to explode and burst on the dance floor, 'scattering its stinking yellow contents over the dead and dying'.[296]

The outcome if the bombs had been of a heavier calibre or if both had exploded can be imagined. Much was made of this incident in the media although this focus on the upper classes struck down whilst enjoying themselves did not find favour in all quarters. Barbara Nixon, a warden in Finsbury acknowledged that this 'was a gory incident, but the same week another dance hall about a mile to the east of us was hit and there were nearly 200 casualties. This time there were only 10/6d frocks, and a few lines in the paper followed by, 'It is feared there were several casualties.' Local feeling was rather bitter.'[297] I have not been able to identify the location of this incident, but fourteen people were killed at the *Thatched House* pub in Essex Road, Islington that same night. A bomb fell through a first-floor window, demolishing the public and private bars and penetrating to the basement. It is also possible that the incident referred to could be that at the Princes Dance Hall in Southgate a week later even if geographically the location doesn't match. However, the *Daily Express*[298] describes how a smaller and obviously more downmarket restaurant was bombed on 8/9 March, and among the dead were the owner, waiting staff and customers. This was probably in Dean Street, Soho, where eleven fatalities are listed in the Civilian War Dead Roll of Honour.

Another controversial aspect of the bombing of the Cafe de Paris was a delay in the arrival of rescue and ambulance services, seemingly because many trapped casualties were anticipated – a normal scenario in the heavy old buildings of the West End – whereas this was not the case here as the bomb had been a small

---

296 Fitzgibbon, *The Blitz* (1970)
297 Nixon, *Raiders Overhead* (1980)
298 10 March 1941

one and blast rather than falling masonry caused the injuries. There are reports of looting even as rescuers tended to the injured, documented by Fitzgibbon.[299]

Altogether there were well over 200 fatalities in London. In the City of London, the Cloak Lane police station in Cannon Street was hit at 21.35, with four policemen being killed. Liverpool Street Station was hit at the same time and later three railway workers were killed when a delayed action bomb exploded there. Bishopsgate telephone exchange was put out of action. Buckingham Palace had five bombs fall nearby at 20.56, the North Lodge being damaged and a policeman on duty killed. A bomb which hit Garland's Hotel in Suffolk Street, Westminster killed three people, and badly damaged much of the building. Lancaster House, Westminster Abbey, York House, St. James' Palace, the Foreign Office and the India Office were all damaged.

Also hit in this raid were flats in north-west London (probably Pembroke Hall in Hendon), and seven died in Brinsley Road, Harrow. Incidents also occurred in Kensington and Lambeth. Hornsey had fourteen fatalities, a stick of bombs having fallen across Stroud Green causing fifty-nine casualties in all. Twenty-two were killed in Bermondsey, mainly at Fort Buildings, Southwark Park Road, and sixteen in Southwark, mainly at Manor Place. Twelve died in Wandsworth at the Currie House shelter and twelve at Victoria Buildings in Stratford. A family of five died at Basing Place, Shoreditch, and a total of thirty-two in various incidents in Stepney. A stick of bombs fell across Chingford causing a number of serious incidents, demolishing seventeen houses and sixteen flats, although fortunately casualties were few.

There was a concentration of bombs around Waterloo

299 Fitzgibbon, *The Blitz* (1970).

Station, headquarters of the Southern Railway. By 21.00 all lines were out of service and thereafter services had to start and terminate at Clapham Junction. Normal working of steam services was achieved by 11.00 on the Sunday, and all services were working by 16.00 on Monday. The LPTB Metropolitan line was closed between Kensington High Street and Notting Hill Gate. At Kings Cross two high explosive bombs hit the sub-surface Metropolitan line station killing a worker and blocking the track, although damage was not serious.

The next morning's situation report noted 'Barnes and Croydon Fire Brigades reported what appeared to be a new type of incendiary bomb, which exploded on impact throwing up a number of rockets to a height of about 200 feet, the rockets dying out before reaching the ground. Lewisham wardens report I.B.'s burning with red glare which were more difficult to extinguish than the usual type. One of these are (sic) available for inspection at Lewisham Police Station.' No other mentions of or explanations for these phenomena can be found.

Only two serious fires were recorded, at the Glico Petroleum Works in West Ham (20 pumps) and in Brixton Road, Lambeth. A bomb in Wolseley Road, Romford caused a large crater and much damage, with a number of casualties including five fatalities.

10 March 1941
Two members of a bomb disposal team were killed and two injured when a bomb exploded at King Edward Street in the City of London.

11 March 1941
Although activity was widespread over the UK, no significant incidents were recorded in London, although 'yellow bombs' were reported to have fallen in Holborn and in south London.

15 March 1941

This was a short raid, the period of alert being from 20.25 to 23.10, and only a small number of aircraft participated. This may have been the reason why so many people were about when at 20.40 three bombs fell in Green Lanes, Southgate, blasting a trolleybus which was just setting down passengers opposite the Princes Dance Hall. The bombs fell in Green Lanes between Tottenhall Road and Princes Avenue, another at the junction of Green Lanes and Sidney Avenue and the third at 62/68 Green Lanes. Forty-three people, mainly local, were killed and forty seriously injured. The Civilian War Dead Roll of Honour records for Southgate all say 'died at Green Lanes' which is rather vague as Green Lanes is a very long road. Nine fatalities are listed under Edmonton, mostly people who died later at the North Middlesex Hospital. It seems all but one of the fatalities were outside in the street or were passengers on the bus rather than in the dance hall or neighbouring properties. A personal account in the BBC Peoples War archive although not mentioning dates, appears to refer to this incident and indicates that the dance hall itself was badly blasted. In addition, a large number of shop buildings in the vicinity were destroyed.

Elsewhere in London, the raid mainly targeted the eastern suburbs and the docks, and there was one serious and thirty-six medium fires. A bomb hit a First Aid post in Westhorne Avenue, Eltham, killing nine people – three nurses, three first aid attendants and three patients. A police box was hit in Dog Kennel Hill, Camberwell, killing five people including one policeman. In Romford, over 500 incendiaries of the explosive type were scattered over the town, and high explosive bombs caused damage at Oldchurch Hospital.

18/19 March

The main Luftwaffe attacks were directed at Hull and

Scarborough, with a subsidiary attack by about thirty-five aircraft on London. The only significant incident in London occurred in Hurstwood Road, Hendon, where eight people were killed.

19/20 March 1941

A cloudless misty night, but no moon. This raid is sometimes referred to as 'the Wednesday', although this name is usually given to the raid that occurred four weeks later on 16/17 April. Both raids were equally devastating. The 1942 official publication *Front Line* identifies 16 April as 'the Wednesday', as do most other sources. However, given that the raid of 19 March was a very severe ordeal for the east of London, which was only lightly affected by the raid of 16 April, it is understandable that 19 March was 'the Wednesday' for many people in that area. Cyril Demarne is one of those people; he records 'a spectacularly heavy raid to mark the opening of the spring offensive'[300].

It was the heaviest raid on London since 15 October, and the worst in terms of casualties in the London Blitz to date. Massive fires and explosions were observed by the crews of the attacking aircraft. 479 aircraft dropped 470 tons of high explosive and 122,292 incendiaries in a raid that lasted from 20.10 to 01.58. The absence of moonlight led to the attackers employing flares for target illumination. The raid was notable for its concentration in terms of area and time, and for the quantity of incendiaries dropped, the largest number to be dropped on Britain to date. Four 2,500 kg bombs were also dropped, according to German records.[301] It appears these bombs were targeted at the West India Dock and one of them fell in Poplar, causing massive destruction in the Cording Street area, but it is not known

---

300 Demarne in Ramsey ed., *The Blitz Then and Now Vol.2* (1988)
301 Ramsey ed., *The Blitz Then and Now Vol.2 (*1988)

where the others fell. 1,881 fires were caused including three conflagrations (two in Poplar and one in Greenwich), ten major fires and fifty-three serious fires. Fatality totals vary in different sources but it seems from the Civilian War Dead Roll of Honour that about 750 people were killed in London. Subsequently the War Cabinet recorded a perception that 'full use was not being made of Anderson shelters.' This was always going to be an issue once raids became less frequent.

The worst impact of the raid was on east and south-east London, particularly West Ham where nearly 200 people died after twelve pairs of parachute mines caused tremendous devastation in residential streets. The police report[302] for the K Division (Plaistow, Canning Town and Custom House areas) of West Ham gives some idea of the massive cost in terms of human lives and property destroyed. Eighty people were killed and 100 seriously injured here. Fifty high explosive bombs fell and fifteen parachute mines, in addition to around 2,000 incendiaries. Fires were started at the Bromley-by-Bow Gas Works of the Gas Light and Coke company, and eleven local authorities were left without gas supplies for several days as a result of the damage. Mines are recorded as destroying 100 houses in South Moulton Road, eighty in Beckton Road, 200 in York Street, 150 in Dale Road and eighty in Fife Road. This appears a very high level of destruction even for parachute mines so perhaps some of the incidents could have been caused by the other 2,500 kg bombs that were claimed to have been dropped. At 01.25 a fire engine from Beckenham with its entire crew was wiped out by a parachute mine explosion in the Plaistow Road as it proceeded in convoy to a fire in Silvertown. There were many other fatalities in Plaistow Road but it is unclear whether they were as a result of the same incident. At Mann's

---

302 TNA MEPO 8/108

Brewery in Whitechapel, fires destroyed the hop store and vat room. The Taylor Walker brewery in Limehouse was so severely damaged by fire that it was out of action for eighteen months, and Charrington's brewery in Mile End Road was also damaged.

A large number of fires occurred in Poplar, where eighty-five died. Over one hundred people were sheltering at Bullivant's Wharf, a large communal shelter on the Isle of Dogs riverfront off Westferry Road. The shelter took a direct hit and forty-four people were killed and sixty injured. This was the Isle of Dogs' biggest wartime disaster.[303] The City of London Chest Hospital in Approach Road, Bethnal Green, received a direct hit which destroyed the chapel, north wing and nurses' home. About 100 patients had to be moved to the nearby Parmiters School although this had no windows and no power as a result of earlier bombing. There was only one fatality, but further deaths occurred when people were trapped in the basement of a bombed house in Approach Road.[304] St. Paul's Church in Burdett Road was severely damaged.

Fifty-three people died in Stepney, at least fifteen of them at Cowley Gardens. Here, a railway arch shelter was blasted by a bomb falling in the roadway. The rest centre at St. Mary & St. Michael school was also damaged by the same bomb. Incidents also occurred at the Brunton House and Regent House shelters; others died at Canal Road. Twenty died in East Ham at Whittaker Road, Henniker Gardens and St. Bernard's Road.

In the outer eastern suburbs, things were also bad – thirty-five died in Ilford (at Eton Road and Hampton Road), fourteen in Leyton (mainly at Ellingham Road), and ten in Walthamstow. Observers in Chingford noted that 'shortly after the siren sounded, just after 8 o'clock in the evening, large fires began to

---

303 The Island History Trust
304 Taylor & Lloyd, *The East End at War* (2000)

glow in the factory area of Edmonton adjoining the Chingford boundary ...'[305] The Mills Equipment Co in Edmonton was gutted and production ceased, and the Lissen factory and the LCC depot were also damaged. Bombs also fell in residential areas of Edmonton causing nearly fifty casualties, including seven killed. Seventeen incidents occurred in Chingford and fifteen people were killed; the borough was showered with 2,000 incendiaries, which caused fires in homes and shops, and gutted the Brotherhood Hall. Two ARP wardens and two ARP messengers died in Wanstead when a parachute mine fell near Lake House Road, where they were working on an earlier incident. Thousands of incendiaries burned on Wanstead Flats, an area of grassland.[306]

According to Blake, it was the most intensive raid of the Blitz for south-east London.[307] The boroughs affected were Woolwich where there were fifty-seven deaths, Greenwich with thirty-seven and Lewisham with fifty-six. Most of the Lewisham deaths occurred on the Honor Oak estate in Brockley where Hilton House, a modern block of LCC flats, was demolished. The Royal Victoria Victualing Yard in Deptford – thirty-five acres of buildings containing stores – was 70% destroyed, with three firefighters killed. The Royal Arsenal and barracks in Woolwich, RAF Kidbrooke, and the barrage balloon site in Greenwich were also heavily damaged. St. Alfege church in Greenwich, the work of Hawksmoor, was burnt out. Extensive damage by high explosive was caused at Redpath Brown & Co, structural engineers of east Greenwich. Other industrial premises damaged included the Nash paper mills at St Pauls Cray and Peak Frean's biscuit factory in Bermondsey.

305 Warburton, *Chingford at War* (1946)
306 http.//www.wansteadpark.org.uk/wp-content/uploads/2012/10/It_happened_here.pdf
307 Blake, *Red Alert South East London 1939-1945* (1982)

There were fires all over south-east London. At British Ropes at Charlton, five LFS men were injured and at the South Metropolitan Gas Company in Blackwall Lane, two gasholders were damaged. The nurses' home at New Cross Hospital was destroyed by high explosive. In Mayday Gardens, Greenwich, thirty-seven houses were demolished and nine killed. Nine were killed at Heavitree Road, Plumstead where two bombs demolished nineteen houses. Plumstead Institute and the Charlton greyhound stadium were damaged.

There were forty-one deaths in Islington, including seventeen in Kelvin Road. Six policemen were killed at Hornsey Road police station, and at Northwood Hall, a huge modern block of 194 flats in the same road but in the borough of Hornsey, there were forty-one casualties including six deaths. Incidents also occurred in Holloway and Camden Town, where three were killed in Datchet House, Augustus Street. Twenty-four people died in Hackney, where great damage was done to J.C. Ingram's London India Rubber Works, which was entirely turned over to war production, including vital self-sealing fuel tanks for the RAF. Tremendous destruction was caused in the centre of Hackney by a parachute mine that landed in Mare Street. In Hampstead at 20.50 a parachute mine killed three people in North End Way, destroyed Heathlands and Heath Brow and badly damaged the *Jack Straw's Castle* pub and Heath House.

On the railway network, due to the destruction of signals, only one line was left open between London Bridge and New Cross. All lines at the Bricklayers Arms Goods Depot, Bermondsey, were blocked. In the Lewisham district many suburban lines were damaged and services dislocated. Suburban lines of the LNER and LMS serving the eastern districts of London suffered severely, and the Temple Mills marshalling yard in Leyton was put out of action.

Many ships in the docks were damaged or sunk, including

the 4,962-ton British freighter *Nailsea Meadow* (damaged at Victoria Dock, two deaths), the 5,780-ton British freighter *Telesfora De Larringa* (damaged, one death), the 5,248-ton British freighter *Lindenhall* (which caught fire and sank but was later refloated and salvaged) and the Royal Navy auxiliary anti-aircraft ship *HMS Helvellyn* which was sunk.

There were also incidents outside the London Civil Defence region. Two parachute mines fell in Leatherhead, killing one person and injuring twenty-seven including five nuns at St. Andrew's Convent School, which was badly damaged.

British air defences were again ineffectual, only two Luftwaffe aircraft being lost, both as a result of accidents. The MoHS remarked on the effective raids that the Luftwaffe had made on important targets across the country over the previous ten nights. The weekly report by Home Intelligence noted that 'the East End blitz was regarded by the people in the affected districts as the worst they have yet suffered. Many were physically tired at the end of a winter often spent in damaged houses or shelters, with long hours at work. They faced the bombing with resignation, and even in places a listless indifference. On the whole, the homeless showed great patience, though they are less willing than they were to wait in queues for assistance. There was no rush evacuation following the raid.'[308]

20 March 1941

The next night a few raiders attacked London but did not penetrate beyond the outer suburbs in Kent and Essex, although there was one incident in Plumstead when a heavy bomb caused over sixty casualties in Alabama Street including twenty deaths. There was little activity over London for the rest of the month.

---

308 https://moidigital.ac.uk/ Weekly Report by Home Intelligence – No. 25

NINE

THE WEDNESDAY
AND THE SATURDAY

16/17 April 1941 – 'the Wednesday'

That 'the Wednesday' and 'the Saturday' are thus known reflects their significance in setting new records for the aerial attack on London. Fatal casualties for both raids were said to have exceeded 1,000 and these figures reflect the accuracy and concentration of bombing achieved. 'The Wednesday', the name given to the raid on Wednesday 16 April, lasted from 20.50 to 05.18 and was concentrated on central and south London. However, sixty-six local authorities within London were affected. It seems to have been called as retaliation for a RAF raid on Berlin,[309] and was the heaviest raid on London to date – 1,179 were killed in all in London, and 2,230 seriously injured. If German radio described it as 'the greatest raid of all time' at that stage of the war, they

---

309 An RAF raid on 9/10 April had destroyed buildings in the centre of Berlin, including the opera house.

were probably correct. Collier[310] quotes German sources that show 685 aircraft dropped 890 tons of high explosive and 4,200 incendiary canisters.

2,251 fires were started, with eight classified as major and forty-one as serious. Sixty public buildings were destroyed or damaged, together with eighteen hospitals and thirteen churches.[311]

'Among the public buildings damaged were St. Paul's Cathedral, the Houses of Parliament, the Admiralty, the Law Courts and the National Gallery. Many roads were blocked and the railway systems were hit in nineteen places. There were a large number of fires, the most serious being at L.N.E.R Goods Yard in Lisson Grove. Other serious fires were caused at Selfridge's department store, in Bessborough Gardens, Westminster, and at the Kidbrooke R.A.F. Stores Depot. Although many fires were burning at daybreak, the situation was considered to be in hand'.[312]

Of the fatalities, 225 died in Lambeth, 148 in Westminster, over 100 in both Holborn and St. Pancras, ninety-seven in Southwark, seventy-eight in Wandsworth, sixty-six in Islington and fifty-four in Battersea. Chelsea was also badly hit, with fifty-four killed. Forty-five died in Marylebone, thirty-one in Paddington, and twenty-seven in Hampstead. The East End also had some incidents – over fifty died at Thorold Street, Bethnal Green, although few details have been published about what must have been a catastrophic incident. At 03.25 a parachute mine fell on the south side of the street, demolishing nine houses with a further six on the north side being seriously damaged. A street shelter was demolished and two more partially demolished and there was extensive damage in Bethnal Green Road, Turin Street and Satchwell Road[313].

---

310 Collier, *The Defence of the United Kingdom* (1955)
311 Ramsey ed., *The Blitz Then and Now Vol.2* (1988)
312 TNA CAB 66/16/10
313 TNA HO 198/33

There were around thirty deaths in Stepney, twenty-six in Shoreditch and twenty in Hackney. Christ Church in Watney Street, Stepney together with its vicarage was destroyed by a parachute mine. South of the river, thirty-two died in Beckenham, seventy-two in Bromley and seventy-eight in Croydon, but Bermondsey, Greenwich, Woolwich and Deptford were not so badly affected. A dozen deaths in Bermondsey were mainly at the *Royal Oak* pub in Tooley Street.

In the borough of St. Pancras, a parachute mine was dropped on flats in Pancras Square, Pancras Road. These were grim old Victorian blocks dating back to the 1840s. The mine landed in the courtyard between a surface shelter and the flats; as a result, the explosion had maximum effect and out of 200 people, seventy-seven were killed and fifty-two seriously injured. Other premises in the borough hit by mines that night were at Oakley Square and Leeke Street, the latter damaging the LPTB railway bridge near Kings Cross. Twenty people died at Montague Tibbles House, a modern block of flats in Queens Crescent, Kentish Town, when it too was struck by a parachute mine. A woman living opposite recalled that 'the screaming from the trapped and buried people was awful.' St. Pancras Hospital was hit and elsewhere in the borough of St. Pancras incendiaries started fires at Malet Place, the Express Dairy in Tavistock Place, Aldenham Street, Diana Place, Acton Street, Euston Road, Stanley Buildings, and the British Medical Association in Tavistock Square. Maple's department store in Tottenham Court Road was burnt out by a huge fire that threatened the neighbouring University College Hospital.

Four parachute mines fell in Islington, causing heavy casualties in Pembroke Street, Foxham Road and Stroud Green Road. Dennis Street, Carlsbad Street and Rotherfield Street also had incidents and altogether sixty-eight people died in Islington.

The Arsenal football stadium at Highbury was the scene of a 20-pump fire.

Eleven parachute mines fell across the City of Westminster. One serious incident was at Sutherland Terrace and Lillington Street. The whole of Sutherland Terrace including the *Monster* pub was destroyed. A further mine fell amongst rescuers working at the Sutherland Terrace incident. A bomb also fell on firemen working to extinguish a fire at Christ Church, Victoria. A shower of incendiaries fell and ARP wardens put most of these out but fire took hold on the church roof and just above the altar. The organ was also set alight and soon Christ Church began to burn out of control. The next few hours were chaotic. The firemen managed to save the church tower, but not the roof. Whilst attending the blaze – using 100-foot ladders and water hoses – the fire service crews were then hit by a single high explosive bomb which killed one fireman, seriously injured several others and smashed their equipment. The blast reportedly blew a wheel from one of the fire service pumps across the street, hitting a bank opposite.[314]

A parachute mine exploded in Jermyn Street at around 03.10. The Hammam Turkish Baths at 76 Jermyn Street, dating back to 1862, were destroyed and other premises damaged included Fortnum & Mason, the Cavendish Hotel, Dunhill's and the southern end of Piccadilly Arcade. Roads were blocked locally and later a serious fire situation developed when mains water supplies failed. In this incident twenty-three people were injured and seven were killed. One of the fatalities was the popular singer Al Bowlly at his flat at 32 Dukes Court.[315] Of his neighbours in the flats, Lord Auckland, a serving RAF officer was killed, and Judge Gerald de la Pryme Hargreaves seriously

314 Westminster City Archives www.westendatwar.org.uk
315 Westminster City Archives www.westendatwar.org.uk

injured. The annexe of the Regent Palace Hotel at Brewer Street, used for staff accommodation, was damaged with at least eight fatalities.

At 03.25 another mine landed just south of Shaftesbury Avenue, exploding on the Newport Buildings, Newport Place, a large block of flats built in 1883 and located due west of Charing Cross Road. The blast destroyed the adjoining Shaftesbury Theatre (1888) and superficially damaged the Palace Theatre (1891) opposite. Most of the red brick Newport dwellings themselves were demolished with forty-eight dead and more than eighty-three injured. After the raid police were deployed at the site to prevent looting.

Numerous fires broke out, engulfing Christie's auction rooms and other buildings across the borough. St. Peter's church in Eaton Square was damaged, the vicar Austin Thompson being killed in the porch whilst fire-watching (Colville says he was encouraging people to take shelter in the church[316]). Among the well-known buildings destroyed were the historic Stone's Chop House in Panton Street and the Guildhouse in Belgrave Road, and Charing Cross Station hotel and the Royal Courts of Justice were also damaged. The Little Theatre in John Adam Street was badly damaged. At the Palace of Westminster, the Speaker's House received a direct hit, the building being further damaged by a shattered water tank.[317] The damage forced both houses to meet at the Annexe (Church House). The Admiralty building was badly damaged with 100 rooms being put out of use. Two parachute mines fell on the Hyde Park gun site. The Westminster Hospital was damaged by a parachute mine explosion and had to be evacuated.

St. Marylebone's casualties mainly occurred in incidents at

316 Colville, *The Fringes of Power* (1985)
317 Sansom, *The Blitz. Westminster at War* (1990)

Hallam Street, Clipstone Street, Mortimer Street, Northwick Terrace and New Cavendish Street. At the latter, where the most casualties occurred, the *Globe Inn* was amongst the buildings involved. Forty-six people died in all in the borough.

The Abbey, a huge gothic-style Victorian house in Campden Hill Road, Kensington was badly damaged. This may have been the result of a Junkers 88 bomber crashing in Observatory Gardens at 02.15. It was probably hit by AA fire, and the crew were captured after they had landed in the Brompton Road, south Kensington. Another Junkers, probably hit by a night fighter, crashed in Wimbledon. In Paddington, twelve people were killed at Pembridge Mansions, Moscow Road, which was destroyed by a parachute mine, with many nearby buildings being badly damaged including the Greek Orthodox church.

At 05.00 a parachute mine caused much destruction in Eastbourne Terrace and platform 1 of Paddington station, resulting in another twelve (Brooksbank says sixteen) deaths. The mine landed in the approach road, blasting the west side of the station.

'In the early hours of 17th April ... a landmine exploded in the departure roadway, close to the station manager's office ...causing extensive damage. The Company board room and part of the general offices were demolished and severe damage was also sustained by the waiting room on Platform 1, which unfortunately was kept open at night. A number of passengers were trapped beneath the rubble and debris from the blast, and despite the actions of the rescue services a number were killed. In total, 18 people were killed including six members of staff, and a further 97 were injured.

Almost the whole of the side of the station adjacent to Platform 1 was affected by the blast and in reporting the incident to the board, the General Manager listed a number of other offices and premises on the station that were damaged or destroyed in the raid. This list included property occupied by Boots the Chemist, Lyons and Wyman's, as well as Company offices for season tickets, urgent parcels and passenger enquiries. The No. 2 booking office was also wrecked, as was one of the station's buffets. When the landmine exploded at 2.46 am, as ARP and first aid parties went to the scene, other Company staff immediately began the task of clearance and demolition work. With so many casualties, Paddington Borough Council sent additional rescue parties to assist in the removal of the injured from the rubble of the waiting room; further help was given by a detachment of Auxiliary Military Pioneer Corps.[318]

In Brondesbury, at 00.45 parachute mines hit the First Aid Post at the Brondesbury Synagogue, putting it out of action, seriously damaging fifty houses and partially demolishing the Maria Grey Training College. Three people died.

Chelsea experienced a very bad night and the local community was particularly affected by the loss of the Chelsea Old Church. In this notable local incident, the seventeenth century church was almost totally destroyed by a parachute mine, and the church's fire-watching party – four people in all – was wiped out. Extensive damage was caused locally and among the buildings affected was Crosby Hall.[319]

Frances Faviell's autobiographical account *A Chelsea Concerto* contains a vivid but chilling description of this raid during which her home was destroyed. The pregnant Frances Faviell had dined with her husband Richard at a restaurant a short walk from their home in Cheyne Place, Chelsea. They lived there with their dog Vicki, their upstairs neighbours being their good friends Kathleen Marshman, and her recently married daughter Anne and her husband Cecil:

---

318 Bryan, *The Great Western at War 1939-1945* (1995)
319 Crosby Hall is a historic building that originally stood in the City of London. It was moved to Chelsea in 1910

As we walked home enjoying the warm air to our astonishment the sirens went – first in the distance those eerie mournful howls and then nearer until they blasted the still air in full fury. It was five minutes past nine.

Almost immediately there was the sickening roar of a great drove of planes which increased and increased so that we knew there must be hundreds of them. The guns opened up at once – a terrific barrage, so loud that it was difficult to speak, and huge flares – different to any we had seen – were being dropped.

The raid became heavier and heavier after we reached home ... we left the studio and went downstairs to the dining-room in which we still slept when the raid became even more heavy. As it intensified and more and more planes came over I telephoned Kathleen and asked her if she were not going to take shelter over the road in the basement of her little shop. She said she was tired and felt like sleeping in her own bed. Her bedroom, like Anne and Cecil's, was right under the roof. I don't know why I begged her so strongly to come downstairs, offering her a bed in the hall, which we considered the safest place as it had one wall of ferro-concrete and the others were very thick. Richard added his arguments to mine in vain. I asked about Anne and Cecil. 'What d'you expect?' she said, 'they've gone to bed.'

Anne came to the telephone herself; she sounded as if she was in a dilemma. It was quite clear that she did not like the raid – the noise must have been even more deafening up there and with the terrific barrage it would have been quite possible for shell-caps to penetrate the roof. Cecil settled the matter. He quite obviously took the receiver from her, speaking to me himself. 'Have a heart,' he said laughingly. 'It's still our honeymoon – we've got two more days.' 'You can have our bed,' I said, 'if you'll only come down. Richard says it's a terribly heavy raid and that there are droves of German planes. Do come down – anyhow for a while.' 'Sure we'll come down,' he said jokingly. 'Don't worry. We'll come down with the rubble.'

We had never experienced such a night – bombs seemed to rain down – and in the intervals of their explosions which tonight were the loudest and longest we could remember we could hear the guns in the planes as the fighters chased them. The sky was alight with flares, searchlights, and exploding shells – it was a magnificent but appalling sight! The fires which we could see were terrifying – the largest, in the direction of Victoria, was enormous and appeared to be increasing. Behind us, much nearer, there was a terrible blaze in the direction of Burton Court. Wardens kept running by and were heard the revving up of engines from the auxiliary fire-station a few doors down at No. 21. We were keeping a sharp look-out for incendiaries and there seemed to be no watchers about at all. About twenty past eleven we decided to settle down and read for a time. Neither of us felt like going to bed – it was far too noisy and exciting. A warden raced by shouting, and suddenly we heard a shout of 'Lights, lights' from the street. Richard wondered if the recent near explosions had caused the black-out curtains to shift in the studio and he said, 'I'll run up and have a look.'

He had scarcely gone when the lights all went out. There was a strange quiet – a dead hush, and prickles of terror went up my spine as a rustling, crackling, endless sound as of ripping, tearing paper began. I did not know what it was, and I screamed to Richard, 'Come *down, come down!' Before I could hear whether or not he was coming down the stairs, things began to drop – great masses fell – great crashes sounded all round me. I had flung myself down by the bed hiding Vicki under my stomach, trying thus to save her and the coming baby from harm. I buried my face in the eiderdown of the bed as the rain of debris went on falling for what seemed ages … ages, … The bed was covered and so was I – I could scarcely breathe – things fell all round my head – some of it almost choked me as the stuff, whatever it was, reached my neck and my mouth.*

At last there was a comparative silence and with great difficulty I raised my head and shook it free of heavy, choking, dusty stuff. An arm had fallen round my neck – a warm, living arm, and for one moment I thought that Richard had entered in the darkness and was holding me. But when very, very cautiously I raised my hand to it, I found it was a woman's bare arm with two rings on the third finger and it stopped short in a sticky mess. I shook myself free of it. Vicki, who had behaved absolutely perfectly, keeping so still that she could have been dead, became excited now as she smelt the blood. I screamed again, 'Richard, Richard', and to my astonishment he answered quite near me. 'Where are you?' I cried – more things had begun falling. 'At the bottom of the stairs,' he said.

'Keep there. Keep still – there are more things falling,' I cried and buried my head again as more debris fell all round me. At last it appeared to have stopped. I raised my head again – I could see the sky and the searchlights and I knew that the whole of the three upper stories of the house had gone. 'We've been hit,' I said. 'One in a million!' and the only feeling I was conscious of was furious anger.

It was pitch dark — too dangerous to move without some idea of what the position was. I had had my torch in my hand but the blast had thrown it from me. 'Light a match,' I said. 'What about gas?' asked Richard. 'Can't smell any yet — be quick,' I said. He lit several matches, standing, as I saw by their light, in the entrance to the room. The front of the room had blown out — but the wall nearest to the one where I was crouching, the ferro-concrete one, was still there as was the one to the hall. By the light of the matches I saw something more terrifying than the arm which was no partially covered with debris — the light lathes from the ceiling had all fallen down across me — so that their weight had not hurt me at all — but balanced on them were huge blocks and lumps of masonry. If I moved they might all crash down. 'Don't come any nearer,' I shouted to Richard. He said, 'Keep still — I'm going to try and get out — the front door is twisted and jammed.'

I had seen where my best exit passage lay when Richard had lit the matches for me and while he was trying to shift the broken door I began wriggling very, very carefully and cautiously along the floor. It was not easy — for I was not as slim as normally, and I had Vicki. It was so perilous that I thought of loosing her and letting her find her own way out. Had she not behaved so wonderfully I should have been obliged to leave her — for the thought uppermost of anything else in my mind was to save my baby. The baby, hitherto a nebulous dream of the future, now became urgently real and my only thought was of it. I shouted again and again — for if only the heavy rescue would come, as they had always promised me they would if I were buried, I would not have to face this perilous crawl — but no sound came from the streets.

There were constant terrific explosions and things fell each time there was a fresh thud. If I did not get out soon some of those huge blocks were bound to fall on me. I shouted again, 'Help, help,' and so did Richard. The sounds echoed in the darkness and then far away I heard a woman's voice calling … 'They're coming … they'll come …' and it died away and we didn't know if it was to us they would come, because from the thuds and whooshes and violent explosions all round they must have been pretty busy.

'I've got the door open enough to squeeze through,' Richard called. 'Don't light any more matches, I can smell gas,' I warned him. I could not see him – nor he me. 'I'm going to try and crawl through this space to the door,' I said, and I began doing it immediately. I remembered what Tapper (a member of the local heavy rescue squad) told me, 'Test it first, tap it gently,' and his warning, 'Don't go scrabbling at anything in case it all comes down on you.' Very slowly and cautiously I squeezed my way along the tiny tunnel under lathes, on which were balanced the concrete blocks which I had only caught sight of for a split second in the light of the matches. It seemed a life-time. There were two awful moments when my shoulders brushed something and there was a fall of stuff again – and then I was at the door and Richard had caught me and pulled me carefully up. We stood there for a minute clinging together. 'Anne's dead – her arm is in there,' I said. 'I'm afraid they're all dead – the whole stories have gone,' he said. 'D'you think you can walk?'

We now had to squeeze through the jammed door, which he had managed to shift a little. I begged him not to put his weight on it again in case there was another collapse of what was left standing. It was almost impossible *to get out because of the piled-up glass in the entrance to the flats under the archway. I had to climb and even so I could feel the glass cutting my legs. At the back of the archway there was a solid mass of debris – and above it nothing remained of the Marshmans' flat – just this great pile of rubble. I rushed at it crying, 'Kathleen, Kathleen! Cecil! Cecil!' but there wasn't a sound.[320]*

The AFS station near Frances Faviell's home in Cheyne Place was hit and three firemen killed.[321] A further four firemen were killed at the AFS station in Chelsea Square. The infirmary of the Royal Hospital was struck by another parachute mine and eight Chelsea Pensioners were killed including the 100-year-old Henry Rattray. In addition, five members of the hospital staff died.

The borough of Holborn was to experience its worst night of the war and major incidents occurred. St. John the Evangelist church in Red Lion Square was badly damaged by a parachute mine which killed sixteen people who were sheltering there. The church was recognised as the masterpiece of the Victorian architect, J L Pearson. The Metropolitan Electricity Supply power station opposite St. John's was reported damaged and on fire. At 56/59 Red Lion Street 14,000 sq ft of buildings were burnt out.

Old Gloucester Street was hit by another mine which demolished seventeenth century houses at 15/22 Old Gloucester Street and blasted the modern council flats of Bevan House and a local school. The Hotel Russell suffered damage as did the Embassy Cinema in Torrington Place, where the frontage collapsed. In Bloomsbury Street, nos 2-8 received a direct hit and later Oakley House at nos 14-20 was also damaged. Further

---

320 Faviell, *A Chelsea Concerto* (1959)
321 Wallington, *Firemen at War* (1981)

damage occurred at Pitman House in Newton Street, and in Parker Street.

The University area was badly affected. A parachute mine fell in the courtyard of the King George & Queen Elizabeth Victoria League Club in Malet Street which was being used as a hostel for 350 Canadian troops – nearly twenty of them were killed. The RADA theatre was hit and badly damaged, and the National Central Library in Malet Place was destroyed by fire and lost 110,000 books.[322]

By far the worst shelter incident of the night happened soon after 03.00 when a parachute mine fell at the West Central Jewish Girls' Club in Alfred Place. In peacetime this hosted the welfare services of a 'Day Settlement' in daytime, and educational work in the evenings. The club building was flattened and all twenty-seven people sheltering in the basement shelter were trapped. A crowd of anxious relatives gathered, as at the pit-head of a colliery disaster, waiting and hoping to obtain news of rescue work. The rescue operation found that none of those people sheltering had survived. The Western Synagogue next door was severely damaged although the resident caretaker survived.[323]

At 03.24 the Dallas shelter in Ridgmount Place was the scene of yet another tragedy. The firm of J E Dallas & Sons was established there in 1937 and made banjos and ukuleles – George Formby was a customer – and they were also wholesalers of guitars and music publishers. The modern factory building was badly damaged by a high explosive bomb and then gutted by fire, and eight people were killed in the shelter. It is said that the fire spread from the Jewish Club incident.

The eastern part of Holborn adjoining the City of London was ravaged by fires. Wren's St. Andrew's Church, the City

322 Scholey, *Bombs on Holborn* (1998)
323 Barnett, *The Western Synagogue Through Two Centuries (1761-1961)*, (1961)

Temple and Wallis' department store at Holborn Circus were all burnt out. Thavies Inn, a former Inn of Court, was also destroyed by fire. St. Alban the Martyr in Brooke Street was partially destroyed and burnt out, and much of the area to the north of the church was devastated by fires, which because of the lack of water were able to cross over Gray's Inn Road into Gray's Inn itself. A parachute mine fell at flats on the Bourne Estate in Portpool Lane, and forty-seven people were killed. The mine fell between Portpool Buildings and Duncan Buildings and the two blocks were demolished. St. Peter's church in Saffron Hill was also burnt out.

In the City of London, a bomb fell on the north transept of St. Paul's Cathedral, sending debris into the crypt. A parachute mine fell outside the east wall of the cathedral, but fortunately failed to explode.

At Great Percy Street, Finsbury, eleven people died when 'H.E. bombs demolished houses and the basements were flooded with water from a damaged main. Wardens Finch and Mead waded in and were successful in getting several people to safety. The water was rising fast but Mr. Finch continued his work and carried an elderly lady to a window where she was raised to the pavement by helpers on the footway. He then returned through the rising water, which by this time was up to his chest, and although hampered by floating debris, he rescued an elderly man. Finch again returned to search for further victims but without success. He showed great courage and powers of endurance and, with the help of Warden Mead, saved many lives. Both men showed complete disregard of their own safety.'[324] Senior ARP Post Warden Henry Finch was posthumously awarded the George Medal, after he was killed on 10/11 May on duty at Holford Square, Finsbury. He is probably the 'Wally Marshall'

---

324 *London Gazette* 29 August 1941

referred to by Nixon.[325] Another parachute mine fell in Fellows Road, Hampstead, killing twenty-four people.

All over south London there were fires. The Avery Hill Park College and the Pope Street School in Eltham; Battersea gas works where one gasholder was destroyed; Camberwell bus garage and Brixton police station; in Brixton the organ makers Henry Willis, and Fremlin's bottling stores; St. Jude's church in Sarsfield Road, Balham, and the Palladium Cinema in Balham. Wandsworth Town Hall, the Oval cricket ground, the NAAFI in Kennington Lane, and the Bricklayers Arms railway goods depot all fell victim to incendiaries. Carr's biscuit factory in Fulham was extensively damaged.

In Southwark the targets included the South London Palace Music Hall in London Street, and the AFS station in Webber Street, where five AFS personnel were injured. By Waterloo Bridge two firemen were killed and another two injured. Blackfriars School in Gray Street was also hit as were St. Thomas' Hospital, where fires caused much destruction, and County Hall where serious damage was done to the north wing. The Charles Brown Royal Flour Mills and Tuck's India Rubber Works on the Albert Embankment were both damaged by fire. Incidents at Great Dover Street, Grosvenor Terrace and Crampton Street School contributed to a huge death toll in Southwark. At least twenty-four died at the Skipton Street shelter. St. George's Catholic Cathedral in Southwark was burnt out by incendiaries and Lambeth Palace was damaged again. At 01.15 two bombs landed on the air raid shelter in the cellars of Walkling's cake shop, 50/52 The Cut, on the site of where the Young Vic theatre now stands. Forty-seven people were killed. The Dante Road shelter was also hit and Christ Church in Blackfriars Road, Lambeth was burnt out.

---

325 Nixon, *Raiders Overhead* (1980)

At Victoria Station, the 21.05 warning was followed by a busy night with a succession of incidents. After midnight, a parachute was reported on the line at Ebury Bridge, then came two loud explosions – glass fell from the roof and windows were blown out at the central (signal) box. There was a fire at the Grosvenor Hotel (the station hotel) and the office lighting and the gas supply failed in the station. At 04.55 the all clear sounded but an unexploded bomb meant that all lines were blocked; in addition, the signalling had failed.[326] At Waterloo station, the facilities of the London Necropolis Company were badly damaged after avoiding damage to date in the Blitz. The London Necropolis Railway was opened in 1854 to tackle the problem of overcrowding in London's existing graveyards and cemeteries. It was designed to use the railway to move as many burials as possible to the newly built Brookwood Cemetery in Brookwood, Surrey. In the early stages of the air raid the rolling stock stored in the Necropolis siding was burnt, and the railway arch connecting the main line to the Necropolis terminus was damaged, although the terminal building itself remained unscathed. At 22.30 many incendiaries and high explosive bombs struck the central section of the terminus building. While the office building and platforms survived, the workshops, driveway and Chapelle Ardente were destroyed, along with the third-class waiting room.

At 01.50 a bomb hit the Charing Cross Hotel at the same time as many incendiaries fell on the station. Three trains were on fire in the station and a fourth on Hungerford Bridge. The fires were all but extinguished when a parachute mine was discovered entangled with some ironwork on the bridge. A fire under platform 4 was creeping towards the mine and the station had to be evacuated although the fire brigade was able

---

326 Darwin, *War on the line* (1946)

to extinguish the fire. More incendiaries fell on the hotel but firefighting had to be abandoned because of the mine.[327] This also halted underground services and prompted the evacuation of the nearby War Office. As a result of an outstanding act of bravery, the mine was defused by 10.30 the following morning. Temporary Sub-Lieutenant Ernest Oliver 'Mick' Gidden of the Royal Navy Volunteer Reserve received the George Cross for defusing this mine. 'He found the mine had come to rest across the railway's live high voltage line and that he would have to turn it over to reach the fuse. Working from dawn, it took six hours for him to make the device safe, at times having to ease the distorted casing back with a hammer and chisel where it had melted onto the live third rail.'[328]

At Marylebone goods yard, at 03.16 a huge fire gutted the goods warehouse, destroying all interior equipment and vehicles.

The Bromley area received a concentrated attack, beginning at 21.30 when a bomb fell at Bromley Common, destroying or severely damaging ninety homes, ten shops, a pub and Bromley bus garage along with sixty buses. Lansdowne Road, Ravensbourne Road, Nichol Lane and Southover were particularly badly hit and there were seventy-two fatalities in the borough. Then Bromley parish church, dedicated to SS Peter and Paul, where Dr Johnson had buried his wife, was almost totally destroyed by a direct hit. The adjacent Church House was gutted by fire as the fire services were unable to access it because of debris from the church blocking the road. In the Market Square, Dunn's furniture store was burnt out, the fire services finding that water supplies had been cut by broken mains. In fact, the fire situation was critical by 22.30 with nearly 100 fires needing the attention of the fire brigades although reinforcements soon

---

327 Darwin, *War on the line* (1946)
328 *London Gazette* 9 June 1942

arrived from other parts of north Kent. Lord Stamp of Shortlands was killed along with members of his family in Shortlands, Bromley, when a bomb struck the air raid shelter of his home. He was said by some to be the greatest financial economist of his day. A former civil servant, he was chairman of the LMS railway and also a government adviser who had key skills which would have been needed in post-war Britain. Two parachute mines at Downham caused immense damage and at least thirty-three deaths. Twenty-seven died in Chislehurst mainly as a result of a bomb demolishing a ward at Queen Mary's hospital, Sidcup. In the borough of Orpington, the parish church at Farnborough was destroyed by fire and in Mottingham, four parachute mines caused a huge amount of damage.[329]

From Bromley, it was reported to Whitehall that there occurred 'a minor panic on Downham Housing estate in which about one hundred distraught women and children invaded a rest centre reserved for the bombed out'. This was no doubt an outcome of the very heavy raid locally and is an unusual event. Blake comments that exaggerated rumours had been circulating locally and there does not appear to have been a serious problem.[330]

It was also Croydon's worst night of the war with seventy-eight fatalities occurring. At 22.25 a particularly bad incident occurred at the Queen's Road Homes, a hospital for the elderly where a parachute mine caused extensive damage and killed seventeen patients and a member of staff. Another mine fell at Waddon, causing extensive damage to residential property. There were over sixty incidents in Croydon and 230 fires were reported to the fire service.[331] In neighbouring Mitcham at least twenty were killed, including eleven members of 'B' Company,

---

329 Blake, *Bromley in the Front Line* (2005)
330 Blake, *Bromley in the Front Line* (2005)
331 Berwick Sayers, *Croydon in the Second World War* (1949)

57th (Mitcham) Home Guard Battalion, East Surrey Regiment. They died when a parachute mine hit the Tower Creameries building in Commonside East, where they were on duty. This was a factory manufacturing margarine, which was mostly demolished and then gutted by fire. Some of the fatalities appear in the Civilian War Dead Roll of Honour for Croydon. Seven high explosive bombs fell in an area bordered by Park Avenue and Hill Road and caused widespread damage to residential property. Nine people, mainly in Caithness Road were killed, including the ARP Post Warden of the area, and seventeen injured.[332] The *California Hotel* pub in Belmont, Sutton received a direct hit and eight people including the licensee were killed. The nearby Belmont railway station was also destroyed.

Some mystery surrounds two incidents in Poplar. On 17 April fatalities are recorded in the Civilian War Dead Roll of Honour at Coborn Road, Bow, which indicates that this area of London was affected by the raid of 16/17 April. On 18 April twenty-five fatalities are recorded at the Morant Street Shelter in Poplar. However, no air raid took place on this day. An account (which does not mention a date) in the BBC's WW2 People's War archive claims a parachute mine fell nearby and caused the roof of the shelter to collapse. This is certain to be a simple mistake in the Roll regarding the date of the Morant Street incident, which actually happened on the night of 19/20 April. There are other deaths recorded in London on 18 April but most are annotated as being the result of incidents on earlier dates.

Five Southern Railway rail terminals were closed causing chaos for commuters – a mile-long queue at Clapham Junction for the substitute buses was recorded, although their proposed route was in flames and blocked by fire hoses! Waterloo station was without gas, water and lighting. The Waterloo and City

---

332 Merton Historical Society – Bulletin 175, September 2010

Railway (reopened only in March) was shut again. Newspaper trains had to run from Wimbledon and Surbiton. As a result of this and the raid on 19 April, things were not back to normal on the Southern Railway until 26 April.

Many people were left homeless in Finsbury, Holborn, Shoreditch, Stepney and Lewisham. In summary, this raid had slightly better results for the defenders; five German aircraft failed to return. Three were shot down over London by night fighters, one was shot down by AA fire (as described earlier) and a further one crashed near Faversham, Kent.

The Home Intelligence Weekly Reports noted that 'The London raid on Wednesday night found the public mentally unprepared. It was generally believed that heavy raids on the capital were unlikely, for the following reasons:

The enemy bombing tactics were thought to be directed for the present primarily against our ports.

It was suggested that bombers could not be spared from the Balkans.

Our night-fighters' recent successes were beginning to produce a half-hearted hope that the conquest of the night bomber was in sight.

There had been no really heavy raids on London for some time, and as a result, the public had become "unconditioned."

Nevertheless, the effect on the public was not as severe as after the first blitz in September last year.'[333]

19/20 April 1941 – 'the Saturday'

The raid of 19/20 April, known as 'the Saturday' was said to be a birthday present for Hitler, who was fifty-two on 20 April. It was more likely to have been revenge for a raid on Berlin by the RAF on 17 April. It targeted the Docks and East London. Bombing

---

333 https.//moidigital.ac.uk/ Weekly Report by Home Intelligence – No. 29

was concentrated well although as a result of the poor weather accuracy was impaired and several incidents did occur north and west of the City of London, well outside the target area. The raid lasted from 21.15 to 04.15 and for the first and only time in the London Blitz, over 1,000 tonnes of high explosive were dropped. 250 parachute mines were dropped and four 2,500 kg 'Max' bombs and ten of the 1,800 kg type were included in the bomb load. According to Ramsey, the Luftwaffe flew 783 bomber sorties and 153,096 incendiaries were dropped.[334] German sources quoted by Collier[335] indicate this was the largest number of incendiaries dropped in any raid on Britain. It was in fact the heaviest air raid of the war on Britain.

Coming only three days after 'the Wednesday' undoubtedly more people sought shelter, but how effective shelters were against parachute mines and very heavy high explosive bombs can be seen in the casualty lists. There was no 'bombers' moon' but cloud and drizzle, which did not clear until 03.00. To compensate, the attackers used parachute flares; at 22.30 Vere Hodgson finds that 'the whole of Notting Hill was as light as Midsummer Noon!'

'The Saturday' is less well-documented than 'the Wednesday', with fewer personal accounts published, perhaps because its impact was largely on working-class areas of east London and also, connected to this, few famous or historic buildings were hit. Damage was largely to residential and industrial premises. Because of the targeting of east London, many bombs fell in the Docks and on other commercial premises, and in this area much residential property had already been destroyed in earlier raids. This may account for fatalities being rather less numerous than in the raids of 16/17 April and 10/11 May. But there is

---

334 Ramsey, ed., *The Blitz Then and Now Vol.2* (1988)
335 Collier, *The Defence of the UK* (1955)

uncertainty surrounding casualties. Brooksbank quotes 1,208 fatalities which apparently derives from HO 322/134, in fact many sources including Ramsey say that 1,200 fatalities resulted from this raid. However, those listed in the Civilian War Dead Roll of Honour only total some 900. This is rather strange – in the case of the raids on 16/17 April and 10/11 May fatalities quoted in most sources are usually fairly close to the figures in the Roll, although the Roll does not include any military casualties. Twenty-five fatalities in Poplar on 19/20 April have been included (although they are listed incorrectly under 18 April) as have about thirty who died of their injuries over the following week or so. Brooksbank also says 92 died in a shelter in Shoreditch, but it is not stated where this figure originates. This is presumably the Nuttall Street incident – but the figure of 92 seems as Ramsey says, to be the initial estimate of 46 killed plus 46 missing.

Parachute mines fell in the Thames, halting traffic downstream from Tower Bridge. Fires were reported in the boroughs of Westminster, Holborn and St Pancras, but none of these boroughs, along with St Marylebone, the City of London and Finsbury suffered any significant bombing incidents or casualties. Apart from the destruction of the railway bridge in Southwark the boroughs of Southwark and Bermondsey were also relatively unscathed. In the borough of Woolwich, there were fires at the Arsenal, the Royal Arsenal Co-operative Society (RACS) in Powis Street, and at Siemens. Serious damage was caused by fires at the Royal Naval College, Greenwich, Brook Hospital in Shooters Hill Road, the gun site on Woolwich Common, Woolwich Institute in Plumstead and Plumstead High Street LCC school. Rotherhithe town hall was also hit. Twenty-seven people were killed by a high explosive bomb in Saltwell Street, Poplar and although this doesn't tie in with the Civilian War Dead Roll of Honour, it must be the Morant Street shelter incident listed presumably in error on 18 April in the Roll. Barges and ships were on fire in the East India docks. There was destruction in Pitfield Street, Hoxton by high explosive and also in Shoreditch, at the technical institute, public library and baths. Three LFS men were killed at Mulgrove Place school, and three LFS men were injured at the fire station in Sunbury Street, Woolwich. The Bricklayers Arms goods depot was hit, and hospitals hit included St Peter's in Stepney, where staff and patients died after being trapped by fires in the 100-year-old building.

The proportion of heavy bombs dropped is reflected in the number of incidents with a large casualty list. Of the fatalities in the Civilian War Dead Roll of Honour, sixty-six died in East Ham, sixty-five in Shoreditch, fifty in West Ham, fifty-five in Poplar, fifty in Ilford, forty-four in Romford, forty-three in Barking but only around sixteen in Stepney. Thirty-four died in Hackney, mainly at Annis Road and Egerton Road. Twenty died and nearly fifty were seriously injured in Tottenham, mainly at Nursery Street and Beaufoy Road. Leyton, Wanstead and Woodford, and Walthamstow (seventeen killed – four high explosive bombs and four parachute mines were recorded) all had incidents but Edmonton and Chingford were virtually unscathed.

Amongst individual incidents, thirty-six firemen and women were killed at Old Palace School sub-station, St. Leonard's Street, Bromley-by-Bow, when it received a direct hit by a 1,000kg armour-piercing bomb. This is the largest single loss of fire brigade personnel in English history. Twenty-one of the victims were from Beckenham and were there as reinforcements for the local brigade. Thirty-two people died at the *Prince of Wales* pub in Manor Road in Chigwell after it was hit by a parachute mine at 21.45. This was the one of only two incidents involving fatalities to occur in Chigwell parish during the whole war. Many of the victims are buried in St. Mary's churchyard.

In Shoreditch, at Horner House, blocks of flats in Nuttall Street, 'a bomb (not a mine) struck no.14 trench shelter completely demolishing three blocks of flats and part of the nurses' home of St Leonards Hospital. Extensive blast damage to Stringer House a similar block of flats.'[336] Horner House had two trench shelters each holding forty-eight people; those in no.13 shelter escaped but thirteen died in no.14. Over 60 were killed in all. Also badly damaged in the same incident was an electricity sub-station. Six people died at St. Mary's station in Whitechapel Road, Stepney when a bomb struck the entrance. This station had been closed to passenger traffic since 1938 but was one of those brought back into use as a public shelter. In West Ham, a mine falling at the junction of Woodgrange Road and Romford Road completely demolished the *Princess Alice* pub. In East Ham, St Bartholomew's church was gutted by fire, but a couple went ahead with their wedding in the ruins the following day. Both the new and temporary Waterloo bridges were damaged by high explosive. Several sources say these were the only hits on a bridge over the Thames during the Blitz.[337]

In Lambeth, twenty-two people were killed at 214 Kennington Road, which appears to have been an ARP centre as most of the victims were wardens or messengers. Strangely, this incident is not mentioned by Shaw and Mills in their account of the war in Lambeth. Some clues can be found on Jimmy's Lambeth website, although the author seems unaware of the true scope of the incident, as far as casualties were concerned:

'It turns out that Charlie (Rapley) was an Air Raid Warden and on the night of 19th April, 1941 he was on duty at the Vestry

336 TNA HO 198/33 Group 3
337 The temporary bridge replaced the original bridge demolished in 1935. The new bridge was completed in 1942 but not formally opened until 1945.

300

of St Philips at 214 Kennington Road along with his friend, Issie (Israel) Kutz. They had both joined the ARP service at the start of the war in 1939. It seems that Air Raid Wardens were the butt of jokes but these men were the ones above the ground, whilst everyone else was in shelters, just waiting for the bombs to drop on their patch. They would be the first at the scene, bombs still dropping around them, so they could call up the help needed from the emergency services – frequently they were the ones making the initial rescues of trapped people. God knows why people made jokes about them – sounds to me like they were doing a splendidly courageous job. Not only that, they had to act as guards to prevent people looting the bombed premises.

The bomb apparently landed right on the Vestry and killed Charlie and Issie outright – it's believed that a 16-year-old messenger also died from his wounds and also a woman. The role of the boy messengers was to ride bikes through the bombs and rubble to notify the other services of the situation if phone lines were down. The woman was probably there on duty, to co-ordinate phone calls and paper work. Charlie was awarded his medal[338] thanks to the efforts of his brother George, but I wonder whether Issie Kutz was ever awarded his – I'd like to think so'.[339]

Romford and Hornchurch had their worst night of the whole war when the boroughs were hit by ten parachute mines. Essex Road in Collier Row, Romford was particularly badly hit with thirty-eight killed when two rows of terraced houses were completely demolished. In Hornchurch, nine members of the Gill family were killed when their shelter in Brentwood Road was hit. Fifteen people were killed in Poets Road, Highbury. Ilford's casualties included twenty-four killed in Westwood Road.

---

338 He was posthumously awarded his World War 2 Defence Medal
339 Janice Crow on Jimmy's Lambeth website

There were also many casualties in south east London and north Kent, with fifteen being killed in Belvedere and Abbey Wood. There were also fatalities in Crayford and Dartford.

Isolated incidents occurred in north and west London, presumably after attacking aircraft got lost. Suburbs that received bombs included East Finchley and Muswell Hill which were showered by a large number of incendiaries. As a result, the hilltop St. James's church on Muswell Hill Broadway was burnt out and the main roof, organ, choir stalls and many pews were destroyed. Bomb damage on the LTPB Northern line near Highgate station (a bomb shattered the portal of the north exit of the tunnel) restricted traffic to 15 mph. Twenty-four died in New Southgate, where the ARP logbooks state four parachute mines fell, and sixty-eight were seriously wounded. The casualties were mainly in Pevensey Avenue.

In Ealing, at least twenty-two people died in Talbot Road; the circumstances are unclear and this incident is not mentioned by Upton. Only some of the victims have a street number given in the Civilian War Dead Roll of Honour, but contemporary photographs indicate this might have been a shelter incident. There were also six fatalities in Green End Road, Acton.

In Putney Bridge Road, Wandsworth, a bomb struck the *Castle Hotel*, a modern pub that was packed with customers. Shaw and Mills state that forty-two were killed and 141 injured here but do not mention that another bomb fell on a shelter in Wandsworth Park shortly after, killing at least sixteen. The Civilian War Dead Roll of Honour lists a total of fifty-four fatalities in Wandsworth on the night.

Railway damage was mainly to the LMS and LNER tracks in east London and to the Southern Railway's Central and Eastern sections. At 22.15 a parachute mine hit the railway bridge over Southwark Street just south of Blackfriars Bridge and caused the track and supporting girders to collapse into the street below.

This extremely unfortunate incident necessitated extensive and costly reconstruction work which took over a month to complete. This resulted in a major disruption to cross-London goods traffic via the Metropolitan Widened lines. Lt.-Colonel Sir Alan Mount, Chief Inspecting Officer of Railways was clearly convinced that the Germans wanted to destroy the cross-Thames traffic: 'It appears that the enemy has made several attempts to put the MWL at Blackfriars out of use, and with other recent incidents at the river bridges it may indicate deliberate attack on cross-Thames communications.'[340] The Blackfriars signal box was totally destroyed; here, seven men had taken shelter from flagging trains and working points in a military steel shelter protected by sandbags. However, it seems that the door of this shelter was not fully closed and six of the men were killed by blast, the seventh being seriously injured.

Brooksbank also recounts how a parachute mine explosion at Kensal Green stopped all freight services from Willesden to the Southern Railway and the Great Western Railway. This was not cleared until 24 April. All lines into Broad Street station were blocked by high explosive; passenger services, already terminating at Canonbury or Dalston since 17 April, were not resumed until 24 April. However, most railway damage was swiftly repaired.

Described as 'perhaps the most memorable event of the war to the residents of Merstham' two parachute mines fell at South Merstham. One dropped harmlessly on Wells Nursery, but the other exploded on All Saints Green. The explosion, heard for miles, had a devastating effect. All Saints Church was completely destroyed, as was the vicarage and two nearby houses. A total of ten people died in the blast that night. The 84-year-old vicar, who had been reading in his study, suffered severe injuries. One

---

340 Brooksbank, *London Main Line War Damage* (2007)

of his two sisters was killed and the other, like the vicar himself, was in hospital for several months.[341]

Night fighters destroyed a Heinkel 111 bomber which broke up in the air over Wormley, Surrey, and a Junkers 88, which crashed into a garden in Wimbledon.[342]

Probably 148,000 houses in the London region were damaged and destroyed in the two April raids but Titmuss claims that 'social disruption' was kept under greater control with far fewer homeless people in the rest centres than in the previous autumn.[343]

The weekly report by Home Intelligence noted that the two raid-free nights preceding this meant 'there was a marked recovery and a restoration of confidence; feeling was a good deal less upset by Saturday's raid. Arrangements for the care of raid victims worked as well as could be expected under very difficult conditions, and there were few complaints. Since the raids, the number of shelter users has greatly increased, and shelters which were practically empty are now full.[344]'

341 http.//www.merstham.co.uk/merstham/MersthamHistory.htm
342 Ogley, *Surrey at War 1939-1945* (1995)
343 Titmuss *Problems of Social Policy* (1950)
344 https.//moidigital.ac.uk/ Weekly Report by Home Intelligence – No. 29

TEN

MOONLIGHT IN MAY

8-9 May 1941

In an isolated incident at midnight, two high explosive bombs hit St. Vincent's Hospital in Ruislip. This hospital had 219 beds, 75 of which were designated for the Emergency Medical Service. Histories suggest the hospital chapel was destroyed by bombing and rebuilt in 1962.

10-11 May 1941

Barbara Nixon, a warden in Finsbury wrote 'As the May moon grew to full we were all expecting trouble. Would it be worse than April had been? By the Thursday of the second week the moon was brilliant. Nothing happened. On Friday, it was at its zenith, but again it was quiet. Perhaps, we thought, we might be missed this month. But on Saturday we paid for that faint flicker of optimism.'[345] Collier alleges that Hitler was provoked

---

345 Nixon, *Raiders Overhead* (1980)

by Martin Bormann and others into ordering this attack at a late night gathering on the Friday at Hitler's *Berghof* retreat.[346] Conceived on a whim it may have been, but the raid was nevertheless thoroughly planned and executed by Sperrle, despite the short notice he was given.

The sheer scale and perceived viciousness of this raid is remarkable and reflects the success of the Luftwaffe in concentrating on the inner-city boroughs. Target areas were the City of London and the East End, Westminster, and the area centred around the Elephant and Castle, the hub of the road system of south London. This junction, taking its name from the eponymous pub, lies a couple of miles south of London Bridge where five major roads meet.[347]

According to Mortimer,[348] sixty-one boroughs reported incidents. However, fatalities occurred in less than half of the London region's ninety-five boroughs, which is a fair indicator that the vast majority of the bombs fell on those boroughs. It should be noted that both 'the Wednesday' and 'the Saturday' in April were bigger raids both in terms of number of aircraft taking part and the tonnage of bombs dropped. It is also evident that people in some parts of London remained unaware, initially at least, of the intensity of the raid on the affected areas. Blake, looking at the raid from a south-east London perspective, claims that 'much less bombing over-spilled on semi-rural parts of outer London than on many previous occasions.'[349]

However, on May 10/11, compared to the April raids, the number and size of the fires that developed were near catastrophic, with nine fires classed as conflagrations which had the potential to develop into firestorms of the type that were to

---

346 Collier, *The City that wouldn't Die. London May 10-11, 1941* (1959)
347 Mortimer, *The Longest Night 10-11 May 1941* (2005)
348 Mortimer, *ibid*
349 Blake, *Bromley in the Front Line* (2005)

sweep through German cities later in the war. There were also twenty major fires, thirty-seven serious fires and 210 medium fires recorded. The number of incidents with casualties was high across all the boroughs affected, and it has to be remembered that many parts of London were not affected at all. Given that this raid was one of the biggest suffered by London, and that 1,436 fatal casualties resulted, it is surprising there were not more individual incidents with a high number of fatalities. The worst incident appears to have been that at Holford Square, Finsbury, where two parachute mines that fell at around midnight killed over forty people and caused massive destruction. The large number of casualties suffered by Civil Defence workers, the police and the fire services is also significant. Collier claims that only twenty of the fatalities in London were in approved shelters, but the Civilian War Dead Roll of Honour records indicates there were rather more but not at the level of earlier raids. It would appear that many people failed to take cover during this raid. The lack of enemy air activity for the previous four weeks, and the lack of any RAF attack which might have provoked retaliation, had probably induced a false sense of security in London's population. Collier has suggested that as the April raids had seen continuing incidents at shelters, this may have acted as a further discouragement to Londoners.[350] Graves however says that sheltering in the Underground doubled after the April raids to over 100,000 but the numbers had shrunk again before 10 May.[351]

The reasons for the high casualty list should not disguise the fact that the impact of the raid was such that it was acknowledged in many quarters that a repeat on the Sunday night would have had catastrophic consequences. Another raid

350 Collier, *The City That Wouldn't Die* (1959).
351 Graves, *London Transport at War* (1978)

of this severity was widely predicted to have the potential to 'defeat London', or at least bring life in the capital to a halt. This was because of the anticipated damage to utilities, particularly water, communications and transport, not necessarily because of the casualties or destruction of housing that might have resulted.

By the early evening of 10 May, the fire services were aware that the German beams were directed on London, and extra fire appliances were closed in on the capital in readiness. At 22.45 the Luftwaffe's fire-raisers, the pathfinder aircraft of KG100, crossed the coast and shortly afterwards the sirens sounded in the London area. The first bomb of the night was recorded at the Royal Albert Dock at 23.02.

Fatalities included 138 in Southwark, 110 in Westminster, eighty-seven in Camberwell, eighty-five in Lambeth, eighty-four in St. Pancras and seventy-two in Paddington. These were the worst affected boroughs in terms of loss of life.

Holborn was the scene of a huge conflagration in Theobalds Road which destroyed most of the buildings on and behind the north side of the road, including the Bloomsbury cinema and Holborn council's works department in New North Street. In addition, many buildings in Red Lion Square, Lambs Conduit Street and Red Lion Street were destroyed by high explosive or burnt out by incendiaries. Hanway House, a large block of government offices in Red Lion Square, had to be evacuated. In one of the many incidents in the borough of Holborn, the Camden Hotel in Store Street was demolished.

At 12.55 the Royal College of Surgeons at 41 Lincoln's Inn Fields was hit by a high explosive bomb. The British government had purchased the collection of leading anatomist and surgeon John Hunter in 1799 and it was housed in galleries at 35 Lincoln's Inn Fields. The bomb destroyed two rooms of the Hunterian Museum at no. 35 and around half of the entire collection of

6,000 specimens was lost. The salvage on stretchers of valuable pickled body part specimens caused some alarm![352]

Eight pumps were dispatched to the British Museum, which suffered extensive fire damage. Fortunately, many of its exhibits had been removed for safekeeping before the outbreak of war. However, tens of thousands of books were destroyed when fire consumed the South-West Quadrant bookstacks.

The borough of Paddington had serious incidents in Delamere Crescent and Clifton Gardens. Three men of the London Fire Service were killed in the latter incident, where in all fourteen people succumbed to fire and high explosive at a block of flats. The BBC Maida Vale studios, the Imperial Cinema in Edgware Road and Paddington Coroner's Court were all hit.

Bermondsey had sixty-three fatalities including many at the St. John's Estate shelter. Mortimer mentions an incident with many casualties at a shelter at Peek Frean's, the Bermondsey biscuit maker, but this is not identifiable from the Civilian War Dead Roll of Honour, which only lists one AFS man killed at Peek Frean's. The company provided shelters for the area under the factory's railway arches. It is possible that there is confusion with another of the many shelter incidents in this area during the Blitz. Certainly, Peek Frean's, whose factory was in Clements Road, was badly damaged by bombing at this time and was put out of action for three months. Huntley and Palmer, an associated biscuit manufacturing company, had to take over some production from them.

As the night wore on, the fire situation in Southwark became increasingly serious.

'In addition to Southwark Fire Station, a sub-station in Rockingham Street, the policemen's married quarters at the station in Borough High Street, and the local mortuary were also on fire. Borough Market was wrecked by high explosive bombs and a barrage balloon was brought down in Marshalsea Road. In Harper Road the LCC Weights and Measures Office was hit by a parachute mine, killing a fire guard and several others.'[353]

By the early hours of the morning the fire situation at the Elephant and Castle was so bad that occupants of a public shelter had to be quickly evacuated to the Elephant and Castle tube station. Just after midnight Superintendent Adams, in command of 'F' District, arrived at the Elephant and Castle. Freeman, Hardy and Willis's shoe shop and warehouse, and Spurgeon's Tabernacle were already on fire. A heavy fall of incendiaries caused fires to break out in all the six roads meeting at the Elephant and Castle, but fire brigade personnel found all hydrants dry. By 01.00 there were more than thirty broken water mains in the Elephant and Castle district. Adams ordered two water units and set one trailer pump into a 5,000-gallon dam by Spurgeon's Tabernacle, on the west side of the junction, but in five minutes it too was dry. Two more pumps were sent to Manor Place Baths, an emergency supply of 125,000 gallons, just off the Walworth Road. Three others were sent to the Surrey Theatre. The Surrey Theatre in Blackfriars Road had been demolished in 1934 and its basement had been converted into an emergency water supply.

The Manor Place Baths was soon dry and within an hour it was on fire. Adams organised relays from the Thames and the Surrey Canal by Camberwell Road, but this was a time-consuming operation. Four lines of hose had been set up from the three trailer pumps at the Surrey Theatre as well as a scaffolding dam holding 5,000 gallons, into which water was just coming through.

At St George's Circus, the Royal Eye Hospital and the

---

353 Maltman, in *Saved* edition 22 (Summer 2000)

Salvation Army building, either side of the Surrey Music Hall, were on fire. In addition to the three pumps working from the water supply in the basement, several London Fire Brigade appliances were attempting to keep the situation under control. At 02.22, a parachute mine fell in Blackfriars Road causing devastation over a wide area. Seventeen firemen were killed (all three crews of the trailer pumps) and several others were injured. All access to the water supply in the basement of the Surrey Theatre was blocked.

The situation became more and more desperate. A relay to bring water from the Thames at London Bridge was buried when a burning building collapsed. Several fires dealt with earlier re-ignited and the heat and sparks were so intense that a firestorm was feared. 100 pumps had been summoned. Senior fire service personnel met with Herbert Morrison, the Minister for Home Security and decided to use a new kind of emergency steel piping made up in 20ft lengths and able to withstand all forms of attack, including high explosives. This could be laid in 50 minutes and seemed the last hope. By the time the all clear was sounded a good supply of water was coming from the river and from the Surrey Canal. The fires at the Elephant and Castle were gradually brought under control.

A lack of water and a low tide on the river had meant that firemen all over London were helpless to deal with a situation that developed rapidly around them that night.[354]

Fifty-three died in St. Marylebone where serious incidents occurred at Lisson Grove, Mulready Street, Great Titchfield Street and at 43/47 York Terrace in Regents Park. The highest casualties occurred at the latter location with nearly twenty killed amongst a gathering of ninety-nine members of the Group for Sacrifice and Service, who according to Richard

---

354 Maltman, in *Saved* edition 22 (Summer 2000)

Collier had been worshipping the moon under a glass roof![355]
However, some of the fatalities appear to be from the WVS, ARP
and the Observer Corps but there is no explanation of how they
were involved. At 01.45 initial reports were that there were up
to 100 trapped and sixty casualties in this terrace of solidly built
Regency buildings. The incident was not cleared until 09.30 the
next morning.[356] The *Pitts Head* pub in Paddington Street was
totally demolished and the licensee killed.

The Central Synagogue, Hallam Street, was also hit after 23.00
by a single incendiary bomb, which caused a raging fire. The
Central Synagogue was a fine 600-seat Gothic-style Ashkenazi
orthodox synagogue facing Hallam and Great Portland Streets
and consecrated in 1870. Local residents displaced by bombing
were sheltering in its basement. Extensive damage was also
caused in Hallam Street.[357] Post Warden Stanley Barlow of post
D2 in St Marylebone was awarded the George Medal for rescuing
people from under burning buildings. His role in local incidents
that night is documented by Richard Collier.[358] Among Barlow's
wardens was the Nigerian law student E Ita Ekpenyon, later to
document his experiences in his booklet 'Some Experiences of an
African Air-Raid Warden'. Bickenhall Mansions, the large block
of flats diagonally across the road from Baker Street station was
set on fire, the roof being burnt off. Baker Street station itself
was hit by incendiaries and high explosive. Druce's furnishing
store, badly damaged in December, was finished off with further
fires at Baker Street and Blandford Street. Bedford College on
the Inner Circle in Regent's Park was seriously damaged by high
explosive.

---

355 Collier, *The City That Wouldn't Die* (1959)
356 Harris & Bright, *A Wander Through Wartime London. Five Walks
    Revisiting the Blitz* (2010)
357 Westminster City Archives www.westendatwar.org.uk
358 Collier, *The City That Wouldn't Die* (1959)

In Westminster, the Alexandra Hotel in Knightsbridge received direct hits by two bombs at 00.40 and twenty-four people died. The whole building was dangerously unstable and to add to the difficulties facing rescuers, the hotel's registers could not be traced. 'Half the upper storeys of the hotel had cascaded like a landslide across the road', which was now blocked by rubble.[359] The hotel's lifts and staircases having been destroyed, a delicate operation began to rescue guests trapped on the upper storeys. People were not only trapped on the upper floors but also in the basement. Police Constables John McKenning and Reginald Oakes received the George Medal for their part in the rescue.

'A high explosive bomb fell on a building and wrecked the interior. A landing had collapsed on to the ground floor, leaving a chasm 12 feet across and 40 feet deep. Cries for help were coming from a room on the opposite side. Oakes and McKenning obtained a nine-inch plank and carried it up a badly damaged exterior iron staircase to the second floor where it was passed over the gap and they crossed to the other side. By climbing through an opening in the wall about seven feet from the floor Oakes reached the room where four people were trapped. He helped them to climb through on to the plank and across to the other side. The scene of the rescue was immediately over the centre of the bomb crater and the whole of the surrounding portions of the building were liable to collapse. Throughout the operations heavy gunfire shook the building and debris was continually falling. The Constables showed outstanding courage and resourcefulness.'[360]

Twenty-four people also died at Turner Buildings, a big block of LCC flats at Millbank, Westminster. A bomb which hit the Watney brewery in Victoria killed twelve dray horses. In

359 Collier, *The City That Wouldn't Die* (1959)
360 *London Gazette* 5 September 1941

Kensington there were twenty-eight deaths, eighteen of them at Elvaston Place. It is not clear what happened here and among the fatalities are members of the Home Guard, ARP Wardens and police. Collier says fire ignited an unexploded bomb in a basement. In Lambeth, Field's candle and soap factory in Upper Marsh near Waterloo Station with its highly inflammable stocks of animal and vegetable fats, was totally destroyed after a fall of incendiaries overwhelmed the fire watchers and water supplies failed. Farmiloe's Paint Works in Battersea was another of the many industrial premises blazing.

Amongst the famous buildings destroyed was the Queen's Hall, London's leading concert hall, in Portland Place near the BBC. The final performance in the hall had taken place that afternoon when Malcolm Sargent conducted the London Philharmonic Orchestra and the Royal Choral Society in Elgar's *Dream of Gerontius*. About 21.00 an incendiary bomb fell on the roof of the hall and although extinguished it reignited. The fire services could not attend until 02.00 due to the serious fire situations all around, but no water was available. By 02.45 the fire was reported by police as 'very serious, now out of control'.[361] Eventually the hall was completely gutted and the roof collapsed, and concert goers arriving for the Sunday concert were confronted by a total ruin. Because another concert was scheduled for the Sunday, some musicians had left their instruments in the band room overnight, and many were a total loss including the priceless seventeenth century double-bass of the London Philharmonic's principal, Adolf Lotter.

The Houses of Parliament and in fact the whole historic complex of buildings known as the Palace of Westminster was threatened. Incendiaries caused a spectacular blaze in the Victoria Tower. War Reserve Constables Gordon Farrant and

---

361 Collier, *The City That Wouldn't Die* (1959)

Arthur Stead were on fire watch duties in the turret above the Royal Gallery in the House of Lords and were killed when bombs struck the complex, blocking access in the already complicated network of passages. The chamber of the House of Commons was burnt out, but fortunately after much hard work by firefighters the mediaeval roof of Westminster Hall was saved, although a significant area was affected by fire. Collier[362] implies that the fire in the chamber having taken hold, fanned by the underground heating ducts, a decision was taken to contain it and concentrate most of the fifty pumps attending on the fire in the roof of Westminster Hall, where there was a good chance of saving the 1,000-year-old structure. The next day Earl Winterton[363] observed that 'the fire had done its work in a most astonishingly clean fashion. The Chamber itself had completely disappeared, as had the voting lobbies, but the other lobbies and Ministers' rooms close behind the chamber were untouched; the void gave the appearance of having been chiselled out with a knife.'

One of the clock faces of Big Ben was damaged, probably by shrapnel from an AA shell, but the clock continued to chime. Captain Edward Elliot, the House of Lords Resident Staff Superintendent, was also killed. He should not be confused with Colonel Walter Elliott, MP for Kelvingrove, Glasgow, who, quoting his authority as a Privy Councillor, took an axe to an ancient door to allow firefighters access to Westminster Hall. Cocks[364] claims Elliott did not need to do this – a side door was left permanently open for just such an emergency.

Churches destroyed included a further four of the works of Sir Christopher Wren. His famous St. Clement Danes and St. Mary-le-Bow were both burnt out, and also his less well-known St.

362 Collier, *The City That Wouldn't Die* (1959)
363 Winterton, *Orders of the Day* (1953)
364 Cocks, *Mid Victorian Masterpiece* (1977)

Mildred Bread Street and St. Nicholas Cole Abbey. St. Dunstan-in-the–East received a direct hit and the nave collapsed. Wren's St. Stephen's Walbrook is described as destroyed in some sources but was only slightly damaged. The Hawksmoor church, St. George-in-the-East, Stepney, was gutted by fire, as was St. John's Smith Square, Westminster, the work of Thomas Archer. Across the river, both St. Mary's Newington and Spurgeon's Tabernacle were destroyed by fire. Other churches destroyed included the Church of Scotland St. Columba's in Pont Street, Knightsbridge. Holy Trinity in Sloane Street, Chelsea, was badly damaged. The Great Synagogue of London in Duke's Place, Aldgate – built in 1788-90 by James Spiller – was destroyed.

Many other ancient buildings were lost to fire and high explosive. Gray's Inn and the Temple in particular suffered great destruction. In Gray's Inn, the hall, library and chapel were gutted in addition to much of South Square. The famous and beautiful Temple Church, built by the Knights Templar and dedicated in 1185, was gutted. The library roof was set on fire. By this stage of the Blitz, half of the Middle Temple had been destroyed. The Charterhouse, an important collection of historic buildings in Clerkenwell, was even worse hit. Due to a lack of water, fires were able to spread rapidly through the whole complex, most of which was gutted.

Like Wren churches there is sometimes confusion regarding when City livery company halls were destroyed. O'Brien[365] says five halls were destroyed – those of the Mercers, Salters, Cordwainers, Cutlers and Butchers. However, it appears that the Butchers Hall was destroyed in 1944 by a flying bomb, but the Carpenters' history states their hall was one of those burnt out on 10/11 May. Devonshire House, a fine old Georgian house in Boswell Street, Holborn, housing a museum, was totally

365 O'Brien, *Civil Defence* (1954)

destroyed although the contents had already been moved. The Grand Priory church of St. John of Jerusalem in Clerkenwell was virtually obliterated. In Westminster, the historic Greycoat Hospital (a girls' grammar school) and Westminster School were both badly damaged by fire. At the latter, Great School, Kings College, Kings College Master's House and Ashburnham House were the worst affected.

The Clubland complex in Camberwell was almost completely gutted. Clubland was the product of years of work by the Rev Jimmy Butterworth on behalf of the young people of south London. Its church, cinema, theatre and workshops were all destroyed.

Damage in the City of London was severe, reminiscent of the 29 December raid. The Salvation Army HQ at 101 Queen Victoria Street in the City of London was totally consumed by fire. Another building in this street collapsed into the road, its fall being captured in one of those classic pictures of the Blitz. This was no.23, the premises of John Wood & Son. Some damage had far-ranging effects. The London Commercial Sales Rooms in Mincing Lane were razed. Kynaston says that 'up to that night the City had been as least as much a commercial as a financial centre; subsequently it would be predominantly financial in character.'[366]

Fire damage in the Fleet Street and Fetter Lane areas was particularly extensive. The old houses of Nevill's Court off Shoe Lane, which dated back to 1662 and had survived the Great Fire, were destroyed as was the Moravian Chapel in Fetter Lane and Sergeant's Inn. The premises of the *News Chronicle* and the *News of the World* were on fire, but incredibly Fleet Street managed to publish all the Sunday papers. Ludgate Hill was also severely damaged, the premises of publishers Cassell and

---

366 Kynaston, *The City of London* (2011)

Co being among the casualties, with huge stocks of publications destroyed.

Cable and Wireless's premises in Moorgate were burnt out. Part of the building was struck by incendiaries and fires also began to spread from the neighbouring Tower Chambers. A bomb on Salisbury House blasted out doors and windows encouraging the spread of flames. By 02.00 Electra House had to be abandoned and the danger posed by the fuel store in the basement of Tower Chambers and the discovery of an UXB in Finsbury Square sealed the fate of the building.[367]

The Old Bailey was struck by a bomb which shattered the north-west corner of the building destroying no.2 Court. St. James' Palace and Westminster Abbey were amongst buildings that were less seriously damaged. The chapel and library of Lambeth Palace suffered grave damage, the fire service having greater priority demands on their services locally, particularly at St. Thomas' Hospital. Stone's Chop House in Panton Street, Haymarket was amongst other well-known buildings destroyed.

Islington had serious incidents and over fifty people died in the borough. Halton Mansions in Halton Road, Liverpool Road and Roman Way were the scene of major incidents. Pentonville prison was hit and C-Wing destroyed, and several prisoners were among the thirteen killed. Shoreditch had numerous incidents with eighteen fatalities in Crondall Street, Purcell Street and Whiston Road. Hackney and Stoke Newington escaped relatively lightly.

Chelsea had another difficult night, although it does not seem, as Faviell claims, to have been the worst night of the Blitz for the borough. However, there were many fires and the cumulative effect of the raids of 1940-41 on the population must have been severe. St. Luke's Hospital received a direct hit which

---

367 Graves, *The Thin Red Lines* (1948)

destroyed the operating theatre, two wards, the radiography department, the kitchens, reception areas and the doctors' quarters. Two doctors were among the dead, and the hospital had to be closed. It was one of fourteen hospitals in London to be hit. There were also many casualties in an incident in Basil Street, Chelsea. Neighbouring Fulham was relatively lightly affected but Hammersmith was not so lucky with twenty fatalities. But this represented the extent to which the raid spread westwards.

Two mayors of London boroughs died on duty. Leonard Eaton-Smith, the mayor of Westminster, was visiting trench shelters in Eaton Square when a bomb fell. The doughty Albert Henley, mayor of Bermondsey, had been out in the raid since it began, in the thick of the action, and was killed when a bomb fell near the Town Hall. He earned a posthumous commendation from the King for brave conduct in civil defence.

The effect on London's telecommunications was dire – more than 50% of all telephone trunk circuits and 60% of all out-going toll circuits were put out of action. The Metropolitan Water Board eventually recorded a total of 605 water mains broken. Large areas of London were without water. As far as damage to industrial targets was concerned, seventy-one 'key points' were out of action.[368]

With regard to roads, all east-west routes through the City were impassable, and enormous disruption was caused to bus, trolleybus and tram services. Hundreds of vehicles were damaged. The damage to London's railways was also enormous and such that through routes were not open again until June. All the London main line railway stations were put out of action, with the exception of Marylebone, although this had damage to the station roof and bombs in the goods yard causing restricted working. St. Pancras had two direct hits; at 00.15 a bomb struck

---

368 Collier, *The City That Wouldn't Die* (1959)

between platforms 3 and 4 and penetrated to the King's Cross tunnel which connects the Midland lines to the Metropolitan line. Another bomb fell between platforms 6 and 7, exploding below ground. Extensive damage was done to the station roof and railway coaches, and a passenger was killed in the shelter. Services did not resume until 19 May. All lines into Euston were closed by debris on the line from a bomb which fell on the Hampstead Road bridge.

Severe damage was caused at Kings Cross when a heavy bomb hit the booking hall, which was wrecked with much of the west side of the station blown out. Four members of staff who were on duty as firewatchers were killed and five servicemen were also killed. Some platforms were not back in use until 27 May.

Waterloo had sixteen incidents leaving the station without gas, water, lighting and power. However, the most dangerous scenario occurred as a result of a bomb which penetrated the arches below the station, causing a large fire which spread rapidly, engulfing many areas and reaching the bonded stores where it consumed £30,000 worth of spirits. The fire was not extinguished for five days and caused grave concerns regarding damage to the structure of the station. The station was closed at 00.15, and 240 staff had to be mobilised to cope with the emergency. The extensive structural repairs needed meant that the station wasn't even partially re-opened until 16 May, and not completely back in action until September.

Holborn Viaduct station was gutted by fire and all lines were blocked. At Cannon Street, the station roof and the station hotel were ablaze soon after midnight, and it was decided to bring two trains out of the station onto the bridge over the Thames. Bombs then fell around the trains, nearly toppling them into the river; one engine received a direct hit and the other had to be uncoupled and taken to the other side of the river leaving the remaining carriages to burn until daybreak and the all clear. At Elephant & Castle railway station the station buildings were struck by two bombs, blocking all lines. The station buildings and signal box were burnt out and four staff seriously injured.[369]

At Victoria, there were five delayed action bombs to be tackled, and both the main line and underground stations had to be closed. The west side of Liverpool Street was set on fire.

Much damage was done to the underground railway network particularly to the sub-surface lines in the centre of London. The Circle line at Kings Cross was blocked by debris after a bomb penetrated the tunnel arch and the service was suspended between Baker Street and Kings Cross until 21 July and between Euston Square and King's Cross until 4 October. A bomb through the tunnel between Victoria and St James Park stations closed the line until 21 May. Aldgate station was closed for eleven days due to bomb damage and the Rotherhithe-Surrey Docks service was suspended until 8 June.[370]

Overall, the east of London was not so badly affected by this raid and incidents mainly occurred in boroughs in the old East End. The worst-hit borough was Stepney where there were eighty-eight dead in various incidents including a number at street shelters. Many died at the Chaseley Street shelter (the most serious incident in Stepney – twenty people died), the Friends Shelter, Clayton's Shelter and the Globe Road shelter. In Bethnal Green, there were serious incidents at Arline Street and Columbia Square Buildings. Rego's garment factory and the synagogue on Bethnal Green Road were both destroyed. Thirty-one died in Poplar including several at Poplar Hospital which received a direct hit. Twenty-two were killed in West

---

369 Brooksbank, *London Main Line War Damage* (2007)
370 Graves, *London Transport at War* (1978)

Ham, where some incidents occurred early in the night, and the Conference Hall in West Ham Lane was burnt out, although Queen Mary's hospital next door was saved.

A bomb fell at Tower Pier, a base for the Royal Naval Auxiliary Patrol, where the fire service was relaying water to Whitechapel. Collier relates how the blast spun the fire-pumps into the river, blasting two firemen to pieces. 'The Naval patrol depot, HMS Tower, a 100-ton hulk moored alongside, was sinking fast, her decks awash with blood and oil, strewn with wounded men.'[371] The Port of London Authority building at Trinity Square was badly damaged and its domed rotunda was destroyed.

Reflecting the concentration of the raid in the inner London suburbs, Chingford, Edmonton and Walthamstow were hardly affected and suffered no fatal casualties. However, two clusters of incendiaries falling in the Lea Bridge and Selwyn Avenue areas of Walthamstow resulted in two factories being destroyed by fire at the former location.

Much of south and south-west London apart from the central and riverside boroughs – Bermondsey, Camberwell, Deptford, Lambeth, Greenwich, Southwark and Woolwich – escaped serious damage. One exception was Croydon. Besides incidents in Thornton Heath, Upper Norwood and Addiscombe, eight bombs fell on south Croydon. Two of these bombs fell on the LPTB bus garage which was destroyed by the ensuing fire, along with sixty buses, with eleven of the staff killed. The fire was particularly violent as the buses were fuelled ready for the next morning's service. Some staff were trapped below ground in the inspection pits and desperate attempts were made by rescue workers to reach them. The nearby Carrington Manufacturing Co's factory also blazed, sending burning varnish running down the streets, and the damage totalled £100,000. Total casualties

---

371 Collier, *The City That Wouldn't Die* (1959)

in Croydon were fourteen dead and forty seriously injured. Bombs also fell at Bromley and in the neighbouring areas of Beckenham, Elmers End, Sidcup and West Wickham.

North London was not affected to any great extent but two parachute mines in Muswell Hill caused extensive damage in Leaside Avenue and Woodside Avenue, and killed or seriously injured ten people. Fatalities also occurred in Enfield, Harrow, Hendon and Wembley, and further out at Abbots Langley near Hemel Hempstead. A number of high explosive bombs fell in Hampstead but fortunately all of them failed to explode.

The description of the Holford Square incident at Finsbury by Richard Collier,[372] if somewhat dramatized, gives some clue to the devastation caused by this incident, which was probably the largest, in terms of casualties and destruction, of the night. He claims sixty dead and 116 seriously injured, with a brewery, a convent, two pubs and sixty houses demolished. The quiet, early nineteenth century square was struck by two parachute mines (records indicate one mine was recorded as a bomb, at least initially) which caused immense damage in the square and neighbouring Percy Circus. About thirty-six local residents died in addition to the military personnel manning the barrage balloon site in the square, for whom casualty figures are not available, but who presumably could number up to twenty-four dead if Collier's figures are correct. An account by Barbara Nixon, a Finsbury warden, was first published in 1943 and does not refer to the locality by name. However, it is clearly the Holford Square incident that she refers to on page 142. Nixon gives fifty-two fatalities and mentions that two RAF personnel were killed, and a warden's post destroyed with four wardens killed.[373] Afterwards, Nixon notes that although

372 Collier, *The City That Wouldn't Die* (1959)
373 Nixon, *Raiders Overhead* (1980)

four wardens and a stretcher party member had been killed on duty, the Town Hall officials seemed reluctant to make any official preparations for the burials. However, at the last moment a full Civil Defence parade was authorised for each funeral.[374]

The last bomb of the night fell on New Scotland Yard at 05.37 bringing the records of thousands of criminals down onto the desk of the Commissioner, Sir Philip Game, who fortunately had yet to arrive at work. It was a delayed-action high explosive bomb which landed on the east side of the building, near the entrance on Victoria Embankment and penetrated to the basement. The bomb exploded an hour later, fortunately only causing minor injuries and only doing a small amount of damage.[375]

The fires caused by this raid resulted in 700 acres of destruction – about double that of the Great Fire of London. The final costs of damage in 1941 values – £20 million – were also about double those of the Great Fire. As far as the human cost is concerned, the heavy losses suffered by the fire services are significant. Thirty-six firemen died. Of these, nineteen were killed in Southwark at the Surrey Theatre incident described above. Seventeen policemen also died in various incidents across London.

Anti-aircraft guns expended 4,510 rounds and two bombers were claimed as destroyed. RAF Fighter Command in total dispatched 325 aircraft (not all over London). They initially claimed twenty-eight enemy aircraft destroyed, later this total was amended to eleven. One Hurricane was destroyed, and another Hurricane and a Beaufighter were badly damaged. The Luftwaffe actually lost fourteen aircraft that night, a rather higher figure than on any previous night raid.

---

374 Nixon, *Raiders Overhead* (1980)
375 Westminster City Archives www.westendatwar.org.uk

Those in the boroughs not affected by the raid often remained totally unaware of the great devastation in those areas that were bombed. Some recorded reports of very light casualties or even that other cities had been the target. But news of the immense destruction soon became known and spread rapidly, as those on duty the next morning found.

The Home Intelligence weekly report stated 'Despite the heavy raids on London on May 10th/11th, less depression is evident here than during the early part of last week ... Saturday night's raid was not unexpected, on account of the full moon. The fact that it came at a week-end gave most people a chance to make up lost sleep before returning to work, and there was little outward sign of stress on Monday. The restorative services worked well.'[376]

11 May was a Sunday, and this brought sightseers into central London from around the capital, to the great annoyance of civil defence workers and fire-fighting personnel. In particular, the light-hearted enjoyment the visitors were experiencing was not appreciated neither was their propensity to consume food and drink much needed by those still on duty. Nixon notes that sightseers would ask the police at the nearest railway station the way to the worst bomb damage.[377] On Monday 12 May the *Daily Mail* was gleefully able to report that some 'Blitz idlers' had been injured when a pavement collapsed. That Monday however saw many visitors of a different kind, those whose workplaces had gone forever, trying to find out if their employer would be carrying on or, if not, whether their wages would be paid. Businesses all over London were unable to function because of a lack of gas, water or electricity. 150,000 households were also without these services. The whole of Southwark,

---

376 https.//moidigital.ac.uk/ Home Intelligence Weekly Report No. 32 – May 7th – 14th, 1941
377 Nixon, *Raiders Overhead* (1980)

Bermondsey and north Camberwell was without a gas supply. The Metropolitan Water Board reported over 600 mains broken and that there was no water in vast areas of London.

The overall benefit of the raid to the Luftwaffe was reduced by its failure to follow-up. In what Collier describes as 'the bitterest irony of all …the Luftwaffe had to let the greatest opportunity of the blitz slide by. From start to finish, the whole effort, the lives wasted on both sides, were in vain. Again, Hitler's whim had prevailed. The raid had proved nothing at all.'[378] The Germans gained no real appreciation of the damage caused, and by the time their spy Hans Schmidt reported via Lisbon six weeks later it was too late. However, there is little evidence that any meaningful feedback was received in Germany on any of the damage caused in London during the Blitz.

On 11 May however, the London fire services had to prepare for a possible repetition of the raid. At that time, no one knew of the German plans to invade Russia which would necessitate the diversion of much of the Luftwaffe's bomber force to the east. Those fire service personnel who had been on duty had worked extended hours and were exhausted. All leave was cancelled and 1,000 relief fire personnel and 500 pumps were ordered from Home Office Control, to stand in readiness on the borders of London before darkness fell. As many pumps as could be spared from 'damping down' duties were also held in readiness. A fleet of 100 canteen vans was allocated to provide food and hot drinks to those still on duty. Fires burned for days and the last pumps were not withdrawn until 22 May, although the conflagrations in the City and at the Elephant and Castle were coming under control by the Sunday afternoon. However, the Metropolitan Water Board reported that over 1,000 acres around Shoreditch and London Bridge were entirely without water. Only after two

---

378 Collier, *The City That Wouldn't Die* (1959)

nights without further activity could fire services personnel begin to relax.

Wallington explains the crisis facing fire brigades nationally after the 10/11 May raid. 'In the wake of this almost fatal blow to the capital, many senior fire officers were adamant that never again should London have to face such a risk, which was largely the result of inefficient mobilisation of back-up crews and appliances from other areas'.[379]

Nixon notes when attending the funeral for her colleagues, to and from the crematorium, north London traffic seemed to almost consist entirely of hearses.

June 1941

The remainder of May and June 1941 did not see any raids of significance against London although other parts of the country continued to experience heavy bombing and serious casualties. Just after midnight on 5 June bombs fell in Farnborough village in Kent, but there were no casualties. On 8 June Vere Hodgson noted 'landmine on Chiswick last night and bombs on Acton'.[380] The bombs on Acton, fifteen in all, hit the LPTB's Acton works and Acton Town station at 12.56, but no casualties are recorded. On 22 June Germany launched its invasion of the Soviet Union. At 01.45 that morning possibly the last parachute mine incidents of the war occurred; at least these were the last occasions on which these hated weapons were deliberately aimed at civilian targets. A pair of mines fell at Crockenhill, Kent.

27/28 July 1941

July 1941 saw a rather higher level of enemy activity over the UK. The Luftwaffe having sent most of its bombing fleets to

379 Wallington, *Firemen at War* (1981)
380 Hodgson, *Few Eggs No Oranges* (2010)

support the invasion of the Soviet Union, only about 10 per cent of its original force remained to continue operations against Britain. This was the last raid on London of the 1940/41 Blitz and although it was on a much smaller scale than the four spring raids (60 aircraft took part), nearly one hundred people died, most of them in boroughs in the inner suburbs. Strangely, the number of incidents involving public shelters was high. Once again, the unfortunate borough of Poplar was to suffer badly – over half the night's casualties occurred there. It seems that several public shelters were hit, including that at the Royal National Lifeboat Institution where forty-three people died when this shelter in Broomfield Street was hit at 02.30. The shelter was situated on the ground floor of an old building which was formerly the main workshop for the repair and servicing of the Royal National Lifeboat Institution fleet of lifeboats. When the RNLI moved to a new site in 1936 the building remained empty until 1939, when the Ministry of Food had the upper floors reinforced and used for bulk storage of food stocks. The Poplar Civil Defence Committee had the lower floor adapted to provide a shelter for 160 people.'[381]

Whitman House on the Cornwall Estate, Bethnal Green, was blasted and one person killed, and a direct hit on factories at West Ham caused serious damage. Six people were killed in Mildmay Park, Islington, and other fatalities occurred in Wandsworth and Tolworth. Eight bombs fell in Feltham, hitting the Southern Railway marshalling yards, Hanworth Air Park and the Gresham Transformers factory. Bombs also fell at Beckenham, Bromley and Sidcup, but only Beckenham, where thirty-two bombs fell, had casualties.

When the all clear sounded, it was not clear that this, yet

---

381 East London History Society Newsletter Summer 1999

another pointless raid, marked the end of the London Blitz. But there was not to be another air raid on London until January 1943.

PART 3
CONCLUSIONS

ELEVEN

THE HUMAN COST

Who died? It proved to be truly the people's war, and surprisingly few famous or prominent people died in the London Blitz. Lord Stamp of Shortlands was the only peer of the realm to die in the Blitz when his home in Bromley was destroyed by a direct hit in the raid of 16/17 April 1941. Lionel Hichens, chairman of shipbuilders Cammell Laird was killed at Church House, Westminster, on 14 October 1940. Perhaps tongue in cheek, A D Harvey comes up with Viscountess Charlemont, the former wife of the former Northern Ireland Education Minister, who died at Praed Street station on 13 October 1940![382] The band leader Ken Johnson died in the Café de Paris incident on 8 March 1941 and the singer Al Bowlly died when his flat in Duke Street off Oxford Street was blasted on 16 April 1941. These two celebrities are sometimes confused. The former Liberal MP, John Wodehouse, later 3rd Earl of Kimberley, was also killed on 16 April 1941 at

---

382 Harvey, *Collision of Empires* (1994)

Jermyn Street, Westminster. 100-year-old Chelsea Pensioner Henry Rattray was the oldest person to die in the London Blitz, also on 16 April 1941, and was probably the only centenarian to die in air raids in the whole country. Tragically however, hundreds of infants under two years old were to die in air raids in the United Kingdom.

Maybe the rich and famous did avoid the bombs by getting out of London, or perhaps they had better shelters. They were unlikely to have used communal public shelters of the type that was hit so many times. It is interesting to read that on the night of the great raid of 10/11 May 1941 Lord President of the Council Sir John Anderson and Minister of Labour Ernest Bevin were in the Citadel, an especially secure refuge for the Cabinet at Faraday Building in the City of London.[383] Montagu Norman, Governor of the Bank of England, repaired to his bank's vaults. Both Duff Cooper, the Minister of Information, and the Foreign Secretary, Lord Halifax, took shelter in the basement gym of the Dorchester Hotel on Park Lane, which had been turned into an air-raid dormitory.[384]

The role of the Blitz in breaking down Britain's class structures has often been highlighted. It brought people into contact with people from other social strata for the first time. It also exposed many British people to class antagonism for the first time, and to the realities of class distinction which already horrified more liberal people. When a colleague of a Mass Observation diarist asked someone to help a bombed-out woman, she is livid when asked 'what class was she, exactly?'[385] But another writer, an otherwise compassionate observer, refers to an air-raid victim as a 'slum woman'. But she is ready to defend a bereaved and homeless air raid victim against a censorious and uncaring

383 Collier, *The City that Wouldn't Die* (1959)
384 Gardiner, *The Blitz* (2010)
385 Mosley, *London Under Fire 1939-1945* (1972)

clergyman. Class distinction was very much on the minds of the authorities who were very concerned about the 'working classes' and how they might react under aerial bombardment.

Even eighty years after the Blitz, strong feelings are expressed about the lack of recognition and commemoration of its victims, and the lack of information about tragic incidents, and there is justifiable concern about the accuracy of casualty statistics, and whether any cover-ups have occurred. With over fifty incidents in the London Blitz having over twenty fatalities it is clear that for most of them very little has been done to commemorate the victims. Fatality figures in the Civilian War Dead Roll of Honour seem to accurately reflect actual deaths in the incidents but there is very little visual or written recognition. The perception that the victims were forgotten is understandable.

In the post-war years there seemed little interest in commemoration and even in recording the events of 1939-45 as they affected the civilian population. After the collection of oral history began in earnest in the 1970s contextualisation did not become an issue although it must have been obvious that behind the personal stories there was much background information missing. People are astonished to read about the large and tragic loss of life in familiar suburban settings, of which they were completely unaware and perhaps this has reinforced suspicions of cover-up. Post-war official accounts were sometimes brief, impersonal and matter of fact. One brief local history publication covering two pre-1965 London boroughs has a fair amount of space devoted to generic information about wartime Britain – call-up, evacuation, rationing etc. The local impact of the Blitz of 1940-41 is covered but in no great detail. Over 540 civilians in the two boroughs which are the subject of the book died as a result of the enemy bombardments in World War 2 but this catastrophic loss of life is not really brought home or acknowledged in the text.

There is general agreement that the sheer enormity of London's ordeal in the Blitz and the huge cost in terms of human lives is still not recorded or commemorated adequately in today's London. No central memorial has been dedicated to commemorate the citizens of London who gave their lives in the London Blitz of 1940-41 and the other aerial attacks on the capital. City of London councillor Marianne Fredericks pursued a long campaign to get a Civilian Memorial Garden on the river bank at Wapping – the Hermitage Memorial Park. Its centrepiece is a 'dove' sculpture, the work of acclaimed local sculptor Wendy Taylor, and the park was opened in July 2008. This modest effort is the nearest London has to a civilian memorial although it specifically commemorates east Londoners. It is also of concern that for many significant events of the Blitz, there is no official written or recorded account surviving.

The origin of the Civilian War Dead Roll of Honour 1939-1945 is described on the Westminster Abbey website:

By a supplemental charter dated 7 February 1941 the Imperial War Graves Commission was empowered to collect and record the names of civilians who died from enemy action during World War II. Using information supplied by the Registrar-General and local authorities an initial list of 43,000 names was compiled covering just the period of the Battle of Britain in 1940 and the big air raids of 1940-41. In 1942, this was made available to the public for consultation and comment. An understanding that the Roll should eventually be placed in Westminster Abbey was reached with the Dean and Chapter at about this time, but it was decided that this should not happen until the list had been made complete at the end of hostilities. The first six volumes were handed over to the Dean and Chapter by the Duke of Gloucester, President of the Imperial War Graves Commission, at a short ceremony in the Jerusalem Chamber (part of the Deanery) on 21 February 1956; the final volume was added to the showcase in 1958.

The Roll consists of seven leather-bound volumes (the work of the binder, Roger Powell) containing printed details of 66,375 fatalities. Entries are not arranged chronologically but by county, and within county by local government areas (many of which have changed since 1945). The lists are then alphabetical by surname and give details of the residential address, place of death and family relationship (e.g., "wife of...", "son of..."). One volume covers deaths on board ship and deaths abroad (including civilian deaths in prison camps). This volume also has addenda for all seven volumes. The books are kept just outside the entrance to St George's Chapel at the west end of Westminster Abbey. At a service on 23rd May 2017 to mark the centenary of the Commonwealth War Graves Commission two supplementary books were processed through the Abbey and presented to the Dean at the High Altar. These contain several hundred new names uncovered by recent research, many of whom died overseas and had been missed from the original listings.

The Commission's 'Debt of Honour Register', which includes all the names on the Civilian War Dead Roll of Honour, can be searched via the internet at www.cwgc. org. Another copy of the Roll is held by the Imperial War Museum and can be consulted by appointment in the Museum's library.

The Roll of Honour for the 28,000 Americans stationed in the UK who gave their lives throughout the *war is in St Paul's Cathedral, in the American Memorial Chapel.'*[386]

The People of London memorial by Richard Kindersley, carved from a three-ton block of Irish limestone, commemorates the people of London who died in the Blitz 1939-1945 and is located outside St Paul's Cathedral. Dedicated in 1999, it is inscribed 'Remember before God the people of London 1939-1945.'

The National Firefighters Memorial dating from 1991 is composed of three bronze statues depicting firefighters in action at the height of the Blitz. It is located on the Jubilee Walkway to the south of St Paul›s Cathedral and can be approached via the Millennium Footbridge. The monument, originally the concept of Cyril Demarne, was commissioned by the Firefighters Memorial Charitable Trust and sculpted by John W. Mills. Firemen and firewomen of the London Civil Defence Region in World War 2 are well served by today's fire service and its associated charities. The Civil Defence organisations have not benefited in a similar way as they were largely disbanded after the war.

The Civilian War Dead Roll of Honour lists all civilians who died 'as a result of enemy action' in World War 2. There are some points to bear in mind when looking at these casualty figures which appear in the Commonwealth War Graves Commission (CWGC) Civilian War Dead records for the London Civil Defence region. The records are an excellent source of information but are not always straightforward to interpret, as deaths are usually recorded in the borough in which they occurred but sometimes in the borough in which the victim normally resided. Sometimes pressure on the emergency services or hospitals necessitated casualties not being taken to their local hospital.

---

386 Westminster Abbey website https.//www.westminster-abbey.org/

Those who died in hospital are invariably recorded at the location of the hospital and the entry, although giving the victim's home address, may not contain any indication of where the incident in which they were injured occurred. Casualties were sometimes taken to one of the emergency hospitals established around outer London; but some boroughs did not have any hospital of their own, and all casualties needing hospitalization would have been taken out of the borough. Unidentified fatalities are problematical. Also problematical is the recording of fatalities during the initial few months of the Blitz as a death recorded on a particular day might have occurred during the previous night's raid or in daytime on the day concerned. There is also a need to be aware that the Ministry of Home Security Daily Intelligence Reports record events in 24-hour periods, commencing at 06.00.

Some victims of a particular raid may not have died for some time after the incident occurred, though it seems that the majority of casualties who were to die after admission to hospital did so within a few days of arrival. This perhaps reflects that in those days, trauma treatment was relatively limited in its effectiveness. For example, in the period 21 April to 9 May 1941, there were actually no air raids with fatalities in London. Of the ninety-three fatalities listed for boroughs in the London region that occurred in that period, most died in the period 21 April to 25 April from injuries received in the raids of 16/17 and 19/20 April.

For air raid victims, the local coroner would record that their death was due to war operations, and this reason then appeared on the death certificate. In the Civilian War Dead Roll of Honour, no reason for a death is given. Casualties of war-related incidents are also listed, for example those who died when British aircraft crashed on residential areas and those in the fire, police and Civil Defence services who died 'in service' as a result of illnesses contracted on duty, or in accidents. Therefore, the Roll is more than just a list of civilians killed as a result of enemy action. Police, fire personnel and civil defence workers killed in air raids are included on the Roll but any military personnel, whether on duty or on leave, are not, and separate figures for them have never been made available. Children killed when trespassing onto mined areas or when tampering with live bombs or ammunition were not always included. However, I have noticed that a boy who was killed by falling clay whilst seeking souvenirs in a bomb crater is included.[387]

Often the source of the casualty figures given in publications is unclear, and they do not always tally with the Civilian War Dead Roll of Honour. The total fatalities for the great raid on 10/11 May are given as 1,436 in most sources; the figures for the raids of 16/17 April and 19/20 April are not so precise. In fact, the figures for 19/20 April are usually said to be 'over 1,000' and in one source as 1,208, but the Civilian War Dead Roll of Honour only lists some 850, although others may have died later or at out-of-London hospitals.

Figures for seriously injured (admitted to hospital) and slightly injured (treated at a First Aid Post) are less reliable, reflecting the difficulty of recording all injuries in air raid conditions. Generally, for each fatal casualty there was on average one or two seriously injured casualties. Serious injuries are not documented in detail but it can be readily assumed that these encompassed a wide range, with some resulting in long-term disabilities and life-changing outcomes for the victims. Some of those thought to have been seriously injured were found to be only slightly injured when they reached hospital. Victims of air raids were likely to be covered in dirt when extricated from bombed buildings.

---

387 Warburton, *Chingford at War* (1946) recounts the incident but does not list the victim with the other air raid fatalities. However, he does now appear on the Civilian War Dead Roll of Honour.

Recognition awards were formally announced in the *London Gazette*, usually two or three months after the event. Presumably for security reasons few details are included as to the location and date of the event, therefore some detective work is required to link the recipient to an incident. A general narrative is given of the circumstances including some rather strange descriptions as 'a working-class block of flats' as if an incident at an up-market block of flats might have demanded a greater or lesser degree of bravery!

THE CHALLENGE OF THE BLITZ

Did the Blitz on London have any role in shaping the course of the war? Blitzing London was not effective as a military strategy even if it had considerable propaganda value on the German home front. The London Blitz opened with a heavy raid but it wasn't anything approaching a knockout blow. The subsequent 57-night ordeal was not anticipated by the British but after the first few weeks, the organisation of a response strategy meant that the Civil Defence services could mostly cope with the aftermath of nightly air raids. Daylight bombing which could have been accurate and thus more effective rapidly became impossible due to RAF supremacy. As it was, isolated daylight raids by a few aircraft usually had no effect even if they inevitably led to tragedies when civilians were killed. The Luftwaffe suffered increasing problems with weather and serviceability of aircraft, even if losses of aircraft to the British defences were low.

Fifty-seven nights of dusk to dawn Blitz had a cumulative effect on the population although the raids became increasingly less focussed and were absorbed by the vast acreage of Greater London. Their capacity to work was seriously impacted by lack of sleep. From November 1940, the raids were curtailed by the weather (this had been remarkably favourable to the attackers in the Autumn of 1940) and the sporadic raids on London in the next few months had limited impact because of their small scale and because they didn't affect all areas. The increase in attacks on the provinces also diluted the effort against London. The Blitz certainly wasn't a victory for the Luftwaffe.

Individual raids could have a great impact but their effectiveness owed more to chance or luck when serious incidents occurred; the Bank station incident on 11 January 1941 was sheer bad luck. Conversely, others could be used for British propaganda, for example when hospitals were hit. 29 December 1940 was a significant raid but despite the devastation caused it ended early enough for the fires to be got under control. The low tides hampered fire-fighting at the beginning of the raid, but during the raid the tide came in. In reality, other than in telecommunications, the City as a target had little value except historic and symbolic, and thus this raid could be turned to the advantage of British propaganda.

Railways were central to London's functioning and in some ways the presence of four railway companies rather than a national system helped although movement of traffic between the companies was vulnerable. There was no 'London Central' station but each railway company had one or more stations around the fringes of central London. Brooksbank[388] has confirmed how the professionalism and efficiency of these companies greatly aided recovery from raids which posed relatively few serious operational challenges.

One senses relief in government circles that after the first few weeks of the London Blitz there were no major concerns – in fact, by the end of September 1940 most problem areas were in hand and Senior Regional Commissioner Sir Ernest Gowers

---

388 Brooksbank *London Main Line War Damage* (2007)

was able to congratulate the civil defence and fire services accordingly. After mid-September, no major fire situations arose until 29 December. One real problem was water and although the actual supplies remained adequate, the breakages of mains that occurred were not anticipated. A similar situation arose with gas. Electricity supplies were maintained well and power stations sustained surprisingly little damage. The sewage network was not so fortunate. The Northern Outfall sewer at Abbey Mills, Stratford in east London was breached on 23 September and sewage discharged into the river Lea, but this turned out not to be as catastrophic as might be imagined.

It was the effect on the people that was most anticipated and feared. So why was so much hostility was directed at the government and local authorities after the Blitz began, and why has this continued to the present day? They were condemned as incompetent, secretive and uncaring, and chastised for putting a false spin on events. Undoubtedly a high degree of dissatisfaction with officialdom (rather than government) existed in many quarters in wartime Britain. This was by no means solely a left-wing view. Alleged harsh treatment of would-be shelterers at the beginning of the Blitz added to the dissatisfaction but reflected the panicked response of the authorities. From at least the organisational point of view this is perhaps unfair because they couldn't cater for the unknown. The government made extensive and detailed plans, but they also had to persuade local authorities to buy into these plans, and in addition the reality turned out to be somewhat different to the scenarios envisaged in the plans.

There were three main areas of criticism:

Firstly, the government's ARP preparation and shelter provision was alleged to be inadequate. Much criticism revolved around whether 'inadequate' provision was made particularly disadvantageous to the working classes in east London. The issue of the provision of shelters for civilians was a complex one and perceptions of its shortcomings were seized upon by those anxious to decry government intentions. Their basic stance was that the government had not provided sufficient shelters and those provided were inadequate. In February 1941 Sir Ernest Gowers explained this to MPs from the London Civil Defence Region. 'The plans made by the government were based on a policy of dispersal – of shelter at the home – and public shelter was only intended for those who might be caught in the street during a raid and unable to get home.'[389] It was further envisaged when developing air raid shelter policy that raids would be in daytime and comparatively short, and that the bombers would always get through. Short, sharp and heavy daytime raids were expected from day 1, and therefore shelters needed to be readily accessible. Experiences during the first year of war (the phoney war) gave little indication as to what format an attack would take, or if it would differ from that planned for. But Gowers also acknowledged that the shelter programme was incomplete and also that many Anderson shelters had become unusable due to water ingress. However, also working against the government's shelter policy were people who understandably wanted to shelter in company rather than in solitude. Therefore, it took time to convert the shelters to dormitories. Gowers was at pains to point out that only a small proportion of Londoners ever used public shelters.

After the Blitz commenced it was clear that the actual experience would be rather different to that planned for. Daytime attacks would lead to the attackers suffering unsustainable losses, and they soon dwindled to insignificance. The prolonged night raiding that followed – fifty-seven nights of continuous attack –was not anticipated. This meant people were led to

---

389 Woolven, *Civil Defence in London 1935-1945 Annex A* (2001)

seek shelter, irrespective of warnings, towards nightfall and stay there until morning. The Government had argued against using the tubes and later against deep shelters, and both lines of argument (which had hitherto prevailed) were, therefore, no longer entirely valid. An aerial attack on day 1 was a strong possibility but the commitments of the Luftwaffe in Poland made it unlikely. Shelters designed for short sharp daylight attacks were not equipped for long stays. Long night attacks had no precedent and needed different provision, which could not be made quickly – the construction of deep shelters was a long-term project. Much effort had to put into preparation for gas, a form of attack which could still not be ruled out even at the end of the 1940-41 Blitz. The accessibility of deep shelters when only ten minutes warning of an attack from northern France and Belgium could be given was a problem. Negatives regarding communal shelters often ignore the fact that most purpose-built shelters were safe from all but a direct hit but many direct hits were sustained. Many victims would have survived if they had stayed at home even if their home didn't have a shelter.

Secondly, it was alleged that the government kept the public in the dark and covered up bad news. How effective and therefore significant this was is open to question. Even with limited media news output, most news got around. There was an obvious need to avoid disclosing details of the accuracy/ effectiveness of enemy air raids, although some critics clearly do not accept this. More controversial was talking down the true impact of some raids although this was disliked for different reasons. The Ministry of Home Security played down the severity of some raids, a strategy that did not go down too well with Londoners. Not all might agree that publication of a large casualty list might be detrimental to morale. Morale was in any case a little-understood topic, but few acknowledged this at the time. 'Morale' and 'moral' were sometimes confused. Similar problem arose in the provinces where some hard-hit towns were not named whilst others were for propaganda purposes. Describing a raid as 'unsuccessful' might provoke a further raid to remedy the earlier lack of success! To avoid people feeling defenceless and unable to retaliate, the government via the press liked to boast that AA guns (which at least could be heard) or night fighters scared off attackers even if they didn't actually bring them down. However, the reality was that there was little practical retaliation possible. As far as the press were concerned, newspapers of the Blitz era tended to sanitise news, but did not avoid bad news, for example by trying to balance family tragedies with lucky escapes. They concentrated on small scale bombing incidents involving non-essential targets, hits on churches, schools, hospitals. No mention was made of industrial targets, communications etc. The St. Paul's bombing made the headlines in the *Evening Standard* on 10 October 1940, complete with a picture of the damage. Locations were disguised, for example 'south-east England' or 'a London suburb'. In some 'personal' stories, the names of people seemed to have been altered as they cannot be traced in the civilian war dead rolls of honour. Delays in publication of photographs were determined by the censor who also edited them as deemed appropriate. Damage but not total devastation could be shown, and certainly not dead bodies. Some press photographs were never released for publication, or not for several years. The Bank incident on 11 January 1941 was referred to as at a subway which technically it was, although like most it doubled as entrances to 'underground' stations. Readers in the USA would have equated the two.

Thirdly, the treatment of bombed out and displaced people was said to be poor. Gowers admitted that 'over-insurance against damage to the person and under-insurance against damage to homes ... presented us with the grave problem of looking after the unwounded people who had lost their homes and the lesser problem of repairing these homes.' This had not been high on the pre-war agenda because cataclysmic raids with large numbers of casualties were predicted; these were not expected, one presumes, to leave many survivors. The number displaced by unexploded bombs, again not predicted, added considerably to the problem. Not only was there a proportion of 'delayed action' bombs dropped but in addition many more bombs failed to explode although intended to do so. German efficiency was not evident. Although British society was changing, 'poor law' attitudes, bureaucracy and maintaining 'distance' from suffering were still common. With their perceived lack of empathy and compassion, Britain's leaders were seen as starchy and remote. Britain was a considerably more uptight and reserved nation than it is today. Better or at least more people-orientated leaders, for example Herbert Morrison were beginning to emerge.

The bombing attacks on Guernica, Rotterdam and Warsaw were all terrible experiences for the civilians but the latter two attacks were in direct support of military operations – enemy tanks and troops were closing in on those cities with no English Channel in their way. It was thought that the bomber would always get through – technical developments in aircraft design, radar etc were accelerating but only in the 1930s did one significant thing change: fighter aircraft were able to outrun bombers. Henceforth bombers could only get through without heavy losses at night, with consequent effect on accuracy. Radar aids for attackers started to help accuracy but were soon countered; for defenders it took longer before night fighters became effective. There were questions both regarding the intention and the capabilities of the enemy which were no clearer in September 1940 than they were a year earlier. One only can deduce that Hitler did not wish to destroy Britain by bombing and that his military commanders had little enthusiasm for the value of non-strategic attacks on a civil population.

Three years later the RAF was heavily attacking Germany. Max

Hastings condemns 'the chauvinistic assumption upon which the RAF founded its area-bombing campaign, that Germans were liable to moral collapse in a way that the British proved in 1940 they were not, was shown to be totally unfounded.'[390] Albert Speer, later Hitler's minister for armaments and war production was qualified to state that 'the vast but pointless area bombing had achieved no important effect on the German war effort by early 1944.' Also, of importance was the failure by the USAAF to repeat the attacks on Schweinfurt ball-bearing factories, the British failure to prevent the recovery of Hamburg and to follow up the Dams raids by impeding the repairs work. The Allies were inexplicably failing just as their German opponents had done.

Surprisingly, civilians everywhere appeared to get used to bombing although the first experience was always traumatic, so probably most people who did not experience personal loss remained relatively upbeat. To go back to Chingford, that quiet suburb in north-east London with virtually no targets for the attacking bombers. 19/20 March was Chingford's last significant raid of the Blitz and no further fatalities were to occur in the borough until the V1 offensive began in June 1944. Chingford was not affected by the raids of 16/17 April and 10/11 May, but on 19/20 April a single incident occurred and two people were taken to hospital. By the end of the war virtually all Chingford's 11,275 rateable dwellings were damaged and 103 of its citizens dead as a result of bombing. What was the point?

WRITING ABOUT THE BLITZ

Accounts of the Blitz have tended to polarise around social history (with a strong input from the personal memories of

---

390 Hastings, *Bomber Command* (1979)

those who lived through the Blitz) or to a lesser extent, around 'military' accounts of the Luftwaffe bombing attacks. The latter emphasise the forces involved, the tonnage of bombs dropped, the casualties caused and the damage inflicted. There have been relatively few accounts combining these two aspects, and many personal accounts contain common errors on the 'military' aspects which go uncorrected in the editing. This may reflect a lack of appreciation of the true facts behind the events at the time.

Front Line appeared in 1942 and was the official account of the 1940-41 Blitz on the United Kingdom. It was written (anonymously) for the Ministry of Home Security by Clem Leslie, who was chief Public Relations Officer at the Ministry of Home Security. A friend of Herbert Morrison, Leslie has a certain style and compassion and uses some telling images, which makes this booklet much more than a mere propaganda tract. Official histories were published by the government after the war, and the two volumes entitled *Civil Defence* and *The Defence of the UK* are of most relevance here. Whilst the authors had access to documents denied to the general public, the volumes make for quite bland reading, with a heavy emphasis on the smoothness and efficiency of civil administration in coping with the demands of war. Neither volume provides a comprehensive account of the Blitz on London. Titmuss' account *Problems of Social Policy* is far more penetrating, perhaps because in its very title it acknowledges the reality. Dr Robin Woolven's thesis *Civil Defence in London 1935-1945* analyses the performance of the ARP organisation, a topic that the official histories do not cover adequately.

After the war, many people wished to forget the ordeal that they as civilians went through and despite the huge popularity of books and films about various British military triumphs and endeavours, little appeared about the Blitz as it affected civilians.

Constantine Fitzgibbon's book *The Blitz*, which did not appear until 1957, was the first book dedicated to the London Blitz, but it is by no means a comprehensive account. When it was written most official records were still restricted under the thirty-year rule and could not be accessed by the general public including journalists and writers. In all honesty, when official papers were declassified not many great revelations emerged, but many issues remained less than clear. Fitzgibbon's book certainly doesn't contain any of the myths, but it does contain detailed first-hand accounts of the bombing as it affected Londoners in various parts of the capital. These include the Café de Paris incident, the incident when a parachute mine dropped outside the BBC on 8 December 1940, and the bombing of Chelsea Old Church on 16 April 1941. There was little information available as to the effectiveness of the Blitz raids on London and their success in hitting strategic targets such as the railways. Other early Blitz books were *The City that wouldn't die*, Richard Collier's account of the raid of 10/11 May 1941 and the excellent autobiographical *A Chelsea Concerto* by Frances Faviell[391], which both appeared in 1959. Leonard Mosley's 1971 *Backs to the Wall* (the title was changed to the perhaps more suitable *London under Fire 1939-1945* the following year) incorporates a combination of various personal stories. There is a rather curious and disproportionate emphasis on the complexities surrounding the presence of the 'fighting French' in wartime London. Following the stories of both rich and working-class Londoners, as well as drawing on Mass Observation diaries, Mosley set the pattern for many such books over the next few decades. Mosley, like Collier, was a journalist, and does not spare us the intrigues. Alfred Price's *Blitz on Britain 1939-1945* (1977) is a 'military' account,

---

391 Frances Faviell was the penname of Olivia Parker. She died shortly after the publication of her book.

covering the technical aspects of the bombing campaign against Britain, as does John Ray's *The Night Blitz* (1996), which is perhaps more of a textbook although none the worse for that. If like me you ask 'what was the point' you are referred to Richard Overy's *The Bombing War*, his excellent account of the strategy behind the various bombing campaigns that ravaged Europe in World War 2.

Many books about the Blitz rely heavily on personal memories, often quoted verbatim. Those written at the time are the most reliable in terms of accuracy, even though wartime censorship and restriction of information mean that the writer may not have been full informed on the background to events and would not have been permitted to give information on the location of 'incidents.' Those people working for the Civil Defence services would have had access to the most reliable information. Barbara Nixon's 1943 *Raiders Overhead* gives an account of the author's experiences as a warden in Finsbury but this locality is not identified in her book and was not disclosed until it was reprinted in 1980. Streets are not named or the names have been changed, although many locations can be identified without much trouble. There is of course no mention of 'land mines' in Miss Nixon's book, even though references to them are only thinly disguised – 'two enemy objects dropped close together, exploded on the surface'![392] Miss Nixon also uses pseudonyms for the characters who appear in her book. Often people were not named in these early accounts, including many of the heroes and heroines of the Blitz, and they can make rather dry reading. For example, *Raiders over Sheffield* is an excellent account written at the time but not published until 1980. It also does not refer to anyone – residents, victims, ARP personnel,

---

392 Nixon, *Raiders Overhead* (1980)

local government officials – by name.[393]Other accounts were perhaps over-effusive and sentimental in their praise of the community spirit of much attacked towns and cities. Fortunately, most follow a sensible middle path.

The 1970s and the opening of government records under the 'thirty-year rule' set off a new wave of books which continued through to the 50th anniversary of the Blitz. Angus Calder's *The People's War* describes the effect of the war on Britain's population. Norman Longmate's *How We Lived Then* covers the British civilian experience in war in great and accurate detail, drawing on hundreds of personal reminiscences. Both books provide definitive and comprehensive guides to how the war affected all aspects of civilian life. Personal accounts and memories came thick and fast at this time but when written up after thirty to fifty years invariably have inaccuracies. Even ten years ago a writer was appealing for reminiscences of a particular Blitz raid, although sixty years had elapsed since it happened!

Accounts of personal experiences by ordinary citizens are very valuable, their personal theories about issues regarding the Blitz, which can get into their accounts, are less valuable and can be wrong. One of the main problems is that individuals have been apt to incorporate as fact the rumours and hearsay which constitute the 'myths' that had circulated since the war. The editors of such accounts do not always bear in mind the potential inaccuracies and may be oblivious to the 'myths' that are being perpetuated. But in a few cases, it is just the failure of memory after the passage of time and confusion between dates and places. Also, it is little use if the linking text is full of inaccuracies – if the editor doesn't know his subject, 'myths' are again perpetuated. One exception is *The War on our Doorstep* by Harriet Salisbury, which in addition to many accounts of

---

393 Walton & Lamb, *Raiders over Sheffield* (1980)

Blitz experiences, includes many valuable insights into the way people lived in the East End during the early part of the twentieth century. These form an essential background to understanding how they endured the Blitz.

All students of the Blitz should be grateful to Winston Ramsey, editor of *The Blitz Then and Now*, three massive volumes that appeared over the period 1987 to 1990 and which provided the first comprehensive account of the Blitz on Britain from both the civilian and military points of view. Few key events of the Blitz escape the attentions of Mr Ramsey's team, and we should be particularly appreciative of their contribution to the pictorial record of the Blitz, as they discovered and identified many uncaptioned pictures of London's damaged buildings and married them to present-day pictures. At the time of the Blitz newspapers and news agencies took many pictures of bomb damage. There was a 28-day embargo on publication and many were not captioned at the time presumably because they were either not used or were not submitted to or passed by the censor. Others were published but without precise identification of locality.

Of the personal accounts, much value is found in those of Notting Hill-based charity worker Vere Hodgson. Her book *Few Eggs and no Oranges* is based on material from her diaries of the period, although some writers had drawn on these before Miss Hodgson published her book in 1983. Gwladys Cox, a housewife living in West Hampstead, is one of many eye-witnesses whose letters and diaries are deposited at the Imperial War Museum in London. Another is the Reverend John Markham, Rector of St. Peter's Church, Walworth whose 50-page memoir was written in the 1970s. The diaries of Anthony Heap, deposited at the London Metropolitan Archives, also are full of valuable post-raid observations, gathered first-hand even if the author's opinions are sometimes less than likeable. Bill Hoodless' *Air Raid. A diary and stories from the Essex Blitz* is notable for the inclusion of his mother's diary of the blitz in Upminster which records over 500 soundings of the sirens. Also of interest is Ruby Side Thompson, resident in nearby Romford, who writes extensively about her personal and family situation in her diaries, although much of this is not war-related. But like Mrs Hoodless, she was an ordinary civilian. This is hardly a true London blitz diary as Romford was an Essex market town, outside the London Civil Defence region. Still, it was on the enemy flight path and Romford suffered badly, usually at the same time as London, although Mrs Thompson's home escapes damage. Fortunately, perhaps, as she does not mention having a shelter to use during raids, and when the bombing comes near, it has a traumatic effect on her, reducing her to uncontrollable vomiting![394]

Mass Observation diaries were said to have been 'produced by inexperienced people in very difficult conditions'[395] but this isn't borne out by for example those chosen by Simon Garfield for his three wartime anthologies *We are at War*, *Private Battles* and *Our Hidden Lives*. His chosen diarists certainly have a degree of literary fluency. In most cases, in addition to living outside the most heavily bombed areas, they have an unexpectedly relaxed approach to their wartime work responsibilities, which probably allowed them to devote more time to their Mass Observation diaries. Inevitably Mass Observation correspondents included some conscientious objectors and others who did not appear to be 100% behind the wartime government, and this was seized upon by denigrators of Mass Observation both during the war and after.

Much criticism of Mass Observation arose from its reports on bombed cities – when teams of observers went into the

---

394 Washuk, ed., *World War II London Blitz Diary vol. 1 – 4*
395 Calder, *The Peoples War* (1971)

cities post-raid, rather than the written-up diaries of individual correspondents. It has to be said that Mass Observation reports on most blitzed cities do not seem very controversial, but those in authority did not like them. It was inevitable that some cities were better prepared than others and coped better with the aftermath of air raids. Southampton was one that was not, and with the release of Mass Observation findings after thirty years a storm of protest was unleashed, although a (non-MO) report on the city by Inspector-General of Air Raid Precautions, John Hodsoll, attracted the most criticism.

In some cases, twenty years or more went by before eye witnesses revisited their wartime experiences. Len Jones is quoted at length by Mack and Humphries in their *London at War*.[396] His account was written in response to appeals in connection with their London Weekend Television 'London at War' programme in 1985. Mr Jones was so traumatized by his experiences when the Blitz began in Poplar that he was unable to revisit them until 40 years after the event.

By the time of the great revival of interest in the 1980s and 1990s some eye witnesses were no longer with us, and their memories are lost for ever. Many major events of the Blitz were not recorded officially or at least in any great detail at the time, and many local authority records have been lost or destroyed, particularly before or during the merger of boroughs in the London local government restructuring in the 1960s. Only in the last decade have some of the major events of the London Blitz received official recognition in the form of memorial plaques and commemorative events to mark the huge loss of life that occurred. Overall though, London's civilian losses are still to receive adequate permanent remembrance.

'Official' histories from the local authorities and their Civil

---

396 A follow-up to the LWT 'London at War' programme

Defence organisations are few and far between. After the war, some boroughs wanted to produce them but naturally at the time there were conflicting priorities and the expense could not be justified. Walthamstow was one of the first in London although government restrictions still meant some information could not be included, much to the frustration of its author, local councillor Ross Wyld. According to Peter Watt, in Romford local newspaper editor Glyn Richards had to overcome a great deal of bureaucracy and red tape to publish his *Ordeal in Romford* in October 1945.[397] Walthamstow's neighbour, Chingford, waited a little longer and was able to produce a very comprehensive volume in 1946. Although this is somewhat dull and impersonal, it does give a good impression of how Civil Defence was organised and operated in a small borough. Of particular interest is the degree to which the whole population was involved in Civil Defence activity – hundreds of Chingford's citizens 'did their bit' in some way. Local accounts can be full of civic pride and focus on officialdom – *Chingford at War* has plenty of photographs of civic dignitaries and ARP personnel, but none of the borough's decorated war heroes including those of the Blitz.

After the war, comprehensive accounts were written by Civil Defence officials in the boroughs of St Pancras and Islington, but neither author could get them published at the time. Eventually, the St Pancras account by Charles Allen Newbery was published by the Camden History Society in 2006,[398] but the Islington account by W Eric Adams has yet to be published. Croydon's history of 1949 by the borough librarian, W Berwick Sayers, is a worthy literary endeavour, although impersonal – he does not mention that he sustained serious injuries in a

397 Watt, *Hitler v Havering* (1994)
398 Newbery, *Wartime St Pancras. a London borough defends itself* (2006)

bombing incident at Croydon Town Hall that put him out of action for five months! All local authorities had similar Civil Defence structures, but it was their efficiency that was to vary. This was not always reflected in published accounts which were often full of uncritical praise for the local response to the ordeal of bombing.

Unfortunately, a few more recent accounts are disappointingly thin and concentrate almost exclusively on the 'civilian experience' of evacuation, rationing and call-up and it is sometimes difficult not to lose sight of the hundreds of fatalities that occurred in the boroughs concerned.

Some local newspapers produced accounts of the Blitz in their locality, but it wasn't until the 50th anniversary of the Blitz that many of the compilations by local historians were published. But given the number of local authorities contained within the London Civil Defence region, there are still parts of London where the wartime ordeal has yet to be put adequately into print. Of the many books about London boroughs in the Blitz, published in the 1980s and 1990s, those by Lewis Blake covering south-east London are particularly comprehensive. However, many of the inner-city boroughs in particular lack a comprehensive account of the Blitz as it affected them, but in all fairness, some published accounts do not claim to be comprehensive. Westminster has the most thorough coverage. Not only does it have novelist William Sansom's eloquent account of Civil Defence in Westminster during the war years, the Westminster Archive has used a lottery grant to compile *West End at War*, a website featuring bombing incidents that occurred in the former boroughs of Westminster and St Marylebone. This began as part of a project to mark the 70th anniversary of the Blitz, and it is able to draw on the extensive civil defence records preserved by the boroughs.[399]

---

399 http://www.westendatwar.org.uk/

Keith Scholey's brief account *Bombs on Holborn* for the Camden History Society stands out because he tries to apply a sense of proportion when examining the intensity of bombing on this central London borough. *Fire and Water* edited by H S Ingham is a very good anthology of fire service memories first published in 1942 and also shows what high literary standards were to be found in the AFS in wartime. Cecil Madden's selection *The Blitz. 20 Survivors' Stories* is also notable because his subjects were working in theatres and carrying on with their professions in the evenings during the London Blitz. It is not clear when the accounts were collected and although Madden died in 1987 his book was not published until 2017.

A number of books have appeared that cover the large raids of the London Blitz, those on 7 September 1940, 29 December 1940 and 10/11 May 1941 have each been the subject of detailed studies. It's difficult to make a book out of a single air raid, and in at least one of the books there is clearly confusion over when exactly specific incidents occurred. For example, although much damage in the City of London occurred on 29 December 1940, further extensive destruction occurred on 10/11 May 1941 and in other raids, and on a number of occasions some of Wren's churches were to succumb to enemy bombing.

London boroughs are now very anxious to preserve and enhance their collections of wartime records. This was not always the case unfortunately, and few records survive in some localities, policies on retention of records having varied considerably. For example, it appears that the former borough of St. Pancras disposed of all its photographs pertaining to bombing incidents, before the formation of the new London Borough of Camden which incorporates St. Pancras. David Haunton says 'the detailed local records for Merton and Morden Urban District were discarded when the London Borough of Merton was formed in 1965 – no public-spirited and/or indignant person took them home to preserve them (as happened in Wimbledon).'[400]

This has caused problems for those writing about wartime in current London boroughs for example Ealing and Barnet, as it has proved difficult to merge the records of the 'old' boroughs where records are in different formats and are in different states of preservation.

Hitler Passed This Way is a booklet containing 170 'before and after' photographs of blitzed London from the London Evening News archive. The 'after' pictures show the various scenes of destruction as they were after the war and before any reconstruction had started. Some fascinating photographs of surviving Blitz era signage appear on the Blitzwalkers blog http.//blitzwalkers.blogspot.co.uk/, including notices giving directions to public shelters. Much shrapnel damage can still be found by careful observers.

Sean Dettman's blog[401] has an interesting post in which he explores how various national publications in the USA covered the Blitz. Dettmann says 'National publications capitalised on the American public's fascination with underground shelters. Images of Londoners sleeping in underground cities left a lasting impression on the US public ... these images had a very positive effect on their readership.' Although it no doubt helped keep the United States on Britain's side, it probably also contributed to the myths. Some US correspondents were aware that not all the British public were heroic and Eric Sevareid in his *Not So Wild a Dream* was ready to point out it would 'do them less than justice to suggest that none of them at any time betrayed stark fear or that there were no individual cases of hysteria and panic.'

---

400 Haunton, in Merton Historical Society Bulletins 166
401 http.//www.whenthosewerethedays.blogspot.co.uk/

House of Commons Speaker Bernard Weatherill, in his foreword to the 1991 book on the Houses of Parliament in wartime[402] said 'you can destroy a man's house, but in doing so, you may well preserve or strengthen his spirit' and went on to describe how the House proceeded to routine business the next morning, and concluded that the destruction of the Chamber interfered 'not one whit' with the resolve to prosecute the war until a successful conclusion.

The same might be said of the effect of the Blitz on London as a whole.

---

402 Jennifer Tanfield, *In Parliament 1939-50*

PART 4

THE LEGACY

TWELVE

BLITZED LONDON TODAY

The changes to the cityscape of London that resulted from the Blitz are still apparent although the few visible original remnants of the Blitz era – the shelters and various public notices, never numerous, are disappearing. Paul Talling's *Derelict London* website[403] gives a useful insight into the remnants. A number of commemorative plaques can be found and some are detailed below. A few years ago, Alan Brooks attempted to record these remnants of the Blitz, although his research is confined to the metropolitan boroughs.[404] Some plaques commemorate specific bombing incidents and have only been put up fairly recently. Others are cemetery memorials commemorating civilian deaths and most of those

---

403 https.//www.derelictlondon.com/war---bunkers-and-pillboxes.html
404 Brooks, *London at War* (2011)

for the metropolitan boroughs are located away from the borough concerned. Unfortunately, many of the older cemetery memorials are not in good condition, and in general, visibility and access are often issues with memorials. The Shoreditch memorial in New Southgate cemetery has been reported as in a poor state of repair and a campaign to reinstate it elsewhere has been started.[405] A few of the more recent Blitz plaques are not accurate and there is sometimes a lack of care evident in the wording of the inscriptions.

It is not so easy to identify where the bombs fell in the Blitz by merely looking at the buildings that occupy a site today. Too much wholesale redevelopment has taken place in the past twenty years including the replacement of many post-Blitz buildings, particularly in the City of London, Camden and Westminster. Some guidance can be obtained from *the London County Council Bomb Damage Maps 1939-1945* by Laurence Ward. This valuable book also shows how relatively lightly some Metropolitan boroughs were affected by the Blitz of 1940-41.

The Bomb Sight project has attempted to map all incidents and covers the period 7 October 1940 to 6 June 1941. The project has scanned original 1940s bomb census maps, geo-referenced the maps and digitally captured the geographical locations of all the falling bombs recorded on the original map. Bomb Sight was created by collaboration between Dr Catherine Jones, University of Portsmouth Stepping into Time Project and The National Archives. Its creation was funded by JISC – Joint Information Service Committee. However, it does not claim to map every bomb, and does not cover the very important first month of the London Blitz. A confusing issue is the use of political wards within today's London boroughs to identify locations.

---

405 Brooks, *London at War* (2011)

The City of London's historic buildings suffered badly. Twenty-three of its forty-nine churches were badly damaged or destroyed along with twenty-five of the thirty-six livery halls.[406] It should be borne in mind that not all of the City's churches were built by Sir Christopher Wren. The Great Fire which gave rise to their construction did not destroy the whole of the pre-1666 City, and some churches pre-date the Fire, and others were built or rebuilt by other architects. At the end of the war the Port of London had been devastated. Bombs had caused damage valued at £13.5 million based on pre-war prices and half of all storage and one third of all warehousing in the docks had been lost. In Surrey Commercial Docks, 176 sheds had been completely destroyed and fifty-seven others had to be demolished. Tarpaulins and prefabricated huts were being used as makeshift cover for goods[407].

The following reviews what has happened since the war on the sites of some of the incidents covered in my chronology of the Blitz.

16 July 1940 – a planter was inaugurated at The Drive, Loughton in July 2015 commemorating the two people killed.

7/8 September 1940. The advent of North Sea gas in the 1970s meant the end of gas production from coal at Beckton and other gasworks in London. A new memorial for the victims of the tragedy at Columbia Market was unveiled in 2015 at the Rose Garden between Sivill House and Ravenscroft Park. The Columbia Market was demolished in 1958. A temporary church was built within the walls of St. Matthew's, Bethnal Green and this was dedicated in the 1950s. Later it was decided to rebuild

406 Bradley & Pevsner, *The Buildings of England. London 1. The City of London* (1997)
407 Port of London Authority website http.//www.pla.co.uk/

the church and it was re-consecrated on 15 July 1961. As a result of the destruction at Keiller's factory at Tay Wharf Silvertown the chocolate and confectionery trade was transferred to Dundee whilst preserves manufacture restarted after a few months.

8/9 September 1940. Madame Tussauds waxworks exhibition was restored and re-opened later in the year, but the cinema was never re-built. Today, the Planetarium occupies the site. K block of the Peabody estate in John Fisher Street, Stepney was not rebuilt after the war and the site remained vacant until 2012/14 when Peabody erected Darbishire Place, a residential block. St. Michael and All Angels Church in Sydenham was rebuilt in 1955/56.

9/10 September 1940. A plaque to commemorate the fifteen AFS men killed at Poplar Fire Station was unveiled in 2011. St. Mary Islington was rebuilt and rededicated in 1956. The Dulwich Society marked its fiftieth year by placing twelve plaques around Dulwich at the sites of significant civilian loss of life in World War 2; in September 2013 the incident at Wheatland House, Dog Kennel Hill was commemorated.

10/11 September 1940. The Wenlock brewery closed in 1961 and was demolished. The site is occupied by storage units belonging to the British Museum.

12 September 1940. St. Catherine Coleman on Westway, Shepherds Bush was rebuilt in 1959, and is now known as St. Katherine's.

13 September 1940. Queen Anne's Mansions, at one time the tallest residential blocks in Britain, were demolished in 1973.

17 September 1940. John Lewis's was completely rebuilt in 1958-

1960. Through tremendous efforts by staff, the other Oxford Street stores were able to resume trading within a few days.

18/19 September 1940. After the war, Cubitt Town School was rebuilt and later, it became home to St. Luke's School. On 8 December 2008, a Service of Remembrance was held in the school, and a plaque was unveiled, bearing the names of all those who died on the night of 18/19 September 1940. The wartime sacrifice of two female firefighters was honoured in the naming of a new Isle of Dogs development by Swan Housing which features two blocks named after teenagers Violet Pengelly and Joan Bartlett who were among the first women to sign up to the Auxiliary Fire Service in 1938.[408]

St. James, Stoke Newington Road was not rebuilt and the West Hackney parish was amalgamated with St Barnabas, Shacklewell, in 1955.

19 September 1940. On Sunday 19 September 2010, over seventy people attended a commemorative event in Lordship Recreation Ground, Tottenham. A Downhills Shelter memorial was finally dedicated in July 2014.

24 September 1940. Further damage was caused to St. Anne's Soho in later raids. The tower survived and St. Anne's was rededicated in 1991 as a church and community centre. The Queen's Theatre was restored and reopened in 1959. It is now the Sondheim Theatre.

25 September 1940. The *Sun Inn* in Hammersmith was rebuilt in 1960 but demolished in 2013. An article on the Indy R's website indicates that a memorial plaque was proposed.

---

408 The Island History Trust

26 September 1940. The *Queen's Arms* pub in Kilburn was rebuilt in 1958.

27/28 September 1940. Holland House, Kensington has been left much as it was after the site was cleared and tidied up, with only the east wing intact. It is no longer used as a youth hostel.

30 September 1940. The *Two Brewers* pub in Ponders End was never rebuilt. A memorial garden on the site was officially opened on Tuesday 30 September 2014 by Cliff Short, who was 14 years old at the time and had helped fire fighters retrieve bodies from the wreckage.

1/2 October 1940. The Holborn Restaurant was demolished in 1955 and replaced by Civil Aviation House, which in turn was replaced by shops and flats more recently. It is unclear as to the extent of the damage to the restaurant in 1940 and whether it continued to trade. The *Hare and Hounds* in Hampstead reopened in temporary premises in 1941 and was completely rebuilt in 1968. It closed about twenty years ago and was replaced with a block of flats.

3 October 1940. St. Quintin Park station was permanently closed.

7 October 1940. Ealing Abbey Church was eventually restored and reopened in 1962.

8 October 1940. The Nelson rotunda staircase at Somerset House was reconstructed to great acclaim by architect Albert Richardson in 1952.

9/10 October 1940. St. Matthew's Hospital, Shoreditch was evacuated and remained empty for the next two years. After it was reopened, further damage was done in the Little Blitz of 1944, and it finally closed in 1995. The 70th anniversary of the wartime bombing of Spriggs Oak House in Epping was commemorated with a Service of Remembrance, organised by the Royal British Legion.

12/13 October 1940. Brooke House in Clapton was further damaged later in the war and despite its exceptional architectural interest, it was demolished in 1954.

13/14 October 1940. The Coronation Avenue flats in Stoke Newington Road were rebuilt after the war in matching architectural style. There is a plaque on Coronation Avenue, on the corner of Stoke Newington Road and Victorian Road, next to the police station, dedicated in May 2011. The memorial in Abney Park Cemetery was restored and rededicated at a ceremony on Remembrance Day 2013, sixty-five years after the disaster. The *Prince of Wales* in Lambeth was repaired and reopened but was further damaged in 1944 and closed.

14/15 October 1940. Emergency repairs were made to 55 Broadway and it remained in service as LPTB's headquarters. Major restoration was subsequently completed so successfully that today no trace of its wartime damage is visible. It continues in use as the head office of London Underground Ltd. The surface buildings at Balham tube station were rebuilt after the war. The Holborn Empire was never rebuilt and shops and offices occupy the site. St. James's Piccadilly remained a roofless shell for nearly seven years. In 1941, services resumed after a temporary roof was constructed over parts of the south aisle. St. James's famous altar carvings, altar piece and organ casing had been protected prior to the raid and survived. Likewise, air raid precautions taken by the staff ensured that the church's marble font – in which poet and painter William Blake and 18th century Prime Minister William Pitt the Elder had been baptised – also survived. The Carlton Club moved to premises in St James's Street where it remains to this day.

15/16 October 1940. The Dutch church in Austin Friars, City of London, was rebuilt in modern style in 1954. Dame Alice Owen's School, Finsbury was eventually rebuilt after the war, but was subsequently relocated to Potters Bar. The building now houses the City and Islington College. At Morley College, Maufe's 1930s extension survived. The remains of the Victorian building were cleared and a new college building designed by Charles Cowles-Voysey and Brandon Jones was completed in 1958 and opened by Queen Elizabeth, the Queen Mother. The remnants of the screen and gallery of Middle Temple Hall were gathered into two hundred sacks and stored until they could be painstakingly reassembled after the war. The hall was restored by Sir Edward Maufe and reopened in 1949. The Inn's Library was irretrievably damaged and had to be demolished. The burnt-out Temple Church and Master's House were restored in the period 1947-1957. By the end of the war the Middle Temple had lost 122 of its 285 sets of chambers. St. Mary, Haggerston, built to the designs of John Nash in 1827, was not rebuilt and the site is now occupied by a playground.

19 October 1940. The badly damaged St. Philip's Church, Dalston, was demolished after the war and the parish was united with Holy Trinity.

26 October 1940. Curzon Street House was shored up and one wing was demolished after the incident. The building suffered further blast damage in the raid of 10/11 May 1941.

28 October 1940. St. Peter's Walworth was temporarily repaired in the weeks following the bombing. It was restored and rededicated in 1953. The names of those who died in the crypt are commemorated by a plaque.

1 November 1940. In July 2006, a plaque was unveiled by Cis Keefe at Lansbury Lawrence Primary School, Poplar, now occupying the site of the old school building, in memory of Joan Ridd and those who lost their lives with her.

6 November 1940. Kilburn police station was reopened in a temporary building in 1965 which in turn was replaced by a new building in 1980. In 2010 a ceremony was held to unveil a memorial plaque. A plaque on the Henry Cavendish School, Hydethorpe Road, Balham, commemorates the thirteen men and women who died at the AFS station that once occupied the school.

12 November 1940. The Granada, Wandsworth Road was closed for repairs but before it could re-open it was severely damaged by bombing in May 1941. It remained closed until 1949. It later became a bingo club and today it is the Southbank Club, a fitness centre.

16 November 1940. Wandsworth fire station, although temporarily restored in 1942, was eventually replaced with a new building in 1955. St. Saviour's Church in Ealing was not rebuilt after the war and the parish was combined with Christ Church.

18 November 1940. A memorial plaque to the thirty men of the King's Own Scottish Borderers is located in St. Mary's church, Theydon Bois. The memorial was unveiled on 18 November 1998.

8 December 1940. All Hallows Barking was rebuilt and re-dedicated in 1957 and is now known as All Hallows-by-the-Tower, appropriately perhaps as it is nowhere near Barking[409]! Repairs to All Souls, Langham Place were not completed until 1951. The Langham Hotel was given emergency repairs, and after the war was used by the BBC, but only in recent years has it been restored to luxury standards. The destroyed parts of Maybury Mansions in Marylebone were rebuilt after the war. The Druces site was redeveloped as Michael House in 1957, serving as the UK headquarters of Marks & Spencer until 2005. St. John's Waterloo and St. John's East Dulwich were both restored ten years after their wartime destruction.

11 December 1940. Today the site of the Hovis Mill in Grosvenor Road is occupied by the Rivermill and Crown Reach housing developments.

13 December 1940. The bomb disposal teams killed in Manor Park are commemorated by a plaque, presented to the Salisbury Road Primary School on 13 December 2000 by the Bomb Disposal Branch of The Royal Engineers Association with the co-operation and participation of the Manor Park Branch of The Royal British Legion. It commemorates the sixtieth anniversary of the incident.

29 December 1940. This raid played an important role in shaping the future of the post-war City. Trinity House was restored and reopened by the Queen on 21 October 1953 – Trafalgar Day.

16 January 1941. Ravenscourt House in Hammersmith was demolished after the war.

---

409 The church was in fact founded from Barking Abbey in Essex

17/18 January 1941. The *Kentish Arms* pub was rebuilt after the war and is now called *Mabel's*.

13 February 1941. Eventually the whole area of West Hendon including the streets devastated by the 2,500kg bomb was cleared and rebuilt in the 1960s. I have seen a claim that a memorial garden (the 'York Memorial Park') was dedicated where the bomb fell but has been obliterated in a more recent redevelopment of the area. However, York Park was in existence before the war and lay to the south of Ravenstone Road, and it is not referred to anywhere as a memorial park. Ramsey says no memorial was ever dedicated locally, although it seems that annual memorial services were held at the site of the incident for several years.

8/9 March 1941. The Café de Paris re-opened in 1948. What remained of Garland's Hotel was destroyed a month later in the raid on 16/17 April and the site is now occupied by offices.

19 March 1941. A plaque to remember those who died at Bullivant's Wharf, Isle of Dogs is now on view on the river walkway between Hutchins Street and Cuba Street. St. Mary and St. Michael Junior School in Stepney was destroyed by a V2 rocket in 1945. *Jack Straw's Castle* in Hampstead was rebuilt in 1962. It is no longer a pub.

16/17 April 1941. The Abbey was demolished after the war and is now the site of Kensington Central Library, built in 1959. Chelsea Old Church was also rebuilt and rededicated in 1959. The seven AFS firemen who died in Chelsea are commemorated by a plaque on Chelsea Fire Station in the Kings Road. Maple's department store in Tottenham Court Road was rebuilt in the 1950s but was replaced by another ultra-modern building by R Seifert & Partners in the 1980s. Maple's ceased trading in 1997.

All the houses in Thorold Street, Bethnal Green were so severely damaged they had to be demolished. The street no longer exists and its site is covered by a post-war estate, completed in 1954. St. George's Catholic Cathedral in Southwark was rebuilt and consecrated in 1958. South London Palace Music Hall was eventually demolished in 1955. A memorial to the fifty-four people who died when two bombs hit the air raid shelter of Walkling's cake shop in The Cut, Lambeth, was rededicated on Thursday 21 June 2007 to mark its installation on the rebuilt Young Vic theatre.[410] Christ Church in Blackfriars Road, Lambeth was rebuilt in 1959. The London Necropolis Company's facility at Waterloo station was never used again, and the undamaged office buildings were sold. Today, the site of Pancras Square is occupied by flats called The Chenies. Christ Church Victoria remained an empty burnt-out ruin for the rest of the war. The remains of the church tower, as well as the adjoining vicarage, were pulled down in 1954, and a telephone exchange and a new Post Office were opened at the north end of the site in 1962. A small sign in the corner of Christ Church Gardens recalls the church's Blitz story. The site of Newport Buildings is now occupied by a multi-storey car park, businesses and flats.

Pevsner[411] called St. John's, Red Lion Square 'a very impressive ruin' but despite proposals to preserve it, what remained of the church was eventually demolished in 1961. The whole area around Red Lion Square was substantially redeveloped after the war. It was decided that St. Andrew's church at Holborn Circus would be restored 'stone for stone and brick for brick' to Wren's original designs, and the church eventually re-opened in 1961. RADA's

410 London SE1 Community website https.//www.london-se1.co.uk
411 Pevsner, *The Buildings of England* (1952)

performances were moved to the City Literary Institute until the new Vanbrugh Theatre was opened by Her Majesty Queen Elizabeth the Queen Mother. There is a small plaque, now in the London Museum of Jewish Life, commemorating the Jewish Club members who died at Alfred Place. The Jewish Girls' Club, the Western Synagogue and J E Dallas & Sons relocated to other premises. None of them was to return to its original site after the war.[412] The Towers Creamery in Mitcham was rebuilt after the war but later closed after which the buildings were used for industrial purposes. After the site was redeveloped for housing, a memorial plaque and garden were dedicated in 2012 to commemorate those who died. The *California* in Belmont, Sutton was rebuilt in 1956.

19 April 1941. In Wandsworth, the *Castle* was rebuilt in 1959 and again in 2003 when it was renamed the *Boathouse*. There is a memorial plaque in Brewhouse Street. St. James' church at Muswell Hill was restored after the war and was rededicated by the Bishop of London on 24 October 1952. In April 1997, Firemen Remembered, along with the London Fire Brigade, dedicated a plaque to the memory of the firemen who died at Old Palace School, Bromley-by-Bow. St. Peter's Hospital in Stepney was seriously damaged by a V1 flying bomb in 1944, and never re-opened. In Merstham, Canadian engineers built Canada Hall as a temporary church, giving the building its unique 'prairies' architecture. A new church was built in the 1950s and Canada Hall became instead the church hall.

10 May 1941. Despite Pevsner's somewhat gloomy assessment of the damage done[413], the Charterhouse was faithfully restored by

---

412 Bloomsbury blitzed. Graham Greene; 'Dallas'; and the Jewish tragedy in Alfred Place by David A Hayes and Ruth E Hayes, Camden History Review 39, 2015.

413 Pevsner, *The Buildings of England. London 1* (1957)

the architects, Seely and Paget, opening its doors again in 1951. It now takes its place as one of the most important monuments of London. The Grey Coat Hospital girls' school was unoccupied, the girls having been evacuated to Surrey. It was rebuilt and re-opened in 1955. St. John's Smith Square was restored for use as a concert hall, re-opening in 1969. In Knightsbridge, Agriculture House was built on the site of the Alexandra Hotel in 1954 but this was in turn demolished in 1993 and replaced by Nos 25 & 27 Knightsbridge.[414]St. Mary's Newington was rebuilt in 1958 next to the ruins of the old church. St. Columba's in Pont Street was rebuilt in 1958 to a design by Sir Edward Maufe, the architect of Guildford Cathedral. St. George-in-the-East, Stepney, was restored and rededicated on 26 April 1964. The Central Synagogue used temporary premises for a number of years before it was rebuilt on the Hallam Street site in 1958. Cable and Wireless's premises at Electra House in Moorgate were not used again and the company transferred its operations to Electra House on Victoria Embankment. The Salvation Army HQ in Queen Victoria Street was rebuilt and reopened in 1963. At the Palace of Westminster, the stained-glass window in St. Stephen's Porch is the main memorial to members and staff of both Houses, including police officers, who died in World War 2. The window was designed by Sir Ninian Comper and replaced the original Pugin window which was destroyed in December 1940.[415] The damage in Holford Square, Finsbury, was so comprehensive that the entire site was eventually cleared and no trace of the square remains today. The process of rebuilding the Royal College of Surgeons after the war was slow and with much of the collection lost, the new college building devoted more space to research. Gray's Inn was extensively restored in the 1950s.

---

414 Westminster City Archives www.westendatwar.org.uk
415 http.//www.parliament.uk/about/living-heritage/building/cultural-collections/memorials/in-the-collection/world-war-ii/wwii-window/

Other buildings

In September 1940 (I have been unable to establish an exact date), Cecil Sharp House, the London headquarters of the English Folk Dance and Song Society in Regents Park Road, was partially demolished by a bomb which destroyed most of the upper storey and part of the main hall of the building, which had only been completed in 1929. Re-building began early in 1950.

Pymmes Park House, an Elizabethan mansion in Edmonton was destroyed by fire in 1940, but no sources give a date. It seems the fire may not have been a result of enemy action.

The imposing Lancaster House in St. James', dating from 1825 and housing the London Museum at the time of the Blitz, was damaged on a number of occasions, Dorothy Hood noted after the war that it was 'scarred and pitted.'[416]

Overall, London's theatres and cinemas did not suffer too badly in the Blitz and fortunately, no disasters involving loss of life occurred. However, the Kingsway Theatre, damaged on 10/11 May 1941 never reopened and was demolished in 1959. Bomb damage temporarily closed several including the Old Vic from 1941 until 1950. The Duke of York's Theatre was also closed due to bomb damage in 1940 but reopened in 1943. The Royal Court Theatre was closed between 1940 and 1952 due to bomb damage, although it had been used as a cinema for some time. The Shaftesbury Theatre was not rebuilt after the war and since 1983 the Soho Fire Station has occupied the site. The Embassy cinema in Tottenham Court Road, seriously damaged on 16 April, had only opened in 1939. It was not rebuilt and the site is now part of University College. The Little Theatre in John Adam Street which was badly damaged on 16/17 April had been created by Gertrude Kingston in the former Coutts' banking

416 Hood, *London is Invincible* (1946)

hall. It was demolished in 1949. The original architects T.P. Bennett & Son were brought back to restore the Odeon cinema in Haverstock Hill, Hampstead, which was eventually re-opened on 13 December 1954. The Playhouse Cinema in Greenford was extensively damaged in October 1940. It seems that although it was eventually repaired and re-opened, it closed for good in the 1950s.

APPENDIX A

LONDON LOCAL AUTHORITIES IN 1940-41

Post 1965 London Borough	LONDON CIVIL DEFENCE REGION Pre 1965 Boroughs & local authorities as in World War 2	Notes on later reorganisations
Barnet	Barnet UD East Barnet UD Finchley MB Hendon MB Friern Barnet UD	
Barking and Dagenham	Barking MB Dagenham MB	
Bexley	Bexley MB Erith MB Crayford UD Chislehurst and Sidcup UD*	*Chislehurst was transferred to Bromley in 1965.
Brent	Wembley MB Willesden MB	
Bromley	Bromley MB Beckenham MB Orpington UD Penge UD Chislehurst and Sidcup UD*	*Sidcup was transferred to Bexley in 1965.

Camden	Hampstead Holborn St. Pancras	
City of London	City of London	
Croydon	Croydon CB Coulsdon and Purley UD	
Ealing	Acton MB Ealing MB Southall MB	
Enfield	Edmonton MB Enfield UD Southgate MB	
Greenwich	Greenwich MB Woolwich MB	
Hackney	Hackney Shoreditch Stoke Newington	
Hammersmith	Fulham Hammersmith	
Haringey	Hornsey MB Tottenham MB Wood Green MB	
Harrow	Harrow UD	
Havering	(Romford UD Hornchurch UD)	Neither of the pre-1965 boroughs were in the London Civil Defence Region.
Hillingdon	Hayes and Harlington UD Ruislip-Northwood UD Uxbridge UD Yiewsley and West Drayton UD	
Hounslow	Brentford and Chiswick MB Heston and Isleworth MB Feltham UD	
Islington	Islington Finsbury	
Kensington and Chelsea	Kensington Chelsea	

Kingston upon Thames	Kingston upon Thames MB Maldon and Coombe MB Surbiton MB	
Lambeth	Lambeth Part of Wandsworth*	*Clapham and most of Streatham were transferred from the borough of Wandsworth in 1965.
Lewisham	Lewisham Deptford	
Merton	Mitcham MB Merton and Malden UD Wimbledon MB	
Newham	East Ham CB West Ham CB Barking MB	North Woolwich was transferred from the former Woolwich MB in 1965.
Redbridge	Ilford MB Wanstead and Woodford MB Dagenham MB Chigwell UD (a small part)	
Richmond upon Thames	Barnes MB Richmond MB Twickenham MB	
Southwark	Bermondsey Camberwell Southwark	
Sutton	Beddington & Wallington MB Carshalton UD Sutton and Cheam MB	
Tower Hamlets	Bethnal Green Poplar Stepney	
Waltham Forest	Chingford MB Leyton MB Walthamstow MB	

Wandsworth	Battersea Wandsworth*	*Clapham and Streatham were transferred to the London Borough of Lambeth in 1965.
Westminster	Paddington St. Marylebone Westminster	
Post 1974 Local Authorities	**Pre 1974 local authorities as in 1944 (authorities not in the London Civil Defence Region are not listed).**	
Epping Forest (from 1974)	Chigwell UD (greater part) Waltham Holy Cross UD	Later renamed Waltham Abbey
Hertsmere (from 1974)	Elstree RD (created 1941) Bushey UD Potters Bar UD Watford RD (Aldenham)	
Broxbourne (from 1974)	Cheshunt UD Hoddesdon UD	
Spelthorne (from 1974)	Staines UD Sunbury on Thames UD	Transferred to Surrey in 1965
Elmbridge (from 1974)	Esher UD	
Epsom & Ewell	Epsom & Ewell MB	
Reigate & Banstead (from 1965)	Banstead UD	

CB   County Borough
MB   Municipal Borough
RD   Rural District
UD   Urban District
Other pre-1965 boroughs shown were Metropolitan Boroughs

APPENDIX B

ANALYSIS OF 'DISASTERS' IN LONDON, SEPTEMBER TO NOVEMBER 1940(BOMBING INCIDENTS WITH OVER 20 FATALITIES)

Type of shelter	Number of incidents	Number killed
Strutted basements	8	420
Subways, arches etc	3	201
Trenches	7	248
Surface shelters	2	84
Tube (underground) stations	2	90
Railway Stations	2	66
Hospitals & rest centres	8	352
Dwellings	5	120
Unspecified	4	92
Totals	**41**	**1673**

Source: HO 186/1862

APPENDIX C

MAJOR BOMBING INCIDENTS IN LONDON 1940-41

Date	Location	Borough	No Killed
07/09/1940	Keetons Road School	Bermondsey	35
08/09/1940	Columbia Market shelter	Bethnal Green	43
08/09/1940	Peabody Buildings, John Fisher Street	Stepney	78
09/09/1940	Cadogan House, Beaufort Street	Chelsea	61
10/09/1940	South Hallsville School	Poplar	78
11/09/1940	Albion Way shelter	Lewisham	36
11/09/1940	Central Hall	Greenwich	23
16/09/1940	Neptune Street shelter	Bermondsey	21
16/09/1940	Linsey Street Arch shelter	Bermondsey	26
19/09/1940	Downhills shelter	Tottenham	42
22/09/1940	Orsett House shelter	Lambeth	25
23/09/1940	Risinghill Street	Finsbury	30
23/09/1940	742 Romford Road, Manor Park	East Ham	30

24/09/1940	Stansfield House, Frampton Street	St Marylebone	31
25/09/1940	Sun Inn, Askew Road	Hammersmith	21
08/10/1940	High Holborn	Holborn	32
08/10/1940	St. Matthew's Hospital	Shoreditch	33*
13/10/1940	Bounds Green Underground Station	Wood Green	17
13/10/1940	Coronation Avenue flats, 157-161 High Street	Stoke Newington	154
14/10/1940	Balham Underground Station	Wandsworth	67
15/10/1940	Dame Alice Owen's School shelter, Goswell Rd	Finsbury	91[§]
15/10/1940	Prospect Terrace, Grays Inn Rd	St Pancras	30
15/10/1940	Morley College, Westminster Bridge Road	Lambeth	57
15/10/1940	Barnsbury Road	Islington	24
15/10/1940	Kennington Park trench shelters	Lambeth	50
18/10/1940	Rose & Crown PH, Crown Lane	Lambeth	21
29/10/1940	St. Peter's Church, Liverpool Grove, Walworth	Southwark	65
09/11/1940	Kings Cross Goods Station	St Pancras	21
11/11/1940	Great Peter Street	Westminster	25
12/11/1940	Sloane Square Station	Westminster	34
16/11/1940	Huntingdon Street	Islington	22
24/11/1940	Liberal Club, Scarbrook Road	Croydon	25
08/12/1940	Maybury Mansions	St Marylebone	21
11/12/1940	Rogers House, Page Street	Westminster	23
11/01/1941	Bank Underground Station	City of London	56

11/01/1941	Bishopsgate	City of London	43
16/01/1941	92 Westminster Bridge Road	Lambeth	37
13/02/1941	Ravenstone Road	Hendon	85
17/02/1941	Stainer Street Arch	Bermondsey	68
08/03/1941	Café de Paris	Westminster	34
15/03/1941	Green Lanes	Palmers Green	42
16/04/1941	Montague Tibbles House, Queens Crescent	St Pancras	20
16/04/1941	Pancras Square flats	St Pancras	77
16/04/1941	Lillington Street, Pimlico	Westminster	40
16/04/1941	Newport Buildings, Shaftesbury Avenue	Westminster	48
16/04/1941	Thorold Street	Bethnal Green	53
16/04/1941	Jewish Club, Alfred Place	Holborn	27
16/04/1941	Portpool Lane	Holborn	47
16/04/1941	Fellows Road	Hampstead	24
16/04/1941	Walkling's, The Cut	Lambeth	47
19/04/1941	Horner House, Nuttall Street	Shoreditch	46
19/04/1941	Prince of Wales PH, Manor Road	Chigwell	36
19/04/1941	Castle PH, Putney Bridge Road	Wandsworth	48
19/04/1941	Old Palace School, Bromley by Bow	Poplar	36
19/04/1941	Saltwell Street	Poplar	27
19/04/1941	Kennington Road	Lambeth	22
19/04/1941	Essex Road	Romford	38
19/04/1941	Talbot Road	Ealing	22
10/05/1941	Alexandra Hotel, Knightsbridge	Westminster	24
10/05/1941	Turner Buildings	Westminster	24
10/05/1941	Holford Square	Finsbury	35#

NOTES

* The total may be much higher. Fatalities from St. Matthew's Hospital that were recorded at other hospitals for example St. Leonard's cannot always be identified as victims of the former incident.
$ A figure of 109 is also quoted
# Does not include military casualties (barrage balloon site)

Excludes fatalities outside the London Civil Defence Region.
PH = Public house

BIBLIOGRAPHY

PUBLISHED SOURCES

General Accounts
Anon., *Front Line 1940-1941* (HMSO, 1942)

Bradley, S & Pevsner, N., *The Buildings of England. London 1. The City of London* (Penguin Books, 1997)

Brooks, A., *London at War* (Wharncliffe Books, 2011)

Brooksbank, B., *London Main Line War Damage* (Harrow. Capital Transport, 2007).

Calder, A., *The Peoples War* (Panther Books, 1971)

Calder, A., *The Myth of the Blitz* (Pimlico, 1992)

Churchill, W., *Their Finest Hour* (Cassell 1950)

Collier, B., *The Defence of the UK* (HMSO, 1955)

Collier, R., *The City that wouldn't Die. London May 10-11, 1941* (Collins, 1959)

Cooper, N., *London Underground at War* (Amberley Publishing, 2014)

Fitzgibbon, C., *The Blitz* (Macdonald, 1970)

Gardiner, J., *The Blitz. The British under attack* (Harper Press, 2010)

Garfield, S., *Private Battles* (Ebury Press, 2007)

Gaskin, M., *Blitz. The Story of 29th December 1940* (Faber and Faber, 2005)

Graves, C., *London Transport at War* (Oldcastle Books, 1989)

Gregg, J., *The Shelter of the Tubes* (Capital Transport, 2001)

Harris, C & Bright, N., *A Wander Through Wartime London. Five Walks Revisiting the Blitz* (Pen & Sword, 2010)

Harris, C., *Blitz Diary* (The History Press, 2010)

Harrisson, T., *Living through the Blitz* (Penguin, 1978)

Harvey, A.D., *Collision of Empires* (Phoenix, 1994)

Hay, I., *The Post Office Went to War* (HMSO, 1946)

Hill, M., & Alexander, J., *The Blitz on Britain* (Transatlantic Press, 2010)

Holloway, S., *Courage High. A history of fire fighting in London* (HMSO, 1992)

Hood, D., *London is Invincible* (Hutchinson, 1946)

Ingham, H. S., ed. *Fire and Water* (Firestorm Publications, 1992)

Jenkins, R., *Churchill* (Macmillan, 2001)

Jenkins, S., *A Short History of London* (Viking, 2019)

Johnson, D., *The City Ablaze. The Second Great Fire of London 29th December 1940* (William Kimber, 1980)

Jones, I., *London bombed, blitzed and blown up* (Frontline, 2016)

Levine, J., *Forgotten Voices of the Blitz and the Battle for Britain* (Random House, 2007)

Mackay, R., *Half the Battle. Civilian Morale in Britain during the Second World War* (Manchester University Press, 2002)

Mortimer, G., *The Longest Night 10-11 May 1941* (Weidenfeld & Nicolson 2005)

Mosley, L., *London Under Fire 1939-1945* (Pan Books, 1972)

Murray, W., *Luftwaffe. Strategy for Defeat 1939-45* (1985)

O'Brien, T., *Civil Defence* (HMSO, 1958)

Overy, R., *The Bombing War. Europe 1939-1945* (Penguin Books, 2014)

Owen, J., *Danger UXB. The Heroic Story* (Hachette Digital, 2010)

Pevsner, N., *The Buildings of England. London 1. The City of London* (Penguin Books, 1957)

Price, A., *Blitz on Britain 1939-1945* (Purnell Book Services Limited, 1977)

Ramsey, W., ed., *The Blitz Then and Now Vol.1* (After the Battle, 1987)

Ramsey, W., ed., *The Blitz Then and Now Vol.2* (After the Battle, 1988)

Ramsey, W., ed., *The Blitz Then and Now Vol.3* (After the Battle, 1990)

Ramsey, W., ed., *Epping Forest Then and Now* (After the Battle, 1986)

Ray, J., *The Night Blitz 1940-41* (Castle Books, 2004)

Smith, L., *Young Voices* (Penguin, 2007)

Smyth, Sir J., *The George Cross* (Arthur Barker, 1968)

St George Saunders, H., *The Royal Air Force 1939-45 vol. III* (HMSO, 1954)

Stansky, P., *The First Day of the Blitz. September 7, 1940* (Yale University Press, 2007)

Titmuss, R., *Problems of Social Policy* (HMSO, 1950)

Trench, R., *London before the Blitz* (Weidenfeld and Nicolson, 1989)

Waller, J., & Vaughan-Rees, M., *Blitz. The Civilian War 1940-45*

(Macdonald Optima, 1990)
Wallington, N., *Firemen at War* (David & Charles, 1981)
White, J., *London in the 20th Century* (The Bodley Head, 2001)
Wicks, B., *Waiting for the All Clear* (Bloomsbury, 1990)
Ziegler, P., *London at War 1939-1945* (Sinclair-Stevenson, 1995)

Local histories

Bard, R., *Elstree & Borehamwood Through Time* (Amberley, 2011)
Barnfield, P., *When the Bombs Fell* (Borough of Twickenham Local History Society, 2001)
Berwick-Sayers, W. C., *Croydon in the Second World War* (The Croydon Corporation, 1949)
Blake, L., *Red Alert South East London 1939-1945* (Lewis Blake, 1982)
Blake, L., *Bromley in the Front Line* (Bromley Libraries, 2005)
Bright, N., *Southwark in the Blitz* (Amberley, 2016)
Camden History Society *Hampstead at War* (1977)
Carter, E. J., *Diary of an Air Raid Warden* (Waltham Abbey Historical Society, 2009)
Clegg, C., and Marshall, J., *The World War II bombing of Feltham, Hanworth & Bedfont* (John Klewer, 2013)
Fowler, S., *Richmond at War* (The Richmond Local History Society, 2015)
Golden, J., *Hackney at War* (The History Press, 1995)
Hasker, L., *Fulham in the Second World War* (Fulham and Hammersmith Historical Society, 2005)
Haunton, D., *Bombs on Merton* (Merton & Morden Historical Society Bulletins 165-168, 2008)
Hornsey Historical Society Bulletin no.33. *Home Fires. A North London Suburb at War* 1992
Lewey, F., *Cockney Campaign* (Stanley Paul & Co., 1944)
Mack, J., and Humphries, S., *London at War* (Guild Publishing, 1985)
Newbery, C. A., *Wartime St Pancras. a London borough defends itself* (Camden History Society, 2006)
Nixon, B., *Raiders Overhead* (Scolar/Gulliver, 1980)
Ogley, R., *Surrey at War 1939-1945* (Froglets, 1995)
Plastow, N., *Safe as Houses. Wimbledon at War 1939-1945* (Wimbledon Society Museum Press, 1994)
Reboul, P. & Heathfield, J., *Days of Darkness. The London Borough of Barnet at War* (Sutton Publishing, 2005)
Richards, G., *Ordeal in Romford* (Romford Mutual Help Association, 1945)

Rootes, A., *Front Line County. Kent at War 1939-45* (Robert Hale, 1980)

Sansom, W., *The Blitz. Westminster at War* (Oxford University Press, 1990)

Scholey, K., *Bombs on Holborn* (London. Camden History Review, vol. 22, 1998)

Shaw, A., & Mills, J., *"We served" War-time Wandsworth and Battersea 1939-1945* (Wandsworth Borough Council, 1989)

Taylor, R., and Lloyd, C., *The East End at War* (Sutton, 2000)

Upton, D., *Ealing, Acton & Southall at War* (The History Press, 2009)

Warburton, S., *Chingford at War* (Chingford Borough Council, 1946)

Watt, P., *Hitler v Havering* (Carlton Armitage Press, 1994)

Whitehead, J., *Brent's War* (Brent Council, 1995)

Wyld, R., *The War over Walthamstow* (London Borough of Waltham Forest, 1989)

Autobiographical

Lord Alanbrooke, *War Diaries 1939-1945* (Phoenix, 2002)

Colville, J., *The Fringes of Power* (Hodder & Stoughton, 1985)

Demarne, C., *The London Blitz. A Fireman's Tale* (Battle of Britain Prints International Ltd, 1991)

Faviell, F., *A Chelsea Concerto* (Cassell, 1957)

Ferguson, R., *Royal Borough* (Jonathan Cape, 1950)

Harris, A., *Bomber Offensive* (Pen & Sword, 2005)

Henrey, Mrs R., *The Siege of London* (Temple Press, 1946)

Hodgson, V., *Few Eggs and no Oranges* (Persephone Books, 2010)

Kops, B., *The World is a Wedding* (MacGibbon & Kee, 1963)

Leutze, J., ed., *The London Observer. The Journal of General Raymond E Lee* (Hutchinson, 1972)

Lees-Milne, J., *Diaries, 1942-1954* (John Murray, 2006)

Macbeth, G., *A Child of the War* (Jonathan Cape, 1987)

Morrison, M., *A Very Private Diary. A Nurse in Wartime* (W&N 2015)

Pile, General Sir F., *Ack-Ack* (Harrap, 1949)

Others

Anon, *Tragedy at Bethnal Green 1943* (The Stationery Office, 1999)

Barnett, A., *The Western Synagogue Through Two Centuries (1761-1961)*, (Vallentine Mitchell, 1961)

Bryan, T., *The Great Western at War 1939-1945* (Patrick Stephens, 1995)

Cocks, Sir Barnett, *Mid Victorian Masterpiece* (Hutchinson, 1977)

Darwin, *War on the Line* (Southern Railway 1946)

Glover, B., *Brewing for Victory* (Lutterworth Press, 1995)

Graves, C., *The Thin Red Lines* (Standard Art Book Co., 1946)

Hayward, J., *Myths and Legends of the Second World War* (Sutton Publishing, 2003)

Kynaston, N., *City of London* (Chatto & Windus, 2011)

Longmate, N., *Air Raid* (Hutchinson, 1976)

Longmate, N., *How We Lived Then* (Arrow Books 1973)

Longmate, N., *The Doodlebugs* (Hutchinson, 1981)

Matthews, W., *St. Paul's Cathedral in Wartime* (Hutchinson 1946)

Nash, George C., *The L.M.S. at war* (LMS, 1946)

Salisbury, H., *The War on our Doorstep* (Ebury Press, 2012)

St George Saunders, H., *Ford at War* (Hodder & Stoughton, 1946)

Serocold, W. P., *The Story of Watney's* (Watney Combe Reid Ltd, 1949)

Stourton, E., *Auntie's War. The BBC during the Second World War* (Doubleday, 2017)

Tanfield, J., *In Parliament 1939-50* (HMSO, 1991)

Walton, M., & Lamb, J P., *Raiders over Sheffield* (Sheffield City Libraries, 1980)

Winterton, Earl, *Orders of the Day* (Cassell, 1953)

WEBSITE SOURCES AND ARTICLES

Acton History Group website http.//www.actonhistory.co.uk

Dettman, S., http.//www.whenthosewerethedays.blogspot.co.uk/

Simkin, J., *Crime in Wartime (1997)* Spartacus Educational Publishers Ltd

Pateman, R., *Kennington's forgotten tragedy* (Friends of Kennington Park c2007)

The Newham Story http.//www.newhamstory.com/

Enfield at War. History of Enfield in World War 1 and 2 https.// enfieldatwar.wordpress.com/

http.//www.nickmetcalfe.co.uk/gallantry-during-the-blitz-29-december-1940

Washuk, V., ed., *World War II London Blitz Diary vol. 1 – 4*

Talling, P., *Derelict London* website https.//www.derelictlondon.com/ war---bunkers-and-pillboxes.html

Westminster at War http://www.westendatwar.org.uk/

MoI Digital a History of the Ministry of Information, 1939-46
https://moidigital.ac.uk/

UNPUBLISHED SOURCES

Adams, W Eric., *Civil Defence in Islington 1938-1945* in Islington Local
    History Centre.
Woolven, R., *Civil Defence in London 1935-1945. The Formation and
    Implementation of the Policy for, and the Performance of, the Air
    Raid Precautions (later Civil Defence) Services in the London
    Region* (Department of War Studies King's College, London 2001)

ARCHIVAL SOURCES

Imperial War Museum
2769 Private Papers of Mrs G Cox

The London Metropolitan Archives
Heap, Anthony, *Diaries of Anthony Heap.* Note. since this book was
    researched, the London Record Society has published *The London
    Diary of Anthony Heap, 1931-1945*, edited by Dr Robin Woolven.
LCC/FB/WAR/02
LCC/FB/WAR/03
MCC/CD/WAR/1

The National Archives
CAB 65/9
CAB 66/16/10
HO 186/149
HO186/1862
HO 186/641
HO 198/33
HO 202
HO 203/3
HO 203/4 24.6.40-29.9.40

HO 203/5 29.9.40-31.12.40
HO 203/6 1.1.41-31.3.41
HO 203/7 1.4.41-31.5.41
MEPO 4/126